Data Visualization with Python and JavaScript

Scrape, Clean, Explore & Transform Your Data

Kyran Dale

Beijing · Boston · Farnham · Sebastopol · Tokyo

Data Visualization with Python and JavaScript

by Kyran Dale

Published by O'Reilly Media, Inc., 1005 Gravenstein Highway North, Sebastopol, CA 95472.

O'Reilly books may be purchased for educational, business, or sales promotional use. Online editions are also available for most titles (*http://safaribooksonline.com*). For more information, contact our corporate/institutional sales department: 800-998-9938 or *corporate@oreilly.com*.

Editors: Dawn Schanafelt and Meghan Blanchette
Production Editor: Kristen Brown
Copyeditor: Gillian McGarvey
Proofreader: Rachel Monaghan

Indexer: Judith McConville
Interior Designer: David Futato
Cover Designer: Karen Montgomery
Illustrator: Rebecca Demarest

July 2016:   First Edition

Revision History for the First Edition
2016-06-29:   First Release

See *http://oreilly.com/catalog/errata.csp?isbn=9781491920510* for release details.

978-1-491-92051-0

[LSI]

Table of Contents

Preface... ix

Introduction... xv

1. Development Setup... 1
The Accompanying Code   1
Python   1
JavaScript   5
Databases   6
Integrated Development Environments   8
Summary   8

Part I.   Basic Toolkit

2. A Language-Learning Bridge Between Python and JavaScript... 13
Similarities and Differences   14
Interacting with the Code   15
Basic Bridge Work   18
Differences in Practice   42
A Cheat Sheet   54
Summary   56

3. Reading and Writing Data with Python..................... 59
Easy Does It   59
Passing Data Around   60
Working with System Files   61

CSV, TSV, and Row-Column Data Formats   62
JSON   65
SQL   69
MongoDB   79
Dealing with Dates, Times, and Complex Data   84
Summary   86

4. Webdev 101. 87
The Big Picture   87
Single-Page Apps   88
Tooling Up   88
Building a Web Page   93
Chrome's Developer Tools   102
A Basic Page with Placeholders   105
Scalable Vector Graphics   109
Summary   125

Part II.   Getting Your Data

5. Getting Data off the Web with Python. 129
Getting Web Data with the requests Library   129
Getting Data Files with requests   130
Using Python to Consume Data from a Web API   134
Using Libraries to Access Web APIs   140
Scraping Data   146
Getting the Soup   149
Selecting Tags   149
Summary   159

6. Heavyweight Scraping with Scrapy. 161
Setting Up Scrapy   163
Establishing the Targets   164
Targeting HTML with Xpaths   165
A First Scrapy Spider   171
Scraping the Individual Biography Pages   177
Chaining Requests and Yielding Data   180
Scrapy Pipelines   185
Scraping Text and Images with a Pipeline   187
Summary   194

Part III.   Cleaning and Exploring Data with Pandas

7. Introduction to NumPy. **197**
The NumPy Array   198
Creating Array Functions   204
Summary   206

8. Introduction to Pandas. **207**
Why Pandas Is Tailor-Made for Dataviz   207
Why Pandas Was Developed   207
Heterogeneous Data and Categorizing Measurements   208
The DataFrame   210
Creating and Saving DataFrames   214
Series into DataFrames   223
Panels   225
Summary   226

9. Cleaning Data with Pandas. **229**
Coming Clean About Dirty Data   229
Inspecting the Data   231
Indices and Pandas Data Selection   235
Cleaning the Data   239
The Full clean_data Function   256
Saving the Cleaned Dataset   257
Summary   259

10. Visualizing Data with Matplotlib. **261**
Pyplot and Object-Oriented Matplotlib   261
Starting an Interactive Session   262
Interactive Plotting with Pyplot's Global State   264
Figures and Object-Oriented Matplotlib   269
Plot Types   274
Seaborn   282
Summary   291

11. Exploring Data with Pandas. **293**
Starting to Explore   294
Plotting with Pandas   296
Gender Disparities   297
National Trends   304
Age and Life Expectancy of Winners   316

The Nobel Diaspora   323
Summary   325

Part IV.   Delivering the Data

12. Delivering the Data. **329**
    Serving the Data   330
    Delivering Static Files   336
    Dynamic Data with Flask   340
    Using Static or Dynamic Delivery   344
    Summary   344

13. RESTful Data with Flask. **347**
    A RESTful, MongoDB API with Eve   348
    Delivering Data to the Nobel Prize Visualization   356
    RESTful SQL with Flask-Restless   361
    Summary   365

Part V.   Visualizing Your Data with D3

14. Imagining a Nobel Visualization. **369**
    Who Is It For?   369
    Choosing Visual Elements   370
    Menu Bar   371
    Prizes by Year   372
    A Map Showing Selected Nobel Countries   373
    A Bar Chart Showing Number of Winners by Country   375
    A List of the Selected Winners   375
    The Complete Visualization   377
    Summary   378

15. Building a Visualization. **379**
    Preliminaries   380
    The HTML Skeleton   382
    CSS Styling   386
    The JavaScript Engine   390
    Running the Nobel Prize Visualization App   404
    Summary   405

16. Introducing D3—The Story of a Bar Chart. 407
Framing the Problem   408
Working with Selections   408
Adding DOM Elements   412
Leveraging D3   418
Measuring Up with D3's Scales   418
Unleashing the Power of D3 with Data Binding   423
The enter Method   425
Accessing the Bound Data   429
The Update Pattern   430
Axes and Labels   436
Transitions   442
Summary   447

17. Visualizing Individual Prizes. 449
Building the Framework   449
Scales   450
Axes   451
Category Labels   452
Nesting the Data   454
Adding the Winners with a Nested Data-Join   456
A Little Transitional Sparkle   460
Summary   463

18. Mapping with D3. 465
Available Maps   466
D3's Mapping Data Formats   467
D3 Geo, Projections, and Paths   471
Putting the Elements Together   477
Updating the Map   481
Adding Value Indicators   484
Our Completed Map   487
Building a Simple Tooltip   488
Summary   491

19. Visualizing Individual Winners. 493
Building the List   494
Building the Bio-Box   497
Summary   500

20. The Menu Bar. **503**
Creating HTML Elements with D3   504
Building the Menu Bar   504
Summary   514

21. Conclusion. **515**
Recap   515
Future Progress   518
Final Thoughts   521

A. Moving from Development to Production. **523**

Index. **545**

Preface

The chief ambition of this book is to describe a data visualization (dataviz) toolchain that, in the era of the Internet, is starting to predominate. The guiding principle of this toolchain is that whatever insightful nuggets you have managed to mine from your data deserve a home on the web browser. Being on the Web means you can easily choose to distribute your dataviz to a select few (using authentication or restricting to a local network) or the whole world. This is the big idea of the Internet and one that dataviz is embracing at a rapid pace. And that means that the future of dataviz involves JavaScript, the only first-class language of the web browser. But JavaScript does not yet have the data-processing stack needed to refine raw data, which means data visualization is inevitably a multilanguage affair. I hope this book provides ammunition for my belief that Python is the natural complementary language to JavaScript's monopoly of browser visualizations.

Although this book is a big one (that fact is felt most keenly by the author right now), it has had to be very selective, leaving out a lot of very cool Python and JavaScript dataviz tools and focusing on the ones I think provide the best building blocks. The number of cool libraries I couldn't cover reflects the enormous vitality of the Python and JavaScript data science ecosystems. Even while the book was being written, brilliant new Python and JavaScript libraries were being introduced, and the pace continues.

I wanted to give the book some narrative structure by setting a data transformation challenge. All data visualization is essentially transformative, and showing the journey from one reflection of a dataset (HTML tables and lists) to a more modern, engaging, interactive, and, fundamentally, browser-based one seemed a good way to introduce key data visualization tools in a working context. The challenge I set was to transform a basic Wikipedia list of Nobel Prize winners into a modern, interactive, browser-based visualization. Thus the same dataset is presented in a more accessible, engaging form. But while the creation of the Nobel visualization lent the book a backbone, there were calculated redundancies. For example, although the book uses Flask and the MongoDB-based Python-EVE API to deliver the Nobel data to the browser, I also show how to do it with the SQL-based Flask-RESTless. If you work in the field of dataviz, you will need to be able to engage with both SQL and NoSQL databases, and this book aims to be impartial. Not every library demonstrated was used in transforming the Nobel dataset, but all are ones I have found most useful personally and think you will, too.

So the book is a collection of tools forming a chain, with the creation of the Nobel visualization providing a guiding narrative. You should be able to dip into relevant chapters when and if the need arises; the different parts of the book are self-contained so you can quickly review what you've learned when required.

Conventions Used in This Book

The following typographical conventions are used in this book:

Italic
> Indicates new terms, URLs, email addresses, filenames, and file extensions.

`Constant width`
> Used for program listings, as well as within paragraphs to refer to program elements such as variable or function names, databases, datatypes, environment variables, statements, and keywords.

`Constant width bold`
> Shows commands or other text that should be typed literally by the user.

`Constant width italic`
> Shows text that should be replaced with user-supplied values or by values determined by context.

This element signifies a tip or suggestion.

This element signifies a general note.

This element indicates a warning or caution.

Using Code Examples

Supplemental material (code examples, exercises, etc.) is available for download at *https://github.com/Kyrand/dataviz-with-python-and-js.*

This book is here to help you get your job done. In general, if example code is offered with this book, you may use it in your programs and documentation. You do not need to contact us for permission unless you're reproducing a significant portion of the code. For example, writing a program that uses several chunks of code from this book does not require permission. Selling or distributing a CD-ROM of examples from O'Reilly books does require permission. Answering a question by citing this book and quoting example code does not require permission. Incorporating a significant amount of example code from this book into your product's documentation does require permission.

We appreciate, but do not require, attribution. An attribution usually includes the title, author, publisher, and ISBN. For example: "*Data Visualization with Python and JavaScript* by Kyran Dale (O'Reilly). Copyright 2016 Kyran Dale, 978-1-491-92051-0."

If you feel your use of code examples falls outside fair use or the permission given above, feel free to contact us at *permissions@oreilly.com.*

Safari® Books Online

 *Safari Books Online* is an on-demand digital library that delivers expert content in both book and video form from the world's leading authors in technology and business.

Technology professionals, software developers, web designers, and business and creative professionals use Safari Books Online as their primary resource for research, problem solving, learning, and certification training.

((("Safari® Books Online")))Safari Books Online offers a range of plans and pricing for enterprise, government, education, and individuals.

Members have access to thousands of books, training videos, and prepublication manuscripts in one fully searchable database from publishers like O'Reilly Media, Prentice Hall Professional, Addison-Wesley Professional, Microsoft Press, Sams, Que, Peachpit Press, Focal Press, Cisco Press, John Wiley & Sons, Syngress, Morgan Kaufmann, IBM Redbooks, Packt, Adobe Press, FT Press, Apress, Manning, New Riders, McGraw-Hill, Jones & Bartlett, Course Technology, and hundreds more. For more information about Safari Books Online, please visit us online.

How to Contact Us

Please address comments and questions concerning this book to the publisher:

O'Reilly Media, Inc.
1005 Gravenstein Highway North
Sebastopol, CA 95472
800-998-9938 (in the United States or Canada)
707-829-0515 (international or local)
707-829-0104 (fax)

We have a web page for this book, where we list errata, examples, and any additional information. You can access this page at *http://bit.ly/dataVisualization_PyJS*.

To comment or ask technical questions about this book, send email to *bookquestions@oreilly.com*.

For more information about our books, courses, conferences, and news, see our website at *http://www.oreilly.com*.

Find us on Facebook: *http://facebook.com/oreilly*

Follow us on Twitter: *http://twitter.com/oreillymedia*

Watch us on YouTube: *http://www.youtube.com/oreillymedia*

Acknowledgments

Thanks first to Meghan Blanchette, who set the ball rolling and steered that ball through its first very rough chapters. Dawn Schanafelt then took the helm and did the bulk of the very necessary editing. Kristen Brown did a brilliant job taking the book through production, aided by Gillian McGarvey's impressively tenacious copy editing. Working with such talented, dedicated professionals has been an honor and a privilege—and an education: the book would have been so much easier to write if I'd known then what I know now. Isn't that always the way?

Many thanks to Amy Zielinski for making the author look better than he deserves.

The book benefited from some very helpful feedback. So much thanks to Christophe Viau, Tom Parslow, Peter Cook, Ian Macinnes, and Ian Ozsvald.

I'd also like to thank the valiant bug hunters who answered my appeal during Early Release. At time of writing, these are Douglas Kelley, Pavel Suk, Brigham Hausman, Marco Hemken, Noble Kennamer, Manfredi Biasutti, Matthew Maldonado, and Geert Bauwens.

Introduction

This book aims to get you up to speed with what is, in my opinion, the most powerful data visualization stack going: Python and JavaScript. You'll learn enough about big libraries like Pandas and D3 to start crafting your own web data visualizations and refining your own toolchain. Expertise will come with practice, but this book presents a shallow learning curve to basic competence.

 If you're reading this, I'd love to hear any feedback you have. Please post it to *pyjsdata-viz@kyrandale.com*. Thanks a lot.

You'll also find a working copy of the Nobel visualization the book literally and figuratively builds toward at *http://kyrandale.com/static/pyjs dataviz/index.html*.

The bulk of this book tells one of the innumerable tales of data visualization, one carefully selected to showcase some powerful Python and JavaScript libraries and tools which together form a toolchain. This toolchain gathers raw, unrefined data at its start and delivers a rich, engaging web visualization at its end. Like all tales of data visualization, it is a tale of transformation—in this case, transforming a basic Wikipedia list of Nobel Prize winners into an interactive visualization, bringing the data to life and making exploration of the prize's history easy and fun.

A primary motivation for writing the book is the belief that, whatever data you have and whatever story you want to tell with it, the natural home for the visualizations you transform it into is the Web. As a delivery platform, it is orders of magnitude more powerful than what came before, and this book aims to smooth the passage from desktop- or server-based data analysis and processing to getting the fruits of that labor out on the Web.

But the most ambitious aim of this book is to persuade you that working with these two powerful languages toward the goal of delivering powerful web visualizations is actually fun and engaging.

I think many potential dataviz programmers assume there is a big divide between *web development* and doing what they would like to do, which is program in Python and JavaScript. Web development involves loads of arcane knowledge about markup languages, style scripts, and administration, and can't be done without tools with strange names like *Gulp* or *Yeoman*. I aim to show that, these days, that big divide can be collapsed to a thin and very permeable membrane, allowing you to focus on what you do well: programming stuff (see Figure P-1) with minimal effort, relegating the web servers to data delivery.

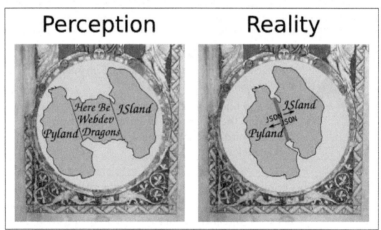

Figure P-1. Here be webdev dragons

Who This Book Is For

First off, this book is for anyone with a reasonable grasp of Python or JavaScript who wants to explore one of the most exciting areas in the data-processing ecosystem right now: the exploding field of data visualization for the Web. It's also about addressing some specific pain points that in my experience are quite common.

When you get commissioned to write a technical book, chances are your editor will sensibly caution you to think in terms of *pain points* that your book could address. The two key pain points of this book are best illustrated by way of a couple of stories, including one of my own and one that has been told to me in various guises by JavaScripters I know.

Many years ago, as an academic researcher, I came across Python and fell in love. I had been writing some fairly complex simulations in C++, and Python's simplicity and power was a breath of fresh air from all the boilerplate Makefiles, declarations, definitions, and the like. Programming became fun. Python was the perfect glue, playing nicely with my C++ libraries (Python wasn't then and still isn't a speed demon) and doing, with consummate ease, all the stuff that is such a pain in low-level languages (e.g., file I/O, database access, and serialization). I started to write all my graphical user interfaces (GUIs) and visualizations in Python, using *wxPython*, *PyQt*, and a whole load of other refreshingly easy toolsets. Unfortunately, although I think some of these tools are pretty cool and would love to share them with the world, the effort required to package them, distribute them, and make sure they still work with modern libraries represents a hurdle I'm unlikely to ever overcome.

At the time, there existed what in theory was the perfect universal distribution system for the software I'd so lovingly crafted—namely, the web browser. Web browsers were (and are) available on pretty much every computer on Earth, with their own built-in, interpreted programming language: write once, run everywhere. But Python didn't play in the web browser's sandpit and browsers were incapable of ambitious graphics and visualizations, being pretty much limited to static images and the odd jQuery (*https://jQuery.com/*) transformation. JavaScript was a "toy" language tied to a very slow interpreter that was good for little *DOM* (*https://en.wikipedia.org/wiki/Document_Object_Model*) tricks but certainly nothing approaching what I could do on the desktop with Python. So that route was discounted, out of hand. My visualizations wanted to be on the Web, but there was no route through.

Fast forward a decade or so and, thanks to an arms race initiated by Google and their V8 engine, JavaScript is now orders of magnitude faster; in fact, it's now an awful lot faster than Python.[1] HTML has also tidied up its act a bit, in the guise of HTML5. It's a lot nicer to work with, with much less boilerplate code. What were loosely followed and distinctly shaky protocols like Scalable Vector Graphics (SVG) have firmed up nicely, thanks to powerful visualization libraries, D3 in particular. Modern browsers are obliged to work nicely with SVG and, increasingly, 3D in the form of *WebGL* and its children such as *THREE.js*. The visualizations I was doing in Python are now possible on your local web browser, and the payoff is that, with very little effort, they can be made accessible to every desktop, laptop, smartphone, and tablet in the world.

So why aren't Pythonistas flocking to get their data out there in a form they dictate? After all, the alternative to crafting it yourself is leaving it to somebody else, something most data scientists I know would find far from ideal. Well, first there's that term *web development*, connoting complicated markup, opaque stylesheets, a whole slew of new tools to learn, IDEs to master. And then there's JavaScript itself, a strange language, thought of as little more than a toy until recently and having something of the neither fish nor fowl to it. I aim to take those pain points head-on and show that you can craft modern web visualizations (often single-page apps) with a very minimal amount of HTML and CSS boilerplate, allowing you to focus on the programming, and that JavaScript is an easy leap for the Pythonista. But you don't have to leap; Chapter 2 is a language bridge that aims to help Pythonistas and JavaScripters bridge the divide between the languages by highlighting common elements and providing simple translations.

The second story is a common one among JavaScript data visualizers I know. Processing data in JavaScript is far from ideal. There are few heavyweight libraries, and although recent functional enhancements to the language make data munging much more pleasant, there's still no real data-processing ecosystem to speak of. So there's a distinct asymmetry between the hugely powerful visualization libraries available (D3, as ever, is the paramount library), and the ability to clean and process any data delivered to the browser. All of this mandates doing your data cleaning, processing, and exploring in another language or with a toolkit like Tableau, and this often

---

[1] See here (*http://bit.ly/291UVme*) for a fairly jaw-dropping comparison.

devolves into piecemeal forays into vaguely remembered Matlab, the steepish learning curve that is R, or a Java library or two.

Toolkits like Tableau (*http://www.tableau.com/*), although very impressive, are often, in my experience, ultimately frustrating for programmers. There's no way to replicate in a GUI the expressive power of a good, general-purpose programming language. Plus, what if you want to create a little web server to deliver your processed data? That means learning at least one new web-development-capable language.

In other words, JavaScripters starting to stretch their data visualization are looking for a complementary data-processing stack that requires the least investment of time and has the shallowest learning curve.

Minimal Requirements to Use This Book

I always feel reluctant to place restrictions on people's explorations, particularly in the context of programming and the Web, which is chock-full of autodidacts (how else would one learn with the halls of academia being light years behind the trends?), learning fast and furiously, gloriously uninhibited by the formal constraints that used to apply to learning. Python and JavaScript are pretty much as simple as it gets, programming-language-wise, and are both top candidates for best first language. There isn't a huge cognitive load in interpreting the code.

In that spirit, there are expert programmers who, without any experience of Python and JavaScript, could consume this book and be writing custom libraries within a week. These are also the people most likely to ignore anything I write here, so good luck to you people if you decide to make the effort.

For beginner programmers, fresh to Python or JavaScript, this book is probably too advanced for you, and I recommend taking advantage of the plethora of books, web resources, screencasts, and the like that make learning so easy these days. Focus on a personal itch, a problem you want to solve, and learn to program by doing—it's the only way.

For people who have programmed a bit in either Python or Java-Script, my advised threshold to entry is that you have used a few libraries together, understand the basic idioms of your language, and can look at a piece of novel code and generally get a hook on what's going on—in other words, Pythonistas who can use a few modules of the standard library, and JavaScripters who can not only use JQuery but understand some of its source code.

Why Python and JavaScript?

Why JavaScript is an easy question to answer. For now and the foreseeable future, there is only one first class, browser-based programming language. There have been various attempts to extend, augment, and usurp, but good old, plain-vanilla JS is still preeminent. If you want to craft modern, dynamic, interactive visualizations and, at the touch of a button, deliver them to the world, at some point you are going to run into JavaScript. You might not need to be a Zen master, but basic competence is a fundamental price of entry into one of the most exciting areas of modern data science. This book hopes to get you into the ballpark.

Why Not Python on the Browser?

There are currently some very impressive initiatives aimed at enabling Python-produced visualizations, often built on Matplotlib (*http://matplotlib.org/*), to run in the browser. They achieve this by converting the Python code into JavaScript based on the canvas or svg drawing contexts. The most popular and mature of these are Bokeh (*http://bokeh.pydata.org/en/latest/*) and the recently open-sourced Plotly (*https://plot.ly*). While these are both brilliant initiatives, I feel that in order to do web-based dataviz, you have to bite the JavaScript bullet to exploit the increasing potential of the medium. That's why, along with space constraints, I'm not covering the Python-to-JavaScript dataviz converters.

While there is some brilliant coding behind these JavaScript converters and many solid use cases, they do have big limitations:

- Automated code conversion may well do the job, but the code produced is usually pretty impenetrable for a human being.

- Adapting and customizing the resulting plots using the powerful browser-based JavaScript development environment is likely to be very painful.

- You are limited to the subset of plot types currently available in the libraries.

- Interactivity is very basic at the moment. Stitching this together is better done in JavaScript, using the browser's developer tools.

Bear in mind that the people building these libraries have to be Java-Script experts, so if you want to understand anything of what they're doing and eventually express yourself, then you'll have to get up to scratch with some JavaScript.

My basic take-home message regarding Python-to-JavaScript conversion is that it has its place but would only be generally justified if JavaScript were 10 times harder to program than it is. The fiddly, iterative process of creating a modern browser-based data visualization is hard enough using a first-class language without having to negotiate an indirect journey through a second-class one.

Why Python for Data Processing

Why you should choose Python for your data-processing needs is a little more involved. For a start, there are good alternatives as far as data processing is concerned. Let's deal with a few candidates for the job, starting with the enterprise behemoth Java.

Java

Among the other main, general-purpose programming languages, only *Java* offers anything like the rich ecosystem of libraries that Python does, with considerably more native speed too. But while *Java* is a lot easier to program in than languages like C++, it isn't, in my opinion, a particularly nice language to program in, having rather too much in the way of tedious boilerplate code and excessive verbiage. This sort of thing starts to weigh heavily after a while and makes for a hard slog at the code face. As for speed, Python's default interpreter is slow, but Python is a great *glue* language that plays nicely with other languages. This ability is demonstrated by the big Python data-processing libraries like *NumPy* (and its dependent, *Pandas*), *Scipy*, and the like, which use C++ and Fortran libraries to do the heavy lifting while providing the ease of use of a simple, scripting language.

R

The venerable R has, until recently, been the tool of choice for many data scientists and is probably Python's main competitor in the space. Like Python, R benefits from a very active community, some great tools like the plotting library ggplot, and a syntax specially crafted for data science and statistics. But this specialism is a double-edged sword. Because R was developed for a specific purpose, it means that if, for example, you wish to write a web server to serve your R-processed data, you have to skip out to another language with all the attendant learning overheads, or try to hack something together in a round-hole/square-peg sort of way. Python's general-purpose nature and its rich ecosystem mean one can do pretty much everything required of a data-processing pipeline (JS visuals aside) without having to leave its comfort zone. Personally, it is a small sacrifice to pay for a little syntactic clunkiness.

Others

There are other alternatives to doing your data processing with Python, but none of them come close to the flexibility and power afforded by a general-purpose, easy-to-use programming language with a rich ecosystem of libraries. While, for example, mathematical programming environments such as Matlab and Mathematica have active communities and a plethora of great libraries, they hardly count as general purpose, because they are designed to be used within a closed garden. They are also proprietary, which means a significant initial investment and a different vibe to Python's resoundingly open source environment.

GUI-driven dataviz tools like Tableau (*http://www.tableau.com/*) are great creations but will quickly frustrate someone used to the freedom to programming. They tend to work great as long as you are singing from their songsheet, as it were. Deviations from the designated path get painful very quickly.

Python's Getting Better All the Time

As things stand, I think a very good case can be made for Python being the budding data scientist's language of choice. But things are not standing still; in fact, Python's capabilities in this area are growing at an astonishing rate. To put it in perspective, I have been programming in Python for over 15 years and have grown used to being surprised if I can't find a Python module to help solve a problem at hand, but I find myself surprised at the growth of Python's data-processing abilities, with a new, powerful library appearing weekly. To give an example, Python has traditionally been weak on statistical analysis libraries, with R being far ahead. Recently a number of powerful modules, such as *StatsModel*, have started to close this gap fast.

So Python is a thriving data-processing ecosystem with pretty much unmatched general purpose, and it's getting better week by week. It's understandable why so many in the community are in a state of such excitement—it's pretty exhilarating.

As far as visualization in the browser, the good news is that there's more to JavaScript than its privileged, nay, exclusive place in the web ecosystem. Thanks to an interpreter arms race that has seen performance increase in staggering leaps and bounds and some powerful visualization libraries such as D3, which would complement any language out there, JavaScript now has serious chops.

In short, Python and JavaScript are a wonderful complement for data visualization on the Web, each needing the other to provide a vital missing component.

What You'll Learn

There are some big Python and JavaScript libraries in our dataviz toolchain, and comprehensive coverage of them all would require a number of books. Nevertheless, I think that the fundamentals of most libraries, and certainly the ones covered here, can be grasped fairly quickly. Expertise takes time and practice but the basic knowledge needed to be productive is, so to speak, low-hanging fruit.

In that sense, this book aims to give you a solid backbone of practical knowledge, strong enough to take the weight of future development. I aim to make the learning curve as shallow as possible and get you over the initial climb with the practical skills needed to start refining your art.

This book emphasizes pragmatism and best practice. It's going to cover a fair amount of ground, and there isn't enough space for too many theoretical diversions. I will aim to cover those aspects of the libraries in the toolchain that are most commonly used, and point you to resources for the other stuff. Most libraries have a hard core of functions, methods, classes, and the like that are the chief, functional subset. With these at your disposal, you can actually do stuff. Eventually, you'll find an itch you can't scratch with those, at which time good books, documentation, and online forums will be your friend.

The Choice of Libraries

I had three things in mind while choosing the libraries used in the book.

1. Open source and free as in beer (*http://www.howtogeek.com/howto/31717/what-do-the-phrases-free-speech-vs.-free-beer-really-mean/*)—you shouldn't have to invest any extra money to learn with this book.
2. Longevity—generally well-established, community-driven, and popular.
3. Best of breed (assuming good support and an active community), at the sweet spot between popularity and utility.

The skills you learn here should be relevant for a long time. Generally, the obvious candidates have been chosen—libraries that write their own ticket, as it were. Where appropriate, I will highlight the alternative choices and give a rationale for my selection.

Preliminaries

A few preliminary chapters are needed before beginning the transformative journey of our Nobel dataset through the toolchain. These cover the basic skills necessary to make the rest of the toolchain chapters run more fluidly. The first few chapters cover the following:

Chapter 2
> Building a language bridge between Python and JavaScript

Chapter 3
> How to pass around data with Python, through various file formats and databases

Chapter 4
> Covering the basic web development needed by the book

These chapters are part tutorial, part reference, and it's fine to skip straight to the beginning of the toolchain, dipping back where needed.

The Dataviz Toolchain

The main part of the book demonstrates the data-visualization toolchain, which follows the journey of a dataset of Nobel Prize winners from raw, freshly scraped data to engaging, interactive JavaScript visualization. During the collection process, the refinement and transformation of a number of big libraries are demonstrated, summarized in Figure P-2. These libraries are the industrial lathes of our toolchain: rich, mature tools that demonstrate the power of the Python+JavaScript dataviz stack. The following sections contain a brief introduction to the five stages of our toolchain and their major libraries.

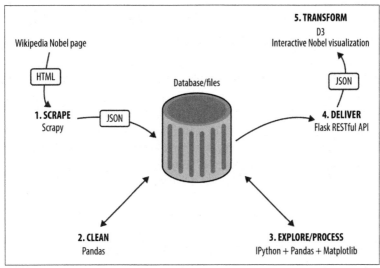

Figure P-2. The dataviz toolchain

1. Scraping Data with Scrapy

The first challenge for any data visualizer is getting hold of the data they need, whether by request or to scratch a personal itch. If you're very lucky, this will be delivered to you in pristine form, but more often than not you have to go find it. I'll cover the various ways you can use Python to get data off the Web (e.g., web APIs or Google spreadsheets). The Nobel Prize dataset for the toolchain demonstration is scraped from its Wikipedia pages using Scrapy.[2]

Python's Scrapy is an industrial-strength scraper that does all the data throttling and media pipelining, which are indispensable if you plan on scraping significant amounts of data. Scraping is often the only way to get the data you are interested in, and once you've mastered Scrapy's workflow, all those previously off-limits datasets are only a spider away.[3]

2. Cleaning Data with Pandas

The dirty secret of dataviz is that pretty much all data is dirty, and turning it into something you can use may well occupy a lot more time than anticipated. This is an unglamorous process that can easily steal over half your time, which is all the more reason to get good at it and use the right tools.

Pandas is a huge player in the Python data-processing ecosystem. It's a Python data-analysis library whose chief component is the Data Frame, essentially a programmatic spreadsheet. Pandas extends NumPy, Python's powerful numeric library, into the realm of heterogeneous datasets, the kind of categorical, temporal, and ordinal information that data visualizers have to deal with. As well as being great for interactively exploring your data (using its built-in Matplotlib plots), Pandas is well suited to the drudge-work of cleaning data, making it easy to locate duplicate records, fix dodgy date-strings, find missing fields, and so on.

3. Exploring Data with Pandas and Matplotlib

Before beginning the transformation of your data into a visualization, you need to understand it. The patterns, trends, and anomalies hidden in the data will inform the stories you are trying to tell with it, whether that's explaining a recent rise in year-by-year widget sales or demonstrating global climate change.

---

2 Web scraping (*https://en.wikipedia.org/wiki/Web_scraping*) is a computer software technique to extract information from websites, usually involving getting and parsing web pages.

3 Scrapy's controllers are called spiders.

In conjunction with *IPython*, the Python interpreter on steroids, Pandas and Matplotlib (with additions such as Seaborn) provide a great way to explore your data interactively, generating rich, inline plots from the command line, slicing and dicing your data to reveal interesting patterns. The results of these explorations can then be easily saved to file or database to be passed on to your JavaScript visualization.

4. Delivering Your Data with Flask

Once you've explored and refined your data, you'll need to serve it to the web browser, where a JavaScript library like D3 can transform it. One of the great strengths of using a general-purpose language like Python is that it's as comfortable rolling a web server in a few lines of code as it is crunching through large datasets with special-purpose libraries like NumPy and Scipy.[4] *Flask* is Python's most popular lightweight server and is perfect for creating small, RESTful[5] APIs that can be used by JavaScript to get data from the server, in files or databases, to the browser. As I'll demonstrate, you can roll a RESTful API in a few lines of code, capable of delivering data from SQL or NoSQL databases.

5. Transforming Data into Interactive Visualizations with D3

Once the data is cleaned and refined, we have the visualization phase, where selected reflections of the dataset are presented, ideally allowing the user to explore them interactively. Depending on the data, this might involve bar charts, maps, or novel visualizations.

D3 is JavaScript's powerhouse visualization library, arguably one of the most powerful visualization tools irrespective of language. We'll use D3 to create a novel Nobel Prize visualization with multiple elements and user interaction, allowing people to explore the dataset for items of interest. D3 can be challenging to learn, but I hope to bring you quickly up to speed and ready to start honing your skills in the doing.

---

4 The scientific Python library, part of the NumPy ecosystem.

5 REST is short for Representational State Transfer, the dominant style for HTTP-based web APIs and much recommended.

Smaller Libraries

In addition to the big libraries covered, there is a large supporting cast of smaller libraries. These are the indispensable smaller tools, the hammers and spanners of the toolchain. Python in particular has an incredibly rich ecosystem, with small, specialized libraries for almost every conceivable job. Among the strong supporting cast, some particularly deserving of mention are:

requests
> Python's go-to HTTP library, fully deserving its motto "HTTP for humans." requests is far superior to urllib2, one of Python's included batteries.

SQLAlchemy
> The best Python SQL toolkit and object-relational mapper (ORM) there is. It's feature rich and makes working with the various SQL-based databases a relative breeze.

Seaborn
> A great addition to Python's plotting powerhouse Matplotlib, adding some very useful plot types including some statistical ones of particular use to data visualizers. It also adds arguably superior aesthetics, overriding the Matplotlib defaults.

crossfilter
> Even though JavaScript's data-processing libraries are a work in progress, a few really useful ones have emerged recently, with crossfilter being a stand-out. It enables very fast filtering of row-columnar datasets and is ideally suited to dataviz work, which is unsurprising because one of its creators is Mike Bostock, the father of D3.

Using the Book

Although the book's different parts follow a process of data transformation, this book doesn't need to be read cover to cover. The first part provides a basic toolkit for Python- and JavaScript-based web dataviz and will inevitably have content that is familiar to many readers. Cherry-pick for the stuff you don't know and dip back as required (there will be link backs further on, as required). The language learning bridge between Python and JavaScript will be unnecessary for those seasoned in both languages, although there may still be some useful nuggets.

The remaining parts of the book, following our toolchain as it transforms a fairly uninspiring web list into a fully fledged, interactive D3 visualization, are essentially self-contained. If you want to dive immediately into Part III and some data cleaning and exploration with Pandas, go right ahead, but be aware that it assumes the existence of a dirty Nobel Prize dataset. You can see how that was produced by Scrapy later if that fits your schedule. Equally, if you want to dive straight into creating the Nobel-viz app in parts Part IV and Part V, be aware that they assume a clean Nobel Prize dataset.

Whatever route you take, I suggest eventually aiming to acquire all the basic skills covered in the book if you intend to make dataviz your profession.

A Little Bit of Context

This is a practical book and assumes that the reader has a pretty good idea of what he or she wants to visualize and how that visualization should look and feel, as well as a desire to get cracking on it, unencumbered by too much theory. Nevertheless, drawing on the history of data visualization can both clarify the central themes of the book and add valuable context. It can also help explain why now is such an exciting time to be entering the field, as technological innovation is driving novel dataviz forms, and people are grappling with the problem of presenting the increasing amount of multidimensional data generated by the Internet.

Data visualization has an impressive body of theory behind it and there are some great books out there that I recommend you read (see "Recommended Books" on page xxxii for a little selection). The practical benefit of understanding the way humans visually harvest information cannot be overstated. It can be easily demonstrated, for example, that a pie chart is almost always a bad way of presenting comparative data and a simple bar chart is far preferable. By conducting psychometric experiments, we now have a pretty good idea of how to trick the human visual system and make relationships in the data harder to grasp. Conversely, we can show that some visual forms are close to optimal for amplifying contrast. The literature, at its very least, provides some useful rules of thumb that suggest good candidates for any particular data narrative.

In essence, good dataviz tries to present data, collected from measurements in the world (empirical) or as the product of abstract mathematical explorations (e.g., the beautiful fractal patterns of the *Mandlebrot set* (*https://en.wikipedia.org/wiki/Mandelbrot_set*)), in such a way as to draw out or emphasize any patterns or trends that might exist. These patterns can be simple (e.g., average weight by country), or the product of sophisticated statistical analysis (e.g., data clustering in a higher dimensional space).

In its untransformed state, we can imagine this data floating as a nebulous cloud of numbers or categories. Any patterns or correlations are entirely obscure. It's easy to forget but the humble spreadsheet (Figure P-3 a) is a data visualization—the ordering of data into row-columnar form an attempt to tame it, make its manipulation easier, and highlight discrepancies (e.g., actuarial bookkeeping). Of course, most people are not adept at spotting patterns in rows of numbers so more accessible, visual forms were developed to engage with our visual cortex, the prime human conduit for information about the world. Enter the bar chart, pie chart,[6] and line chart. More imaginative ways were employed to distill statistical data in a more accessible form, one of the most famous being Charles Joseph Minard's visualization of Napoleon's disastrous Russian campaign of 1812 (Figure P-3 b).

The tan-colored stream in Figure P-3 b shows the advance of Napoleon's army on Moscow; the black line shows the retreat. The thickness of the stream represents the size of Napoleon's army, thinning as casualties mounted. A temperature chart below is used to indicate the temperature at locations along the way. Note the elegant way in which Minard has combined multidimensional data (casualty statistics, geographical location, and temperature) to give an impression of the carnage, which would be hard to grasp in any other way (imagine trying to jump from a chart of casualties to a list of locations and make the necessary connections). I would argue that the chief problem of modern interactive dataviz is exactly the same as that faced by Minard: how to move beyond conventional one-dimensional bar charts (perfectly good for many things) and

---

6 William Playfair's *Statistical Breviary* of 1801 having the dubious distinction of originating the pie chart.

develop new ways to communicate cross-dimensional patterns effectively.

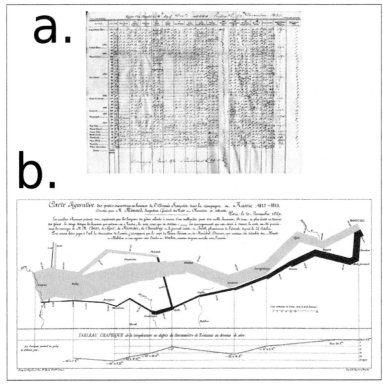

Figure P-3. (a) An early spreadsheet and (b) Joseph Minard's visualization of Napoleon's Russian campaign of 1812

Until quite recently, most of our experience of charts was not much different from those of Charles Minard's audience. They were pre-rendered and inert, and showed one reflection of the data, hopefully an important and insightful one but nevertheless under total control of the author. In this sense, the replacement of real ink points with computer screen pixels was only a change in the scale of distribution.

The leap to the Internet just replaced newsprint with pixels, the visualization still being unclickable and static. Recently, the combination of some powerful visualization libraries (D3 being preeminent among them) and a massive improvement in JavaScript's performance have opened the way to a new type of visualization, one that is easily accessible and dynamic, and actually encourages exploration and discovery. The clear distinction between data exploration and presentation is blurred. This new type of data visualization is the focus of this book and the reason why dataviz for the Web is such an exciting area right now. People are trying to create new ways to visualize data and make it more accessible/useful to the end user. This is nothing short of a revolution.

Summary

Dataviz on the Web is an exciting place to be right now with innovations in interactive visualizations coming thick and fast, and many (if not most) of them being developed with D3. JavaScript is the only browser-based language, so the cool visuals are by necessity being coded in it (or converted into it). But JavaScript lacks the tools or environment necessary for the less dramatic but just as vital element of modern dataviz: the aggregation, curation, and processing of the data. This is where Python rules the roost, providing a general-purpose, concise, and eminently readable programming language with access to an increasing stable of first-class data-processing tools. Many of these tools leverage the power of very fast, low-level libraries, making Python data processing fast as well as easy.

This book introduces some of those heavyweight tools, as well as a host of other smaller but equally vital tools. It also shows how Python and JavaScript in concert represent the best dataviz stack out there for anyone wishing to deliver their visualizations to the Internet.

Up next is the first part of the book, covering the preliminary skills needed for the toolchain. You can work through it now or skip ahead to Part II and the start of the toolchain, referring back when needed.

Recommended Books

Here are a few key data-visualization books to whet your appetite, covering the gamut from interactive dashboards to beautiful and insightful infographics.

- Tufte, Edward. *The Visual Display of Quantitative Information.* Graphics Press, 1983.

- Ware, Colin. *Information Visualization: Perception for Design.* Morgan Kaufmann, 2004.
- Rosenberg, Daniel. *Cartographies of Time: A History of the Timeline.* Princeton Architectural Press, 2012.
- Few, Stephen. *Information Dashboard Design: Displaying Data for at-a-glance Monitoring.* Analytics Press, 2013.
- Cairo, Alberto. *The Functional Art.* New Riders, 2012.
- Bertin, Jacques. *Semiology of Graphics: Diagrams, Networks, Maps.* Esri Press, 2010.

## CHAPTER 1

Development Setup

This chapter covers the downloads and software installations needed to use this book, and sketches out a recommended development environment. As you'll see, this isn't as onerous as it might once have been. I'll cover Python and JavaScript dependencies separately and give a brief overview of cross-language IDEs.

The Accompanying Code

There's a GitHub repository for the bulk of the code covered in this book, including the full Nobel Prize visualization. To get hold of it, just perform a git clone (*https://git-scm.com/docs/git-clone*) to a suitable local directory:

```
$ git clone https://github.com/Kyrand/
    dataviz-with-python-and-js.git
```

This should create a local *dataviz-with-python-and-js* directory with the key source code covered by the book.

Python

The bulk of the libraries covered in the book are Python-based, but what might have been a challenging attempt to provide comprehensive installation instructions for the various operating systems and their quirks is made much easier by the existence of Continuum Analytics' (*https://www.continuum.io/*) *Anaconda*, a Python platform that bundles together most of the popular analytics libraries in a convenient package.

Anaconda

Installing some of the bigger Python libraries used to be a challenge all in itself, particularly those such as NumPy that depend on complex low-level C and Fortran packages. That's why the existence of Anaconda is such a godsend. It does all the dependency checking and binary installs so you don't have to. It's also a very convenient resource for a book like this.

Python 2 or 3?

Right now, Python is in transition to version 3, a process that is taking longer than many would like. This is because Python 2+ works fine for many people, a lot of code will have to be converted,[1] and up until recently some of the big libraries, such as NumPy and Scipy, only worked for Python 2.5+.

Now that most of the major libraries are compatible with Python 3, it would be a no-brainer to recommend that version for this book. Unfortunately, one of the few holdouts is Scrapy, a big tool on our toolchain,[2] which you'll learn about in Chapter 6. I don't want to oblige you to run two versions, so for that reason we'll be using the version 2 Anaconda package.

I will be using the new print function,[3] which means all the non-Scrapy code will work fine with Python 3.

To get your free Anaconda install, just navigate your browser to *https://www.continuum.io/downloads*, choose the version for your operating system (as of late 2015, we're going with Python 2.7), and follow the instructions. Windows and OS X get a graphical installer (just download and double-click), whereas Linux requires you to run a little bash script:

```
$ bash Anaconda-2.3.0-Linux-x86_64.sh
```

I recommend sticking to defaults when installing Anaconda.

---

1 There are a number of pretty reliable automatic converters out there.

2 The Scrapy team is working hard to rectify this. Scrapy relies on Python's Twisted, an event-driven networking engine also making the journey to Python 3+ compatibility.

3 This is imported from the __future__ module (i.e., from __future__ import print_function).

Checking the Anaconda Install

The best way to check that your Anaconda install went well is to try firing up an IPython session at the command line. How you do this depends on your operating system:

At the Windows command prompt:

```
C:\Users\Kyran>ipython
```

At the OS X or Linux prompt:

```
$ ipython
```

This should produce something like the following:

```
kyran@Tweedledum:~/projects/pyjsbook$ ipython
Python 2.7.10 |Anaconda 2.3.0 (64-bit)|
          (default, May 28 2015, 17:02:03) Type
"copyright", "credits" or "license" for more information.

IPython 3.2.0 -- An enhanced Interactive Python.  Anaconda is
brought to you by Continuum Analytics.  Please check out:
http://continuum.io/thanks and
https://anaconda.org
...
```

Most installation problems will stem from a badly configured environment PATH variable. This PATH needs to contain the location of the main *Anaconda* directory and its *Scripts* subdirectory. In Windows, this should look something like:

```
'...C:\\Anaconda;C:\\Anaconda\Scripts...
```

You can access and adjust the environment variables in Windows 7 by typing **environment variables** in the program's search field and selecting "Edit environment variables" or in XP via Control Panel→System→ Advanced→Environment Variables.

In OS X and Linux systems, you should be able to set your PATH variable explicitly by appending this line to the *.bashrc* file in your home directory:

```
export PATH=/home/kyran/anaconda/bin:$PATH
```

Installing Extra Libraries

Anaconda contains almost all the Python libraries covered in this book (see here (*http://docs.continuum.io/anaconda/pkg-docs*) for the full list of Anaconda libraries). Where we need a non-Anaconda library, we can use pip (*https://pypi.python.org/pypi/pip*) (short for Pip Installs Python), the de facto standard for installing Python libraries. Using pip to install is as easy as can be. Just call pip install followed by the name of the package from the command line and it should be installed or, with any luck, give a sensible error:

```
$ pip install dataset
```

Virtual Environments

Virtual environments (*http://docs.python-guide.org/en/latest/dev/virtualenvs/*) provide a way of creating a sandboxed development environment with a particular Python version and/or set of third-party libraries. Using these virtual environments avoids polluting your global Python with these installs and gives you a lot more flexibility (you can play with different package versions or change your Python version if need be). The use of virtual environments is becoming a best practice in Python development, and I strongly suggest that you follow it.

Anaconda comes with a conda system command that makes creating and using virtual environments easy. Let's create a special one for this book, based on the full Anaconda package:

```
$ conda create --name pyjsviz anaconda
...
#
# To activate this environment, use:
# $ source activate pyjsviz
#
# To deactivate this environment, use:
# $ source deactivate
#
```

As the final message says, to use this virtual environment you need only source activate it (for Windows machines you can leave out the source):

```
$ source activate pyjsviz
discarding /home/kyran/anaconda/bin from PATH
prepending /home/kyran/.conda/envs/pyjsviz/bin to PATH
(pyjsviz) $
```

Note that you get a helpful cue at the command line to let you know which virtual environment you're using.

The conda command can do a lot more than just facilitate virtual environments, combining the functionality of Python's pip installer and `virtualenv` command, among other things. You can get a full rundown here (*http://conda.pydata.org/docs/using/using.html*).

JavaScript

The good news is that you don't need much JavaScript software at all. The only must-have is the Chrome/Chromium web browser, which is used in this book. It offers the most powerful set of developer tools of any current browser and is cross-platform.

To download Chrome, just go here (*https://www.google.com/chrome/browser/desktop/*) and download the version for your operating system. This should be automatically detected.

If you want something slightly less Google-fied, then you can use Chromium, the browser based on the open source project from which Google Chrome is derived. You can find up-to-date instructions on installation here (*https://www.chromium.org/getting-involved/download-chromium*) or just head to the main download page (*https://download-chromium.appspot.com/*). Chromium tends to lag Chrome feature-wise but is still an eminently usable development browser.

Content Delivery Networks

One of the reasons you don't have to worry about installing JavaScript libraries is that the ones used in this book are available via content delivery networks (CDN). Rather than having the libraries installed on your local machine, the JavaScript is retrieved by the browser over the Web, from the closest available server. This should make things very fast—faster than if you served the content yourself.

To include a library via CDN, you use the usual `<script>` tag, typically placed at the bottom of your HTML page. For example, the following call adds the latest (as of late 2015) version of D3:

```
<script
  src="https://cdnjs.cloudflare.com/ajax/libs/d3/3.5.6/d3.min.js"
  charset="utf-8">
</script>
```

Installing Libraries Locally

If you need to install JavaScript libraries locally, because, for example, you anticipate doing some offline development work or can't guarantee an Internet connection, there are a number of fairly simple ways to do so.

You can just download the separate libraries and put them in your local server's static folder. This is a typical folder structure. Third-party libraries go in the *static/libs* directory off root, like so:

```
nobel_viz/
└── static
    ├── css
    ├── data
    ├── libs
    │   └── d3.min.js
    └── js
```

If you organize things this way, to use D3 in your scripts now requires a local file reference with the <script> tag:

```
<script src="/static/libs/d3.min.js"></script>
```

Databases

This book shows how to interact with the main SQL databases and MongoDB (*https://www.mongodb.org/*), the chief nonrelational or NoSQL (*https://en.wikipedia.org/wiki/NoSQL*) database, from Python. We'll be using SQLite (*https://www.sqlite.org/*), the brilliant file-based SQL database. Here are the download details for SQLite and MongoDB:

SQLite
    A great, file-based, serverless SQL database. It should come standard with OS X and Linux. For Windows, follow this guide (*http://www.tutorialspoint.com/sqlite/sqlite_installation.htm*).

MongoDB
    By a long shot, the most popular NoSQL database. Installation instructions here (*http://docs.mongodb.org/manual/installa tion/*).

Note that we'll be using Python's SQLAlchemy (*http://www.sqlalchemy.org/*) SQL library either directly or through libraries that build on it. This means we can convert any SQLite examples to another SQL backend (e.g., MySQL (*https://www.mysql.com/*) or

PostgreSQL (*http://www.postgresql.org/*)) by changing a configuration line or two.

Installing MongoDB

MongoDB can be a little trickier to install than some databases, but it is well worth the effort. Its JSON-like document storage makes it a natural for web-based dataviz work.

For OS X users, check out this guide (*http://www.choskim.me/how-to-install-mongodb-on-apples-mac-os-x/*), which fills out a few details from the official docs.

This Windows-specific guide (*https://docs.mongodb.org/manual/tuto rial/install-mongodb-on-windows/*) from the official docs should get your MongoDB server up and running. You will probably need to use administrator privileges to create the necessary data directories and so on.

More often than not these days, you'll be installing MongoDB to a Linux-based server, most commonly an Ubuntu variant, which uses the Deb (*https://en.wikipedia.org/wiki/Deb_(file_format)*)) file format to deliver its packages. The official MongoDB docs (*https:// docs.mongodb.org/manual/tutorial/install-mongodb-on-ubuntu/*) do a good job covering an Ubuntu install.

MongoDB uses a *data* directory to store to and, depending how you install it, you may need to create this yourself. On OS X and Linux boxes, the default is a *data* directory off the root directory, which you can create using mkdir as a superuser (sudo):

```
$ sudo mkdir /data
$ sudo mkdir /data/db
```

You'll then want to set ownership to yourself:

```
$ sudo chown 'whoami' /data/db
```

With Windows, installing the MongoDB Community Edition (*http://bit.ly/1S9am86*), you can create the necessary *data* directory with the following command:

```
$ md \data\db
```

The MongoDB server will often be started by default on Linux boxes; otherwise, on Linux and OS X the following command will start a server instance:

```
$ mongod
```

On Windows Community Edition, the following, run from a command prompt, will start a server instance:

```
C:\mongodb\bin\mongod.exe
```

Integrated Development Environments

As I explain in "The Myth of IDEs, Frameworks, and Tools" on page 90, you don't need an IDE to program in Python or JavaScript. The development tools provided by modern browsers, Chrome in particular, mean you only really need a good code editor to have pretty much the optimal setup. It's free as in beer too.

For Python, I have tried a few IDEs but they've never stuck. The main itch I was trying to scratch was a decent debugging system. Setting breakpoints in Python with a text editor isn't particularly elegant, and using the command-line debugger pdb feels a little too old school sometimes. Nevertheless, Python's logging is so easy and effective that breakpoints became an edge case that didn't justify leaving my favorite editor,[4] which does pretty decent code completion and solid syntax highlighting.

In no particular order, here are a few that I've tried and not disliked:

PyCharm (https://www.jetbrains.com/pycharm/)
This option offers solid code assistance and good debugging.

PyDev (http://pydev.org/)
If you like Eclipse and can tolerate its rather large footprint, this might well be for you.

WingIDE (http://www.wingware.com/)
This is a solid bet, with a great debugger and incremental improvements over a decade-and-a-half's worth of development.

Summary

With free, packaged Python distributions such as Anaconda, and the inclusion of sophisticated JavaScript development tools in freely

---

4 Emacs with VIM key bindings.

available web browsers, the necessary Python and JavaScript elements of your development environment are a couple of clicks away. Add a favorite editor and a database of choice,[5] and you are pretty much good to go. There are additional libraries, such as node.js, that can be useful but don't count as essential. Now that we've established our programming environment, the next chapters will teach the preliminaries needed to start our journey of data transformation along the toolchain, starting with a language bridge between Python and JavaScript.

---

5 SQLite is great for development purposes and doesn't need a server running on your machine.

Basic Toolkit

This first part of the book provides a basic toolkit for the toolchain to come and is part tutorial, part reference. Given the fairly wide range of knowledge in the target audience, there will probably be things covered that you already know. My advice is just to cherry-pick the material to fill any gaps in your knowledge and maybe skim what you already know as a refresher.

If you're confident you already have the basic toolkit at hand, feel free to skip to the start of our journey along the toolchain in Part II.

## CHAPTER 2

A Language-Learning Bridge Between Python and JavaScript

Probably the most ambitious aspect of this book is that it deals with two programming languages. Moreover, it only requires that you are competent in one of these languages. This is only possible because Python and JavaScript (JS) are fairly simple languages with much in common. The aim of this chapter is to draw out those commonalities and use them to make a learning bridge between the two languages such that core skills acquired in one can easily be applied to the other.

After showing the key similarities and differences between the two languages, I'll show how to set up a learning environment for Python and JS. The bulk of the chapter will then deal with core syntactical and conceptual differences, followed by a selection of patterns and idioms that I use often while doing data visualization work.

Similarities and Differences

Syntax differences aside, Python and JavaScript actually have a lot in common. After a short while, switching between them can be almost seamless.[1] Let's compare the two from a data visualizer's perspective:

These are the chief similarities:

- They both work without needing a compilation step (i.e., they are interpreted).
- You can use both with an interactive interpreter, which means you can type in lines of code and see the results right away.
- Both have garbage collection.
- Neither language has header files, package boilerplate, and so on.
- Both are primarily developed with a text editor—not an IDE.
- In both, functions are first-class citizens, which can be passed as arguments.

These are the key differences:

- Possibly the biggest difference is that JavaScript is single-threaded and non-blocking (*http://bit.ly/1tADn8E*), using asynchronous I/O. This means that simple things like file access involve the use of a callback function.
- JS is used essentially in web development and until very recently was browser-bound,[2] but Python is used almost everywhere.
- JS is the only first-class language in web browsers, Python being excluded.
- Python has a comprehensive standard library, whereas JS has a limited set of utility objects (e.g., JSON, Math).

---

1 One particularly annoying little gotcha is that while Python uses pop to remove a list item, it uses append—not push—to add an item. JavaScript uses push to add an item, whereas append is used to concatenate arrays.

2 The ascent of node.js (*https://nodejs.org/en/*) has extended JavaScript to the server.

- Python has fairly classical object-oriented classes, whereas JS uses prototypes.
- JS lacks general-purpose data-processing libs.[3]

The differences here emphasize the need for this book to be bilingual. Javascript's monopoly of browser dataviz needs the complement of a conventional data-processing stack. And Python has the best there is.

Interacting with the Code

One of the great advantages of Python and JavaScript is that because they are interpreted on the fly, you can interact with them. Python's interpreter can be run from the command line, whereas JavaScript's is generally accessed from the web browser through a console, usually available from the built-in development tools. In this section, we'll see how to fire up a session with the interpreter and start trying out your code.

Python

By far, the best Python interpreter is IPython (*http://ipython.org/*), which comes in three shades: the basic terminal version, an enhanced graphical version, and a Notebook. The Notebook is a wonderful and fairly recent innovation, providing a browser-based interactive computational environment. There are pros and cons to the different versions. The command line is fastest to scratch a problematic itch but lacks some bells and whistles, particularly embedded plotting courtesy of *Matplotlib* (*http://matplotlib.org/*) and friends. The makes it suboptimal for *Pandas*-based data-processing (*http://pandas.pydata.org/*) and data visualization work. Of the other two, both are better for multiline coding (e.g., trying out functions) than the basic interpreter, but I find the graphical Qt console more intuitive, having a familiar command line rather than executable cells.[4] The great boon of the Notebook is session persistence and the possibility of web access.[5] The ease with which one can share pro-

---

3 This is changing with libraries like Crossfilter, but JS is far behind Python, R, and others.

4 This version is based on the Qt GUI library (*http://www.qt.io*).

5 At the cost of a running a Python interpreter on the server.

gramming sessions, complete with embedded data visualizations, makes the Notebook a fantastic teaching tool as well as a great way to recover programming context.

You can start them at the command line like this:

```
$ ipython [qt | notebook]
```

Options can be empty for the basic command-line interpreter, -qt for a Qt-based graphical version, and -notebook for the browser-based Notebook. You can use any of the three IPython alternatives for this section, but for serious interactive data processing, I generally find myself gravitating to the Qt console for sketches or the Notebook if I anticipate an extensive project.

The IPython notebook has recently been spun into Project Jupyter (*http://jupyter.org*). A Jupyter notebook can be started from the command line with:

```
$ jupyter notebook
```

JavaScript

There are lots of options for trying out JavaScript code without starting a server, though the latter isn't that difficult. Because the JavaScript interpreter comes embedded in all modern web browsers, there are a number of sites that let you try out bits of JavaScript along with HTML and CSS and see the results. *JSBin* (*https://jsbin.com*) is a good option. These sites are great for sharing code and trying out snippets, and usually allow you to add libraries such as *D3.js*.

If you want to try out code one-liners or quiz the state of live code, browser-based consoles are your best bet. With Chrome, you can access the console with the key combo Ctrl-Shift-J. As well as trying little JS snippets, the console allows you to drill down into any objects in scope, revealing their methods and properties. This is a great way to quiz the state of a live object and search for bugs.

One disadvantage of using online JavaScript editors is losing the power of your favorite editing environment, with linting, familiar keyboard shortcuts, and the like (see Chapter 4). Online editors tend to be rudimentary, to say the least. If you anticipate an extensive JavaScript session and want to use your favorite editor, the best bet is to run a local server.

First, create a project directory—called *sandpit*, for example—and add a minimal HTML file that includes a JS script:

```
sandpit
├── index.html
└── script.js
```

The *index.html* file need only be a few lines long, with an optional div placeholder on which to start building your visualization or just trying out a little DOM manipulation.

```
<!-- index.html -->
<!DOCTYPE html>
<meta charset="utf-8">

<div id='viz'></div>

<script type="text/javascript" src="script.js" async></script>
```

You can then add a little JavaScript to your *script.js* file:

```
// script.js
var data = [3, 7, 2, 9, 1, 11];
var sum = 0;
data.forEach(function(d){
    sum += d;
});

console.log('Sum = ' + sum);
// outputs 'Sum = 33'
```

Start your development server in the project directory:

```
$sandpit python -m SimpleHTTPServer
Serving HTTP on 0.0.0.0 port 8000 ...
```

Then open your browser at *http://localhost:8000*, press Ctrl-Shift-J (Cmd-Opt-J on OS X) to access the console and you should see Figure 2-1, showing the logged output of the script (see Chapter 4 for further details).

Figure 2-1. Outputting to the Chrome console

Now that we've established how to run the demo code, let's start building a bridge between Python and JavaScript. First, we'll cover the basic differences in syntax. As you'll see, they're fairly minor and easily absorbed.

Basic Bridge Work

In this section, I'll contrast the basic nuts and bolts of programming in the two languages.

Style Guidelines, PEP 8, and use strict

Where JavaScript style guidelines are a bit of a free-for-all (with people often defaulting to those used by a big library like jQuery), Python has a Python Enhancement Proposal (PEP) dedicated to it. I'd recommend getting acquainted with PEP-8 but not submitting totally to its leadership. It's right about most things, but there's room for some personal choice here. There's a handy online checker here (*http://pep8online.com/*), which will pick up any infractions of PEP-8.

In Python, you should use four spaces to indent a code block. JavaScript is less strict, but two spaces is the most common indent.

One recent addition to JavaScript (Ecmascript 5) is the 'use strict' directive, which imposes strict mode. This mode enforces some good JavaScript practice, which includes catching accidental global declarations, and I thoroughly recommend its use. To use it, just place the string at the top of your function or module:

```
(function(foo){
  'use strict';
  // ...
}(window.foo = window.foo || {}));
```

CamelCase Versus Underscore

JS conventionally uses CamelCase (e.g., processStudentData) for its variables, whereas Python, in accordance with PEP-8, uses underscores (e.g., process_student_data) in its variable names (see Section B in Examples 2-3 and 2-4). By convention (and convention is more important in the Python ecosystem than JS), Python uses capitalized CamelCase for class declarations (see the following example), uppercase for constants, and underscores for everything else:

```
FOO_CONST = 10
class FooBar(object): # ...
```

```python
def foo_bar():
    baz_bar = 'some string'
```

Importing Modules, Including Scripts

Using other libraries in your code, either your own or third-party, is fundamental to modern programming, which makes it all the more surprising that JavaScript doesn't really have a mechanism for doing it.[6] Python has a simple import system that, on the whole, works pretty well.

The good news on the JavaScript front is that Ecmascript 6, the next version of the language, does address this issue, with the addition of import and export statements. Ecmascript 6 will be getting browser support soon, but as of late 2015 you need a converter to Ecmascript 5, such as Babel.js (*https://babeljs.io/*). Meanwhile, although there have been many attempts to create a reasonable client-side modular system, none have really achieved critical mass and all are a little awkward to use. For now, I recommend using the well-established HTML <script> tag to include scripts. So to include the D3 visualization library, you would add this tag to your main HTML file, conventionally *index.html*:

```html
<!DOCTYPE html>
<meta charset="utf-8">
...
    <script src="http://d3js.org/d3.v3.min.js"></script>
```

You can include the script anywhere in your HTML file, but it's best practice to add scripts after the body (div tags, etc.) section.[7] Note that the order of the <script> tags is important. If a script is dependent on a module (e.g., it uses the D3 library), its <script> tag must be placed after that of the module. In other words, big library scripts, such as jQuery and D3, will be included first.

Python comes with "batteries included," a comprehensive set of libraries covering everything from extended data containers (collections) to working with the family of CSV files (csv). If you want to use one of these, just import it using the import keyword:

---

6 The constraint of having to deliver JS scripts over the Web via HTTP is largely responsible for this.

7 This means any blocking-script-loading calls occur after the page's HTML has rendered.

```
In [1]: import sys

In [2]: sys.platform
Out[2]: 'linux2'
```

If you don't want to import the whole library or want to use an alias, you can use the as and from keywords instead:

```
import pandas as pd
from csv import DictWriter, DictReader
from numpy import * ❶

df = pd.read_json('data.json')
reader = DictReader('data.csv')
md = median([12, 56, 44, 33])
```

❶ This imports all the variables from the module into the current namespace and is almost always a bad idea. One of the variables could mask an existing one, and it goes against the Python best practice of explicit being better than implicit. One exception to this rule is if you are using the Python interpreter interactively. In this limited context, it may make sense to import all functions from a library to cut down on key presses; for example, importing all the math functions (from math import *) if doing some Python math hacking.

If you import a nonstandard library, Python uses sys.path to try to find it. sys.path consists of:

- The directory containing the importing module (current directory)
- The PYTHONPATH variable, containing a list of directories
- The installation-dependent default, where libraries installed using pip or easy_install will usually be placed

Big libraries are often packaged, divided into submodules. These submodules are accessed by dot notation:

```
import matplotlib.pyplot as plt
```

Packages are constructed from the filesystem via *__init__.py* files, usually empty, as shown in Example 2-1. The presence of an init file makes the directory visible to Python's import system.

Example 2-1. Building a Python package

```
mypackage
├── __init__.py
...
├── core
|   └── __init__.py
|   ...
...
└── io
    ├── __init__.py
    └── api.py
    ...
    └── tests
        └── __init__.py
        └── test_data.py
        └── test_excel.py ❶
        ...
...
```

❶ You would import this module using `from mypack age.io.tests import test_excel`.

You can access packages on `sys.path` from the root directory (that's `mypackage` in Example 2-1) using dot notation. A special case of `import` is intrapackage references. The *test_excel.py* submodule in Example 2-1 can import submodules from the `mypackage` package both absolutely and relatively:

```
from mypackage.io.tests import test_data ❶
from . import test_data ❷
import test_data ❷
from ..io import api ❸
```

❶ Imports the *test_data.py* module absolutely, from the package's head directory.

❷ An explicit (`. import`) and implicit relative import.

❸ A relative import from a sibling package of *tests*.

Keeping Your Namespaces Clean

The variables defined in Python modules are encapsulated, which means that unless you import them explicitly (e.g., `from foo import baa`), you will be accessing them from the imported module's namespace using dot notation (e.g., `foo.baa`). This modularization of the global namespace is quite rightly seen as a very good thing and plays to one of Python's key tenets: the importance of explicit statements over implicit. When analyzing someone's Python code you should be able to see exactly where a class, function, or variable has come from. Just as importantly, preserving the namespace limits the chance of conflicting or masking variables—a big potential problem as code bases get larger.

One of the main criticisms of JavaScript, and a fair one, is that it plays fast and loose with namespace conventions. The most egregious example of this is that variables declared outside of functions or missing the var keyword[8] are global rather than confined to the script in which they are declared. There are various ways to rectify this situation, but the one I use and recommend is to make each of your scripts a self-calling function. This makes all variables declared via var local to the script/function, preventing them from polluting the global namespace. Any objects, functions, and variables you want to make available to other scripts can be attached to an object that is part of the global namespace.

Example 2-2 demonstrates a module pattern. The boilerplate head and tail (labeled ❶ and ❸) effectively create an encapsulated module. This pattern is far from a perfect solution to modular JavaScript but is the best compromise I know until Ecmascript 6 and a dedicated import system becomes standard. One obvious disadvantage is that the module is part of the global namespace, which means, unlike in Python, there is no need to explicitly import it.

Example 2-2. A module pattern for JavaScript

```
(function(nbviz) { ❶
    'use strict';
    // ...
    nbviz.updateTimeChart = function(data) { ❷
    // ...
}(window.nbviz = window.nbviz || {})); ❸
```

❶ Receives the global nbviz object.

---

8 You can eliminate the possibility of a missing var by using the Ecmascript 5 'use strict' directive.

❷ Attaches the `updateTimeChart` method to the global `nbviz` object, effectively *exporting* it.

❸ If an `nbviz` object exists in the global (window) namespace, pass it into the module function; otherwise, add it to the global namespace.

Outputting "Hello World!"

By far the most popular initial demonstration of any programming language is getting it to print or communicate "Hello World!" in some form, so let's start with getting output from Python and JavaScript.

Python's output couldn't be much simpler, but version 3 sees a change to the `print` statement, making it a proper function:[9]

```
# In Python 2
print 'Hello World!'

# In Python 3
print('Hello World!')
```

You can use Python 3's print function in Python 2 by importing it from the __future__ module:

```
from __future__ import print_function
```

If you're not using Python 3, then this is a sensible approach. The new print function is here to stay and it's best to get used to it now.

JavaScript has no print function, but you can log output to the browser console:

```
console.log('Hello World!');
```

Simple Data Processing

A good way to get an overview of the language differences is to see the same function written in both. Examples 2-3 and 2-4 show a small, contrived example of data munging in Python and JavaScript, respectively. We'll use these to compare Python and JS syntax.

---

9 This is a good thing for reasons outlined in PEP 3105 (*https://www.python.org/dev/peps/pep-3105/*).

Example 2-3. Simple data munging with Python

```python
from __future__ import print_function

# A
student_data = [
    {'name': 'Bob', 'id':0, 'scores':[68, 75, 56, 81]},
    {'name': 'Alice', 'id':1, 'scores':[75, 90, 64, 88]},
    {'name': 'Carol', 'id':2, 'scores':[59, 74, 71, 68]},
    {'name': 'Dan', 'id':3, 'scores':[64, 58, 53, 62]},
]

# B
def process_student_data(data, pass_threshold=60,
                         merit_threshold=75):
    """ Perform some basic stats on some student data. """

    # C
    for sdata in data:
        av = sum(sdata['scores'])/float(len(sdata['scores']))
        sdata['average'] = av

        if av > merit_threshold:
            sdata['assessment'] = 'passed with merit'
        elif av > pass_threshold:
            sdata['assessment'] = 'passed'
        else:
            sdata['assessment'] = 'failed'
        # D
        print("%s's (id: %d) final assessment is: %s"%(
            sdata['name'], sdata['id'], sdata['assessment'].upper()))

# E
if __name__ == '__main__':
    process_student_data(student_data)
```

Example 2-4. Simple data munging with JavaScript

```javascript
// A (note deliberate and valid inconsistency in keys: some quoted
// and some unquoted)
var studentData = [
    {name: 'Bob', id:0, 'scores':[68, 75, 76, 81]},
    {name: 'Alice', id:1, 'scores':[75, 90, 64, 88]},
    {'name': 'Carol', id:2, 'scores':[59, 74, 71, 68]},
    {'name': 'Dan', id:3, 'scores':[64, 58, 53, 62]},
];

// B
function processStudentData(data, passThreshold, meritThreshold){
    passThreshold = typeof passThreshold !== 'undefined'?\
    passThreshold: 60;
```

```
meritThreshold = typeof meritThreshold !== 'undefined'?\
meritThreshold: 75;

// C
data.forEach(function(sdata){
    var av = sdata.scores.reduce(function(prev, current){
        return prev+current;
    },0) / sdata.scores.length;
    sdata.average = av;

    if(av > meritThreshold){
        sdata.assessment = 'passed with merit';
    }
    else if(av > passThreshold){
        sdata.assessment = 'passed';
    }
    else{
        sdata.assessment = 'failed';
    }
    // D
    console.log(sdata.name + "'s (id: " + sdata.id +
      ") final assessment is: " +
        sdata.assessment.toUpperCase());
});

}

// E
processStudentData(studentData);
```

String Construction

Section D in Examples 2-3 and 2-4 show the standard way to print output to the console or terminal. JavaScript has no print statement but will log to the browser's console through the console object.

```
console.log(sdata.name + "'s (id: " + sdata.id +
  ") final assessment is: " + sdata.assessment.toUpperCase());
```

Note that the integer variable id is coerced to a string, allowing concatenation. Python doesn't perform this implicit coercion, so attempting to add a string to an integer in this way gives an error. Instead, explicit conversion to string form is achieved through one of the str or repr functions.

In section A of Example 2-3, the output string is constructed wit C type formatting. String (%s) and integer (%d) placeholders are provided by a final tuple (%(...)):

```
print("%s's (id: %d) final assessment is: %s"
    %(sdata['name'], sdata['id'], sdata['assessment'].upper()))
```

These days, I rarely use Python's `print` statement, opting for the much more powerful and flexible `logging` module, which is demonstrated in the following code block. It takes a little more effort to use, but it is worth it. Logging gives you the flexibility to direct output to a file and/or the screen, adjusting the logging level to prioritize certain information, and a whole load of other useful things. Check out the details here (*https://docs.python.org/2/howto/logging.html*).

```
import logging
logger = logging.getLogger(__name__) ❶
//...
logger.debug('Some useful debugging output')
logger.info('Some general information')

// IN INITIAL MODULE
logging.basicConfig(level=logging.DEBUG) ❷
```

❶ Creates a logger with the name of this module.

❷ You can set the logging level, an output file as opposed to the default to screen.

Significant Whitespace Versus Curly Brackets

The syntactic feature most associated with Python is significant whitespace. Whereas languages like C and JavaScript use whitespace for readability and could easily be condensed into one line,[10] in Python leading spaces are used to indicate code blocks and removing them changes the meaning of the code. The extra effort required to maintain correct code alignment is more than compensated for by increased readability—you spend far longer reading than writing code and the easy reading of Python is probably the main reason why the Python library ecosystem is so healthy. Four spaces is pretty much mandatory (see PEP 8) and my personal preference is for what is known as *soft tabs*, where your editor inserts (and deletes) multiple spaces instead of a tab character.[11]

---

10 This is actually done by JavaScript compressors to reduce the file size of downloaded web pages.

11 The soft versus hard tab debate generates controversy, with much heat and little light. *PEP 8* stipulates spaces, which is good enough for me.

In the following code, the indentation of the `return` statement must be four spaces by convention:[12]

```
def doubler(x):
    return x * 2
#   |<-this spacing is important
```

JavaScript doesn't care about the number of spaces between statements and variables, using curly brackets to demark code blocks, the two doubler functions in this code being equivalent:

```
var doubler = function(x){
    return x * 2;
}

var doubler=function(x){return x*2;}
```

Much is made of Python's whitespace, but most good coders I know set up their editors to enforce indented code blocks and a consistent look and feel. Python merely enforces this good practice. And, to reiterate, I believe the extreme readability of Python code contributes as much to Python's supremely healthy ecosystem as its simple syntax.

Comments and doc-strings

To add comments to code, Python uses hashes, #:

```
# ex.py, a single informative comment

data = {} # Our main data-ball
```

By contrast, JavaScript uses the C language convention of double backslashes (//) or /* ... */ for multiline comments:

```
// script.js, a single informative comment
/* A multiline comment block for
function descriptions, library script
headers, and the like */
var data = {}; // Our main data-ball
```

In addition to comments, and in keeping with its philosophy of readability and transparency, Python has documentation strings (docstrings) by convention. The `process_student_data` function in Example 2-3 has a triple-quoted line of text at its top that will auto-

---

12 It could be two or even three spaces, but this number must be consistent throughout the module.

matically be assigned to the function's __doc__ attribute. You can also use multiline doc-strings.

```python
def doubler(x):
    """This function returns double its input."""
    return 2 * x

def sanitize_string(s):
    """This function replaces any string spaces
    with '-' after stripping any whitespace
    """
    return s.strip().replace(' ', '-')
```

Doc-strings are a great habit to get into, particularly if you are working collaboratively. They are understood by most decent Python editing toolsets and are also used by such automated documentation libraries as *Sphinx* (*http://sphinx-doc.org/*). The string-literal doc-string is accessible as the doc property of a function or class.

Declaring Variables, var

In Section A of Examples 2-3 and 2-4, the declaration of the student data requires a var keyword for JavaScript. We could dispense with the var and the script would run fine, but we would be in danger of being skewered by JS gotcha number one: any variables declared without var are attached to the global namespace, or window object, which means they can easily mask or be masked by any other variables sharing the same name. This possibility of namespace pollution is a big problem for JS and the reason you should get a good linter to warn of missing vars. You should also use Ecmascript's 'use strict' directive to force all variables to be declared with var (see "Style Guidelines, PEP 8, and use strict" on page 18).

Strictly speaking, JS statements should be terminated with a semicolon as opposed to Python's newline. You will see examples where the semicolon is dispensed with, and modern browsers will usually do the right thing here, but there are risks involved (e.g., it can trip up code minifiers and compressors that remove whitespace). I'm in the semicolon camp, but many smart people seem to make do without them.

Declare all variables to be used in a function at its top. JavaScript has *variable hoisting*, which means variables are processed before any other code. This means declaring them anywhere in the function is equivalent to declaring them at the top. This can result in weird errors and confusion. Explicitly placing vars at the top avoids this.

Strings and Numbers

The *name* strings used in the student data (see Section A of Examples 2-3 and 2-4) will be interpreted as UCS-2 (the parent of unicode UTF-16) in JavaScript,[13] a string of bytes in Python 2, and Unicode (UTF-8 by default) in Python 3.[14]

Both languages allow single and double quotes for strings. If you want to include a single or double quote in the string, then enclose with the alternative, like so:

```
pub_name = "The Brewer's Tap"
```

The scores in Section A of Example 2-4 are stored as JavaScript's one numeric type, double-precision 64-bit (IEEE 754) floating-point numbers. Although JavaScript has a parseInt conversion function, when used with floats,[15] it is really just a rounding operator, similar to floor. The type of the parsed number is still number:

```
var x = parseInt(3.45); // 'cast' x to 3
typeof(x); // "number"
```

Python has three numeric types: the 32-bit int, to which the student scores are cast, a float equivalent (IEE 754) to JS's number, and a long for arbitrary precision integer arithmetic. This means that

---

13 The quite fair assumption that JavaScript uses UTF-16 has been the cause of much bug-driven misery. See here (*https://mathiasbynens.be/notes/javascript-encoding*) for an interesting analysis.

14 The change to Unicode strings in Python 3 is a big one. Given the confusion that often attends Unicode de/encoding, it's worth reading a little bit about it (*https://docs.python.org/3/howto/unicode.html*).

15 parseInt can do quite a bit more than round. For example, parseInt(*12.5px*) gives 12, first removing the *px* and then casting the string to a number. It also has a second radix argument to specify the base of the cast. See here (*https://developer.mozilla.org/en-US/docs/Web/JavaScript/Reference/Global_Objects/parseInt*) for the specifics.

Python can represent any integer, whereas JavaScript is more limited.[16] Python's casting changes type:

```
foo = 3.4 # type(foo) -> float
bar = int(3.4) # type(bar) -> int
```

The nice thing about Python and JavaScript numbers is that they are easy to work with and usually do what you want. If you need something more efficient, Python has the *NumPy* library, which allows fine-grained control of your numeric types (you'll learn more about NumPy in Chapter 7). In JavaScript, aside from some cutting-edge projects, you're pretty much stuck with 64-bit floats.

Booleans

Python differs from the JavaScript and the C class languages in using named boolean operators. Other than that, they work pretty much as expected. This table gives a comparison:

Python	bool	True	False	not	and	or
JavaScript	boolean	true	false	!	&&	+`

Python's capitalized `True` and `False` is an obvious trip-up for any JavaScripter and vice versa, but any decent syntax highlighting should catch that, as should your code linter.

Rather than always returning boolean true or false, both Python and JavaScript and/or expressions return the result of one of the arguments, which may of course be a boolean value. Table 2-1 shows how this works, using Python to demonstrate.

Table 2-1. Python's boolean operators

Operation	Result
x or y	if x is false, then y, else x
x and y	if x is false, then x, else y
not x	if x is false, then `True`, else `False`

This fact allows for some occasionally useful variable assignments:

---

16 Because all numbers in JavaScript are floating point, it can only support 53-bit integers. Using larger integers (such as the commonly used 64 bit) can result in discontinuous integers. See *http://www.2ality.com/2012/07/large-integers.html* for further information.

```
rocket_launch = True
(rocket_launch == True and 'All OK') or 'We have a problem!'
Out:
'All OK'

rocket_launch = False
(rocket_launch == True and 'All OK') or 'We have a problem!'
Out:
'We have a problem!'
```

Data Containers: Dicts, Objects, Lists, Arrays

Roughly speaking, JavaScript objects can be used like Python dicts, and Python lists like JavaScript arrays. Python also has a tuple container, which functions like an immutable list. Here are some examples:

```
# Python
d = {'name': 'Groucho', 'occupation': 'Ruler of Freedonia'}
l = ['Harpo', 'Groucho', 99]
t = ('an', 'immutable', 'container')

// JavaScript
d = {'name': 'Groucho', 'occupation': 'Ruler of Freedonia'}
l = ['Harpo', 'Groucho', 99]
```

As shown in Section A of Examples 2-3 and 2-4, while Python's dict keys must be quote-marked strings (or hashable types), JavaScript allows you to omit the quotes if the property is a valid identifier (i.e., not containing special characters such as spaces and dashes). So in our studentData objects, JS implicitly converts the property 'name' to string form.

The student data declarations look pretty much the same and, in practice, are used pretty much the same, too. The key difference to note is that while the curly-bracketed containers in the JS student Data look like Python dicts, they are actually a shorthand declaration of JS objects (*https://developer.mozilla.org/en-US/docs/Web/JavaScript/Guide/Working_with_Objects*), a somewhat different data container.

In JS data visualization, we tend to use arrays of objects as the chief data container and here, JS objects function much as a Pythonista would expect. In fact, as demonstrated in the following code, we get the advantage of both dot notation and key-string access, the former being preferred where applicable (keys with spaces or dashes needing quoted strings):

```
var foo = {bar:3, baz:5};
foo.bar; // 3
foo['baz']; // 5, same as Python
```

It's good to be aware that although they can be used like Python dictionaries, JavaScript objects are much more than just containers (aside from primitives like strings and numbers, pretty much everything in JavaScript is an object).[17] But in most dataviz examples you see, they are used very much like Python dicts.

Table 2-2 converts basic list operations.

Table 2-2. Lists and arrays

JavaScript array (a)	Python list (l)
a.length	len(l)
a.push(item)	l.append(item)
a.pop()	l.pop()
a.shift()	l.pop(0)
a.unshift(item)	l.insert(0, item)
a.slice(start, end)	l[start:end]
a.splice(start, howMany, i1, …)	l[start:end] = [i1, …]

Functions

Section B of Examples 2-3 and 2-4 shows a function declaration. Python uses `def` to indicate a function:

```
def process_student_data(data, pass_threshold=60,
                         merit_threshold=75):
    """ Perform some basic stats on some student data. """
    ...
```

whereas JavaScript uses `function`:

```
function processStudentData(data, passThreshold, meritThreshold){
    passThreshold = typeof passThreshold !== 'undefined'?
      passThreshold: 60;
    meritThreshold = typeof meritThreshold !== 'undefined'?
      meritThreshold: 75;
    ...
}
```

---

17 This makes iterating over their properties a little trickier than it might be. See here (*http://stackoverflow.com/questions/8312459/iterate-through-object-properties*) for more details.

Both have a list of parameters. With JS, the function code block is indicated by the curly brackets { ... }; with Python, the code block is defined by a colon and indentation.

JS has an alternative way of defining a function called the *function expression*, which you may see in examples:

```
var processStudentData = function( ...){
```

The differences are subtle enough not to worry about for now.[18] For what it's worth, I tend to use function expressions pretty much exclusively.

Function parameters is an area where Python's handling is a great deal more sophisticated than JavaScript's. As you can see in `pro cess_student_data` (Section B in Example 2-3), Python allows default arguments for the parameters. In JavaScript, all parameters not used in the function call are declared as *undefined*. In order to set a default value for these, we have to perform a distinctly hacky conditional (ternary) expression:

```
function processStudentData(data, passThreshold, meritThreshold){
    passThreshold = typeof passThreshold !== 'undefined'?
    passThreshold: 60;
    ...
```

The good news for JavaScripters is that the latest version of JavaScript, based on Ecmascript 6 and coming very soon, allows Python-like default parameters (*https://developer.mozilla.org/en/docs/Web/JavaScript/Reference/Functions/default_parameters*):

```
function processStudentData(data, passThreshold=60,
    meritThreshold=75){
    ...
```

Iterating: for Loops and Functional Alternatives

Section C in Examples 2-3 and 2-4 shows our first major departure, demonstrating JavaScript's functional chops.

Python's `for` loops are simple, intuitive, and effective on any iterator, such as arrays and `dicts`. One gotcha with `dicts` is that standard iteration is by key, not items. For example:

---

18 For the curious, there's a nice summation here (*https://javascriptweblog.wordpress.com/2010/07/06/function-declarations-vs-function-expressions/*).

```python
foo = {'a':3, 'b':2}
for x in foo:
    print(x)
# outputs 'a' 'b'
```

To iterate over the key-value pairs, use the dict's items method like so:

```python
for x in foo.items():
    print(x)
# outputs key-value tuples ('a', 3) ('b' 2)
```

You can assign the key/values in the for statement for convenience. For example:

```python
for key, value in foo.items():
```

Because Python's for loop works on anything with the correct iterator plumbing, you can do cool things like loop over file lines:

```python
for line in open('data.txt'):
    print(line)
```

Coming from Python, JS's for loop is a pretty horrible, unintuitive thing. Here's an example:

```javascript
for(var i in ['a', 'b', 'c']){
  console.log(i)
}
# outputs 1, 2, 3
```

JS's for .. in returns the index of the array's items, not the items themselves. To compound matters, for the Pythonista, the order of iteration is not guaranteed, so the indices could be returned in non-consecutive order.

Even iterating over an object is trickier than it might have been. Unlike Python's dicts, objects could have inherited properties from the prototyping chain, so you should use a hasOwnProperty guard to filter these out, like so:

```javascript
var obj = {a:3, b:2, c:4};
for (var prop in obj) {
  if( obj.hasOwnProperty( prop ) ) {
    console.log("o." + prop + " = " + obj[prop]);
  }
}
// out: o.a = 3, o.b = 2, o.c = 4
```

Shifting between Python and JS for loops is hardly seamless, demanding you keep on the ball. The good news is that you hardly need to use JS for loops these days. In fact, I almost never find the need. That's because JS has recently acquired some very powerful first-class functional abilities, which have more expressive power and less scope for confusion with Python and, once you get used to them, quickly become indispensable.[19]

Section C in Example 2-4 demonstrates forEach( ), one of the *functional* methods available to modern JavaScript arrays.[20] forEach( ) iterates over the array's items, sending them in turn to an anonymous callback function defined in the first argument, where they can be processed. The true expressive power of these functional methods comes from chaining them (maps, filters, etc.), but already we have a cleaner, more elegant iteration with none of the awkward bookkeeping of old.

The callback function receives index and the original array as an optional second argument.

```
data.forEach(function(currentValue, index){//---
```

Whereas JS arrays have a set of native functional iterator methods (map, reduce, filter, every, sum, reduceRight), Objects—in their guise as pseudo-dictionaries—don't. If you want to iterate over Object key-value pairs, then I'd recommend using underscore,[21] the most frequently used functional library for JS and almost as ubiquitous as jQuery. Underscore methods are accessed with the shorthand _, like this:

```
_.each(obj, function(value, key){
    // do something with the data..
```

This does introduce a library dependency, but this type of iteration is very common in data-visualization work and underscore has lots of other goodies. Along with jQuery, it has pretty much honorary JS standard-library status.

---

19 This is one area where JS beats Python hands down and which finds many of us wishing for similar functionality in Python.

20 Added with Ecmascript 5 and available on all modern browsers.

21 I use lodash, which is functionally identical.

Conditionals: if, else, elif, switch

Section C in Examples 2-3 and 2-4 shows Python and JavaScript conditionals in action. Aside from JavaScript's bracket fetish, the statements are very similar; the only real difference being Python's extra `elif` keyword, a convenient conjunction of `else if`.

Though much requested, Python does not have the `switch` statement found in most high-level languages. JS does, allowing you to do this:

```
switch(expression){
    case value1:
    // execute if expression === value1
    break; // optional end expression
    case value2:
    //...
    default:
    // if other matches fail
```

File Input and Output

JavaScript has no real equivalent of file input and output (I/O), but Python's is as simple as could be:

```
# READING A FILE
f = open("data.txt") # open file for reading

for line in f: # iterate over file lines
    print(line)

lines = f.readlines() # grab all lines in file into array
data = f.read() # read all of file as single string

# WRITING TO A FILE
f = open("data.txt", 'w')
# use 'w' to write, 'a' to append to file
f.write("this will be written as a line to the file")
f.close() # explicitly close the file
```

One much recommended best practice is to use Python's `with`, as context manager when opening files. This ensures they are closed automatically when leaving the block, essentially providing syntactic sugar for a `try`, `except`, `finally` block. Here's how to open a file using `with`, `as`:

```
with open("data.txt") as f:
    lines = f.readlines()
    ...
```

Classes and Prototypes

Possibly the cause of more confusion that any other topic is JavaScript's choice of prototypes rather than classical classes as its chief object-oriented programming (OOP) element. I have come to appreciate the concept of prototypes, if not its JS implementation, which could have been cleaner. Nevertheless, once you get the basic principle, you may find that it is actually a better mental model for much of what we do as programmers than classical OOP paradigms.

I remember, when I first started my forays into more advanced languages like C++, falling for the promise of OOP, particularly class-based inheritance. Polymorphism was all the rage and Shape classes were being subclassed to rectangles and ellipses, which were in turn subclassed to more specialized squares and circles.

It didn't take long to realize that the clean class divisions found in the textbooks were rarely found in real programming and that trying to balance generic and specific APIs quickly became fraught. In this sense, I find composition and mix-ins much more useful as a programming concept than attempts at extended subclassing and often avoid all these by using functional programming techniques, particularly in JavaScript. Nevertheless, the class/prototype distinction is an obvious difference between the two languages, and the more you understand its nuances, the better you'll code.[22]

Python's classes are fairly simple affairs and, as with most of the language, easy to use. I tend to think of them these days as a handy way to encapsulate data with a convenient API, and rarely extend subclassing beyond one generation. Here's a simple example:

```python
class Citizen(object):

    def __init__(self, name, country): ❶
        self.name = name
        self.country = country

    def print_details(self):
        print('Citizen %s from %s'%(self.name, self.country))
```

---

22 I mentioned to a talented programmer friend that I was faced with the challenge of explaining prototypes to Python programmers and he pointed out that most JavaScripters could probably do with some pointers too. There's a lot of truth in this and many JSers do manage to be productive by using prototypes in a *classy* way, hacking their way around the edge cases.

```
c = Citizen('Groucho M.', 'Freedonia') ❷
c.print_details()
Out:
Citizen Groucho M. from Freedonia
```

❶ Python classes have a number of double-underscored special methods, __init__ being the most common, called when the class instance is created. All instance methods have a first, explicit self argument (you could name it something else, but it's a very bad idea), which refers to the instance. In this case, we use it to set name and country properties.

❷ Creates a new Citizen instance, initialized with name and country.

Python follows a fairly classical pattern of class inheritance. It's easy to do, which is probably why Pythonistas make a lot of use of it. Let's customize the Citizen class to create a (Nobel Prize) Winner class with a couple of extra properties:

```
class Winner(Citizen):

    def __init__(self, name, country, category, year):
        super(Winner, self).__init__(name, country) ❶
        self.category = category
        self.year = year

    def print_details(self):
        print('Nobel winner %s from %s, category %s, year %s'\
        %(self.name, self.country, self.category,\
        str(self.year)))


w = Winner('Albert E.', 'Switzerland', 'Physics', 1921)
w.print_details()
Out:
Nobel prize-winner Albert E. from Switzerland, category Physics,
year 1921
```

❶ We want to reuse the superclass Citizen's __init__ method, using this Winner instance as self. The super method scales the inheritance tree one branch from its first argument, supplying the second as instance to the class-instance method.

I think the best article I have read on the key difference between JavaScript's prototypes and classical classes is Reginald Braithwaite's "OOP, JavaScript, and so-called Classes" (*http://raganwald.com/2015/05/11/javascript-classes.html*). This quote sums up the difference between classes and prototypes as nicely as any I've found:

> The difference between a prototype and a class is similar to the difference between a model home and a blueprint for a home.

When you instantiate a C++ or Python class, a blueprint is followed, creating an object and calling its various constructors in the inheritance tree. In other words, you start from scratch and build a nice, pristine new class instance.

With JavaScript prototypes, you start with a model home (object) that has rooms (methods). If you want a new living room, you can just replace the old one with something in better colors. If you want a new conservatory, then just make an extension. But rather than building from scratch with a blueprint, you're adapting and extending an existing object.

With that necessary theory out of the way and the reminder that object inheritance is useful to know but hardly ubiquitous in dataviz, let's see a simple JavaScript prototype object in Example 2-5.

Example 2-5. A simple JavaScript object

```
var Citizen = function(name, country){ ❶
  this.name = name; ❷
  this.country = country;
};

Citizen.prototype = { ❸
  printDetails: function(){
    console.log('Citizen ' + this.name + ' from ' + this.country);
  }
};

var c = new Citizen('Groucho M.', 'Freedonia'); ❹

c.printDetails();
Out:
Citizen Groucho M. from Freedonia

typeof(c) # object
```

❶ JavaScript has no classes[23] so object instances are built from functions or objects.

❷ this is an implicit reference to the *calling context* of the function. For now, it behaves as you would expect and even though it looks a little like Python's self, the two are quite different, as we'll see.

❸ The methods specified here will both override any prototypical methods up the inheritance chain and be inherited by any objects derived from Citizen.

❹ new is used to create a new object, set its prototype to that of the Citizen constructor function, and then call the Citizen constructor function on the new object.

self Versus this

At first glance, it would be easy enough to assume that Python's self and JavaScript's this are essentially the same, the latter being an implicit version of the former, which is supplied to all class instance methods. Actually, this and self are significantly different. Let's use our bilingual Citizen class to demonstrate.

Python's self is a variable supplied to each class method (you can call it anything you like, but it's not advisable), representing the class instance. But this is a keyword that refers to the object calling the method. This calling object can be different from the method's object instance, and JavaScript provides the call, bind, and apply (*https://developer.mozilla.org/en-US/docs/Web/JavaScript/Reference/Global_Objects/Function*) function methods to allow you to exploit this fact.

Let's use the call method to change the calling object of a print_details method and therefore the reference for this, used in the method to get the citizen's name:

```
var groucho = new Citizen('Groucho M.', 'Freedonia');
var harpo = new Citizen('Harpo M.', 'Freedonia');
```

---

23 As of Ecmascript 6, this will change with the addition of the class keyword, a piece of syntactic sugar generating a lot of heat and not much light right now.

```
groucho.print_details.call(harpo);
Out:
"Citizen Harpo M. from Freedonia"
```
So JavaScript's `this` is a much more malleable proxy than Python's `self`, offering more freedom but also the responsibility of tracking calling context and, should you use it, making sure `new` is always used in creating objects.[24]

I included Example 2-5, which shows `new` in JavaScript object instantiation, because you will run into its use a fair deal. But the syntax is already a little awkward and gets quite a bit worse when you try to do inheritance. Ecmascript 5 introduced the `Object.cre ate` method, a better way to create objects and to implement inheritance. I'd recommend using it in your own code, but `new` will probably crop up in some third-party libraries.

Let's use `Object.create` to create a `Citizen` and its `Winner` inheritor. To emphasize, JavaScript has many ways to do this, but Example 2-6 shows the cleanest I have found and my personal pattern.

Example 2-6. Prototypical inheritance with Object.create

```
var Citizen = { ❶
    setCitizen: function(name, country){
        this.name = name;
        this.country = country;
        return this;
    },
    printDetails: function(){
        console.log('Citizen ' + this.name + ' from ',\
        + this.country);
    }
};

var Winner = Object.create(Citizen);

Winner.setWinner = function(name, country, category, year){
    this.setCitizen(name, country);
    this.category = category;
    this.year = year;
```

---

24 This is another reason to use Ecmascript 5's `'use strict;'` injunction, which calls attention to such mistakes.

```
    return this;
};

Winner.printDetails = function(){
    console.log('Nobel winner ' + this.name + ' from ' +
    this.country + ', category ' + this.category + ', year ' +
    this.year);
};

var albert = Object.create(Winner)
    .setWinner('Albert Einstein', 'Switzerland', 'Physics', 1921);

albert.printDetails();
Out:
Nobel winner Albert Einstein from Switzerland, category
Physics, year 1921
```

❶ Citizen is now an object rather than a constructor function. Think of this as the base house for any new buildings such as Winner.

To reiterate, prototypical inheritance is not seen that often in Java-Script dataviz, particularly the 800-pound gorilla D3 with its emphasis on declarative and functional patterns, with *raw* unencapsulated data being used to stamp its impression on the web page.

The tricky class/prototype comparison concludes this section on basic syntactic differences. Now let's look at some common patterns seen in dataviz work with Python and JS.

Differences in Practice

The syntactic differences between JS and Python are important to know and thankfully outweighed by their syntactic similarities. The meat and potatoes of imperative programming, loops, conditionals, data declaration, and manipulation is much the same. This is all the more so in the specialized domain of data processing and data visualization where the languages' first-class functions allow common idioms.

What follows is a less-than-comprehensive list of some important patterns and idioms seen in Python and JavaScript, from the perspective of a data visualizer. Where possible, a translation between the two languages is given.

Method Chaining

A common JavaScript idiom is *method chaining*, popularized by its most popular library, jQuery, and much used in D3. Method chaining involves returning an object from its own method in order to call another method on the result, using dot notation:

```
var sel = d3.select('#viz')
    .attr('width', '600px')  ❶
    .attr('height', '400px')
    .style('background', 'lightgray');
```

❶ The `attr` method returns the D3 selection that called it, which is then used to call another `attr` method.

Method chaining is not much seen in Python, which generally advocates one statement per line in keeping with simplicity and readability.

Enumerating a List

Often it's useful to iterate through a list while keeping track of the item's index. Python has the very handy `enumerate` keyword for just this reason:

```
names = ['Alice', 'Bob', 'Carol']

for i, n in enumerate(names):
    print('%d: %s'%(i, n))

Out:
0: Alice
1: Bob
2: Carol
```

JavaScript's list methods, such as `forEach` and the functional `map`, `reduce`, and `filter`, supply the iterated item and its index to the callback function:

```
var names = ['Alice', 'Bob', 'Carol'];

names.forEach(function(n, i){
    console.log(i + ': ' + n);
});

Out:
0: Alice
1: Bob
2: Carol
```

Tuple Unpacking

One of the first cool tricks Python initiates come across uses tuple unpacking to switch variables:

```
(a, b) = (b, a)
```

Note that the brackets are optional. This can be put to more practical purpose as a way of reducing the temporary variables, such as in a Fibonacci function:

```python
def fibonacci(n):
    x, y = 0, 1
    for i in range(n):
        print(x)
        x, y = y, x + y
```

If you want to ignore one of the unpacked variables, use an underscore:

```python
winner = 'Albert Einstein', 'Physics', 1921, 'Swiss'

name, _, _, nationality = winner
```

Tuple unpacking has a slew of use cases. It is also a fundamental feature of the language and not available in JavaScript.

Collections

One of the most useful Python "batteries" is the `collections` module. This provides some specialized container datatypes to augment Python's standard set. It has a `deque`, which provides a list-like container with fast appends and pops at either end; an `OrderedDict`, which remembers the order entries were added; a `defaultdict`, which provides a factory function to set the dictionary's default; and a `Counter` container for counting hashable objects, among others. I find myself using the last three a lot. Here are a few examples:

```python
from collections import Counter, defaultdict, OrderedDict

items = ['F', 'C', 'C', 'A', 'B', 'A', 'C', 'E', 'F']

cntr = Counter(items)
print(cntr)
cntr['C'] -=1
print(cntr)
Out:
Counter({'C': 3, 'A': 2, 'F': 2, 'B': 1, 'E': 1})
Counter({'A': 2, 'C': 2, 'F': 2, 'B': 1, 'E': 1})
```

```
d = defaultdict(int) ❶

for item in items:
    d[item] += 1 ❷

d
Out:
defaultdict(<type 'int'>, {'A': 2, 'C': 3, 'B': 1, 'E': 1, 'F': 2})


OrderedDict(sorted(d.items(), key=lambda i: i[1])) ❸
Out:
OrderedDict([('B', 1), ('E', 1), ('A', 2), ('F', 2), ('C', 3)]) ❹
```

❶ Sets the dictionary default to an integer, with value 0 by default.

❷ If the item-key doesn't exist, its value is set to the default of 0 and 1 added to that.

❸ Gets the list of items in the dictionary d as key-value tuple pairs, sorts using the integer value, and then creates an `OrderedDict` with the sorted list.

❹ The `OrderedDict` remembers the (sorted) order of the items as they were added to it.

You can get more details on the `collections` module from here (*https://docs.python.org/2/library/collections.html*).

There is a recent JavaScript library that emulates the Python `collec tions` module. You can find it here (*https://github.com/seriesoftubes/pycollections.js*). As of late 2015, it is a very new but impressive piece of work, worth checking out even if you just want to extend your JavaScript knowledge.

If you want to replicate some of Python's `collections` function using more conventional JavaScript libraries, underscore (or its functionally identical replacement lodash[25]) is a good place to start. These libraries offer some enhanced functional programming utilities. Let's take a quick look at this very handy tool.

---

25 My personal choice for performance reasons.

Underscore

Underscore is probably the most popular JavaScript library after the ubiquitous jQuery and offers a bevy of functional programming utilities for the JavaScript dataviz programmer. The easiest way to use underscore is to use a content delivery network (CDN) to load it remotely (these loads will be cached by your browser, making things very efficient for common libraries), like so:

```
<script src="https://cdnjs.cloudflare.com/ajax/libs/
underscore.js/1.8.3/underscore-min.js"></script>
```

Underscore has loads of useful functions. There is, for example, a countBy method, which serves the same purpose as the Python's collections counter just discussed:

```
var items = ['F', 'C', 'C', 'A', 'B', 'A', 'C', 'E', 'F'];

_.countBy(items) ❶
Out:
Object {F: 2, C: 3, A: 2, B: 1, E: 1}
```

❶   Now you see why the library is called underscore.

As we'll now see, the inclusion in modern JavaScript of native functional methods (map, reduce, filter) and a forEach iterator for arrays has made underscore slightly less indispensable, but it still has some great utilities to augment vanilla JS. With a little chaining, you can produce extremely terse but very powerful code. Underscore was my gateway drug to functional programming in JavaScript, and the idioms are just as addictive today. Check out underscore's repertoire of utilities here (*http://underscorejs.org/*).

Let's have a look at underscore in action, tackling a more involved task:

```
journeys = [
  {period:'morning', times:[44, 34, 56, 31]},
  {period:'evening', times:[35, 33]},},
  {period:'morning', times:[33, 29, 35, 41]},
  {period:'evening', times:[24, 45, 27]}},
  {period:'morning', times:[18, 23, 28]}}
];

var groups = _.groupBy(journeys, 'period');
var mTimes = _.pluck(groups['morning'], 'times');
mTimes = _.flatten(mTimes); ❶
var average = function(l){
```

```
var sum = _.reduce(l, function(a,b){return a+b},0);
return sum/l.length;
};
console.log('Average morning time is ' + average(mTimes));
Out:
Average morning time is 33.81818181818182
```

❶ Our array of morning times arrays ([[44, 34, 56, 31], [33...]]) needs to be *flattened* into a a single array of numbers.

Functional Array Methods and List Comprehensions

I find myself using underscore a lot less since the addition, with Ecmascript 5, of functional methods to JavaScript arrays. I don't think I've used a conventional for loop since then, which, given the ugliness of JS for loops, is a very good thing.

Once you get used to processing arrays functionally, it's hard to consider going back. Combined with JS's anonymous functions, it makes for very fluid, expressive programming. It's also an area where method chaining seems very natural. Let's look at a highly contrived example:

```
var nums = [1, 2, 3, 4, 5, 6, 7, 8, 9, 10];

var sum = nums.filter(function(o){ return o%2 }) ❶
  .map(function(o){ return o * o}) ❷
  .reduce(function(a, b){return a+b}); ❸

console.log('Sum of the odd squares is ' + sum);
```

❶ Filters the list for odd numbers (i.e., returning 1 for the modulus (%) 2 operation).

❷ map produces a new list by applying a function to each member (i.e., [1, 3, 5...] → [1, 9, 25...]).

❸ reduce processes the resultant mapped list in sequence, providing the current (in this case, summed) value (a) and the item value (b). By default, the initial value of the first argument (a) is 0.

Python's powerful list comprehensions can emulate the previous example easily enough:

```
nums = range(10)  ❶

odd_squares = [x * x for x in nums if x%2]  ❷
sum(odd_squares)  ❸
Out:
165
```

❶ Python has a handy built-in range keyword, which can also take
a start, end, and step (e.g., range(2, 8, 2) → [2, 4, 6])

❷ The if condition tests for oddness of x, and any numbers passing this filter are squared and inserted into the list.

❸ Python also has a built-in and often used sum statement.

 Python's list comprehensions can use recursive
control structures, such as applying a second
for/if expression to the iterated items.
Although this can create terse and powerful
lines of code, it goes against the grain of Python's
readability and I discourage its use. Even simple
list comprehensions are less than intuitive and,
as much as it appeals to the leet hacker in all of
us, you risk creating incomprehensible code.

Python's list comprehensions work well for basic filtering and mapping. They do lack the convenience of JavaScript's anonymous functions (which are fully fledged, with their own scope, control blocks,
exception handling, etc.), but there are arguments against the use of
anonymous functions. For example, they are not reusable and, being
unnamed, they make it hard to follow exceptions and debug. See
here (*http://bit.ly/1Yxkej3*) for some persuasive arguments. Having
said that, for libraries like D3, replacing the small, throwaway
anonymous functions used to set DOM attributes and properties
with named ones would be far too onerous and would just add to
the boilerplate.

Python does have functional lambda expressions, which we'll look at
in the next section, but for full functional processing in Python by
necessity and JavaScript for best practice, we can use named functions to increase our control scope. For our simple odd-squares
example, named functions are a contrivance—but note that they

increase the first-glance readability of the list comprehension, which
becomes much more important as your functions get more complex.

```
def is_odd(x):
    return x%2

def sq(x):
    return x * x

sum([sq(x) for x in l if is_odd(x)])
```

With JavaScript, a similar contrivance can also increase readability
and facilitate DRY code:[26]

```
var isOdd = function(x){ return x%2; };

sum = l.filter(isOdd)
...
```

Map, Reduce, and Filter with Python's Lambdas

Although Python lacks anonymous functions, it does have *lambdas*,
which are nameless expressions that take arguments. Though lack-
ing the bells and whistles of JavaScript's anonymous functions, these
are a powerful addition to Python's functional programming repertoire, especially when combined with its functional methods.

 Python's functional built-ins (`map`, `reduce`, `fil`
`ter` methods, and lambda expressions) have a
checkered past. It's no secret that the creator of
Python wanted to remove them from the language. The clamor of disapproval led to their
reluctant preservation. With the recent trend
toward functional programming, this looks like
a very good thing. They're not perfect but are far
better than nothing. And given JavaScript's
strong functional emphasis, they're a good way
to leverage skills acquired in that language.

Python's lambdas take a number of parameters and return an operation on them, using a colon separator to define the function block,
in much the same way that standard Python functions only pared to

---

26 Don't Repeat Yourself (DRY) is a solid coding convention.

the bare essentials and with an implicit return. The following example shows a few lambdas employed in functional programming:

```
from functools import reduce # if using Python 3+

nums = [0, 1, 2, 3, 4, 5, 6, 7, 8, 9]

odds = filter(lambda x: x % 2, nums)
odds_sq = map(lambda x: x * x, odds)
reduce(lambda x, y: x + y, odds_sq) ❶
Out:
165
```

❶ Here, the reduce method provides two arguments to the lambda, which uses them to return the expression after the colon.

JavaScript Closures and the Module Pattern

One of the key concepts in JavaScript is that of the *closure*, which is essentially a nested function declaration that uses variables declared in an outer (but not global) scope that are *kept alive* after the function is returned. Closures allow for a number of very useful programming patterns and are a common feature of the language.

Let's look at possibly the most common usage of closures and one we've already seen exploited in our module pattern (Example 2-2): exposing a limited API while having access to essentially private member variables.

A simple example of a closure is this little counter:

```
function Counter(inc) {
  var count = 0;
  var add = function() { ❶
    count += inc;
    console.log('Current count: ' + count);
  }
  return add;
}

var inc2 = Counter(2); ❷
inc2(); ❸
Out:
Current count: 2
inc2();
Out:
Current count: 4
```

❶ The add function gets access to the essentially private, outer-scope count and inc variables.

❷ This returns an add function with the closure variables, count (0) and inc (2).

❸ Calling inc2 calls add, updating the *closed* count variable.

We can extend the Counter to add a little API. This technique is the basis of JavaScript modules and many simple libraries. In essence, it selectively exposes public methods while hiding private methods and variables, which is generally seen as good practice in the programming world:

```javascript
function Counter(inc) {
  var count = 0;
  var api = {};
  api.add = function() {
    count += inc;
    console.log('Current count: ' + count);
  }
  api.sub = function() {
    count -= inc;
    console.log('Current count: ' + count)
  }
  api.reset = function() {
    count = 0;
    console.log('Count reset to 0')
  }

  return api;
}

cntr = Counter(3);
cntr.add() // Current count: 3
cntr.add() // Current count: 6
cntr.sub() // Current count: 3
cntr.reset() // Count reset to 0
```

Closures have all sorts of uses in JavaScript and I'd recommend getting your head around them—you'll see them a lot as you start investigating other people's code. These are three particularly good web articles that provide a lot of good use cases for closures:

- "Getting Closure" (*http://markdaggett.com/blog/2013/02/25/getting-closure*) by Mark Daggett

- "JavaScript Module Pattern: In-Depth" (*http://www.adequately good.com/JavaScript-Module-Pattern-In-Depth.html*) by Ben Cherry
- "Use Cases for JavaScript Closures" (*https://msdn.microsoft.com/ en-us/magazine/ff696765.aspx*) by Juriy Zaytsev

Python has closures, but they are not used nearly as much as JavaScript's, perhaps because of a few quirks that, though surmountable, make for some slightly awkward code. To demonstrate, Example 2-7 tries to replicate the previous JavaScript counter.

Example 2-7. A first-pass attempt at a Python counter closure

```python
def get_counter(inc):
    count = 0
    def add():
        count += inc
        print('Current count: ' + str(count))
    return add
```

If you create a counter with `get_counter` (Example 2-7) and try to run it, you'll get an `UnboundLocalError`:

```python
cntr = get_counter(2)
cntr()
Out:
...
UnboundLocalError: local variable 'count' referenced before
assignment
```

Interestingly, although we can read the value of `count` within the `add` function (comment out the `count += inc` line to try it), attempts to change it throw an error. This is because attempts to assign a value to something in Python assume it is local in scope. There is no `count` local to the `add` function and so an error is thrown.

In Python 3, we can get around the error in Example 2-7 by using the `nonlocal` keyword to tell Python that `count` is in a nonlocal scope:

```python
...
def add():
    nonlocal count
    count += inc
...
```

In Python 2, we can use a little dictionary hack to allow mutation of our closed variables:

```python
def get_counter(inc):
    vars = {'count': 0}
    def add():
        vars['count'] += inc
        print('Current count: ' + str(vars['count']))
    return add
```

This *hack* works because we are not assigning a new value to `vars` but are instead mutating an existing container, which is perfectly valid even if it is out of local scope.

As you can see, with a bit of effort, JavaScripters can transfer their closure skills to Python. The use cases are similar, but Python, being a richer language with lots of useful batteries included, has more options to apply to the same problem. Probably the most common use of closures is in Python's decorators.

Decorators are essentially function wrappers that extend the function's utility without having to alter the function itself. They're a relatively advanced concept, but you can find a user-friendly introduction on The Code Ship website (*http://thecodeship.com/patterns/guide-to-python-function-decorators/*).

This Is That

One JavaScript hack you'll see a lot of is a consequence of closures and the slippery `this` keyword. If you wish to refer to the outer-scoped `this` in a child function, you must use a proxy because the child's `this` will be bound according to context. The convention is to use `that` to refer to `this`. The code is less confusing than the explanation:

```javascript
function outer(bar){
   this.bar = bar;
   var that = this;
   function inner(baz){
      this.baz = baz * that.bar; ❶
      // ...
```

❶ `that` refers to the outer function's `this`.

This concludes my cherry-picked selection of patterns and hacks that I find myself using a lot in dataviz work. You'll doubtless acquire your own, but I hope these give you a leg up.

A Cheat Sheet

As a handy reference guide, Figures 2-2 to 2-7 include a set of cheat sheets to translate basic operations between Python and JavaScript.

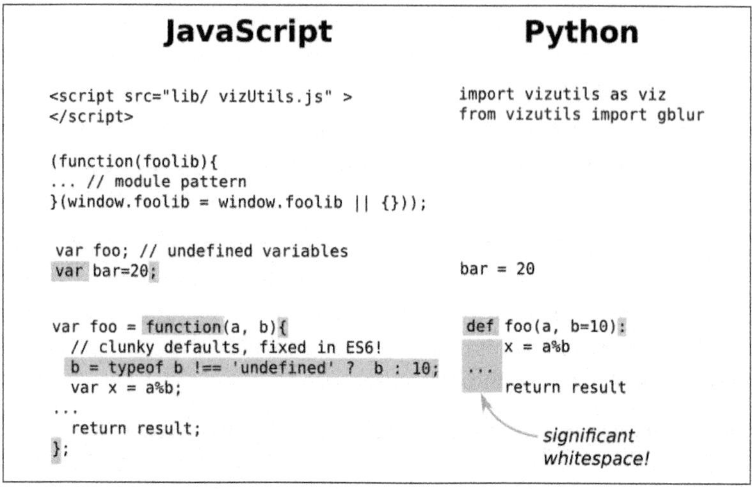

JavaScript	Python
`<script src="lib/ vizUtils.js" >` `</script>`	`import vizutils as viz` `from vizutils import gblur`

`(function(foolib){`
`... // module pattern`
`}(window.foolib = window.foolib || {}));`	

`var foo; // undefined variables`
`var bar=20;`
	`bar = 20`

`var foo = function(a, b){`
`    // clunky defaults, fixed in ES6!`
`    b = typeof b !== 'undefined' ? b : 10;`
`    var x = a%b;`
`    ...`
`    return result;`
`};`
	`def foo(a, b=10):`
	`    x = a%b`
	`    ...`
	`    return result`
	
	`          ↖ significant`
	`            whitespace!`

Figure 2-2. Some basic syntax

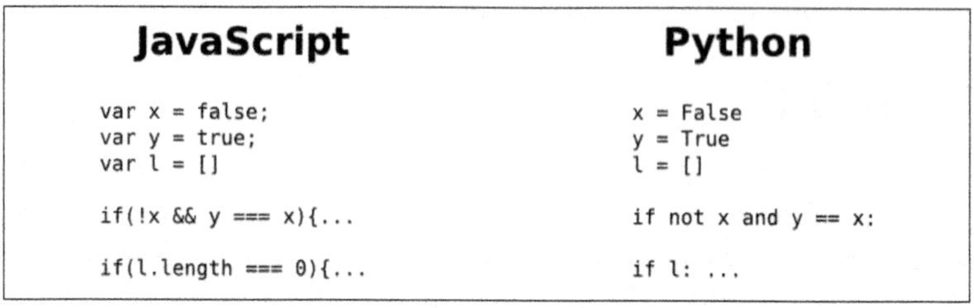

JavaScript	Python

`var x = false;`
`var y = true;`
`var l = []`
	`x = False`
	`y = True`
	`l = []`

`if(!x && y === x){...`	`if not x and y == x:`
`if(l.length === 0){...`	`if l: ...`

Figure 2-3. Booleans

JavaScript   ## Python

camelCase vs underscored

```javascript
var studentData = [
    {'name': 'Bob',
     'scores':[68, 75, 56, 81]},
    {name: 'Alice',
     'scores':[75, 90, 64, 88]},
...];
```

```python
student_data = [
    {'name': 'Bob',
     'scores':[68, 75, 56, 81]},
    {'name': 'Alice',
     'scores':[75, 90, 64, 88]},
...]
```

anonymous functions

line-break

```javascript
studentData.forEach(function(sdata){
    var av = sdata.scores
        .reduce(function(prev, current){
            return prev+current;
        },0) / sdata.scores.length;
    sdata.average = av;
```

```python
s_data = student_data
for data in s_data.items():
    av = sum(data['scores'])\
         /float(len(data['scores'])))
    sdata['average'] = av
```

first-class functional methods

```javascript
console.log(sdata.name + " scored " +
    sdata.average);
```

```python
print("%s scored %d"%
    (sdata.name, sdata.average));
```

```javascript
while(i < 10){
...
}
```

```python
while i < 10:
    ...
```

```javascript
do {
...
}
while(i < 10);
```

```python
while True:
    if i >= 10:
        break
```

Figure 2-4. Loops and iterations

JavaScript   ## Python

```javascript
if(x === 'foo'){
    ...}
else if(x === 'bar'){
    ...}
else{
    ...}
```

```python
if x == 'foo':
    ...
elif x == 'bar':
    ...
else:
    ...
```

```javascript
if(x === foo && y !== bar){...
```

```python
if x == foo and y != bar:
    ...
```

```javascript
if(['foo', 'bar', 'baz']
    .indexOf(s) != -1){...
```

```python
if s in ['foo', 'bar', 'baz']:
    ...
```

```javascript
switch(foo){
    case bar:
    ...
    break;
    case baz: ...
    default:
        return false;
}
```

Figure 2-5. Conditionals

JavaScript	Python

``javascript
var l = [1, 2, 3, 4];
l.push('foo'); // [...4, 'foo']
l.pop(); // 'foo', l=[..., 4]
l.slice(1,3) // [2, 3]
l.slice(-3, -1) // [2, 3]
 	
l.map(function(o){ return o*o;})
// [1, 4, 9, 16]
 	
d = {a:1, b:2, c:3};
d.a === d['a'] // 1
d.z // undefined
 	
// OLD BROWSERS
for(key in d){
  if(d.hasOwnProperty(key){
    var item = d[key];
 	
// NEW AND BETTER
Object.keys(d).forEach(key, i){
  var item = d[key];
``
	``python
	l = [1, 2, 3, 4]
	l.append('foo') # [...4, 'foo']
	l.pop() # 'foo', l=[..., 4]
	l[1:3] # [2, 3]
	l[-3:-1] # [2, 3]
	l[0:4:2] # [1, 3] (stride of 2)
	
	[o*o for o in l]
	// [1, 4, 9, 16]
	
	d = {'a':1, 'b':2, 'c':3}
	d['a'] # 1
	d.get('z') # NoneType
	d['z'] # KeyError!
	
	for key, value in d.items(): ...
	for key in d:
	for value in d.values():...
	``

Figure 2-6. Containers

JavaScript	Python

``javascript
var Foo = {
  initFoo: function(bar){
    this.bar = bar;
    return this;
  }
};
 	
var Baz = Object.create(Foo);
 	
Baz.initBaz = function(bar, qux){
  this.initFoo(bar);
  this.qux = qux;
  return this;
};
 	
var baz = Object.create(Baz)
          .initBaz('answer', 42);
``
	``python
	class Foo(object):
	  def __init__(self, bar):
	    self.bar = bar
	
	class Baz(Foo):
	  def __init__(self, bar, qux):
	    super(Baz).__init__(bar)
	    self.qux = qux
	
	baz = Baz('answer', 42)
	baz.bar # 'answer'
	``

Figure 2-7. Classes and prototypes

Summary

I hope this chapter has shown that JavaScript and Python have a lot of common syntax and that most common idioms and patterns from one of the languages can be expressed in the other without too much fuss. The meat and potatoes of programming, iteration, conditionals, and basic data manipulation is simple in both languages, and the translation of functions is straightforward. If you can program in one to any degree of competency, the threshold to entry for the other is low. That's the huge appeal of these simple scripting languages, which have a lot of common heritage.

I provided a list of patterns, hacks, and idioms I find myself using frequently in dataviz work. I'm sure this list has its idiosyncrasies, but I've tried to tick the obvious boxes.

Treat this as part tutorial, part reference for the chapters to come. Anything not covered here will be dealt with when introduced.

## CHAPTER 3

Reading and Writing Data with Python

One of the fundamental skills of any data visualizer is the ability to move data around. Whether your data is in an SQL database, a comma-separated-value (CSV) file, or in some more esoteric form, you should be comfortable reading the data, converting it, and writing it into a more convenient form if need be. One of Python's great strengths is how easy it makes manipulating data in this way. The focus of this chapter is to bring you up to speed with this essential aspect of our dataviz toolchain.

This chapter is part tutorial, part reference, and sections of it will be referred to in later chapters. If you know the fundamentals of reading and writing Python data, you can cherry-pick parts of the chapter as a refresher.

Easy Does It

I remember when I started programming back in the day (using low-level languages like C) how awkward data manipulation was. Reading from and writing to files was an annoying mixture of boilerplate code, hand-rolled kludges, and the like. Reading from databases was equally difficult, and as for serializing data, the memories are still painful. Discovering Python was a breath of fresh air. It wasn't a speed demon, but opening a file was pretty much as simple as it could be:

```
file = open('data.txt')
```

Back then, Python made reading from and writing to files refreshingly easy, and its sophisticated string processing made parsing the data in those files just as easy. It even had an amazing module called Pickle that could serialize pretty much any Python object.

In the years since, Python has added robust, mature modules to its standard library that make dealing with CSV and JSON files, the standard for web dataviz work, just as easy. There are also some great libraries for interacting with SQL databases such as SQL-Alchemy, my thoroughly recommended go-to. The newer NoSQL databases are also well served. MongoDB is the most popular of these newer document-based databases, and Python's pymongo library, which is demonstrated later in the chapter, makes interacting with it a relative breeze.

Passing Data Around

A good way to demonstrate how to use the key data-storage libraries is to pass a single data packet among them, reading and writing it as we go. This will give us an opportunity to see in action the key data formats and databases employed by data visualizers.

The data we'll be passing around is probably the most commonly used in web visualizations, a list of dictionary-like objects (see Example 3-1). This dataset is transferred to the browser in JSON (*https://en.wikipedia.org/wiki/JSON*) form, which is, as we'll see, easily converted from a Python dictionary.

Example 3-1. Our target list of data objects

```
nobel_winners = [
 {'category': 'Physics',
  'name': 'Albert Einstein',
  'nationality': 'Swiss',
  'sex': 'male',
  'year': 1921},
 {'category': 'Physics',
  'name': 'Paul Dirac',
  'nationality': 'British',
  'sex': 'male',
  'year': 1933},
 {'category': 'Chemistry',
  'name': 'Marie Curie',
  'nationality': 'Polish',
  'sex': 'female',
```

```
'year': 1911}
]
```

We'll start by creating a CSV file from the Python list shown in Example 3-1 as a demonstration of reading (opening) and writing system files.

The following sections assume you're in a work directory with a *data* subdirectory at hand. You can run the code from a Python interpreter or file.

Working with System Files

In this section, we'll create a CSV file from a Python list of dictionaries (Example 3-1). Typically, you would do this using the csv module, which we'll demonstrate after this section, so this is just a way of demonstrating basic Python file manipulation.

First let's open a new file, using w as a second argument to indicate we'll be writing data to it.

```
f = open('data/nobel_winners.csv', 'w')
```

Now we'll create our CSV file from the nobel_winners dictionary (Example 3-1):

```
cols = nobel_winners[0].keys() ❶
cols.sort() ❷

with open('data/nobel_winners.csv, 'w') as f: ❸
    f.write(','.join(cols) + '\n') ❹

    for o in nobel_winners:
        row = [str(o[col]) for col in cols] ❺
        f.write(','.join(row) + '\n')
```

❶ Gets our data columns from the keys of the first object (i.e., ['category', 'name', ...]).

❷ Sorts the columns in alphabetical order.

❸ Uses Python's with statement to guarantee the file is closed on leaving the block or if any exceptions occur.

❹ join creates a concatenated string from a list of strings (cols here), joined by the initial string (i.e., "category,name,..").

❺ Creates a list using the column keys to the objects in nobel_win
ners.

Now that we've created our CSV file, let's use Python to read it and
make sure everything is correct:

```
with open('data/nobel_winners.csv') as f:
    for line in f.readlines():
        print(line),              ❶
```

```
Out:
category,name,nationality,sex,year
Physics,Albert Einstein,Swiss,male,1921
Physics,Paul Dirac,British,male,1933
Chemistry,Marie Curie,Polish,female,1911
```

❶ Adding a comma to the end of the print statement inhibits the
addition of an unnecessary newline.

As the previous output shows, our CCSV file is well formed. Let's
use Python's built-in csv module to first read it and then create a
CSV file the right way.

CSV, TSV, and Row-Column Data Formats

Comma-separated values (CSV) or their tab-separated cousins
(TSV) are probably the most ubiquitous file-based data formats and,
as a data visualizer, these will often be the forms you'll receive to
work your magic with. Being able to read and write CSV files and
their various quirky variants, such as pipe- or semicolon-separated
or those using ` in place of the standard double quotes, is a funda-
mental skill; Python's csv module is capable of doing pretty much all
your heavy lifting here. Let's put it through its paces reading and
writing our nobel_winners data:

```
nobel_winners = [
  {'category': 'Physics',
   'name': 'Albert Einstein',
   'nationality': 'Swiss',
   'sex': 'male',
   'year': 1921},
   ...
]
```

Writing our nobel_winners data (see Example 3-1) to a CSV file is a
pretty simple affair. csv has a dedicated DictWriter class that will

turn our dictionaries into CSV rows. The only piece of explicit bookkeeping we have to do is write a header to our CSV file, using the keys of our dictionaries as fields (i.e., "category, name, nationality, sex"):

```python
with open('data/nobel_winners.csv', 'wb') as f:
    fieldnames = nobel_winners[0].keys() ❶
    fieldnames.sort() ❷
    writer = csv.DictWriter(f, fieldnames=fieldnames)
    writer.writeheader() ❸
    for w in nobel_winners:
        writer.writerow(w)
```

❶ You need to explicitly tell the writer which fieldnames (in this case, the 'category', 'name', etc., keys) to use.

❷ We'll sort the CSV header fields alphabetically for readability.

❸ Writes the CSV-file header ("category,name,…").

You'll probably be reading CSV files more often than writing them.[1] Let's read back the *nobel_winners.csv* file we just wrote.

If you just want to use csv as a superior and eminently adaptable file line-reader, a couple of lines will produce a handy iterator, which can deliver your CSV rows as lists of strings:

```python
import csv

with open('data/nobel_winners.csv') as f:
    reader = csv.reader(f)
    for row in reader: ❶
        print(row)
```

```
Out:
['category', 'name', 'nationality', 'sex', 'year']
['Physics', 'Albert Einstein', 'Swiss', 'male', '1921']
['Physics', 'Paul Dirac', 'British', 'male', '1933']
['Chemistry', 'Marie Curie', 'Polish', 'female', '1911']
```

❶ Iterates over the reader object, consuming the lines in the file.

Note that the numbers are read in string form. If you want to manipulate them numerically, you'll need to convert any numeric columns to their respective type, which is integer years in this case.

---

[1] I recommend using JSON over CSV as your preferred data format.

A more convenient way to consume CSV data is to convert the rows into Python dictionaries. This *record* form is also the one we are using as our conversion target (a list of dicts). csv has a handy DictReader for just this purpose:

```python
import csv

with open('data/nobel_winners.csv') as f:
    reader = csv.DictReader(f)
    nobel_winners = list(reader) ❶

nobel_winners

Out:
[{'category': 'Physics', 'nationality': 'Swiss', \
  'year': '1921', 'name': 'Albert Einstein', 'sex': 'male'},
 {'category': 'Physics', 'nationality': 'British', \
  'year': '1933', 'name': 'Paul Dirac', 'sex': 'male'},
 {'category': 'Chemistry', 'nationality': 'Polish', \
  'year': '1911', 'name': 'Marie Curie', 'sex': 'female'}]
```

❶ Inserts all of the reader items into a list.

As the output shows, we just need to cast the dicts year attributes to integers to make nobel_winners conform to the chapter's target data (Example 3-1), thus:

```python
for w in nobel_winners:
    w['year'] = int(w['year'])
```

The csv readers don't infer datatypes from your file, and instead interpret everything as a string. Pandas, Python's preeminent data-hacking library, will try to guess the correct type of the data columns, usually successfully. We'll see this in action in the later dedicated Pandas chapters.

csv has a few useful arguments to help parse members of the CSV family:

dialect
    By default, 'excel'; specifies a set of dialect-specific parameters. excel-tab is a sometimes used alternative.

delimiter
    Files are usually comma-separated, but they could use |, : or ' ' instead.

quotechar
> By default, double quotes are used, but you occasionally find |
> or ` instead.

You can find the full set of csv parameters in the online Python docs
(*https://docs.python.org/2/library/csv.html#csv-fmt-params*).

Now that we've successfully written and read our target data using
the csv module, let's pass on our CSV-derived nobel_winners dict
to the json module.

JSON

In this section we'll write and read our nobel_winners data using
Python's json module. Let's remind ourselves of the data we're using:

```
nobel_winners = [
 {'category': 'Physics',
  'name': 'Albert Einstein',
  'nationality': 'Swiss',
  'sex': 'male',
  'year': 1921},
  ...
 ]
```

For data primitives such as strings, integers, and floats, Python dictionaries are easily saved (or *dumped*, in the JSON vernacular) into
JSON files, using the json module. The dump method takes a Python
container and a file pointer, saving the former to the latter:

```
import json

with open('data/nobel_winners.json', 'w') as f:
    json.dump(nobel_winners, f)

open('data/nobel_winners.json').read()
```

```
Out: '[{"category": "Physics", "name": "Albert Einstein",
"sex": "male", "person_data": {"date of birth": "14th March
1879", "date of death": "18th April 1955"}, "year": 1921,
"nationality": "Swiss"}, {"category": "Physics",
"nationality": "British", "year": 1933, "name": "Paul Dirac",
"sex": "male"}, {"category": "Chemistry", "nationality":
"Polish", "year": 1911, "name": "Marie Curie", "sex":
"female"}]'
```

Reading (or loading) a JSON file is just as easy. We just pass the
opened JSON file to the json module's load method:

```
import json

with open('data/nobel_winners.json') as f:
    nobel_winners = json.load(f)

nobel_winners
Out:
[{u'category': u'Physics',
  u'name': u'Albert Einstein',
  u'nationality': u'Swiss',
  u'sex': u'male',
  u'year': 1921}, ❶
...
```

❶ Note that, unlike in our CSV file conversion, the integer type of the year column is preserved.

json has the methods loads and dumps, which are counterparts to the file access methods, loading JSON strings to Python containers and dumping Python containers to JSON strings.

Dealing with Dates and Times

Trying to dump a datetime object to json produces a TypeError:

```
from datetime import datetime

json.dumps(datetime.now())
Out:
...
TypeError: datetime.datetime(2015, 9, 13, 10, 25, 52, 586792)
is not JSON serializable
```

When serializing simple datatypes such as strings or numbers, the default json encoders and decoders are fine. But for more specialized data such as dates, you will need to do your own encoding and decoding. This isn't as hard as it sounds and quickly becomes routine. Let's first look at encoding your Python datetimes (*https:// docs.python.org/2/library/datetime.html#datetime-objects*) into sensible JSON strings.

The easiest way to encode Python data containing datetimes is to create a custom encoder like the one shown in Example 3-2, which is provided to the json.dumps method as a cls argument. This encoder is applied to each object in your data in turn and converts dates or datetimes to their ISO-format string (see "Dealing with Dates, Times, and Complex Data" on page 84).

Example 3-2. Encoding a Python datetime to JSON

```
import datetime
from dateutil import parser
import json


class JSONDateTimeEncoder(json.JSONEncoder):  ❶
    def default(self, obj):
        if isinstance(obj, (datetime.date, datetime.datetime)):  ❷
            return obj.isoformat()
        else:
            return json.JSONEncoder.default(self, obj)

def dumps(obj):
    return json.dumps(obj, cls=JSONDateTimeEncoder)  ❸
```

❶ Subclasses a JSONEncoder in order to create customized date-handling one.

❷ Tests for a datetime object and if true, returns the isoformat of any dates or datetimes (e.g., *2015-09-13T10:25:52.586792*).

❸ Uses the cls argument to set a custom date encoder.

Let's see how our new dumps method copes with some datetime data:

```
now_str = dumps({'time': datetime.datetime.now()})
now_str
Out:
'{"time": "2015-09-13T10:25:52.586792"}'
```

The time field is correctly converted into an ISO-format string, ready to be decoded into a JavaScript Date object (see "Dealing with Dates, Times, and Complex Data" on page 84 for a demonstration).

While you could write a generic decoder to cope with date strings in arbitrary JSON files,[2] it's probably not advisable. Date strings come in so many weird and wonderful varieties that this is a job best done by hand on what is pretty much always a known dataset.

---

[2] The Python module dateutil has a parser that will parse most dates and times sensibly, and might be a good basis for this.

The venerable `strptime` method, part of the `datetime.datetime`
package, is good for the job of turning a time string in a known format into a Python `datetime` instance:

```
In [0]: time_str = '2012/01/01 12:32:11'

In [1]: dt = datetime.strptime(time_str, '%Y/%m/%d %H:%M:%S') ❶

In [2]: dt
Out[2]: datetime.datetime(2012, 1, 1, 12, 32, 11)
```

❶ `strptime` tries to match the time string to a format string using
various directives such as %Y (year with century) and %H (hour as
a zero-padded decimal number). If successful, it creates a
Python `datetime` instance. See the Python docs (*https://
docs.python.org/2/library/datetime.html#strftime-and-strptime-
behavior*) for a full list of the directives available.

If `strptime` is fed a time string that does not match its format, it
throws a handy `ValueError`:

```
dt = datetime.strptime('1/2/2012 12:32:11', '%Y/%m/%d %H:%M:%S')
-----------------------------------------------------------------
ValueError                     Traceback (most recent call last)
<ipython-input-111-af657749a9fe> in <module>()
----> 1 dt = datetime.strptime('1/2/2012 12:32:11',\
      '%Y/%m/%d %H:%M:%S')
...
ValueError: time data '1/2/2012 12:32:11' does not match
      format '%Y/%m/%d %H:%M:%S'
```

So to convert date fields of a known format into `datetimes` for a
data list of dictionaries, you could do something like this:

```
for d in data:
    try:
        d['date'] = datetime.strptime(d['date'],\
          '%Y/%m/%d %H:%M:%S')
    except ValueError:
        print('Oops! - invalid date for ' + repr(d))
```

Now that we've dealt with the two most popular data file formats,
let's shift to the big guns and see how to read our data from and
write our data to SQL and NoSQL databases.

SQL

For interacting with an SQL database, SQLAlchemy is the most popular and, in my opinion, best Python library. It allows you to use raw SQL instructions if speed and efficiency is an issue, but also provides a powerful object-relational mapping (ORM) that allows you to operate on SQL tables using a high-level, Pythonic API, treating them essentially as Python classes.

Reading and writing data using SQL while allowing the user to treat that data as a Python container is a complicated process, and though SQLAlchemy is far more user-friendly than a low-level SQL engine, it is still a fairly complex library. I'll cover the basics here, using our data as a target, but encourage you to spend a little time reading some of the rather excellent documentation on SQLAlchemy (*http://www.sqlalchemy.org/library.html#reference*). Let's remind ourselves of the nobel_winners dataset we're aiming to write and read:

```
nobel_winners = [
 {'category': 'Physics',
  'name': 'Albert Einstein',
  'nationality': 'Swiss',
  'sex': 'male',
  'year': 1921},
  ...
]
```

Let's first write our target data to an SQLite file using SQLAlchemy, starting by creating the database engine.

Creating the Database Engine

The first thing you need to do when starting an SQLAlchemy session is to create a database engine. This engine will establish a connection with the database in question and perform any conversions needed to the generic SQL instructions generated by SQLAlchemy and the data being returned.

There are engines for pretty much every popular database, as well as a *memory* option, which holds the database in RAM, allowing fast access for testing.[3] The great thing about these engines is that they are interchangeable, which means you could develop your code using the convenient file-based SQLite database and then switch during production to something a little more industrial, such as Postgresql, by changing a single config string. Check SQLAlchemy (*http://docs.sqlalchemy.org/en/rel_1_0/core/engines.html*) for the full list of engines available.

The form for specifying a database URL is:

```
dialect+driver://username:password@host:port/database
```

So, to connect to a 'nobel_prize' MySQL database running on localhost requires something like the following. Note that cre ate_engine does not actually make any SQL requests at this point, but merely sets up the framework for doing so.[4]

```
engine = create_engine(\
            'mysql://kyran:mypsswd@localhost/nobel_prize')
```

We'll use a file-based SQLite database, setting the echo argument to True, which will output any SQL instructions generated by SQL-Alchemy. Note the use of three backslashes after the colon:

```
from sqlalchemy import create_engine

engine = create_engine(\
            'sqlite:///data/nobel_prize.db', echo=True)
```

SQLAlchemy offers various ways to engage with databases, but I recommend using the more recent declarative style unless there are good reasons to go with something more low-level and fine-grained. In essence, with declarative mapping, you subclass your Python SQL-table classes from a base, and SQLAlchemy introspects their structure and relationships. See SQLAlchemy (*http://bit.ly/1tu8qlU*) for more details.

Defining the Database Tables

We first create a Base class using declarative_base. This base will be used to create table classes, from which SQLAlchemy will create

---

3 On a cautionary note, it is probably a bad idea to use different database configurations for testing and production.

4 See details on SQLAlchemy (*http://docs.sqlalchemy.org/en/latest/core/engines.html*) of this *lazy initialization*.

---

the database's table schemas. You can use these table classes to inter-act with the database in a fairly Pythonic fashion:

```
from sqlalchemy.ext.declarative import declarative_base

Base = declarative_base()
```

Note that most SQL libraries require you to formally define table schemas. This is in contrast to such schema-less NoSQL variants as MongoDB. We'll take a look at the Dataset library later in this chap-ter, which enables schemaless SQL.

Using this `Base`, we define our various tables—in our case, a single `Winner` table. Example 3-3 shows how to subclass `Base` and use SQLAlchemy's datatypes to define a table schema. Note the __table name__ member, which will be used to name the SQL table and as a keyword to retrieve it, and the optional custom __repr__ method, which will be used when printing a table row.

Example 3-3. Defining an SQL database table

```
from sqlalchemy import Column, Integer, String, Enum
// ...

class Winner(Base):
    __tablename__ = 'winners'

    id = Column(Integer, primary_key=True)
    name = Column(String)
    category = Column(String)
    year = Column(Integer)
    nationality = Column(String)
    sex = Column(Enum('male', 'female'))

    def __repr__(self):
        return "<Winner(name='%s', category='%s', year='%s')>"\
            %(self.name, self.category, self.year)
```

Having declared our `Base` subclass in Example 3-3, we supply its met adata create_all method with our database engine to create our database.[5] Because we set the echo argument to True when creating the engine, we can see the SQL instructions generated by SQL-Alchemy from the command line:

---

5 This assumes the database doesn't already exist. If it does, `Base` will be used to create new insertions and to interpret retrievals.

```
Base.metadata.create_all(engine)

INFO:sqlalchemy.engine.base.Engine SELECT CAST('test plain
returns' AS VARCHAR(60)) AS anon_1
...
INFO sqlalchemy.engine.base.Engine
CREATE TABLE winners (
        id INTEGER NOT NULL,
        name VARCHAR,
        category VARCHAR,
        year INTEGER,
        nationality VARCHAR,
        sex VARCHAR(6),
        PRIMARY KEY (id),
        CHECK (sex IN ('male', 'female'))
)
...
INFO:sqlalchemy.engine.base.Engine:COMMIT
```

With our new winners table declared, we can start adding winner
instances to it.

Adding Instances with a Session

Now that we have created our database, we need a session to interact
with:

```
from sqlalchemy.orm import sessionmaker

Session = sessionmaker(bind=engine)
session = Session()
```

We can now use our Winner class to create instances and table rows
and add them to the session:

```
albert = Winner(**nobel_winners[0]) ❶
session.add(albert)
session.new ❷
Out:
IdentitySet([<Winner(name='Albert Einstein', category='Physics',
        year='1921')>])
```

❶ Python's handy ** operator unpacks our first nobel_winners
member into key-value pairs: (name='Albert Einstein', cate
gory='Physics'...).

❷ new is the set of any items that have been added to this session.

Note that all database insertions and deletions take place in Python. It's only when we use the commit method that the database is altered.

 Use as few commits as possible, allowing SQL-Alchemy to work its magic behind the scenes. When you commit, your various database manipulations should be summarized by SQL-Alchemy and communicated in an efficient fashion. Commits involve establishing a database handshake and negotiating transactions, which is often a slow process and one you want to limit as much as possible, leveraging SQLAlchemy's bookkeeping abilities to full advantage.

As the new method shows, we have added a Winner to the session. We can remove the object using expunge, leaving an empty IdentitySet:

```
session.expunge(albert) ❶
session.new
Out:
IdentitySet([])
```

❶ Remove the instance from the session (there is an expunge_all method that removes all new objects added to the session).

At this point, no database insertions or deletions have taken place. Let's add all the members of our nobel_winners list to the session and commit them to the database:

```
winner_rows = [Winner(**w) for w in nobel_winners]
session.add_all(winner_rows)
session.commit()
Out:
INFO:sqlalchemy.engine.base.Engine:BEGIN (implicit)
...
INFO:sqlalchemy.engine.base.Engine:INSERT INTO winners (name,
category, year, nationality, sex) VALUES (?, ?, ?, ?, ?)
INFO:sqlalchemy.engine.base.Engine:(u'Albert Einstein',
u'Physics', 1921, u'Swiss', u'male')
...
INFO:sqlalchemy.engine.base.Engine:COMMIT
```

Now that we've committed our nobel_winners data to the database, let's see what we can do with it and how to recreate the target list in Example 3-1.

Querying the Database

To access data, you use the `session`'s `query` method, the result of which can be filtered, grouped, and intersected, allowing the full range of standard SQL data retrieval. You can check out available querying methods in the SQLAlchemy docs (*http://docs.sqlalchemy.org/en/rel_1_0/orm/query.html*). For now, I'll quickly run through some of the most common queries on our Nobel dataset.

Let's first count the number of rows in our winners' table:

```
session.query(Winner).count()
Out:
3
```

Next, let's retrieve all Swiss winners:

```
result = session.query(Winner).filter_by(nationality='Swiss')  ❶
list(result)
Out:
[<Winner(name='Albert Einstein', category='Physics',\
  year='1921')>]
```

❶   `filter_by` uses keyword expressions; its SQL expressions counterpart is `filter`—for example, `filter(Winner.nationality == Swiss)`.

Now let's get all non-Swiss Physics winners:

```
result = session.query(Winner).filter(\
            Winner.category == 'Physics', \
            Winner.nationality != 'Swiss')
list(result)
Out:
[<Winner(name='Paul Dirac', category='Physics', year='1933')>]
```

Here's how to get a row based on ID number:

```
session.query(Winner).get(3)
Out:
<Winner(name='Marie Curie', category='Chemistry', year='1911')>
```

Now let's retrieve winners ordered by year:

```
res = session.query(Winner).order_by('year')
list(res)
Out:
[<Winner(name='Marie Curie', category='Chemistry',\
  year='1911')>,
  <Winner(name='Albert Einstein', category='Physics',\
```

```
year='1921')>,
  <Winner(name='Paul Dirac', category='Physics', year='1933')>]
```

To reconstruct our target list requires a little effort converting the
Winner objects returned by our session query into Python dicts.
Let's write a little function to create a dict from an SQLAlchemy
class. We'll use a little table introspection to get the column labels
(see Example 3-4).

Example 3-4. Converts an SQLAlchemy instance to a dict

```
def inst_to_dict(inst, delete_id=True):
    dat = {}
    for column in inst.__table__.columns:  ❶
        dat[column.name] = getattr(inst, column.name)
    if delete_id:
        dat.pop('id')  ❷
    return dat
```

❶ Accesses the instance's table class to get a list of column objects.

❷ If delete_id is true, remove the SQL primary ID field.

We can use Example 3-4 to reconstruct our nobel_winners target
list:

```
winner_rows = session.query(Winner)
nobel_winners = [inst_to_dict(w) for w in winner_rows]
nobel_winners
Out:
[{'category': u'Physics',
  'name': u'Albert Einstein',
  'nationality': u'Swiss',
  'sex': u'male',
  'year': 1921},
  ...
]
```

You can update database rows easily by changing the property of
their reflected objects:

```
marie = session.query(Winner).get(3)  ❶
marie.nationality = 'French'
session.dirty  ❷
Out:
IdentitySet([<Winner(name='Marie Curie', category='Chemistry',
year='1911')>])
```

❶ Fetches Marie Curie, nationality Polish.

❷ `dirty` shows any changed instances not yet committed to the database.

Let's commit `marie`'s changes and check that her nationality has changed from Polish to French:

```
session.commit()
Out:
INFO:sqlalchemy.engine.base.Engine:UPDATE winners SET
nationality=? WHERE winners.id = ?
INFO:sqlalchemy.engine.base.Engine:('French', 3)
...

session.dirty
Out:
IdentitySet([])

session.query(Winner).get(3).nationality
Out:
'French'
```

In addition to updating database rows, you can delete the results of a query:

```
session.query(Winner).filter_by(name='Albert Einstein').delete()
Out:
INFO:sqlalchemy.engine.base.Engine:DELETE FROM winners WHERE
winners.name = ?
INFO:sqlalchemy.engine.base.Engine:('Albert Einstein',)
1

list(session.query(Winner))
Out:
[<Winner(name='Paul Dirac', category='Physics', year='1933')>,
 <Winner(name='Marie Curie', category='Chemistry',\
 year='1911')>]
```

You can also drop the whole table if required, using the declarative class's `__table__` attribute:

```
Winner.__table__.drop(engine)
```

In this section, we've dealt with a single winners table, without any foreign keys or relationship to any other tables, akin to a CSV or JSON file. SQLAlchemy adds the same level of convenience in dealing with many-to-one, one-to-many, and other database table relationships as it does to basic querying using implicit joins, by supplying the `query` method with more than one table class or explicitly using the query's `join` method. Check out the examples in the SQLAlchemy docs (*http://docs.sqlalchemy.org/en/rel_1_0/orm/ tutorial.html#querying-with-joins*) for more details.

Easier SQL with Dataset

One library I've found myself using a fair deal recently is Dataset (*https://dataset.readthedocs.org/en/latest/*), a module designed to make working with SQL databases a little easier and more Pythonic than existing powerhouses like SQLAlchemy.[6] Dataset tries to provide the same degree of convenience you get when working with schema-less NoSQL databases such as MongoDB by removing a lot of the formal boilerplate, such as schema definitions, which are demanded by the more conventional libraries. Dataset is built on top of SQLAlchemy, which means it works with pretty much all major databases and can exploit the power, robustness, and maturity of that best-of-breed library. Let's see how it deals with reading and writing our target dataset (from Example 3-1).

Let's use the SQLite *nobel_prize.db* database we've just created to put Dataset through its paces. First we connect to our SQL database, using the same URL/file format as SQLAlchemy:

```
import dataset

db = dataset.connect('sqlite:///data/nobel_prize.db')
```

To get our list of winners, we grab a table from our db database, using its name as a key, and then use the find method without arguments to return all winners:

```
wtable = db['winners']
winners = wtable.find()
winners = list(winners)
winners
Out:
[OrderedDict([(u'id', 1), (u'name', u'Albert Einstein'),
(u'category', u'Physics'), (u'year', 1921), (u'nationality',
u'Swiss'), (u'sex', u'male')]), OrderedDict([(u'id', 2),
(u'name', u'Paul Dirac'), (u'category', u'Physics'),
(u'year', 1933), (u'nationality', u'British'), (u'sex',
u'male')]), OrderedDict([(u'id', 3), (u'name', u'Marie
Curie'), (u'category', u'Chemistry'), (u'year', 1911),
(u'nationality', u'Polish'), (u'sex', u'female')])]
```

---

6 Dataset's official motto is "databases for lazy people."

Note that the instances returned by Dataset's `find` method are `Order eddicts`. These useful containers are an extension of Python's `dict` class and behave just like dictionaries except that they remember the order in which items were inserted, meaning you can guarantee the result of iteration, pop the last item inserted, and more. This is a very handy additional functionality.

 One of the most useful Python "batteries" for data-mungers is `collections`, which is where Dataset's `OrderedDicts` come from. The `defaultdict` and `Counter` classes are particularly useful. Check out what's available in the Python docs (*https://docs.python.org/2/library/ collections.html*).

Let's recreate our winners table with `Dataset`, first dropping the existing one:

```
wtable = db['winners']
wtable.drop()

wtable = db['winners']
wtable.find()
Out:
[]
```

To recreate our dropped winners table, we don't need to define a schema as with SQLAlchemy (see "Defining the Database Tables" on page 70). Dataset will infer that from the data we add, doing all the SQL creation implicitly. This is the kind of convenience one is used to when working with collection-based NoSQL databases. Let's use our `nobel_winners` dataset (Example 3-1) to insert some winner dictionaries. We use a database transaction and the `with` statement to efficiently insert our objects and then commit them.[7]

```
with db as tx: ❶
    for w in nobel_winners:
        tx['winners'].insert(w)
```

❶ Use the `with` statement to guarantee the transaction `tx` is committed to the database.

---

7 See this documentation (*https://dataset.readthedocs.org/en/latest/quickstart.html#using-transactions*) for further details of how to use transactions to group updates.

Let's check that everything has gone well:

```
list(db['winners'].find())
Out:
[OrderedDict([(u'id', 1), (u'name', u'Albert Einstein'),
(u'category', u'Physics'), (u'year', 1921), (u'nationality',
u'Swiss'), (u'sex', u'male')]),
...
]
```

The winners have been correctly inserted and their order of insertion preserved by the OrderedDict.

Dataset is great for basic SQL-based work, particularly retrieving data you might wish to process or visualize. For more advanced manipulation, it allows you to drop down into SQLAlchemy's core API using the query method.

On top of its huge convenience, Dataset has a freeze method that is a great asset to budding data visualizers. freeze takes the result of an SQL query and turns it into a JSON or CSV file, which is a very convenient way to start playing around with the data with Java-Script/D3:

```
winners = db['winners'].find()
dataset.freeze(winners, format='csv', \
               filename='data/nobel_winners_ds.csv')

open('data/nobel_winners_ds.csv').read()
Out:
'id,name,category,year,nationality,sex\r\n
1,Albert Einstein,Physics,1921,Swiss,male\r\n
2,Paul Dirac,Physics,1933,British,male\r\n
3,Marie Curie,Chemistry,1911,Polish,female\r\n'
```

Now that we've covered the basics of working with SQL databases, let's see how Python makes working with the most popular NoSQL database just as painless.

MongoDB

Document-centric datastores like MongoDB offer a lot of convenience to data wranglers. As with all tools, there are good and bad use cases for NoSQL databases. If you have data that has already been refined and processed and don't anticipate needing SQL's powerful query language based on optimized table joins, MongoDB will probably prove easier to work with. MongoDB is a particularly good fit for web dataviz because it uses binary JSON (BSON) as its data format. An extension of JSON, BSON can deal with binary data and datetime objects, and plays very nicely with JavaScript.

Let's remind ourselves of the target dataset we're aiming to write and read:

```
nobel_winners = [
 {'category': 'Physics',
  'name': 'Albert Einstein',
  'nationality': 'Swiss',
  'sex': 'male',
  'year': 1921},
  ...
]
```

Creating a MongoDB collection with Python is the work of a few lines:

```
from pymongo import MongoClient

client = MongoClient() ❶
db = client.nobel_prize ❷
coll = db.winners ❸
```

❶   Creates a Mongo client, using the default host and ports.

❷   Creates or accesses the nobel_prize database.

❸   If a *winners* collection exists, this will retrieve it; otherwise (as in our case), it creates it.

Using Constants for MongoDB Access

Accessing and creating a MongoDB database with Python involves the same operation, using dot notation and square-bracket key access:

```
db = client.nobel_prize
db = client['nobel_prize']
```

This is all very convenient, but it means a single spelling mistake, such as noble_prize, could both create an unwanted database and cause future operations to fail to update the correct one. For this reason, I advise using constant strings to access your MongoDB databases and collections:

```
DB_NOBEL_PRIZE = 'nobel_prize'
COLL_WINNERS = 'winners'

db = client[DB_NOBEL_PRIZE]
coll = db[COLL_WINNERS]
```

MongoDB databases run on localhost port 27017 by default but could be anywhere on the Web. They also take an optional username and password. Example 3-5 shows how to create a simple utility function to access our database, with standard defaults.

Example 3-5. Accessing a MongoDB database

```
from pymongo import MongoClient

def get_mongo_database(db_name, host='localhost',\
                    port=27017, username=None, password=None):
    """ Get named database from MongoDB with/out authentication """
    # make Mongo connection with/out authentication
    if username and password:
        mongo_uri = 'mongodb://%s:%s@%s/%s'%\  ❶
        (username, password, host, db_name)
        conn = MongoClient(mongo_uri)
    else:
        conn = MongoClient(host, port)

    return conn[db_name]
```

❶ We specify the database name in the MongoDB URI (Uniform Resource Identifier) as the user may not have general privileges for the database.

We can now create a Nobel Prize database and add our target dataset (Example 3-1). Let's first get a winners collection, using the string constants for access:

```
db = mongo_to_database(DB_NOBEL_PRIZE)
coll = db[COLL_WINNERS]
```

Inserting our Nobel Prize dataset is then as easy as can be:

```
coll.insert(nobel_winners)
Out:
[ObjectId('55f8326f26a7112e547879d4'),
 ObjectId('55f8326f26a7112e547879d5'),
 ObjectId('55f8326f26a7112e547879d6')]
```

The resulting array of ObjectIds can be used for future retrieval, but MongoDB has already left its stamp on our nobel_winners list, adding a hidden id property:[8]

```
nobel_winners
Out:
[{'_id': ObjectId('55f8326f26a7112e547879d4'),
  'category': u'Physics',
  'name': u'Albert Einstein',
  'nationality': u'Swiss',
  'sex': u'male',
  'year': 1921},
  ...
]
```

 MongoDB's ObjectIds have quite a bit of hidden functionality, being a lot more than a simple random identifier. You can, for example, get the generation time of the ObjectId, which gives you access to a handy timestamp:

```
oid = bson.ObjectId()
oid.generation_time
Out: datetime.datetime(2015, 11, 4, 15, 43, 23...
```

Find the full details in the MongoDB documentation (*http://bit.ly/1QbOBKE*).

Now that we've got some items in our winners collection, MongoDB makes finding them very easy, with its find method taking a dictionary query:

```
res = coll.find({'category':'Chemistry'})
list(res)
Out:
[{u'_id': ObjectId('55f8326f26a7112e547879d6'),
  u'category': u'Chemistry',
  u'name': u'Marie Curie',
  u'nationality': u'Polish',
  u'sex': u'female',
  u'year': 1911}]
```

---

8 One of the cool things about MongoDB is that the ObjectIds are generated on the client side, removing the need to quiz the database for them.

There are a number of special dollar-prefixed operators that allow for sophisticated querying. Let's find all the winners after 1930 using the $gt (greater-than) operator:

```
res = coll.find({'year': {'$gt': 1930}})
list(res)
Out:
[{u'_id': ObjectId('55f8326f26a7112e547879d5'),
  u'category': u'Physics',
  u'name': u'Paul Dirac',
  u'nationality': u'British',
  u'sex': u'male',
  u'year': 1933}]
```

You can also use Boolean expression, for instance, to find all winners after 1930 or all female winners:

```
res = coll.find({'$or':[{'year': {'$gt': 1930}},\
{'sex':'female'}]})
list(res)
Out:
[{u'_id': ObjectId('55f8326f26a7112e547879d5'),
  u'category': u'Physics',
  u'name': u'Paul Dirac',
  u'nationality': u'British',
  u'sex': u'male',
  u'year': 1933},
 {u'_id': ObjectId('55f8326f26a7112e547879d6'),
  u'category': u'Chemistry',
  u'name': u'Marie Curie',
  u'nationality': u'Polish',
  u'sex': u'female',
  u'year': 1911}]
```

You can find the full list of available query expressions in the MongoDB documentation (*http://bit.ly/1Yxn5c1*).

As a final test, let's turn our new *winners* collection back into a Python list of dictionaries. We'll create a utility function for the task:

```
def mongo_coll_to_dicts(dbname='test', collname='test',\
                query={}, del_id=True, **kw): ❶

    db = get_mongo_database(dbname, **kw)
    res = list(db[collname].find(query))

    if del_id:
        for r in res:
            r.pop('_id')

    return res
```

❶ An empty `query dict {}` will find all documents in the collection. `del_id` is a flag to remove MongoDB's `ObjectIds` from the items by default.

We can now create our target dataset:

```
mongo_coll_to_dicts(DB_NOBEL_PRIZE, COLL_WINNERS)
Out:
[{u'category': u'Physics',
  u'name': u'Albert Einstein',
  u'nationality': u'Swiss',
  u'sex': u'male',
  u'year': 1921},
  ...
]
```

MongoDB's schema-less databases are great for fast prototyping in solo work or small teams. There will probably come a point, particularly with large code bases, when a formal schema becomes a useful reference and sanity check; and when you are choosing a data model, the ease with which document forms can be adapted is a bonus. Being able to pass Python dictionaries as queries to PyMongo and having access to client-side generated `ObjectIds` are a couple of other conveniences.

We've now passed the `nobel_winners` data in Example 3-1 through all our required file formats and databases. Let's consider the special case of dealing with dates and times before summing up.

Dealing with Dates, Times, and Complex Data

The ability to deal comfortably with dates and times is fundamental to dataviz work but can be quite tricky. There are many ways to represent a date or datetime as a string, each one requiring a separate encoding or decoding. For this reason it's good to settle on one format in your own work and encourage others to do the same. I recommend using the International Standard Organization (ISO) 8601 time format (*http://bit.ly/1OcC731*) as your string representation for dates and times, and using the Coordinated Universal Time (UTC) form (*http://bit.ly/1rtmDOT*).[9] Here's a few examples of ISO 8601 date and datetime strings:

2015-09-23   A date (Python/C format code '%Y-%m-%d')

2015-09-23T16:32:35Z   A UTC (Z after time) date and time ('T%H:%M:%S')

2015-09-23T16:32+02:00 A positive two-hour (+02:00) offset from UTC (e.g., Central European Time)

Note the importance of being prepared to deal with different time zones. These are not always on lines of longitude (see Wikipedia's Time Zone entry (*https://en.wikipedia.org/wiki/Time_zone*)), and often the best way to derive an accurate time is by using UTC time plus a geographic location.

ISO 8601 is the standard used by JavaScript and is easy to work with in Python. As web data visualizers, our key concern is in creating a string representation that can be passed between Python and Java-Script using JSON and encoded and decoded easily at both ends.

Let's take a date and time in the shape of a Python datetime, convert it into a string, and then see how that string can be consumed by JavaScript.

First we produce our Python datetime:

```
from datetime import datetime

d = datetime.now()
d.isoformat()
Out:
'2015-09-15T21:48:50.746674'
```

This string can then be saved to JSON or CSV, read by JavaScript, and used to create a Date object:

```
d = new Date('2015-09-15T21:48:50.746674')
> Tue Sep 15 2015 22:48:50 GMT+0100 (BST)
```

We can return the datetime to ISO 8601 string form with the toISO String method:

---

9 To get the actual local time from UTC, you can store a time zone offset or, better still, derive it from a geocoordinate; this is because time zones do not follow lines of longitude very exactly.

```
d.toISOString()
> "2015-09-15T21:48:50.746Z"
```

Finally, we can read the string back into Python.

If you know that you're dealing with an ISO-format time string, Python's `dateutil` module should do the job.[10] But you'll probably want to sanity-check the result:

```
from dateutil import parser

d = parser.parse("2015-09-15T21:48:50.746Z")
d
Out:
datetime.datetime(2015, 9, 15, 21, 48, 50, 746000, \
tzinfo=tzutc())
```

Note that we've lost some resolution in the trip from Python to JavaScript and back again, the latter dealing in milliseconds, not microseconds. This is unlikely to be an issue in any dataviz work but is good to bear in mind just in case some strange temporal errors occur.

Summary

This chapter aimed to make you comfortable using Python to move data around the various file formats and databases that a data visualizer might expect to bump into. Using databases effectively and efficiently is a skill that takes a while to learn, but you should now be comfortable with basic reading and writing for the large majority of dataviz use cases.

Now that we have the vital lubrication for our dataviz toolchain, let's get up to scratch on the basic web development skills you'll need for the chapters ahead.

---

10 To install, just run `pip install dateutil`. `dateutil` is a pretty powerful extension of Python's `datetime`; check it out on Read the Docs (*https://dateutil.readthedocs.org/en/latest/*).

## CHAPTER 4

Webdev 101

This chapter introduces the core web-development knowledge you will need to understand the web pages you scrape for data and to structure those you want to deliver as the skeleton of your JavaScripted visualizations. As you'll see, a little knowledge goes a long way in modern webdev, particularly when your focus is building self-contained visualizations and not entire websites (see "Single-Page Apps" on page 88 for more details).

The usual caveats apply: this chapter is part reference, part tutorial. There will probably be stuff here you know already, so feel free to skip over it and get to the new material.

The Big Picture

The humble web page, the basic building block of the World Wide Web (WWW)—that fraction of the Internet consumed by humans —is constructed from files of various types. Apart from the multimedia files (images, videos, sound, etc.), the key elements are textual, consisting of Hypertext Markup Language (HTML), Cascading Style Sheets (CSS), and JavaScript. These three, along with any necessary data files, are delivered using the Hypertext Transfer Protocol (HTTP) and used to build the page you see and interact with in your browser window, which is described by the Document Object Model (DOM), a hierarchical tree off which your content hangs. A basic understanding of how these elements interact is vital to building modern web visualizations, and the aim of this chapter is to get you quickly up to speed.

Web development is a big field, and the aim here is not to turn you into a full-fledged web developer. I assume you want to limit the amount of webdev you have to do as much as possible, focusing only on that fraction necessary to build a modern visualization. In order to build the sort of visualizations showcased at d3js.org, published in the *New York Times*, or incorporated in basic interactive data dashboards, you actually need surprisingly little webdev fu. The result of your labors should be easy to add to a larger website by someone dedicated to that job. In the case of small, personal websites, it's easy enough to incorporate the visualization yourself.

Single-Page Apps

Single-page applications (SPAs) are web applications (or whole sites) that are dynamically assembled using JavaScript, often building upon a lightweight HTML backbone and CSS styles that can be applied dynamically using class and id attributes. Many modern data visualizations fit this description, including the Nobel Prize visualization this book builds toward.

Often self-contained, the SPA's root folder can be easily incorporated in an existing website or stand alone, requiring only an HTTP server such as Apache or Nginx.

Thinking of our data visualizations in terms of SPAs removes a lot of the cognitive overhead from the webdev aspect of JavaScript visualizations, allowing us to focus on programming challenges. The skills required to put the visualization on the Web are still fairly basic and quickly amortized. Often it will be someone else's job.

Tooling Up

As you'll see, the webdev needed to make modern data visualizations requires no more than a decent text editor, modern browser, and a terminal (Figure 4-1). I'll cover what I see as the minimal requirements for a webdev-ready editor and nonessential but nice-to-have features.

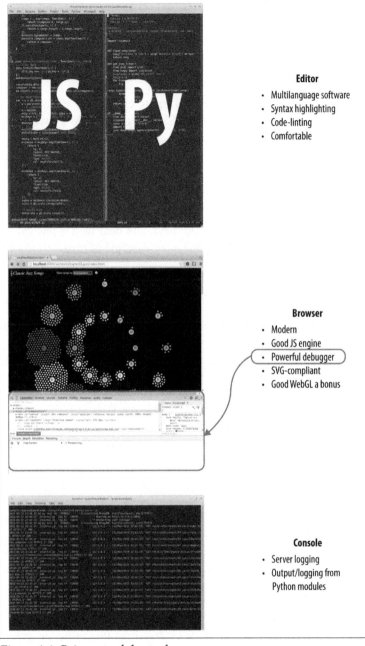

Editor
- Multilanguage software
- Syntax highlighting
- Code-linting
- Comfortable

Browser
- Modern
- Good JS engine
- Powerful debugger
- SVG-compliant
- Good WebGL a bonus

Console
- Server logging
- Output/logging from Python modules

Figure 4-1. Primary webdev tools

My browser development tools of choice are Chrome's web-developer kit (*https://developers.google.com/web/tools/chrome-devtools/*), freely available on all platforms. It has a lot of tab-delineated functionality, the following of which I'll cover in this chapter:

- The *Elements* tab, which allows you to explore the structure of a web page, its HTML content, CSS styles, and DOM presentation
- The *Sources* tab, where most of your JavaScript debugging will take place

You'll need a terminal for output, starting your local web server, and sketching ideas with the IPython interpreter.

Before dealing with what you do need, let's deal with a few things you don't need when setting out, laying a couple of myths to rest on the way.

The Myth of IDEs, Frameworks, and Tools

There is a common assumption among the prospective JavaScripter that to program for the Web requires a complex toolset, primarily an Intelligent Development Environment (IDE), as used by enterprise —and other—coders everywhere. This is potentially expensive and presents another learning curve. The good news is that not only have I never used an IDE to program for the Web, but I can't think of anyone I know in the discipline who does. In all probability, the wonderful web visualizations you have seen, which may have spurred you to pick up this book, were created with nothing more than a humble text editor, a modern web browser for viewing and debugging, and a console or terminal for logging and output.

There is also a common myth that one cannot be productive in Java-Script without using a framework of some kind. At the moment, a number of these frameworks are vying for control of the JS ecosys-tem, sponsored by the various huge companies that created them. These frameworks come and go at a dizzying rate, and my advice for anyone starting out in JavaScript is to ignore them entirely while you develop your core skills. Use small, targeted libraries, such as those in the jQuery ecosystem or Underscore's functional program-ming extensions, and see how far you can get before needing a *my way or the highway* framework. Only lock yourself into a framework to meet a clear and present need, not because the current JS group-

think is raving about how great it is.[1] Another important consideration is that D3, the prime web dataviz library, doesn't really play well
with any of the bigger frameworks I know, particularly the ones that
want control over the DOM.

Another thing you'll find if you hang around webdev forums, Red-
dit lists, and Stack Overflow is a huge range of tools constantly
clamoring for attention. There are JS+CSS minifiers, watchers to
automatically detect file changes and reload web pages during development, among others. While a few of these have their place, in my
experience there are a lot of flaky tools that probably cost more time
in hair-tearing than they gain in productivity. To reiterate, you can
be very productive without these things and should only reach for
one to scratch an urgent itch. Some are keepers, but very few are
even remotely essential for data visualization work.

A Text-Editing Workhorse

First and foremost among your webdev tools is a text editor that you
are comfortable with and which can, at the very least, do syntax
highlighting for multiple languages—in our case, HTML, CSS, Java-
Script, and Python. You can get away with a plain, nonhighlighting
editor, but in the long run it will prove to be a pain. Things like syntax highlighting, code linting, intelligent indentation, and the like
remove a huge cognitive load from the process of programming, so
much so that I see their absence as a limiting factor. These are my
minimal requirements for a text editor:

- Syntax highlighting for all languages you use
- Configurable indentation levels and types for languages (e.g.,
  Python 4 soft tabs, JavaScript 2 soft tabs)
- Multiple windows/panes/tabs to allow easy navigation around
  your code base

If you are using a relatively advanced text editor, all the above
should come as standard with the exception of code linting, which
will probably require a bit of configuration.

---

1 I bear the scars so you don't have to.

My leading candidate for *nice to have* is a decent code linter (*https://en.wikipedia.org/wiki/Lint_%28software%29*). If the mark of a useful tool is how much you would miss its absence, then code linting is easily in my top five. For scripting languages like Python and Java-Script, there's only so much intelligent code analysis that can be achieved syntactically, but just sanity-checking the obvious syntax errors can be a huge time saver. In JavaScript in particular, some mistakes are transparent, in the sense that things will run in spite of them, and will quite often produce confusing error messages. A code linter can save you time here and enforce good practice. Figure 4-2 shows a contrived example of a JavaScript code linter in action.

```
// you should use the function form of 'use strict'
'use strict';
// you included jQuery, but never used it
(function ($) {
    // foo not defined
    foo = 'baa';
    // pub is defined but never used
    var pub = {
        // this is part of an object literal, not an assignment
        init = function(response) {
            // respnse should be response
            console.log(respnse);
        }
    }
    // you're missing a semicolon here
    // also - its jQuery, not jquery
}(jquery))
```

Figure 4-2. A running code linter analyzes the JavaScript continuously, highlighting syntax errors in red and adding a ! to the left of the offending line

A recent addition to Ecmascript 5[2] is a *strict* mode, which enforces a modern JavaScript context. This mode is recognized by most linters and you can invoke it by placing 'use strict' at the top of your program or within a function, to restrict it to that context. Modern browsers should also honor strict mode, throwing errors for non-compliance. In strict mode, trying to assign foo = "bar"; will fail if

---

2 The specification for modern JavaScript is defined by the Ecmascript lineage.

foo hasn't been previously defined. See John Resig's blog (*http://ejohn.org/blog/ecmascript-5-strict-mode-json-and-more/*) for a nice explanation of strict mode.

Browser with Development Tools

One of the reasons an IDE is pretty much redundant in modern webdev is that the best place to do debugging is in the web browser itself, and such is the pace of change there that any IDE attempting to emulate that context will have its work cut out for it. On top of this, modern web browsers have evolved a powerful set of debugging and development tools. Firefox's Firebug led the way but has since been surpassed by Chrome Developer, which offers a huge amount of functionality, from sophisticated (certainly to a Pythonista) debugging (parametric breakpoints, variable watches, etc.) to memory and processor optimization profiling, device emulation (want to know what your web page looks like on a smartphone or tablet?), and a whole lot more. Chrome Developer is my debugger of choice and will be used in this book. Like everything covered, it's free as in beer.

Terminal or Command Prompt

The terminal or command line is where you initiate the various servers and probably output useful logging information. It's also where you'll try out Python modules or run a Python interpreter (*IPython* being in many ways the best).

In OS X and Linux, this window is called a Terminal or xterm. In Windows, it's a command prompt that should be available through clicking Start→All Programs→Accessories.

Building a Web Page

There are four elements to a typical web visualization:

- An HTML skeleton, with placeholders for our programmatic visualization
- Cascading Style Sheets (CSS), which define the look and feel (e.g., border widths, colors, font sizes, placement of content blocks).

- JavaScript to build the visualization
- Data to be transformed

The first three of these are just text files, created using our favorite editor and delivered to the browser by the web server (see Chapter 12). Let's examine each in turn.

Serving Pages with HTTP

The delivery of the HTML, CSS, and JS files that are used to make a particular web page (and any related data files, multimedia, etc.) is negotiated between a server and browser using the Hypertext Transfer Protocol. HTTP provides a number of methods, the most commonly used being GET, which requests a web resource, retrieving data from the server if all goes well or throwing an error if it doesn't. We'll be using GET, along with Python's requests module, to scrape some web page content in Chapter 6.

To negotiate the browser-generated HTTP requests, you'll need a server. In development, you can run a little server locally using Python's command-line initialized SimpleHTTPServer, like this:

```
$ python -m SimpleHTTPServer
Serving HTTP on 0.0.0.0 port 8000 ...
```

This server is now serving content locally on port 8000. You can access the site it is serving by going to the URL *http://localhost:8000* in your browser.

SimpleHTTPServer is a nice thing to have and OK for demos and the like, but it lacks a lot of basic functionality. For this reason, as we'll see in Part IV, it's better to master the use of a proper development (and production) server like Flask (this book's server of choice).

The DOM

The HTML files you send through HTTP are converted at the browser end into a Document Object Model, or DOM, which can in turn be adapted by JavaScript because this programmatic DOM is the basis of dataviz libraries like D3. The DOM is a tree structure, represented by hierarchical nodes, the top node being the main web page or document.

Essentially, the HTML you write or generate with a template is converted by the browser into a tree hierarchy of nodes, each one representing an HTML element. The top node is called the *Document Object* and all other nodes descend in a parent-child fashion. Programmatically manipulating the DOM is at the heart of such libraries as jQuery and the mighty D3, so it's vital to have a good mental model of what's going on. A great way to get the feel for the DOM is to use a web tool such as *Chrome Developer* (my recommended toolset) to inspect branches of the tree.

Whatever you see rendered on the web page, the bookkeeping of the object's state (displayed or hidden, matrix transform, etc.) is being done with the DOM. D3's powerful innovation was to attach data directly to the DOM and use it to drive visual changes (Data-Driven Documents).

The HTML Skeleton

A typical web visualization uses an HTML skeleton, and builds the visualization on top of it using JavaScript.

HTML is the language used to describe the content of a web page. It was first proposed by physicist Tim Berners-Lee in 1980 while he was working at the CERN particle accelerator complex in Switzerland. It uses tags such as <div>, <image>, and <h> to structure the content of the page, while CSS is used to define the look and feel.[3] The advent of HTML5 has reduced the boilerplate considerably, but the essence has remained essentially unchanged over those thirty years.

Fully specced HTML used to involve a lot of rather confusing header tags, but with HTML5 some thought was put into a more user-friendly minimalism. This is pretty much the minimal requirement for a starting template:[4]

```
<!DOCTYPE html>
<meta charset="utf-8">
<body>
```

---

3 You can code style in HTML tags using the style attribute, but it's generally bad practice. It's better to use classes and ids defined in CSS.

4 As demonstrated by Mike Bostock (*http://bost.ocks.org/mike/d3/workshop/#8*), with a hat-tip to Paul Irish.

```
    <!-- page content -->
</body>
```

So we need only declare the document HTML, our character-set 8-bit Unicode, and a <body> tag below which to add our page content. This is a big improvement on the bookkeeping required before and provides a very low threshold to entry as far as creating the documents that will be turned into web pages goes. Note the comment tag form: <!-- comment -->.

More realistically, we would probably want to add some CSS and JavaScript. You can add both directly to an HTML document by using the <style> and <script> tags like this:

```
<!DOCTYPE html>
<meta charset="utf-8">
<style>
    <!-- CSS  -->
</style>
<body>
    <!-- page content -->
    <script>
        <!-- JavaScript -->
    </script>
</body>
```

This single-page HTML form is often used in examples such as the visualizations at d3js.org. It's convenient to have a single page to deal with when demonstrating code or keeping track of files, but generally I'd suggest separating the HTML, CSS, and JavaScript elements into separate files. The big win here, apart from easier navigation as the code base gets larger, is that you can take full advantage of your editor's specific language enhancements such as solid syntax highlighting and code linting (essentially syntax checking on the fly). While some editors and libraries claim to deal with embedded CSS and JavaScript, I haven't found an adequate one.

To use CSS and JavaScript files, we just include them in the HTML using <link> and <script> tags like this:

```
<!DOCTYPE html>
<meta charset="utf-8">
<link rel="stylesheet" href="style.css" />
<body>
    <!-- page content -->
    <script type="text/javascript" src="script.js"></script>
</body>
```

Marking Up Content

Visualizations often use a small subset of the available HTML tags, usually building the page programmatically by attaching elements to the DOM tree.

The most common tag is the `<div>`, marking a block of content. `<div>`s can contain other `<div>`s, allowing for a tree hierarchy, the branches of which are used during element selection and to propagate user interface (UI) events such as mouse clicks. Here's a simple `<div>` hierarchy:

```
<div id="my-chart-wrapper" class="chart-holder dev">
    <div id="my-chart" class="bar chart">
        this is a placeholder, with parent #my-chart-wrapper
    </div>
</div>
```

Note the use of `id` and `class` attributes. These are used when you're selecting DOM elements and to apply CSS styles. IDs are unique identifiers; each element should have only one and there should be only one occurrence of any particular id per page. The class can be applied to multiple elements, allowing bulk selection, and each element can have multiple classes.

For textual content, the main tags are `<p>`, `<h*>`, and `<br>`. You'll be using these a lot. This code produces Figure 4-3:

```
<h2>A Level-2 Header</h2>
<p>A paragraph of body text with a line break here..</br>
and a second paragraph...</p>
```

A Level-2 Header

A paragraph of body-text with a line-break here..
and a second paragraph...

Figure 4-3. An h2 header and text

Header tags are reverse-ordered by size from the largest `<h1>`.

`<div>`, `<h*>`, and `<p>` are what is known as *block elements*. They normally begin and end with a new line. The other class of tag is *inline elements*, which display without line breaks. Images `<img>`, hyperlinks `<a>`, and table cells `<td>` are among these, which include the `<span>` tag for inline text:

```
<div id="inline-examples">
    <img src="path/to/image.png" id="prettypic"> ❶
    <p>This is a <a href="link-url">link</a> to
        <span class="url">link-url</span></p> ❷
</div>
```

❶ Note that we don't need a closing tag for images.

❷ The span and link are continuous in the text.

Other useful tags include lists, ordered <ol> and unordered <ul>:

```
<ol>
    <li>First item</li>
    <li>Second item</li>
</ol>
```

HTML also has a dedicated <table> tag, useful if you want to present raw data in your visualization. This HTML produces the header and row in Figure 4-4:

```
<table id="chart-data">
    <tr> ❶
        <th>Name</th>
        <th>Category</th>
        <th>Country</th>
    </tr>
    <tr> ❷
        <td>Albert Einstein</td>
        <td>Physics</td>
        <td>Switzerland</td>
    </tr>
</table>
```

❶ The header row

❷ The first row of data

Name	Category	Country
Albert Einstein	Physics	Switzerland

Figure 4-4. An HTML table

When you are making web visualizations, the most often used of the tags above are the textual tags, which provide instructions, information boxes, and so on. But the meat of our JavaScript efforts will probably be devoted to building DOM branches rooted on the Scalable Vector Graphics (SVG) <svg> and <canvas> tags. On most modern browsers, the <canvas> tag also supports a 3D *WebGL* context, allowing *OpenGL* visualizations to be embedded in the page.

We'll deal with SVG, the focus of this book and the format used by the mighty D3 library, in "Scalable Vector Graphics" on page 109. Now let's look at how we add style to our content blocks.

CSS

CSS, short for Cascading Style Sheets, is a language for describing the look and feel of a web page. Though you can hardcode style attributes into your HTML, it's generally considered bad practice.[5] It's much better to label your tag with an id or class and use that to apply styles in the stylesheet.

The key word in CSS is *cascading*. CSS follows a precedence rule so that in the case of a clash, the latest style overrides earlier ones. This means the order of inclusion for sheets is important. Usually, you want your stylesheet to be loaded last so that you can override both the browser defaults and styles defined by any libraries you are using.

Figure 4-5 shows how CSS is used to apply styles to the HTML elements. First you select the element using hashes (#) to indicate a unique ID and dots (.) to select members of a class. You then define one or more property/value pairs. Note that the font-family property can be a list of fallbacks, in order of preference. Here we want the browser default font-family of serif (capped strokes) to be replaced with the more modern sans-serif, with Helvetica Neue as our first choice.

---

5 This is not the same as programmatically setting styles, which is a hugely powerful technique that allows styles to adapt to user interaction.

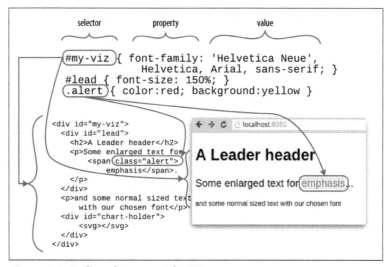

Figure 4-5. Styling the page with CSS

Understanding CSS precedence rules is key to successfully applying styles. In a nutshell, the order is:

1. `!important` after CSS property trumps all.

2. The more specific the better (i.e., ids override classes).

3. The order of declaration: last declaration wins, subject to *1* and *2*.

So, for example, say we have a `<span>` of class `alert`:

```
<span class="alert" id="special-alert">
something to be alerted to</span>
```

Putting the following in our *style.css* file will make the alert text red and bold:

```
.alert { font-weight:bold; color:red }
```

If we then add this to the *style.css*, the id color black will override the class color red, while the class `font-weight` remains bold:

```
#special-alert {background: yellow; color:black}
```

To enforce the color red for alerts, we can use the `!important` directive:[6]

```
.alert { font-weight:bold; color:red !important }
```

If we then add another stylesheet, *style2.css*, after *style.css*:

```
<link rel="stylesheet" href="style.css" type="text/css" />
<link rel="stylesheet" href="style2.css" type="text/css" />
```

with *style2.css* containing the following:

```
.alert { font-weight:normal }
```

then the `font-weight` of the alert will be reverted to `normal` because the new class style was declared last.

JavaScript

JavaScript is the only first-class, browser-based programming language. In order to do anything remotely advanced (and that includes all modern web visualizations), you should have a JavaScript grounding. Other languages that claim to make client-side/ browser programming easier, such as Typescript, Coffeescript, and the like, compile to JavaScript, which means debugging either uses (generally flaky) mapping files or involves understanding the automated JavaScript. 99% of all web visualization examples, the ones you should aim to be learning from, are in JavaScript, and voguish alternatives have a way of fading with time. In essence, good competence in (if not mastery of) JavaScript is a prerequisite for interesting web visualizations.

The good news for Pythonistas is that JavaScript is actually quite a nice language once you've tamed a few of its more awkward quirks.[7] As I showed in Chapter 2, JavaScript and Python have a lot in common and it's usually easy to translate from one to the other.

Data

The data needed to fuel your web visualization will be provided by the web server as static files (e.g., JSON or CSV files) or dynamically

---

6 This is generally considered bad practice and is usually an indication of poorly structured CSS. Use with extreme caution, as it can make life very difficult for codevelopers.

7 These are succinctly discussed in Douglas Crockford's famously short *JavaScript: The Good Parts* (O'Reilly).

through some kind of web API (e.g., RESTful APIs (*https://en.wikipe
dia.org/wiki/Representational_state_transfer*)), usually retrieving the
data server-side from a database. We'll be covering all these forms in
Part IV.

Although a lot of data used to be delivered in XML (*https://en.wikipe
dia.org/wiki/XML*) form, modern web visualization is predomi-
nantly about JSON and, to a lesser extent, CSV or TSV files.

JSON (*https://en.wikipedia.org/wiki/JSON*) (short for JavaScript
Object Notation) is the de facto web visualization data standard and
I recommend you learn to love it. It obviously plays very nicely with
JavaScript, but its structure will also be familiar to Pythonistas. As
we saw in "JSON" on page 65, reading and writing JSON data with
Python is a snap. Here's a little example of some JSON data:

```
{
    "firstName": "Groucho",
    "lastName": "Marx",
    "siblings": ["Harpo", "Chico", "Gummo", "Zeppo"],
    "nationality": "American",
    "yearOfBirth": 1890
}
```

Chrome's Developer Tools

The arms race in JavaScript engines in recent years, which has produced huge increases in performance, has been matched by an
increasingly sophisticated range of development tools built in to the
various browers. Firefox's Firebug led the pack for a while but Chrome's Developer Tools have surpassed it, and are adding functionality
all the time. There's now a huge amount you can do with Chrome's
tabbed tools, but here I'll introduce the two most useful tabs, the
HTML+CSS-focused *Elements* and the JavaScript-focused *Sources*.
Both of these work in complement to Chrome's developer console,
demonstrated in "JavaScript" on page 16.

The Elements Tab

To access the Elements tab, select More Tools→Developer Tools
from the righthand options menu or use the Ctrl-Shift-I keyboard
shortcut.

Figure 4-6 shows the Elements tab at work. You can select DOM elements on the page by using the lefthand magnifying glass and see

their HTML branch in the left panel. The right panel allows you to see CSS styles applied to the element and look at any event listeners that are attached or DOM properties.

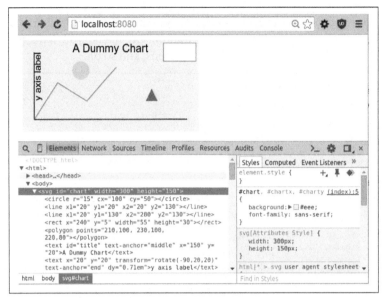

Figure 4-6. Chrome Developer Tools Elements tab

One really cool feature of the Elements tab is that you can interactively change element styling for both CSS styles and attributes.[8] This is a great way to refine the look and feel of your data visualizations.

Chrome's Elements tab provides a great way to explore the structure of a page, finding out how the different elements are positioned. This is good way to get your head around positioning content blocks with the `position` and `float` properties. Seeing how the pros apply CSS styles is a really good way to up your game and learn some useful tricks.

The Sources Tab

The Sources tab allows you to see any JavaScript included in the page. Figure 4-7 shows the tab at work. In the lefthand panel, you

---

8 Being able to play with attributes is particularly useful when trying to get Scalable Vector Graphics (SVG) to work.

can select a script or an HTML file with embedded `<script>` tagged JavaScript. As shown, you can place a breakpoint in the code, load the page, and, on break, see the call stack and any scoped or global variables. These breakpoints are parametric, so you can set conditions for them to trigger, which is handy if you want to catch and step through a particular configuration. On break, you have the standard to step in, out, and over functions, and so on.

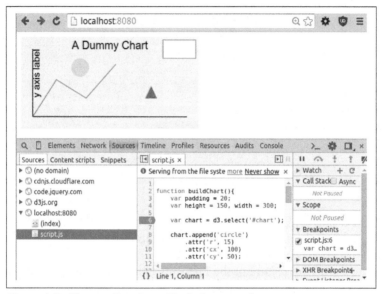

Figure 4-7. Chrome Developer Tools Sources tab

The Sources tab is a fantastic resource and is the main reason why I hardly ever turn to console logging when trying to debug JavaScript. In fact, where JS debugging was once a hit-and-miss black art, it is now almost a pleasure.

Other Tools

There's a huge amount of functionality in those Chrome Developer Tools tabs and they are being updated almost daily. You can do memory and CPU timelines and profiling, monitor your network downloads, and test out your pages for different form factors. But you'll spend 99% of your time as a data visualizer in the Elements and Sources tabs.

A Basic Page with Placeholders

Now that we have covered the major elements of a web page, let's put them together. Most web visualizations start off as HTML and CSS skeletons, with placeholder elements ready to be fleshed out with a little JavaScript plus data (see "Single-Page Apps" on page 88).

We'll first need our HTML skeleton, using the code in Example 4-1. This consists of a tree of <div> content blocks defining three chart-elements: a header, main, and sidebar section.

Example 4-1. The HTML skeleton

```
<!DOCTYPE html>
<meta charset="utf-8">

<link rel="stylesheet" href="style.css" type="text/css" />

<body>

    <div id="chart-holder" class="dev">
      <div id="header">
        <h2>A Catchy Title Coming Soon...</h2>
        <p>Some body text describing what this visualization is all
        about and why you should care.</p>
      </div>
      <div id="chart-components">
        <div id="main">
        A placeholder for the main chart.
        </div><div id="sidebar">
          <p>Some useful information about the chart,
            probably changing with user interaction.</p>
        </div>
      </div>
    </div>

    <script src="script.js"></script>
</body>
```

Now we have our HTML skeleton, we want to style it using some CSS. This will use the classes and ids of our content blocks to adjust size, position, background color, etc. To apply our CSS, in Example 4-1 we import a *style.css* file, shown in Example 4-2.

Example 4-2. CSS styling

```css
body {
    background: #ccc;
    font-family: Sans-serif;
}

div.dev { ❶
    border: solid 1px red;
}

div.dev div {
    border: dashed 1px green;
}

div#chart-holder {
    width: 600px;
    background :white;
    margin: auto;
    font-size :16px;
}

div#chart-components {
    height :400px;
    position :relative; ❷
}

div#main, div#sidebar {
    position: absolute; ❸
}

div#main {
    width: 75%;
    height: 100%;
    background: #eee;
}

div#sidebar {
    right: 0; ❹
    width: 25%;
    height: 100%;
}
```

❶ This dev class is a handy way to see the border of any visual blocks, which is useful for visualization work.

❷ Makes chart-components the relative parent.

❸ Makes the main and sidebar positions relative to chart-components.

❹ Positions this block flush with the right wall of chart-components.

We use absolute positioning of the main and sidebar chart elements (Example 4-2). There are various ways to position the content blocks with CSS, but absolute positioning gives you explicit control over their placement, which is a must if you want to get the look just right.

After specifying the size of the chart-components container, the main and sidebar child elements are sized and positioned using percentages of their parent. This means any changes to the size of chart-components will be reflected in its children.

With our HTML and CSS defined, we can examine the skeleton by firing up Python's single-line SimpleHTTPServer in the project directory, like so:

```
$ python -m SimpleHTTPServer
Serving HTTP on 0.0.0.0 port 8000 ...
```

Figure 4-8 shows the resulting page with the Elements tab open, displaying the page's DOM tree.

The chart's content blocks are now positioned and sized correctly, ready for JavaScript to add some engaging content.

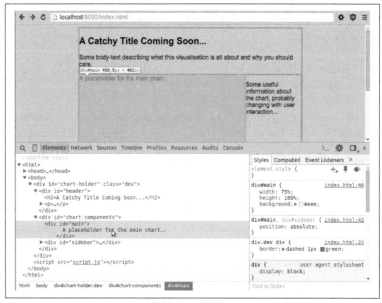

Figure 4-8. Building a basic web page

Filling the Placeholders with Content

With our content blocks defined in HTML and positioned with CSS, a modern data visualization uses JavaScript to construct its interactive charts, menus, tables, and the like. There are many ways to create visual content (aside from image or multimedia tags) in your modern browser, the main ones being:

- Scalable Vector Graphics (SVG) using special HTML tags
- Drawing to a 2D `canvas` context
- Drawing to a 3D `canvas` WebGL context, allowing a subset of OpenGL commands
- Using modern CSS to create animations, graphic primitives, and more.

Because SVG is the language of choice for D3, in many ways the biggest JavaScript dataviz library, many of the cool web data visualizations you have seen, such as those by the *New York Times*, are built using it. Broadly speaking, unless you anticipate having lots (>1,000) of moving elements in your visualization or need to use a specific `canvas`-based library, SVG is probably the way to go.

By using vectors instead of pixels to express its primitives, SVG will generally produce cleaner graphics that respond smoothly to scaling operations. It's also much better at handling text, a crucial consideration for many visualizations. Another key advantage of SVG is that user interaction (e.g., mouse hovering or clicking) is native to the browser, being part of the standard DOM event handling.[9] A final point in its favor is that because the graphic components are built on the DOM, you can inspect and adapt them using your browser's development tools (see "Chrome's Developer Tools" on page 102). This can make debugging and refining your visualizations much easier than trying to find errors in the canvas's relatively black box.

canvas graphics contexts come into their own when you need to move beyond simple graphic primitives like circles and lines, such as when incorporating images like PNGs and JPGs. canvas is usually considerably more performant than SVG, so anything with lots of moving elements[10] is better off rendered to a canvas. If you want to be really ambitious or move beyond 2D graphics, you can even unleash the awesome power of modern graphics cards by using a special form of canvas context, the OpenGL-based WebGL context. Just bear in mind that what would be simple user interaction with SVG (e.g., clicking on a visual element) often has to be derived from mouse coordinates manually, which adds a tricky layer of complexity.

The Nobel Prize data visualization realized at the end of this book's toolchain is built primarily with D3, so SVG graphics are the focus of this book. Being comfortable with SVG is fundamental to modern web-based dataviz, so let's take a little primer.

Scalable Vector Graphics

It doesn't seem long ago that Scalable Vector Graphics seemed all washed up. Browser coverage was spotty and few big libraries were using it. It seemed inevitable that the canvas tag would act as a gateway to full-fledged, rendered graphics based on leveraging the awe-

---

9 With a canvas graphic context, you generally have to contrive your own event handling.

10 This number changes with time and the browser in question, but as a rough rule of thumb, SVG often starts to strain in the low thousands.

some power of modern graphics cards. Pixels—not vectors—would be the building block of web graphics and SVG would go down in history as a valiant but ultimately doomed "nice idea."

D3 might not single-handedly have rescued SVG in the browser, but it must take the lion's share of responsibility. By demonstrating what can be done by using data to manipulate or drive the web page's DOM, it has provided a compelling use case for SVG. D3 really needs its graphic primitives to be part of the document hierarchy, in the same domain as the other HTML content. In this sense it needed SVG as much as SVG needed it.

The <svg> Element

All SVG creations start with an <svg> root tag. All graphical elements, such as circles and lines, and groups thereof, are defined on this branch of the DOM tree. Example 4-3 shows a little SVG context we'll use in upcoming demonstrations, a light-gray rectangle with id chart. We also include the D3 library, loaded from d3js.org and a *script.js* JavaScript file in the project folder.

Example 4-3. A basic SVG context

```
<!DOCTYPE html>
<meta charset="utf-8">
<!-- A few CSS style rules -->
<style>
  svg#chart {
  background: lightgray;
  }
</style>

<svg id="chart" width="300" height="225">
</svg>

<!-- Third-party libraries and our JS script. -->
<script src="http://d3js.org/d3.v3.min.js"></script>
<script src="script.js"></script>
```

Now that we've got our little SVG canvas in place, let's start doing some drawing.

The <g> Element

We can group shapes within our <svg> element by using the group <g> element. As we'll see in "Working with Groups" on page 120, shapes contained in a group can be manipulated together, including changing their position, scale, or opacity.

Circles

Creating SVG visualizations, from the humblest little static bar chart to full-fledged interactive, geographic masterpieces, involves putting together elements from a fairly small set of graphical primitives such as lines, circles, and the very powerful paths. Each of these elements will have its own DOM tag, which will update as it changes.[11] For example, its x and y attributes will change to reflect any translations within its <svg> or group (<g>) context.

Let's add a circle to our <svg> context to demonstrate:

```
<svg id="chart" width="300" height="225">
  <circle r="15" cx="100" cy="50"></circle>
</svg>
```

This produces Figure 4-9. Note that the y coordinate is measured from the top of the <svg> '#chart' container, a common graphic convention.

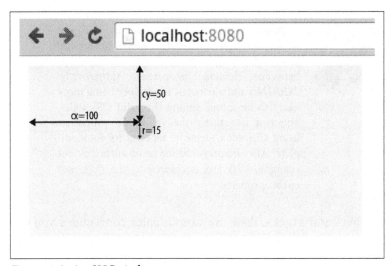

Figure 4-9. An SVG circle

---

11 You should be able to use your browser's development tools to see the tag attributes updating in real time.

Now let's see how we go about applying styles to SVG elements.

Applying CSS Styles

The circle in Figure 4-9 is fill-colored light blue using CSS styling rules:

```
#chart circle{ fill: lightblue }
```

In modern browsers, you can set most visual SVG styles using CSS, including `fill`, `stroke`, `stroke-width`, and `opacity`. So if we wanted a thick, semi-transparent green line (with id `total`) we could use the following CSS:

```
#chart line#total {
    stroke: green;
    stroke-width: 3px;
    opacity: 0.5;
}
```

You can also set the styles as attributes of the tags, though CSS is generally preferable.

```
<circle r="15" cx="100" cy="50" fill="lightblue"></circle>
```

 Which SVG features can be set by CSS and which can't is a source of some confusion and plenty of gotchas. The SVG spec distinguishes between element properties (*http://bit.ly/ 28RR1Ne*) and attributes, the former being more likely to be found among the valid CSS styles. You can investigate the valid CSS properties using Chrome's Elements tab and its autocomplete. Also, be prepared for some surprises. For example, SVG text is colored by the `fill`, not `color`, property.

For `fill` and `stroke`, there are various color conventions you can use:

- Named HTML colors, such as lightblue
- Using HTML hex codes (#RRGGBB); for example, white is #FFFFFF

- RGB values; for example, red = rgb(255, 0, 0)
- RGBA values, where A is an alpha channel (0–1); for example, half-transparent blue is rgba(0, 0, 255, 0.5)

In addition to adjusting the color's alpha channel with RGBA, you can fade the SVG elements using their opacity property. Opacity is used a lot in D3 animations.

Stroke width is measured in pixels by default but can use points.

Lines, Rectangles, and Polygons

We'll add a few more elements to our chart to produce Figure 4-10.

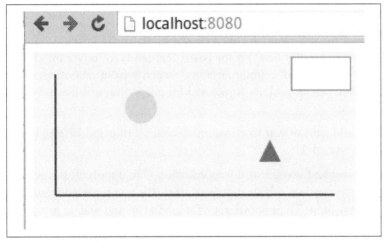

Figure 4-10. Adding a few elements to our dummy chart

First we'll add a couple of simple axis lines to our chart, using the <line> tag. Line positions are defined by a start coordinate (x1, y1) and an end one (x2, y2):

```
<line x1="20" y1="20" x2="20" y2="130"></line>
<line x1="20" y1="130" x2="280" y2="130"></line>
```

We'll also add a dummy legend box in the top-right corner using an SVG rectangle. Rectangles are defined by *x* and *y* coordinates relative to their parent container, and a width and height:

```
<rect x="240" y="5" width="55" height="30"></rect>
```

You can create irregular polygons using the `<polygon>` tag, which takes a list of coordinate pairs. Let's make a triangle marker in the bottom right of our chart:

```
<polygon points="210,100, 230,100, 220,80"></polygon>
```

We'll style the elements with a little CSS:

```
#chart circle {fill: lightblue}
#chart line {stroke: #555555; stroke-width: 2}
#chart rect {stroke: red; fill: white}
#chart polygon {fill: green}
```

Now that we've got a few graphical primitives in place, let's see how we add some text to our dummy chart.

Text

One of the key strengths of SVG over the rasterized `canvas` context is how it handles text. Vector-based text tends to look a lot clearer than its pixelated counterparts and benefits from smooth scaling, too. You can also adjust stroke and fill properties, just like any SVG element.

Let's add a bit of text to our dummy chart: a title and labeled y-axis (see Figure 4-11).

We place text using *x* and *y* coordinates. One important property is the `text-anchor`, which stipulates where the text is placed relative to its x position. The options are `start`, `middle`, and `end`; `start` is the default.

We can use the `text-anchor` property to center our chart title. We set the *x* coordinates at half the chart width and then set the `text-anchor` to `middle`:

```
<text id="title" text-anchor="middle" x="150" y="20">
  A Dummy Chart
</text>
```

As with all SVG primitives, we can apply scaling and rotation transforms to our text. To label our y-axis, we'll need to rotate the text to the vertical (Example 4-4). By convention, rotations are clockwise by degree so we'll want a counterclockwise, –90 degree rotation. By default rotations are around the (0,0) point of the element's container (`<svg>` or group `<g>`). We want to rotate our text around its own position, so first translate the rotation point using the extra arguments to the `rotate` function. We also want to first set the `text-anchor` to the end of the `y axis label` string to rotate about its end point.

Example 4-4. Rotating text

```
<text x="20" y="20" transform="rotate(-90,20,20)"
      text-anchor="end" dy="0.71em">y axis label</text>
```

In Example 4-4, we make use of the text's dy attribute, which, along with dx, can be used to make fine adjustments to the text's position. In this case, we want to lower it so that when rotated counterclockwise it will be to the right of the y-axis.

SVG text elements can also be styled with CSS. Here we set the `font-family` of the chart to `sans-serif` and the `font-size` to 16px, using the `title` id to make that a little bigger:

```
#chart {
background: #eee;
font-family: sans-serif;
}
#chart text{ font-size: 16px }
#chart text#title{ font-size: 18px }
```

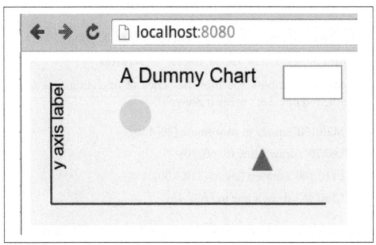

Figure 4-11. Some SVG text

Note that the `text` elements inherit `font-family` and `font-size` from the chart's CSS; you don't have to specify a `text` element.

Paths

Paths are the most complicated and powerful SVG element, enabling the creation of multiline, multicurve component paths that can be closed and filled, creating pretty much any shape you want. A simple example is adding a little chart line to our dummy chart to produce Figure 4-12.

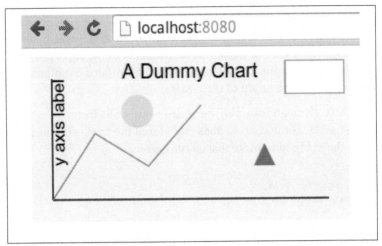

Figure 4-12. A red line path from the chart axis

The red path in Figure 4-12 is produced by the following SVG:

```
<path d="M20 130L60 70L110 100L160 45"></path>
```

The path's d attribute specifies the series of operations needed to make the red line. Let's break it down:

- "M20 130": move to coordinate (20, 130)
- "L60 70": draw a line to (60, 70)
- "L110 100": draw a line to (110, 100)
- "L160 45": draw a line to (160, 45)

You can imagine d as a set of instructions to a pen to move to a point with M raising the pen from the canvas.

A little CSS styling is needed. Note that the fill is set to none; otherwise, to create a fill area, the path would be closed, drawing a line from its end to beginning points, and any enclosed areas filled in with the default color black:

```
#chart path {stroke: red; fill: none}
```

As well as the moveto 'M' and lineto 'L', the path has a number
of other commands to draw arcs, Bézier curves, and the like. SVG
arcs and curves are commonly used in dataviz work, with many of
D3's libraries making use of them.[12] Figure 4-13 shows some SVG
elliptical arcs created by the following code:

```
<svg id="chart" width="300" height="150">
  <path d="M40 40
          A30 40  ❶
          0 0 1  ❷
          80 80
          A50 50  0 0 1  160  80
          A30 30  0 0 1  190  80
  ">
</svg>
```

❶   Having moved to position (40, 40), draw an elliptical arc with x-
    radius 30, y-radius 40, and end point (80, 80).

❷   The last two flags (0, 1) are large-arc-flag, specifying which
    arc of the ellipse to use and sweep-flag, which specifies which
    of the two possible ellipses defined by start and end points to
    use.

---

12 Mike Bostock's chord diagram (*http://bl.ocks.org/mbostock/4062006*) is a nice example,
   and uses D3's chord function.

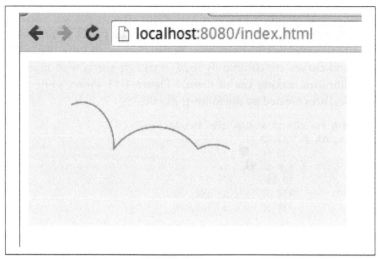

Figure 4-13. Some SVG elliptical arcs

The key flags used in the elliptical arc (`large-arc-flag` and `sweep-flag`) are, like most things geometric, better demonstrated than described. Figure 4-14 shows the effect of changing the flags for the same relative beginning and end points, like so:

```
<svg id="chart" width="300" height="150">
  <path d="M40 80
           A30 40  0 0 1  80 80
           A30 40  0 0 0  120  80
           A30 40  0 1 0  160  80
           A30 40  0 1 1  200  80
        ">
  </svg>
```

Figure 4-14. Changing the elliptic-arc flags

As well as lines and arcs, the path element offers a number of Bézier curves, including quadratic, cubic, and compounds of the two. With a little work, these can create any line path you want. There's a nice run-through on SitePoint (*http://www.sitepoint.com/closer-look-svg-path-data/*) with good illustrations.

For the definitive list of path elements and their arguments, go to the w3 source (*http://www.w3.org/TR/SVG/paths.html*). And for a nice round-up, see Jakob Jenkov's introduction (*http://tutori als.jenkov.com/svg/path-element.html*).

Scaling and Rotating

As befits their vector nature, all SVG elements can be transformed by geometric operations. The most commonly used are rotate, translate, and scale, but you can also apply skewing using skewX and skewY or use the powerful, multipurpose *matrix* transform.

Let's demonstrate the most popular transforms, using a set of identical rectangles. The transformed rectangles in Figure 4-15 are achieved like so:

```
<svg id="chart" width="300" height="150">
  <rect width="20" height="40" transform="translate(60, 55)"
        fill="blue"/>
  <rect width="20" height="40" transform="translate(120, 55),
        rotate(45)" fill="blue"/>
  <rect width="20" height="40" transform="translate(180, 55),
```

```
    scale(0.5)" fill="blue"/>
  <rect width="20" height="40" transform="translate(240, 55),
        rotate(45),scale(0.5)" fill="blue"/>
</svg>
```

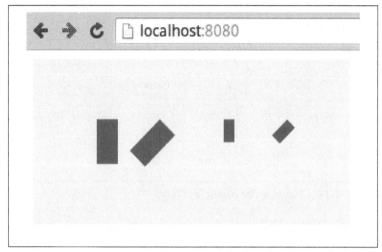

Figure 4-15. Some SVG transforms: rotate(45), scale(0.5), scale(0.5), then rotate(45)

 The order in which transforms are applied is important. A rotation of 45 degrees clockwise folllowed by a translation along the x-axis will see the element moved southeasterly, whereas the reverse operation moves it to the left and then rotates it.

Working with Groups

Often when you are constructing a visualization, it's helpful to group the visual elements. A couple of particular uses are:

- When you require local coordinate schemes (e.g., if you have a text label for an icon and you want to specify its position relative to the icon, not the whole <svg> canvas).

- If you want to apply a scaling and/or rotation transformation to a subset of the visual elements.

SVG has a group <g> tag for this, which you can think of as a mini canvas within the <svg> canvas. Groups can contain groups, allowing for very flexible geometric mappings.[13]

Example 4-5 groups shapes in the center of the canvas, producing Figure 4-16. Note that the position of circle, rect, and path elements is relative to the translated group.

Example 4-5. Grouping SVG shapes

```
<svg id="chart" width="300" height="150">
  <g id="shapes" transform="translate(150,75)">
    <circle cx="50" cy="0" r="25" fill="red" />
    <rect x="30" y="10" width="40" height="20" fill="blue" />
    <path d="M-20 -10L50 -10L10 60Z" fill="green" />
    <circle r="10" fill="yellow">
  </g>
</svg>
```

Figure 4-16. Grouping shapes with SVG <g> tag

If we now apply a transform to the group, all shapes within it will be affected. Figure 4-17 shows the result of scaling Figure 4-16 by a factor of 0.75 and then rotating it 90 degrees, which we achieve by adapting the transform attribute, like so:

---

13 For example, a body group can contain an arm group, which can contain a hand group, which can contain finger elements.

```
<svg id="chart" width="300" height="150">
  <g id="shapes",
     transform = "translate(150,75),scale(0.5),rotate(90)">
     ...
</svg>
```

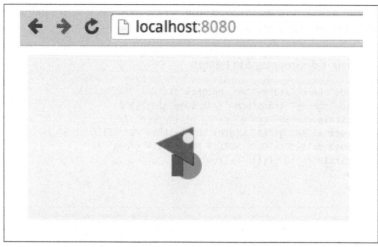

Figure 4-17. Transforming an SVG group

Layering and Transparency

The order in which the SVG elements are added to the DOM tree is
important, with later elements taking precedence, layering over others. In Figure 4-16, for example, the triangle path obscures the red
circle and blue rectangle and is in turn obscured by the yellow circle.

Manipulating the DOM ordering is an important part of JavaScripted dataviz (e.g., D3's insert method allows you to place an SVG
element before an existing one).

Element transparency can be manipulated using the alpha channel
of rgba(R,G,B,A) colors or the more convenient opacity property.
Both can be set using CSS. For overlaid elements, opacity is cumulative, as demonstrated by the color triangle in Figure 4-18, produced
by the following SVG:

```
<style>
  #chart circle { opacity: 0.33 }
</style>

<svg id="chart" width="300" height="150">
  <g transform="translate(150, 75)">
```

```
<circle cx="0" cy="-20" r="30" fill="red"/>
<circle cx="17.3" cy="10" r="30" fill="green"/>
<circle cx="-17.3" cy="10" r="30" fill="blue"/>
</g>
</svg>
```

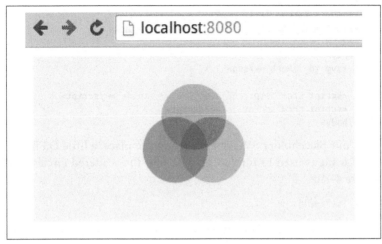

Figure 4-18. Manipulating opacity with SVG

The SVG elements demonstrated here were handcoded in HTML, but in data visualization work they are almost always added programmatically. Thus the basic D3 workflow is to add SVG elements to a visualization, using data files to specify their attributes and properties.

JavaScripted SVG

The fact that SVG graphics are described by DOM tags has a number of advantages over a black box such as the `<canvas>` context. For example, it allows nonprogrammers to create or adapt graphics and is a boon for debugging.

In web dataviz, pretty much all your SVG elements will be created with JavaScript, through a library such as D3. You can inspect the results of this scripting using the browser's Elements tab (see "Chrome's Developer Tools" on page 102), which is a great way to refine and debug your work (e.g., nailing an annoying visual glitch).

As a little taster for things to come, let's use D3 to scatter a few red circles on an SVG canvas. The dimensions of the canvas and circles are contained in a `data` object sent to a `chartCircles` function.

We use a little HTML placeholder for the `<svg>` element:

```
<!DOCTYPE html>
<meta charset="utf-8">

<style>
  #chart circle {fill: red}
</style>

<body>
  <svg id="chart"></svg>

  <script src="http://d3js.org/d3.v3.min.js"></script>
  <script src="script.js"></script>
</body>
```

With our placeholder SVG `chart` element in place, a little D3 in the *script.js* file is used to turn some data into the scattered circles (see Figure 4-19):

```
// script.js

var chartCircles = function(data) {

    var chart = d3.select('#chart');
    // Set the chart height and width from data
    chart.attr('height', data.height).attr('width', data.width);
    // Create some circles using the data
    chart.selectAll('circle').data(data.circles)
        .enter()
        .append('circle')
        .attr('cx', function(d) { return d.x })
        .attr('cy', function(d) { return d.y })
        .attr('r', function(d) { return d.r });
};

var data = {
    width: 300, height: 150,
    circles: [
        {'x': 50, 'y': 30, 'r': 20},
        {'x': 70, 'y': 80, 'r': 10},
        {'x': 160, 'y': 60, 'r': 10},
        {'x': 200, 'y': 100, 'r': 5},
    ]
};

chartCircles(data);
```

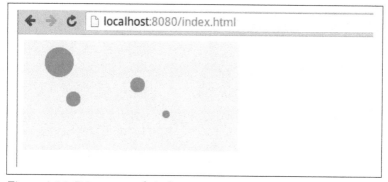

Figure 4-19. D3-generated circles

We'll see exactly how D3 works its magic in Chapter 16. For now, let's summarize what we've learned in this chapter.

Summary

This chapter provided a basic set of modern web-development skills for the budding data visualizer. It showed how the various elements of a web page (HTML, CSS stylesheets, JavaScript, and media files) are delivered by HTTP and, on being received by the browser, combined to become the web page the user sees. We saw how content blocks are described, using HTML tags such as div and p, and then styled and positioned using CSS. We also covered Chrome's Elements and Sources tabs, which are the key browser development tools. Finally we had a little primer in SVG, the language in which most modern web data visualizations are expressed. These skills will be extended when our toolchain reaches its D3 visualization and new ones will be introduced in context.

## PART II

Getting Your Data

In this part of the book we start our journey along the dataviz tool-chain (see Figure II-1), beginning with a couple of chapters on how to get your data if it hasn't been provided for you.

In Chapter 5 we see how to get data off the Web, using Python's requests library to grab web-based files and consume RESTful APIs. We also see how to use a couple of Python libraries that wrap more complex web APIs, namely Twitter (with Python's Tweepy) and Google Docs. The chapter ends with an example of lightweight web scraping (*https://en.wikipedia.org/wiki/Web_scraping*) with the BeautifulSoup library.

In Chapter 6 we use Scrapy, Python's industrial-strength web scra-per, to get the Nobel Prize dataset we'll be using for our web visuali-zation. With this *dirty* dataset to hand, we're ready for the next part of the book, Part III.

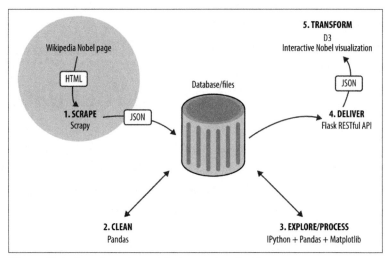

Figure II-1. Our dataviz toolchain: getting the data

## CHAPTER 5

Getting Data off the Web with Python

A fundamental part of the data visualizer's skill set is getting the right dataset in as clean a form as possible. And more often than not these days, this involves getting it off the Web. There are various ways you can do this, and Python provides some great libraries that make sucking up the data easy.

The main ways to get data off the Web are:

- Get a raw data file in a recognized data format (e.g., JSON or CSV) over HTTP
- Use a dedicated API to get the data
- Scrape the data by getting web pages via HTTP and parsing them locally for the required data

This chapter will deal with these ways in turn, but first let's get acquainted with the best Python HTTP library out there: requests.

Getting Web Data with the requests Library

As we saw in Chapter 4, the files that are used by web browsers to construct web pages are communicated via the Hypertext Transfer Protocol (HTTP), first developed by Tim Berners-Lee (*https://en.wikipedia.org/wiki/Tim_Berners-Lee*). Getting web content in order to parse it for data involves making HTTP requests.

Negotiating HTTP requests is a vital part of any general-purpose language, but getting web pages with Python used to be a rather irksome affair. The venerable urllib2 library was hardly user-friendly, with a very clunky API. requests (*http://docs.python-requests.org/en/latest/*), courtesy of Kennith Reitz, changed that, making HTTP a relative breeze and fast establishing itself as the go-to Python HTTP library.

requests is not part of the Python standard library[1] but is part of the Anaconda package (*http://docs.continuum.io/anaconda/pkg-docs*) (see Chapter 1). If you're not using Anaconda, the following pip command should do the job:

```
$ pip install requests
Downloading/unpacking requests
...
Cleaning up...
```

If you're using a Python version prior to 2.7.9, then using requests may generate some Secure Sockets Layer (SSL) (*https://en.wikipedia.org/wiki/SSL*) warnings. Upgrading to newer SSL libraries should fix this:[2]

```
$ pip install --upgrade ndg-httpsclient
```

Now that you have requests installed, you're ready to perform the first task mentioned at the beginning of this chapter and grab some raw data files off the Web.

Getting Data Files with requests

A Python interpreter session is a good way to put requests through its paces, so find a friendly local command line, fire up IPython, and import requests:

```
$ ipython
Python 2.7.5+ (default, Feb 27 2014, 19:37:08)
...

In [1]: import requests
```

---

1 This is actually a deliberate policy (*http://docs.python-requests.org/en/latest/dev/philosophy/#standard-library*) of the developers.

2 There are some platform dependencies that might still generate errors. This Stack Overflow thread (*http://stackoverflow.com/questions/29099404/ssl-insecureplatform-error-when-using-requests-package*) is a good starting point if you still have problems.

To demonstrate, let's use the library to download a Wikipedia page. We use the `requests` library's `get` method to get the page and, by convention, assign the result to a `response` object.

```
response = requests.get(\
"https://en.wikipedia.org/wiki/Nobel_Prize")
```

Let's use Python's `dir` (*https://docs.python.org/3/library/functions.html#dir*) method to get a list of the `response` object's attributes:

```
dir(response)
Out:
...
 'content',
 'cookies',
 'elapsed',
 'encoding',
 'headers',
 ...
 'iter_content',
 'iter_lines',
 'json',
 'links',
 ...
 'status_code',
 'text',
 'url']
```

Most of these attributes are self-explanatory and together provide a lot of information about the HTTP response generated. You'll use a small subset of these attributes generally. Firstly, let's check the status of the response:

```
response.status_code
Out: 200
```

As all good minimal web developers know, 200 is the HTTP status code (*https://en.wikipedia.org/wiki/List_of_HTTP_status_codes*) for OK, indicating a successful transaction. Other than 200, the most common codes are:

401 (Unauthorized)
Attempting unauthorized access

400 (Bad Request)
Trying to access the web server incorrectly

403 (Forbidden)
Similar to 401 but no login opportunity was available

404 (Not Found)
Trying to access a web page that doesn't exist

500 (Internal Server Error)
A general-purpose, catch-all error

So, for example, if we made a spelling mistake with our request, asking to see the SNoble_Prize page, we'd get a 404 (Not Found) error:

```
not_found_response = requests.get(\
"http://en.wikipedia.org/wiki/SNobel_Prize")
not_found_response.status_code
Out: 404
```

With our 200 OK response, from the correctly spelled request, let's look at some of the info returned. A quick overview can be had with the headers property:

```
response.headers
Out: {
    'X-Client-IP': '104.238.169.128',
    'Content-Length': '65820', ...
    'Content-Encoding': 'gzip', ...
    'Last-Modified': 'Sun, 15 Nov 2015 17:14:09 GMT', ...
    'Date': 'Mon, 23 Nov 2015 21:33:52 GMT',
    'Content-Type': 'text/html; charset=UTF-8'...
}
```

This shows, among other things, that the page returned was gzip-encoded and 65 KB in size with Content-Type of text/html, encoded with Unicode UTF-8.

Since we know text has been returned, we can use the text property of the response to see what it is:

```
response.text
Out: u'<!DOCTYPE html>\n<html lang="en"
dir="ltr" class="client-nojs">\n<head>\n<meta charset="UTF-8"
/>\n<title>Nobel Prize - Wikipedia, the free
encyclopedia</title>\n<script>document.documentElement... =
```

This shows that we do indeed have our Wikipedia HTML page, with some inline JavaScript. As we'll see in "Scraping Data" on page 146, in order to make sense of this content, we'll need a parser to read the HTML and provide the content blocks.

`requests` can be a convenient way of getting web data into your program or Python session. For example, we can grab one of the datasets from the huge US government catalog (*https://data.gov*), which often has the choice of various file formats (e.g., JSON or CSV). Picking randomly, here's the data from a 2006–2010 study on food affordability, in JSON format. Note that we check that it has been fetched correctly, with a `status_code` of `200`:

```
response = requests.get(
"https://cdph.data.ca.gov/api/views/6tej-5zx7/rows.json
?accessType=DOWNLOAD")

response.status_code
Out: 200
```

Unfortunately, access to datasets from *data.gov* is a little unreliable. If the example dataset shown is not available, I recommend choosing another and making sure you can access its data using requests.

For JSON data, `requests` has a convenience method, allowing us to access the response data as a Python dictionary. This contains metadata and a list of data items:

```
data = response.json()
data.keys()
Out:
[u'meta', u'data']

data['meta']['view']['description']
Out: u'This table contains data on the average cost of a
market basket of nutritious food items relative to income for
female-headed households with children, for California, its
regions, counties, and cities/towns. The ratio uses data from
the U.S. Department of Agriculture...

data['data'][0]
Out:
[1,
u'4303993D-76F7-4A5C-914E-FDEA4EAB67BA',
...
u'Food affordability for female-headed household with
children under 18 years',
u'2006-2010',
u'1',
u'AIAN',
u'CA',
```

```
u'06',
u'California', ...
```

Now that we've grabbed a raw page and a JSON file off the Web, let's see how to use `requests` to consume a web data API.

Using Python to Consume Data from a Web API

If the data file you need isn't on the Web, there may well be an Application Programming Interface (API) serving the data you need. Using this will involve making a request to the appropriate server to retrieve your data in a fixed format or one you get to specify in the request.

The most popular data formats for web APIs are JSON and XML, though a number of esoteric formats exist. For the purposes of the JavaScripting data visualizer, JavaScript Object Notation (JSON) is obviously preferred (see "Data" on page 101). Lucky for us, it is also starting to predominate.

There are different approaches to creating a web API, and for a few years there was a little war of the architectures among the three main types of APIs inhabiting the Web:

REST (https://en.wikipedia.org/wiki/Representational_state_transfer)
    Short for REpresentational State Transfer, using a combination of HTTP verbs (GET, POST, etc.) and Uniform Resource Identifiers (URIs; e.g., */user/kyran*) to access, create, and adapt data.

XML-RPC (https://en.wikipedia.org/wiki/XML-RPC)
    A remote procedure call (RPC) protocol using XML encoding and HTTP transport.

SOAP (https://en.wikipedia.org/wiki/SOAP)
    Short for Simple Object Access Protocol, using XML and HTTP.

This battle seems to be resolving in a victory for RESTful APIs (*http://en.wikipedia.org/wiki/Representational_state_transfer*), and this is a very good thing. Quite apart from RESTful APIs being more elegant, and easier to use and implement (see "A Simple RESTful API with Flask" on page 340), some standardization here makes it much more likely that you will recognize and quickly adapt to a new API that comes your way. Ideally, you will be able to reuse existing code.

Most access and manipulation of remote data can be summed up by the acronym CRUD (create, retrieve, update, delete), originally coined to describe all the major functions implemented in relational databases. HTTP provides CRUD counterparts with the POST, GET, PUT, and DELETE verbs and the REST abstraction builds on this use of these verbs, acting on a Universal Resource Identifier (URI) (*https://en.wikipedia.org/wiki/Uniform_Resource_Identifier*).

Discussions about what is and isn't a proper RESTful interface can get quite involved, but essentially the URI (e.g., *http://example.com/api/items/2*) should contain all the information required in order to perform a CRUD operation. The particular operation (e.g., GET or DELETE) is specified by the HTTP verb. This excludes architectures such as SOAP, which place stateful information in metadata on the requests header. Imagine the URI as the virtual address of the data and CRUD all the operations you can perform on it.

As data visualizers keen to lay our hands on some interesting datasets, we are avid consumers here, so our HTTP verb of choice is GET and the examples that follow will focus on the fetching of data with various well-known web APIs. Hopefully, some patterns will emerge.

Although the two constraints of stateless URIs and the use of the CRUD verbs is a nice constraint on the shape of RESTful APIs, there still manage to be many variants on the theme.

Using a RESTful Web API with requests

requests has a fair number of bells and whistles based around the main HTTP request verbs. For a good overview, see the requests quickstart (*http://docs.python-requests.org/en/latest/user/quickstart/*). For the purposes of getting data, you'll use GET and POST pretty much exclusively, with GET being by a long way the most used verb. POST allows you to emulate web forms, including login details, field values, etc. in the request. For those occasions where you find yourself driving a web form with, for example, lots of options selectors, requests makes automation with POST easy. GET covers pretty much everything else, including the ubiquitous RESTful APIs (*http://bit.ly/1a1kVX5*), which provide an increasing amount of the well-formed data available on the Web.

Let's look at a more complicated use of `requests`, getting a URL with arguments. The Organisation for Economic Cooperation and Development (OECD) (*http://bit.ly/1WRjrKI*) provides some useful datasets on its site (*https://data.oecd.org/*). These datasets provide mainly economic measures and statistics for the member countries of the OECD, and such data can form the basis of many interesting visualizations. The OECD provides a few of its own, such as one allowing you to compare your country (*http://www.oecd.org/statis tics/compare-your-country.htm*) with others in the OECD.

The OECD web API is described here (*https://data.oecd.org/api/ sdmx-json-documentation/*), and queries are constructed with the dataset name (dsname) and some dot-separated dimensions, each of which can be a number of + separated values. The URL can also take standard HTTP parameters initiated by a ? and separated by &:

```
<root_url>/<dsname>/<dim 1>.<dim 2>...<dim n>
/all?param1=foo&param2=baa..
<dim 1> = 'AUS'+'AUT'+'BEL'...
```

So the following is a valid URL:

```
http://stats.oecd.org/sdmx-json/data/QNA        ❶
/AUS+AUT.GDP+B1_GE.CUR+VOBARSA.Q                 ❷
/all?startTime=2009-Q2&endTime=2011-Q4          ❸
```

❶ Specifies the QNA (Quarterly National Accounts) dataset.

❷ Four dimensions, by location, subject, measure, and frequency.

❸ Data from the second quarter of 2009 to the fourth quarter of 2011.

Let's construct a little Python function to query the OECD's API (Example 5-1).

Example 5-1. Making a URL for the OECD API

```
OECD_ROOT_URL = 'http://stats.oecd.org/sdmx-json/data'

def make_OECD_request(dsname, dimensions, params=None, \
root_dir=OECD_ROOT_URL):
    """ Make a URL for the OECD API and return a response """

    if not params:        ❶
        params = {}

    dim_args = ['+'.join(d) for d in dimensions]    ❷
```

```
dim_str = '.'.join(dim_args)

url = root_dir + '/' + dsname + '/' + dim_str + '/all'
print('Requesting URL: ' + url)
return requests.get(url, params=params) ❸
```

❶ You shouldn't use mutable values, such as {}, for Python function defaults. See here (*http://docs.python-guide.org/en/latest/
writing/gotchas/*) for an explanation of this gotcha.

❷ We first use a Python list comprehension and the join method
to create a list of dimensions, with members concatenated with
plus signs (e.g., [*USA+AUS, ...*]). join is then used again to
concatenate the members of dim_str with periods.

❸ Note that requests' get can take a parameter dictionary as its
second argument, using it to make the URL query string.

We can use this function like so, to grab economic data for the USA
and Australia from 2009 to 2010:

```
response = make_OECD_request('QNA',
    (('USA', 'AUS'),('GDP', 'B1_GE'),('CUR', 'VOBARSA'), ('Q')),
    {'startTime':'2009-Q1', 'endTime':'2010-Q1'})

Requesting URL: http://stats.oecd.org/sdmx-json/data/QNA/
    USA+AUS.GDP+B1_GE.CUR+VOBARSA.Q/all
```

Now, to look at the data, we just check that the response is OK and
have a look at the dictionary keys:

```
if response.status_code == 200:
    json = response.json()
    json.keys()
Out: [u'header', u'dataSets', u'structure']
```

The resulting JSON data is in the SDMX (*https://en.wikipedia.org/
wiki/SDMX*) format, designed to facilitate the communication of
statistical data. It's not the most intuitive format around, but it's
often the case that datasets have a less than ideal structure. The good
news is that Python is a great language for knocking data into shape.
For Python's Pandas library (*http://pandas.pydata.org/*) (see Chapter 8), there is pandaSDMX (*https://pypi.python.org/pypi/
pandaSDMX*), which currently handles the XML-based format.

The OECD API is essentially RESTful with all of the query being
contained in the URL and the HTTP verb GET specifying a fetch
operation. If a specialized Python library isn't available to use the

API (e.g., Tweepy for Twitter), then you'll probably end up writing something like Example 5-1. requests is a very friendly, well-designed library and can cope with pretty much all the manipulations required to use a web API.

Getting Country Data for the Nobel Dataviz

There are some national statistics that will come in handy for the Nobel Prize visualization we're using our toolchain to build. Population sizes, three-letter international codes (e.g., GDR, USA), and geographic centers are potentially useful when you are visualizing an international prize and its distribution. REST countries (*https://rest countries.eu/*) is a handy RESTful web resource with various international stats. Let's use it to grab some data.

Requests to REST countries take the following form:

```
https://restcountries.eu/rest/v1/<field>/<name>?<params>
```

As with the OECD API (see Example 5-1), we can make a simple calling function to allow easy access to the API's data, like so:

```
REST_EU_ROOT_URL = "http://restcountries.eu/rest/v1"

def REST_country_request(field='all', name=None, params=None):

    headers={'User-Agent': 'Mozilla/5.0'} ❶

    if not params:
        params = {}

    if field == 'all':
        return requests.get(REST_EU_ROOT_URL + '/all')

    url = '%s/%s/%s'%(REST_EU_ROOT_URL, field, name)
    print('Requesting URL: ' + url)
    response = requests.get(url, params=params, headers=headers)

    if not response.status_code == 200: ❷
        raise Exception('Request failed with status code ' \
        + str(response.status_code))

    return response
```

❶ It's usually a good idea to specify a valid User-Agent in the header of your request. Some sites will reject the request otherwise.

❷ Before returning the response, make sure it has an OK (200) HTTP code; otherwise, raise an exception with a helpful message.

With the REST_country_request function in hand, let's get a list of all the countries using the US dollar as currency:

```
response = REST_country_request('currency', 'usd')
response.json()
Out:
[{u'alpha2Code': u'AS',
  u'alpha3Code': u'ASM',
  u'altSpellings': [u'AS',
  ...
  u'capital': u'Pago Pago',
  u'currencies': [u'USD'],
  u'demonym': u'American Samoan',
  ...
  u'latlng': [12.15, -68.266667],
  u'name': u'Bonaire',
  ...
  u'name': u'British Indian Ocean Territory',
  ...
  u'name': u'United States Minor Outlying Islands',
  ...
```

The full dataset at REST countries is pretty small, so for convenience we'll make a copy and store it locally to MongoDB and our *nobel-prize* database using the get_mongo_database method from "MongoDB" on page 79:

```
db_nobel = get_mongo_database('nobel_prize')
col = db_nobel['country_data'] # country data collection

# Get all the RESTful country-data
response = REST_country_request()
# Insert the JSON objects straight to our collection
col.insert(country_data)
Out:
[ObjectId('5665a1ef26a7110b79e88d49'),
 ObjectId('5665a1ef26a7110b79e88d4a'),
 ...
```

With our country data inserted into its MongoDB collection, let's again find all the countries using the US dollar as currency:

```
res = col.find({'currencies':{'$in':['USD']}})
list(res)
Out:
[{u'_id': ObjectId('5665a1ef26a7110b79e88d4d'),
```

```
u'alpha2Code': u'AS',
u'alpha3Code': u'ASM',
u'altSpellings': [u'AS',
...
u'currencies': [u'USD'],
u'demonym': u'American Samoan',
u'languages': [u'en', u'sm'],
...
```

Now that we've rolled a couple of our own API consumers, let's take a look at some dedicated libraries that wrap some of the larger web APIs in an easy-to-use form.

Using Libraries to Access Web APIs

requests is capable of negotiating with pretty much all web APIs and often a little function like Example 5-1 is all you need. But as the APIs start adding authentication and the data structures become more complicated, a good wrapper library can save a lot of hassle and reduce the tedious bookkeeping. In this section, I'll cover a couple of the more popular wrapper libraries (*https://en.wikipedia.org/ wiki/Wrapper_library*) to give you a feel for the workflow and some useful starting points.

Using Google Spreadsheets

It's becoming more common these days to have live datasets *in the cloud*. So, for example, you might find yourself required to visualize aspects of a Google spreadsheet that is the shared data pool for a group. My preference is to get this data out of the Google-plex and into Pandas to start exploring it (see Chapter 11), but a good library will let you access and adapt the data *in-place*, negotiating the web traffic as required.

Gspread (*https://github.com/burnash/gspread*) is the best known Python library for accessing Google spreadsheets and makes doing so a relative breeze.

You'll need OAuth 2.0 (*https://en.wikipedia.org/wiki/OAuth*) credentials to use the API.[3] The most up-to-date guide can be found here (*http://bit.ly/292nobI*). Following those instructions should provide a JSON file containing your private key.

---

3 OAuth1 access has been deprecated recently.

You'll need to install `gspread` and the latest Python OAuth2 client library. Here's how to do it with `pip`.

```
$ pip install gspread
$ pip install --upgrade oauth2client
```

Depending on your system, you may also need PyOpenSSL:

```
$ pip install PyOpenSSL
```

See Read the Docs (*http://bit.ly/28W0XqK*) for more details and troubleshooting.

 Google's API assumes that the spreadsheets you are trying to access are owned or shared by your API account, not your personal one. The email address to share the spreadsheet with is available at your Google developers console (*http://bit.ly/28SSIbd*) and in the JSON credentials key needed to use the API. It should look something like `account-1@My Project...iam.gserviceac count.com`.

With those libraries installed, you should be able to access any of your spreadsheets with just a few lines. I'm using the Microbe-scope spreadsheet, which you can see here (*http://bit.ly/1UgxdpH*). Example 5-2 shows how to load the spreadsheet.

Example 5-2. Opening a Google spreadsheet

```
import json
import gspread
from oauth2client.client import SignedJwtAssertionCredentials

json_key = json.load(open('gspread_credentials.json')) ❶
scope = ['https://spreadsheets.google.com/feeds']

credentials = SignedJwtAssertionCredentials(\
    json_key['client_email'],json_key['private_key'], scope)

gc = gspread.authorize(credentials)

ss = gc.open('Microbe-scope') ❷
```

❶ The JSON credentials file is the one provided by Google services, usually of the form *My Project-b8ab5e38fd68.json*.

❷ Here we're opening the spreadsheet by name. Alternatives are open_by_url or open_by_id. See here (*http://gspread.readthe docs.org/en/latest/index.html#gspread.Client*) for details.

Now that we've got our spreadsheet, we can see the worksheets it contains:

```
ss.worksheets()
Out: [<Worksheet 'bugs' id:od6>,
<Worksheet 'outrageous facts' id:o74cw7y>,
<Worksheet 'physicians per 1,000' id:okzh6fp>,
<Worksheet 'amends' id:ogkk64p>]

ws = ss.worksheet('bugs')
```

With the worksheet **bugs** selected from the spreadsheet, **gspread** allows you to access and change column, row, and cell values (assuming the sheet isn't read-only). So we can get the values in the second column with the **col_values** command:

```
ws.col_values(1)
Out: [None,
'grey = not plotted',
'Anthrax (untreated)',
'Bird Flu (H5N1)',
'Bubonic Plague (untreated)',
'C.Difficile',
'Campylobacter',
'Chicken Pox',
'Cholera',...
```

 If you get a **BadStatusLine** error while accessing a Google spreadsheet with **gspread**, it is probably because the session has expired. Reopening the spreadsheet should get things working again. This outstanding **gspread** issue (*http://bit.ly/ 291Vlch*) provides more information.

Although you can use **gspread**'s API to plot directly, using a plot library like Matplotlib, I prefer to send the whole sheet to Pandas, Python's powerhouse programmatic spreadsheet. This is easily achieved with **gspread**'s **get_all_records**, which returns a list of item dictionaries. This list can be used directly to initialize a Pandas **DataFrame** (see "The DataFrame" on page 210):

```
df = pd.DataFrame(ws.get_all_records())
df.info()
```

```
Out:
<class 'pandas.core.frame.DataFrame'>
Int64Index: 41 entries, 0 to 40
Data columns (total 23 columns):
                                    41 non-null object
average basic reproductive rate     41 non-null object
case fatality rate                  41 non-null object
infectious dose                     41 non-null object
...
upper R0                            41 non-null object
viral load in acute stage           41 non-null object
yearly fatalities                   41 non-null object
dtypes: object(23)
memory usage: 7.7+ KB
```

In Chapter 11 we'll see how to interactively explore a DataFrame's data.

Using the Twitter API with Tweepy

The advent of social media has generated a lot of data and an interest in visualizing the social networks, trending hashtags, and media storms contained in them. Twitter's broadcast network is probably the richest source of cool data visualizations and its API provides tweets[4] filtered by user, hashtag, date, and the like.

Python's Tweepy is an easy-to-use Twitter library that provides a number of useful features, such as a StreamListener class for streaming live Twitter updates. To start using it, you'll need a Twitter access token, which you can acquire by following the instructions at the Twitter docs (*https://dev.twitter.com/oauth/overview/application-owner-access-tokens*) to create your Twitter application. Once this application is created you can get the keys and access tokens for your app by clicking on the link at your Twitter app page (*https://apps.twitter.com/*).

Tweepy typically requires the four authorization elements shown here:

```
# The user credential variables to access Twitter API
access_token = "2677230157-Ze3bWuBAw4kwoj4via2dEntU86...TD7z"
access_token_secret = "DxwKAvVzMFLq7WnQGnty49jgJ39Acu...paR8ZH"
```

---

4 The free API is currently limited to around 350 requests per hour (*https://dev.twitter.com/rest/public/rate-limiting*).

```
consumer_key = "pIorGFGQHShuYQtIxzYWk1jMD"
consumer_secret = "yLc4Hw82G0Zn4vTi4q8pSBcNyHkn35BfIe...oVa4P7R"
```

With those defined, accessing tweets could hardly be easier. Here we
create an OAuth `auth` object using our tokens and keys and use it to
start an API session. We can then grab the latest tweets from our
timeline:

```
In [0]: import tweepy

        auth = tweepy.OAuthHandler(consumer_key,\
                                   consumer_secret)
        auth.set_access_token(access_token, access_token_secret)

        api = tweepy.API(auth)

        public_tweets = api.home_timeline()
        for tweet in public_tweets:
            print tweet.text

RT @Glinner: Read these tweets https://t.co/QqzJPsDxUD
Volodymyr Bilyachat https://t.co/VIyOHlje6b +1 bmeyer
#javascript
RT @bbcworldservice: If scientists edit genes to
make people healthier does it change what it means to be
human? https://t.co/Vciuyu6BCx h…
RT @ForrestTheWoods:
Launching something pretty cool tomorrow. I'm excited. Keep
...
```

Tweepy's `API` class offers a lot of convenience methods, which you
can check out in the Tweepy docs (*http://docs.tweepy.org/en/v3.2.0/
api.html#api-reference*). A common visualization is using a network
graph to show patterns of friends and followers among Twitter sub-
populations. The Tweepy methods `follower_ids` (get all users following) and `friends_ids` (get all users being followed) can be used
to construct such a network:

```
my_follower_ids = api.follower_ids() ❶

for id in my_followers_ids:
    followers = api.follower_ids(id) ❷
    # ...
```

❶ Gets a list of your followers' ids (e.g., [1191701545,
1554134420, …]).

❷ The first argument to `follower_ids` can be an id or screen
name.

By mapping followers of followers, you can create a network of connections that might just reveal something interesting about groups and subgroups clustered about a particular individual or subject. There's a nice example of just such a Twitter analysis on Gabe Sawhney's blog (*http://gabesawhney.com/visualizing-twitter-clusters-with-gephi-update/*).

One of the coolest features of Tweepy is its StreamListener class, which makes it easy to collect and process filtered tweets in real time. Live updates of Twitter streams have been used by many memorable visualizations, such as tweetping (*http://tweetping.net/*). Let's set up a little stream to record tweets mentioning Python, JavaScript, and Dataviz and save it to a MongoDB database using the get_mongo_database method from "MongoDB" on page 79:

```python
# ...
from tweepy.streaming import StreamListener
import json

# ...

class MyStreamListener(StreamListener):
    """ Streams tweets and saves to a MongoDB database """

    def __init__(self, api, **kw):
        self.api = api
        super(tweepy.StreamListener, self).__init__()
        self.col = get_mongo_database('tweets', **kw)['tweets'] ❶

    def on_data(self, tweet):
        self.col.insert(json.loads(tweet)) ❷

    def on_error(self, status):
        return True # keep stream open


auth = tweepy.OAuthHandler(consumer_key, consumer_secret)
auth.set_access_token(access_token, access_token_secret)
api = tweepy.API(auth)
stream = tweepy.Stream(auth, MyStreamListener(api))

# Start the stream with track list of keywords
stream.filter(track=['python', 'javascript', 'dataviz'])
```

❶ The extra kw keywords allow us to pass the MongoDB-specific host, port, and username/password arguments to the stream listener.

❷ The data is a raw JSON string that needs decoding before inserting into our *tweets* collection.

Now that we've had a taste of the kind of APIs you might run into during your search for interesting data, let's look at the primary technique you'll use if, as is often the case, no one is providing the data you want in a neat, user-friendly form: scraping data with Python.

Scraping Data

Scraping is the chief metaphor used for the practice of getting data that wasn't designed to be programmatically consumed off the Web. It is a pretty good metaphor because scraping is often about getting the balance right between removing too much and too little. Creating procedures that extract just the right data, as cleanly as possible, from web pages is a craft skill and often a fairly messy one at that. But the payoff is access to visualizable data that often cannot be acquired in any other way. Approached in the right way, scraping can even have an intrinsic satisfaction.

Why We Need to Scrape

In an ideal virtual world, online data would be organized in a library, with everything cataloged through a sophisticated Dewey Decimal System for the web page. Unfortunately for the keen data hunter, the Web has grown organically, often unconstrained by considerations of easy data access for the budding data visualizer. So, in reality, the Web resembles a big mound of data, some of it clean and usable (and thankfully this percentage is increasing) but much of it poorly formed and designed for human consumption. And humans are able to parse the kind of messy, poorly formed data that our relatively dumb computers have problems with.[5]

Scraping is about fashioning selection patterns that grab the data we want and leave the rest behind. If we're lucky, the web pages containing the data will have helpful pointers, like named tables, specific identities in preference to generic classes, and so on. If we're

---

5 Much of modern Machine Learning and Artificial Intelligence (AI) research is dedicated to creating computer software that can cope with messy, noisy, fuzzy, informal data but, as of this book's publication, there's no off-the-shelf solution I know of.

unlucky, then these pointers will be missing and we will have to resort to using other patterns or, in the worst case, ordinal specifiers such as *third table in the main div.* These are obviously pretty fragile, and will break if somebody adds a table above the third.

In this section, we'll tackle a little scraping task, to get the some Nobel Prize winners data. We'll use Python's best-of-breed BeautifulSoup for this lightweight scraping foray, saving the heavy guns of Scrapy for the next chapter.

 The fact that data and images are on the Web does not mean that they are necessarily free to use. For our scraping examples we'll be using Wikipedia, which allows full reuse under the Creative Commons license (*https://en.wikipe dia.org/wiki/Creative_Commons_license*). It's a good idea to make sure anything you scrape is available and, if in doubt, contact the site maintainer. You may be required to at least cite the original author.

BeautifulSoup and lxml

Python's key lightweight scraping tools are *BeautifulSoup* and *lxml*. Their primary selection syntax is different but, confusingly, each can use the other's parsers. The consensus seems to be that lxml's parser is considerably faster, but BeautifulSoup's might be more robust when dealing with poorly formed HTML. Personally, I've found lxml to be robust enough and its syntax, based on xpaths (*https://en.wikipedia.org/wiki/XPath*), more powerful and often more intuitive. I think for someone coming from web development, familiar with CSS and jQuery, selection based on CSS selectors is much more natural. Depending on your system, lxml is usually the default parser for BeautifulSoup. We'll be using it in the following sections.

BeautifulSoup is part of the Anaconda packages (see Chapter 1) and easily installed with pip:

```
$ pip install beautifulsoup4
```

A First Scraping Foray

Armed with requests and BeautifulSoup, let's give ourselves a little task to get the names, years, categories, and nationalities of all the

Nobel Prize winners. We'll start at the main Wikipedia Nobel Prize page (*http://en.wikipedia.org/wiki/List_of_Nobel_laureates*). Scrolling down shows a table with all the laureates by year and category, which is a good start to our minimal data requirements.

Some kind of HTML explorer is pretty much a must for web scraping and the best I know is Chrome's web developer's Elements tab (see "The Elements Tab" on page 102). Figure 5-1 shows the key elements involved in quizzing a web page's structure. We need to know how to select the data of interest, in this case a Wikipedia table, while avoiding other elements on the page. Crafting good selector patterns is the key to effective scraping, and highlighting the DOM element using the element inspector gives us both the CSS pattern and, with a right-click, the xpath. The latter is a particularly powerful syntax for DOM element selection and the basis of our industrial-strength scraping solution, *Scrapy*.

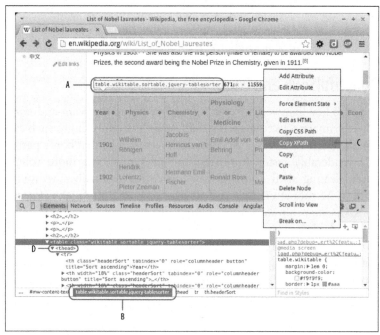

Figure 5-1. Wikipedia's main Nobel Prize Page: A and B show the wikitable's CSS selector. Right-clicking and selecting C (Copy XPath) gives the table's xpath (//*[@id="mw-content-text"]/table[1]). D shows a thead tag generated by jQuery.

Getting the Soup

The first thing you need to do before scraping the web page of interest is to parse it with BeautifulSoup, converting the HTML into a tag
tree hierarchy or soup:

```
from bs4 import BeautifulSoup
import requests

BASE_URL = 'http://en.wikipedia.org'
# Wikipedia will reject our request unless we add
# a 'User-Agent' attribute to our http header.
HEADERS = {'User-Agent': 'Mozilla/5.0'}

def get_Nobel_soup():
    """ Return a parsed tag tree of our Nobel prize page """
    # Make a request to the Nobel page, setting valid headers
    response = requests.get(
        BASE_URL + '/wiki/List_of_Nobel_laureates',
        headers=HEADERS)
    # Return the content of the response parsed by BeautifulSoup
    return BeautifulSoup(response.content, "lxml")  ❶
```

❶ The second argument specifies the parser we want to use,
   namely lxml's.

With our soup in hand, let's see how to find our target tags.

Selecting Tags

BeautifulSoup offers a few ways to select tags from the parsed soup,
with subtle differences that can be confusing. Before demonstrating
the selection methods, let's get the soup of our Nobel Prize page:

```
soup = get_Nobel_soup()
```

Our target table (see Figure 5-1) has two defining classes, wikitable
and sortable (there are some unsortable tables on the page). We
can use BeautifulSoup's find method to find the first table tag with
those classes. find takes a tag name as its first argument and a dictionary with class, id, and other identifiers as its second:

```
In[3]: soup.find('table', {'class':'wikitable sortable'})
Out[3]:
<table class="wikitable sortable">
<tr>
<th>Year</th>
...
```

Although we have successfully found our table by its classes, this method is not very robust. Let's see what happens when we change the order of our CSS classes:

```
In[4]: soup.find('table', {'class':'sortable wikitable'})
# nothing returned
```

So find cares about the order of the classes, using the class string to find the tag. If the classes were specified in a different order—something that might well happen during an HTML edit, then the find fails. This fragility makes it difficult to recommend the BeautifulSoup selectors, such as find and find_all. When doing quick hacking, I find lxml's CSS selectors (*http://lxml.de/cssselect.html*) easier and more intuitive.

Using the soup's select method (available if you specified the lxml parser when creating it), you can specify an HTML element using its CSS class, id, and so on. This CSS selector is converted into the xpath syntax lxml uses internally.[6]

To get our wikitable, we just select a table in the soup, using the dot notation to indicate its classes:

```
In[5]: soup.select('table.sortable.wikitable')
Out[5]:
[<table class="wikitable sortable">
 <tr>
 <th>Year</th>
 ...
 ]
```

Note that select returns an array of results, finding all the matching tags in the soup. lxml provides the select_one convenience method if you are selecting just one HTML element. Let's grab our Nobel table and see what headers it has:

```
In[8]: table = soup.select_one('table.sortable.wikitable')

In[9]: table.select('th')
Out[9]:
[<th>Year</th>,
 <th width="18%"><a href="/wiki/..._in_Physics..</a></th>,
 <th width="16%"><a href="/wiki/..._in_Chemis..</a></th>,
```

---

6 This CSS selection syntax should be familiar to anyone who's used JavaScript's jQuery (*https://jquery.com/*) library and is also similar to that used by D3 (*https://d3js.org/*).

```
    ...
]
```

As a shorthand for select, you can call the tag directly on the soup; so these two are equivalent:

```
table.select('th')
table('th')
```

With lxml's parser, BeautifulSoup provides a number of different filters for finding tags, including the simple string name we've just used, searching by regular expression (*https://en.wikipedia.org/wiki/ Regular_expression*), using a list of tag names, and more. See this comprehensive list (*http://www.crummy.com/software/Beauti fulSoup/bs4/doc/#kinds-of-filters*) for more details.

As well as lxml's select and select_one, there are 10 BeautfulSoup convenience methods for searching the parsed tree. These are essentially variants on find and find_all that specify which parts of the tree they search. For example, find_parent and find_parents, rather than looking for descendents down the tree, look for parent tags of the tag being searched. All 10 methods are available in the BeautifulSoup official docs (*http://www.crummy.com/software/Beau tifulSoup/bs4/doc/#find-parents-and-find-parent*).

Now that we know how to select our Wikipedia table and are armed with lxml's selection methods, let's see how to craft some selection patterns to get the data we want.

Crafting Selection Patterns

Having successfully selected our data table, we now want to craft some selection patterns to scrape the required data. Using the HTML explorer, you can see that the individual winners are contained in <td> cells, with an href <a> link to Wikipedia's bio-pages (in the case of individuals). Here's a typical target row with CSS classes that we can use as targets to get the data in the <td> cells.

```
<tr>
 <td align="center">
  1901
 </td>
 <td>
  <span class="sortkey">
   Röntgen, Wilhelm
  </span>
  <span class="vcard">
```

```
<span class="fn">
 <a href="/wiki/Wilhelm_R%C3%B6ntgen" \
    title="Wilhelm Röntgen">
  Wilhelm Röntgen
 </a>
 </span>
 </span>
</td>
<td>
...
</tr>
```

If we loop through these data cells, keeping track of their row (year) and column (category), then we should be able to create a list of winners with all the data we specified except nationality.

The following get_column_titles function scrapes our table for the Nobel category column headers, ignoring the first Year column. Often the header cell in a Wikipedia table contains a web-linked 'a' tag; all the Nobel categories fit this model, pointing to their respective Wikipedia pages. If the header is not clickable, we store its text and a null href:

```
def get_column_titles(table):
    """ Get the Nobel categories from the table header """
    cols = []
    for th in table.select_one('tr').select('th')[1:]: ❶
        link = th.select_one('a')
        # Store the category name and any Wikipedia link it has
        if link:
            cols.append({'name':link.text,\
                         'href':link.attrs['href']})
        else:
            cols.append({'name':th.text, 'href':None})
    return cols
```

❶ We loop through the table head, ignoring the first Year column ([1:]). This selects the column headers shown in Figure 5-2.

Let's make sure get_column_titles is giving us what we want:

```
get_column_titles(wikitable)
Out:
[{'href': '/wiki/List_of_Nobel_laureates_in_Physics',
  'name': u'Physics'},
 {'href': '/wiki/List_of_Nobel_laureates_in_Chemistry',
  'name': u'Chemistry'}, ...
```

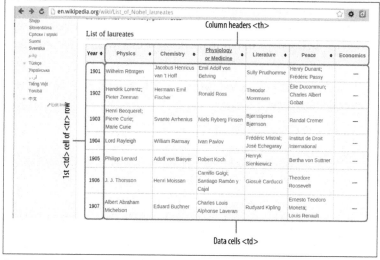

Figure 5-2. Wikipedia's table of Nobel Prize winners

```python
def get_Nobel_winners(table):
    cols = get_column_titles(table)
    winners = []
    for row in table.select('tr')[1:-1]: ❶
        year = int(row.select_one('td').text) # Gets 1st <td>
        for i, td in enumerate(row.select('td')[1:]): ❷
            for winner in td.select('a'):
                href = winner.attrs['href']
                if not href.startswith('#endnote'):
                    winners.append({
                        'year':year,
                        'category':cols[i]['name'],
                        'name':winner.text,
                        'link':winner.attrs['href']
                    })
    return winners
```

❶ Gets all the Year rows, starting from the second, corresponding to the rows in Figure 5-2.

❷ Finds the <td> data cells shown in Figure 5-2.

Iterating through the year rows, we take the first Year column and then iterate over the remaining columns, using enumerate to keep track of our index, which will map to the category column names. We know that all the winner names are contained in an <a> tag but that there are occasional extra <a> tags beginning with #endnote, which we filter for. Finally we append a year, category, name, and link dictionary to our data array. Note that the winner selector has an `attrs` dictionary containing, among other things, the `<a>` tag's href.

Let's confirm that `get_Nobel_winners` delivers a list of Nobel Prize winner dictionaries:

```
In [0]: get_Nobel_winners(wikitable)
[{'category': u'Physics',
  'link': '/wiki/Wilhelm_R%C3%B6ntgen',
  'name': u'Wilhelm R\xf6ntgen',
  'year': 1901},
 {'category': u'Chemistry',
  'link': '/wiki/Jacobus_Henricus_van_%27t_Hoff',
  'name': u"Jacobus Henricus van 't Hoff",
  'year': 1901},
 {'category': u'Physiology\nor Medicine',
  'link': '/wiki/Emil_Adolf_von_Behring',
  'name': u'Emil Adolf von Behring',
  'year': 1901},
 ...
```

Now that we have the full list of Nobel Prize winners and links to their Wikipedia pages, we can use these links to scrape data from the individuals' biographies. This will involve making a largish number of requests, and it's not something we really want to do more than once. The sensible and respectful[7] thing is to cache the data we scrape, allowing us to try out various scraping experiments without returning to Wikipedia.

Caching the Web Pages

It's easy enough to rustle up a quick cacher in Python, but as often as not it's easier still to find a better solution written by someone else and kindly donated to the open source community. `requests` has a nice plugin called `requests-cache` that, with a few lines of configuration, will take care of all your basic caching needs.

First we install the plugin using `pip`:

```
$ pip install --upgrade requests-cache
```

---

7 When scraping, you're using other people's web bandwidth, which ultimately costs them money. It's just good manners to try to limit your number of requests.

requests-cache uses monkey-patching (*http://stackoverflow.com/questions/5626193/what-is-a-monkey-patch*) to dynamically replace parts of the requests API at runtime. This means it can work transparently. You just have to install its cache and then use requests as usual, with all the caching being taken care of. Here's the simplest way to use requests-cache:

```
import requests
import requests_cache

requests_cache.install_cache()
# use requests as usual...
```

The install_cache method has a number of useful options, including allowing you to specify the cache backend (sqlite, memory, mongdb, or redis) or set an expiry time (expiry_after) in seconds on the caching. So the following creates a cache named nobel_pages with an sqlite backend and pages that expire in two hours (7,200 s).

```
requests_cache.install_cache('nobel_pages',\
                    backend='sqlite', expire_after=7200)
```

requests-cache will serve most of your caching needs and couldn't be much easier to use. For more details, see the official docs (*https://requests-cache.readthedocs.org/en/latest/user_guide.html*) where you'll also find a little example of request throttling, which is a useful technique when doing bulk scraping.

Scraping the Winners' Nationalities

With caching in place, let's try getting the winners' nationalities, using the first 50 for our experiment. A little get_nationality() function will use the winner links we stored earlier to scrape their page and then use the infobox shown in Figure 5-3 to get the Nationality attribute.

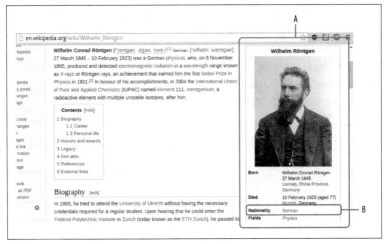

Figure 5-3. Scraping a winner's nationality

When scraping, you are looking for reliable patterns and repeating elements with useful data. As we'll see, the Wikipedia infoboxes for individuals are not such a reliable source, but clicking on a few random links certainly gives that impression. Depending on the size of the dataset, it's good to perform a few experimental sanity checks. You can do this manually, but, as mentioned at the start of the chapter, this won't scale or improve your craft skills.

Example 5-3 takes one of the winner dictionaries we scraped earlier and returns a name-labeled dictionary with a `Nationality` key if one is found. Let's run it on the first 50 winners and see how often a `Nationality` attribute is missing:

Example 5-3. Scraping the winner's country from their biography page

```python
def get_winner_nationality(w):
    """ scrape biographic data from the winner's wikipedia page """
    data = get_url('http://en.wikipedia.org' + w['link'])
    soup = BeautifulSoup(data)
    person_data = {'name': w['name']}
    attr_rows = soup.select('table.infobox tr')    ❶
    for tr in attr_rows:                            ❷
        try:
            attribute = tr.select_one('th').text
```

```
        if attribute == 'Nationality':
            person_data[attribute] = tr.select_one('td').text
    except AttributeError:
        pass

    return person_data
```

❶ We use a CSS selector to find all the `<tr>` rows of the table with class infobox.

❷ Cycles through the rows looking for a Nationality field.

Example 5-4 shows that 14 of the 50 first winners failed our attempt to scrape their nationality. In the case of the Institut de Droit International, national affiliation may well be moot, but Theodore Roosevelt is about as American as they come. Clicking on a few of the names shows the problem (see Figure 5-4). The lack of a standardized biography format means synonyms for *Nationality* are often employed, as in Marie Curie's *Citizenship*; sometimes no reference is made, as with Niels Finsen; and Randall Cremer has nothing but a photograph in his infobox. We can discard the infoboxes as a reliable source of winners' nationalities but, as they appeared to be the only regular source of potted data, this sends us back to the drawing board. In the next chapter, we'll see a successful approach using Scrapy and a different start page.

Example 5-4. Testing for scraped nationalities

```
wdata = []
# test first 50 winners
for w in winners[:50]:
    wdata.append(get_winner_nationality(w))
missing_nationality = []
for w in wdata:
    # if missing 'Nationality' add to list
    if not w.get('Nationality'):
        missing_nationality.append(w)
# output list
missing_nationality

[{'name': u'\xc9lie Ducommun'},
 {'name': u'Charles Albert Gobat'},
 {'name': u'Marie Curie'},
 {'name': u'Niels Ryberg Finsen'},
 {'name': u'Randal Cremer'},
 {'name': u'Institut de Droit International'},
```

```
{'name': u'Bertha von Suttner'},
{'name': u'Theodore Roosevelt'},
...
```

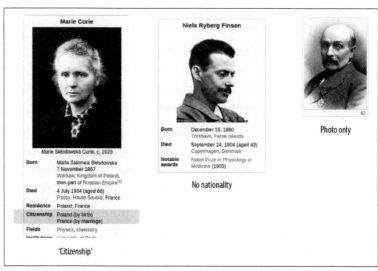

Figure 5-4. Winners without a recorded nationality

Although Wikipedia is a relative free-for-all, production-wise, where data is designed for human consumption, you can expect a lack of rigor. Many sites have similar gotchas and as the datasets get bigger, more tests may be needed to find the flaws in a collection pattern.

Although our first scraping exercise was a little artificial in order to introduce the tools, I hope it captured something of the slightly messy spirit of web scraping. The ultimately abortive pursuit of a reliable Nationality field for our Nobel dataset could have been forestalled by a bit of web browsing and manual HTML-source trawling. However, if the dataset were significantly larger and the failure rate a bit smaller, then programmatic detection, which gets easier and easier as you become acquainted with the scraping modules, really starts to deliver.

This little scraping test was designed to introduce BeautifulSoup, and shows that collecting the data we set ourselves requires a little more thought, which is often the case with scraping. In the next chapter, we'll wheel out the big gun, *Scrapy*, and, with what we've learned in this section, harvest the data we need for our Nobel Prize visualization.

Summary

In this chapter, we've seen examples of the most common ways in which data can be sucked out of the Web and into Python containers, databases, or Pandas datasets. Python's requests library is the true workhorse of HTTP negotiation and a fundamental tool in our dataviz toolchain. For simpler, RESTful APIs, consuming data with requests is a few lines of Python away. For the more awkward APIs, such as those with potentially complicated authorization, a wrapper library like Tweepy (for Twitter) can save a lot of hassle. Decent wrappers can also keep track of access rates and, where necessary, throttle your requests. This is a key consideration, particularly when there is the possibility of blacklisting unfriendly consumers.

We also started our first forays into data scraping, which is often a necessary fallback where no API exists and the data is for human consumption. In the next chapter, we'll get all the Nobel Prize data needed for the book's visualization using Python's Scrapy, an industrial-strength scraping library.

Heavyweight Scraping with Scrapy

As your scraping goals get more ambitious, hacking solutions with BeautifulSoup and requests can get very messy very fast. Managing the scraped data as requests spawn more requests gets tricky, and if your requests are being made synchronously, things start to slow down rapidly. A whole load of problems you probably hadn't anticipated start to make themselves known. It's at this point that you want to turn to a powerful, robust library that solves all these problems and more. And that's where Scrapy comes in.

Where BeautifulSoup is a very handy little penknife for fast and dirty scraping, Scrapy is a Python library that can do large-scale data scrapes with ease. It has all the things you'd expect, like built-in caching (with expiration times), asynchronous requests via Python's Twisted web framework, User-Agent randomization, and a whole lot more. The price for all this power is a fairly steep learning curve, which this chapter is intended to smooth, using a simple example. I think Scrapy is a powerful addition to any dataviz toolkit and really opens up possibilities for web data collection, but if you don't have any need for heavyweight scraping fu right now, it's fine to assume we've collected our Nobel Prize data and proceed to Part III. Otherwise, let's buckle our seat belts and see what a real scraping engine can do.

In "Scraping Data" on page 146, we managed to scrape a dataset containing all the Nobel Prize winners by name, year, and category. We did a speculative scrape of the winners' linked biography pages, which showed that extracting the country of nationality was going to be difficult. In this chapter, we'll set the bar on our Nobel Prize data a bit higher and aim to scrape objects of the form shown in Example 6-1.

Example 6-1. Our targeted Nobel JSON object

```
{
  "category": "Physiology or Medicine",
  "country": "Argentina",
  "date_of_birth': "8 October 1927",
  "date_of_death': "24 March 2002",
  "gender": "male",
  "link": "http:\/\/en.wikipedia.org\/wiki\/C%C3%A9sar_Milstein",
  "name": "C\u00e9sar Milstein",
  "place_of_birth": "Bah\u00eda Blanca , Argentina",
  "place_of_death": "Cambridge , England",
  "text": "C\u00e9sar Milstein , Physiology or Medicine, 1984",
  "year": 1984
}
```

In addition to this data, we'll aim to scrape prize winners' photos (where applicable) and some potted biographical data (see Figure 6-1). We'll be using the photos and body text to add a little character to our Nobel Prize visualization.

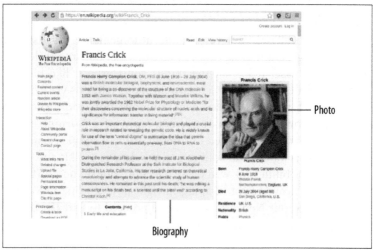

Figure 6-1. Scraping targets for the prize winners' pages

Setting Up Scrapy

Scrapy should be one of the Anaconda packages (see Chapter 1) so you should already have it on hand. If that's not the case, then you can install it with the following conda command line:

```
$ conda install -c https://conda.anaconda.org/anaconda scrapy
```

If you're not using Anaconda, a quick pip install will do the job:[1]

```
$ pip install scrapy
```

With Scrapy installed, you should have access to the scrapy command. Unlike the vast majority of Python libraries, Scrapy is designed to be driven from the command line within the context of a scraping project, defined by configuration files, scraping spiders, pipelines, and so on. Let's generate a fresh project for our Nobel Prize scraping, using the startproject option. This is going to generate a project folder, so make sure you run it from a suitable work directory:

```
$ scrapy startproject nobel_winners
New Scrapy project 'nobel_winners' created in:
    /home/kyran/workspace/.../scrapy/nobel_winners

You can start your first spider with:
    cd nobel_winners
    scrapy genspider example example.com
```

As the output of startproject says, you'll want to switch to the *nobel_winners* directory in order to start driving Scrapy.

Let's take a look at the project's directory tree:

```
nobel_winners
├── nobel_winners
│   ├── __init__.py
│   ├── items.py
│   ├── pipelines.py
│   ├── settings.py
│   └── spiders
│       └── __init__.py
└── scrapy.cfg
```

---

1 See the Scrapy install docs (*http://doc.scrapy.org/en/latest/intro/install.html*) for platform-specific details.

As shown, the project directory has a subdirectory with the same name and a config file *scrapy.cfg*. The *nobel_winners* subdirectory is a Python module (containing an *__init__.py* file) with a few skeleton files and a *spiders* directory, which will contain your scrapers.

Establishing the Targets

In "Scraping Data" on page 146, we tried to scrape the Nobel winners' nationalities from their biography pages but found they were missing or inconsistently labeled in many cases (see Chapter 5). Rather than get the country data indirectly, a little Wikipedia searching shows a way through. There is a page (*http://en.wikipedia.org/wiki/List_of_Nobel_laureates_by_country*) that lists winners by country. The winners are presented in titled, ordered lists (see Figure 6-2), not in tabular form, which makes recovering our basic name, category, and year data a little harder. Also the data organization is not ideal (e.g., the country header titles and winner lists aren't in useful, separate blocks). As we'll see, a few well-structured Scrapy queries will easily net us the data we need.

Figure 6-2 shows the starting page for our first spider along with the key elements it will be targeting. A list of country name titles (A) is followed by an ordered list (B) of their Nobel Prize–winning citizens.

In order to scrape the list data, we need to fire up our Chrome browser's development tools (see "The Elements Tab" on page 102) and inspect the target elements using the Elements tab and its inspector (magnifying glass). Figure 6-3 shows the key HTML targets for our first spider: header titles (h2) containing a country name and followed by an ordered list (ol) of winners (li).

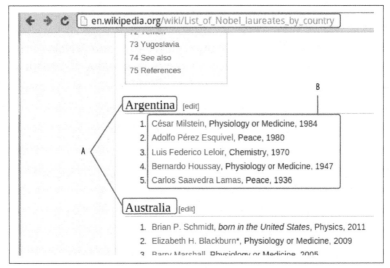

Figure 6-2. Scraping Wikipedia's Nobel Prizes by nationality

Figure 6-3. Finding the HTML targets for the wikilist

Targeting HTML with Xpaths

Scrapy uses xpaths (*https://en.wikipedia.org/wiki/XPath*) to define its HTML targets. Xpath is a syntax for describing parts of an X(HT)ML document, and while it can get rather complicated, the basics are straightforward and will often solve the job at hand.

You can get the xpath of an HTML element by using Chrome's Elements tab to hover over the source and then right-clicking and selecting Copy Xpath. For example, in the case of our Nobel Prize wikilist's country names (h2 in Figure 6-3), selecting the xpath of Argentina (the first country) gives the following:

```
//*[@id="mw-content-text"]/h2[1]
```

We can use the following xpath rules to decode it:

`//E`
> Element `<E>` anywhere in the document (e.g., `//img` gets all images on the page)

`//E[@id="foo"]`
> Select element `<E>` with id `foo`

`//*[@id="foo"]`
> Select any element with id `foo`

`//E/F[1]`
> First child element `<F>` of element `<E>`

`//E/*[1]`
> First child of element `<E>`

Following these rules shows that our Argentinian title `//*[@id="mw-content-text"]/h2[1]` is the first header (h2) child of a DOM element with id `mw-content-text`. This is equivalent to the following HTML:

```
<div id="mw-content-text">
    <h2>
        ...
    </h2>
    ...
</div>
```

Note that unlike Python, the xpaths don't use a zero-based index but make the first member *1*.

Testing Xpaths with the Scrapy Shell

Getting your xpath targeting right is crucial to good scraping and can involve a degree of iteration. Scrapy makes this process much easier by providing a command-line shell, which takes a URL and

creates a response context in which you can try out your xpaths, like
so:

```
$ scrapy shell
  https://en.wikipedia.org/wiki/
  List_of_Nobel_laureates_by_country


2015-12-15 17:42:12+0000 [scrapy] INFO: Scrapy 0.24.4 started
(bot: nobel_winners)
...
2015-12-15 17:42:12+0000 [default] INFO: Spider opened
2015-12-15 17:42:13+0000 [default] DEBUG: Crawled (200)
<GET https://en.wikip...List_of_Nobel_laureates_by_country>
(referer: None)
[s] Available Scrapy objects:

[s]   crawler   <scrapy.crawler.Crawler object at 0x3a8f510>
[s]   item {}
[s]   request   <GET https://...Nobel_laureates_by_country>
[s]   response  <200 https://...Nobel_laureates_by_country>
[s]   settings  <scrapy.settings.Settings object at 0x34a98d0>
[s]   spider    <Spider 'default' at 0x3f59190>

[s] Useful shortcuts:
[s]   shelp()   Shell help (print this help)
[s]   fetch(req_or_url) Fetch request (or URL) and update local
objects
[s]   view(response)   View response in a browser

In [1]:
```

Now we have an IPython-based shell with code-complete and syntax
highlighting in which to try out our xpath targeting. Let's grab all the
<h2> headers on the wiki page:

```
In [1]: h2s = response.xpath('//h2')
```

The resulting h2s is a SelectorList (*http://doc.scrapy.org/en/latest/
topics/selectors.html#scrapy.selector.SelectorList*), a specialized Python
list object. Let's see how many headers we have:

```
In [2]: len(h2s)
Out[2]: 76
```

We can grab the first Selector (*http://doc.scrapy.org/en/latest/topics/
selectors.html#topics-selectors-ref*) object and query its methods and
properties in the Scrapy shell by pressing Tab after appending a dot:

```
In [3] h2 = h2s[0]
In [4] h2.
```

```
h2.css              h2.namespaces      h2.remove_namespaces
h2.text             h2.extract         h2.re
h2.response         h2.type            h2.register_namespace
h2.select           h2.xpath
```

You'll often use the extract method to get the raw result of the xpath selector:

```
In [5]: h2.extract()
Out[5]: u'<h2>Contents</h2>'
```

This shows that our first <h2> header is that of the table of contents for our list of winners by country. Let's look at the second header:

```
In [6]: h2s[1].extract()
Out[6]:
u'<h2>
  <span class="mw-headline" id="Argentina">Argentina</span>
  <span class="mw-editsection">
  <span class="mw-editsection-bracket">
  ...
  </h2>'
```

This shows that our country headers start on the second <h2> and contain a span with class mw-headline. We can use the presence of the mw-headline class as a filter for our country headers and the contents as our country label. Let's try out an xpath, using the selector's text method to extract the text from the mw-headline span. Note that we use the xpath method of the <h2> selector, which makes the xpath query relative to that element.

```
In [7]: h2_arg = h2s[1]
In [8]: country = h2_arg.xpath(\
                   'span[@class="mw-headline"]/text()')\
.extract()
In [9]: country
Out[9]: [u'Argentina']
```

The extract method returns a list of possible matches, in our case the single 'Argentina' string. By iterating through the h2s list, we can now get our country names.

Assuming we have a country's <h2> header, we now need to get the <ol> ordered list of Nobel winners following it (Figure 6-2 B). Handily, the xpath following-sibling selector can do just that. Let's grab the first ordered list after the Argentina header:

```
In [10]: ol_arg = h2_arg.xpath('following-sibling::ol[1]')
Out[10]: ol_arg
```

```
[<Selector xpath='following-sibling::ol[1]' data=u'<ol>\n<li>
<a href="/wiki/C%C3%A9sar_Milst'>]
```

Looking at the truncated data for `ol_arg` shows that we have selected an ordered list. Note that even though there's only one `Selector`, `xpath` still returns a `SelectorList`. For convenience, you'll generally just select the first member directly:

```
In [11]: ol_arg = h2_arg.xpath('following-sibling::ol[1]')[0]
```

Now that we've got the ordered list, let's get a list of its member `<li>` elements:

```
In [12]: lis_arg = ol_arg.xpath('li')
In [13]: len(lis_arg)
Out[13]: 5
```

Let's examine one of those list elements using `extract`. As a first test, we're looking to scrape the name of the winner and capture the list element's text.

```
In [14]: li = lis_arg[0] # select the first list element
In [15]: li.extract()
Out[15]:
u'<li><a href="/wiki/C%C3%A9sar_Milstein"
        title="C\xe9sar Milstein">C\xe9sar Milstein</a>,
        Physiology or Medicine, 1984</li>'
```

Extracting the list element shows a standard pattern: a hyperlinked name to the winner's Wikipedia page followed by a comma-separated winning category and year. A robust way to get the winning name is just to select the text of the list element's first `<a>` tag:

```
In [16]: name = li.xpath('a//text()')[0].extract()
In [17]: name
Out[17]: u'C\xe9sar Milstein'
```

It's often useful to get all the text in, for example, a list element, stripping the various HTML `<a>`, `<span>`, and other tags. `descendent-or-self` gives us a handy way of doing this, producing a list of the descendents' text:

```
In [18]: list_text = li.xpath('descendant-or-self::text()')\
.extract()
In [19]: list_text
Out[19]: [u'C\xe9sar Milstein', u', Physiology or Medicine,'\
'1984']
```

We can get the full text by joining the list elements together:

```
In [20]: ' '.join(list_text)
Out[20]: u'C\xe9sar Milstein , Physiology or Medicine, 1984'
```

Note that the first item of list_text is the winner's name, giving us another way to access it if, for example, it were missing a hyperlink.

Now that we've established the xpaths to our scraping targets (the name and link text of the Nobel Prize winners), let's incorporate them into our first Scrapy spider.

Selecting with Relative Xpaths

As just shown, Scrapy xpath selections return lists of selectors which, in turn, have their own xpath methods. When using the xpath method, it's important to be clear about relative and absolute selections. Let's make the distinction clear using the Nobel page's table of contents as an example.

The table of contents has the following structure:

```
<div id='toc'... >
  <ul ... >
   <li ... >
     <a href='Argentina'> ... </a>
   </li>
   ...
  </ul>
</div>
```

We can select the table of contents of the Nobel wikipage using a standard xpath query on the response, and getting the div with id toc.

```
In [21]: toc = response.xpath('//div[@id="toc"]')[0]
```

If we want to get all the country <li> list tags, we can use a relative xpath on the selected toc div. The following two are equivalent, both selecting children of the current selection relatively:

```
In [22]: lis = toc.xpath('.//ul/li')
In [23]: lis = toc.xpath('ul/li')
In [24]: len(lis)
Out[24]: 76 # the number of countries in the table of contents
```

A common mistake is to use a nonrelative xpath selector on the current selection, which selects from the whole document, in this case getting all unordered (<ul>) <li> tags:

```
In [25]: lis = toc.xpath('//ul/li')
In [26]: len(lis)
Out[26]: 212
```

Errors made from mistaking relative and nonrelative queries crop up a lot in the forums, so it's good to be very aware of the distinction and watch those dots.

 Getting the right xpath expression for your target element(s) can be a little tricky, and those difficult edge cases can demand a complex nest of clauses. The use of a well-written cheat sheet can be a great help here, and thankfully there are many good xpath ones. A very nice selection can be found here (*http://bit.ly/28KxCoO*), with this color-coded one (*http://bit.ly/1UAmlS4*) being particularly useful.

A First Scrapy Spider

Armed with a little xpath knowledge, let's produce our first scraper aiming to get the country and link text for the winners (Figure 6-2 A and B).

Scrapy calls its scrapers *spiders*, each of which is a Python module placed in the *spiders* directory of your project. We'll call our first scraper *nwinner_list_spider.py*:

```
.
├── nobel_winners
│   ├── __init__.py
│   ├── items.py
│   ├── pipelines.py
│   ├── settings.py
│   └── spiders
│       |— __init__.py
│       └── nwinners_list_spider.py <---
└── scrapy.cfg
```

Spiders are subclassed `scrapy.Spider` classes, and any placed in the *spiders* directory will be automatically detected by Scrapy and made accessible by name to the `scrapy` command.

The basic Scrapy spider shown in Example 6-2 follows a pattern you'll be using with most of your spiders. First you subclass a Scrapy `item` to create fields for your scraped data (section A in Example 6-2). You then create a named spider by subclassing scrapy.Spider (section B in Example 6-2). You will use the spider's name when calling scrapy from the command line. Each spider has a parse method, which deals with the HTTP requests to a list of start URLs contained in a start_url class attribute. In our case, the start URL is the Wikipedia page for Nobel laureates by country.

Example 6-2. A first Scrapy spider

```python
# nwinners_list_spider.py

import scrapy
import re
# A. Define the data to be scraped
class NWinnerItem(scrapy.Item):
    country = scrapy.Field()
    name = scrapy.Field()
    link_text = scrapy.Field()

# B Create a named spider
class NWinnerSpider(scrapy.Spider):
    """ Scrapes the country and link text of the Nobel-winners. """

    name = 'nwinners_list'
    allowed_domains = ['en.wikipedia.org']
    start_urls = [
        "http://en.wikipedia.org ... of_Nobel_laureates_by_country"
    ]
    # C A parse method to deal with the HTTP response
     def parse(self, response):

        h2s = response.xpath('//h2')  ❶

        for h2 in h2s:
            country = h2.xpath('span[@class="mw-headline"]'\
            'text()').extract()  ❷
            if country:
                winners = h2.xpath('following-sibling::ol[1]')  ❸
                for w in winners.xpath('li'):
                    text = w.xpath('descendant-or-self::text()')\
                    .extract()
                    yield NWinnerItem(
                        country=country[0], name=text[0],
                        link_text = ' '.join(text)
                    )
```

❶ Gets all the <h2> headers on the page, most of which will be our target country titles.

❷ Where possible, gets the text of the `<h2>` element's child `<span>` with class `mw-headline`.

❸ Gets the list of country winners.

The `parse` method in Example 6-2 receives the response from an HTTP request to the Wikipedia Nobel Prize page and yields Scrapy items, which are then converted to JSON objects and appended to the output file, a JSON array of objects.

Let's run our first spider to make sure we're correctly parsing and scraping our Nobel data. First navigate to the *nobel_winners* root directory (containing the *scrapy.cfg* file) of the scraping project. Let's see what scraping spiders are available:

```
$ scrapy list
nwinners_list
```

As expected, we have one `nwinners_list` spider sitting in the *spiders* directory. To start it scraping, we use the `crawl` command and direct the output to a *nwinners.json* file. By default, we get a lot of Python logging information accompanying the crawl:

```
$ scrapy crawl nwinners_list -o nobel_winners.json
2015- ... [scrapy] INFO: Scrapy started (bot: nobel_winners)
2015- ... [scrapy] INFO: ... features available: ssl, http11
...
2015- ... [nwinners_list] INFO: Closing spider (finished)
2015- ... [nwinners_list] INFO: Dumping Scrapy stats:
        {'downloader/request_bytes': 551,
         'downloader/request_count': 2,
         'downloader/request_method_count/GET': 2,
         'downloader/response_bytes': 45469,

         ...
         'item_scraped_count': 1075, ❶
2015- ... [nwinners_list] INFO: Spider closed (finished)
```

❶ We scraped 1,075 Nobel winners from the page.

The output of the scrapy `crawl` shows 1,075 items successfully scraped. Let's look at our JSON output file to make sure things have gone according to plan:

```
$ head nobel_winners.json
[{"country": "Argentina",
  "link_text": "C\u00e9sar Milstein , Physiology or Medicine,"\
  " 1984",
  "name": "C\u00e9sar Milstein"},
```

```
{"country": "Argentina",
 "link_text": "Adolfo P\u00e9rez Esquivel , Peace, 1980",
 "name": "Adolfo P\u00e9rez Esquivel"},
  ...
```

As you can see, we have an array of JSON objects with the four key fields present and correct.

Now that we have a spider that successfully scrapes the list data for all the Nobel winners on the page, let's start refining it to grab all the data we are targeting for our Nobel Prize visualization (see Example 6-1 and Figure 6-1).

First, let's add all the data we plan to scrape as fields to our scrapy.Item:

```
    ...
    class NWinnerItem(scrapy.Item):
        name = scrapy.Field()
        link = scrapy.Field()
        year = scrapy.Field()
        category = scrapy.Field()
        country = scrapy.Field()
        gender = scrapy.Field()
        born_in = scrapy.Field()
        date_of_birth = scrapy.Field()
        date_of_death = scrapy.Field()
        place_of_birth = scrapy.Field()
        place_of_death = scrapy.Field()
        text = scrapy.Field()
    ...
```

It's also sensible to simplify the code a bit and use a dedicated function, process_winner_li, to process the winners' link text. We'll pass a link selector and country name to it and return a dictionary containing the scraped data:

```
    ...
    def parse(self, response):

        h2s = response.xpath('//h2')

        for h2 in h2s:
            country = h2.xpath('span[@class="mw-headline"]'\
            text()').extract()
            if country:
                winners = h2.xpath('following-sibling::ol[1]')
                for w in winners.xpath('li'):
                    wdata = process_winner_li(w, country[0])
                        ...
```

Embracing Regexes

Some people, when confronted with a problem, think "I know,
I'll use regular expressions." Now they have two problems.

—Jamie Zawinskie

The preceding quote is a hoary old classic but does sum up how
many people feel about regular expressions (regexes) (*https://
en.wikipedia.org/wiki/Regular_expression*). Regexes use a sequence
of characters to define a search expression used for string matching.
Both Python and JavaScript have built-in handling of them.

In Python, the re module provides a number of regex methods. A
common task might be to find all the email addresses in a document, recognizing email strings by the form *foo@bar.com*. Let's create a regex to find them, breaking down the process:[2]

```
In [12]: txt = 'Feel free to contact me at '\
' pyjdataviz@kyrandale.com with any feedback.'

In [13]: re.findall(r'[\w\.-]+@[\w\.-]+', txt)
Out[13]: ['pyjdataviz@kyrandale.com']
```

The findall method takes a regex string (with an *r* prepended) as
its first argument and the text to search as its second. The email
search pattern uses the following rules:

\w   Matches an alphanumeric string containing numbers and upper and lowercase
     letters (regex shorthand is [0-9a-zA-Z_])

\   Escapes a special character

\.   Matches a dot

-    Matches a hyphen

+   Matches one or more of the square-bracketed strings

Taken together, these rules match any two strings connected by @
and containing alphanumeric characters or dots or hyphens. This is
obviously a pretty broad pattern (e.g., .@. would provide a match)

---

2 There are some handy online tools for testing regexes, some of them programming-
language-specific. Pyregex (*http://www.pyregex.com/*) is a good Python one, with a
handy cheat sheet included.

that you might want to refine. For example, you could use `r'[\w \.-]@gmail.com` if you were searching for only Gmail addresses.

Although the syntax of regexes can be challenging at first, the fact is that web scraping is often about pattern-matching messy and underspecified data, and a regex is pretty much tailor-made for many of the jobs that crop up. You can probably hack your way around them, but embracing them a little will make your life that much easier, and the good news is that a little goes a long way. See Example 6-3 for some examples.

The `process_winner_li` method is shown in Example 6-3. A `wdata` dictionary is filled with information extracted from the winner's `li` tag, using a couple of regexes to find the prize year and category.

Example 6-3. Processing a winner's list item

```python
# ...
import re
BASE_URL = 'http://en.wikipedia.org'
# ...
def process_winner_li(w, country=None):
    """
    Process a winner's <li> tag, adding country of birth or
    nationality, as applicable.
    """
    wdata = {}

    wdata['link'] = BASE_URL + w.xpath('a/@href').extract()[0]  ❶

    text = ' '.join(w.xpath('descendant-or-self::text()')
        .extract())
    # get comma-delineated name and strip trailing whitespace
    wdata['name'] = text.split(',')[0].strip()

    year = re.findall('\d{4}', text)  ❷
    if year:
        wdata['year'] = int(year[0])
    else:
        wdata['year'] = 0
        print('Oops, no year in ', text)

    category = re.findall(
            'Physics|Chemistry|Physiology or Medicine|Literature|'\
            'Peace|Economics',
                text)  ❸
    if category:
```

```
          wdata['category'] = category[0]
      else:
          wdata['category'] = ''
          print('Oops, no category in ', text)

      if country:
          if text.find('*') != -1: ❹
              wdata['country'] = ''
              wdata['born_in'] = country
          else:
              wdata['country'] = country
              wdata['born_in'] = ''

      # store a copy of the link's text string
      # for any manual corrections
      wdata['text'] = text
      return wdata
```

❶ To grab the href attribute from the list item's <a> tag (<li><a
   href=/wiki…>[winner name]</a>…), we use the xpath attribute
   referent @.

❷ Here, we use re, Python's built-in regex library, to find the four-
   digit year strings in the list item's text.

❸ Another use of the regex library to find the Nobel prize category
   in the text.

❹ An asterisk following the winner's name is used to indicate that
   the country is the winner's by birth—not nationality—at the
   time of the prize (e.g., "William Lawrence Bragg*, Physics,
   1915" in the list for Australia).

Example 6-3 returns all the winners' data available on the main
Wikipedia Nobels by Country page—that is, the name, year, category, country (country of birth or country of nationality when awarded the prize), and a link to the individual winners' pages. We'll
need to use this last information to get those biographical pages and
use them to scrape our remaining target data (see Example 6-1 and
Figure 6-1).

Scraping the Individual Biography Pages

The main Wikipedia Nobels by Country page gave us a lot of our
target data, but the winner's date of birth, date of death (where appli-

cable), and gender are still to be scraped. It is hoped that this information is available, either implicitly or explicitly, on their biography pages (for nonorganization winners). Now's a good time to fire up Chrome's Elements tab and take a look at those pages to work out how we're going to extract the desired data.

We saw in the last chapter (Chapter 5) that the visible information boxes on individual's pages are not a reliable source of information and are often missing entirely. Until recently,[3] a hidden persondata table (see Figure 6-4) gave fairly reliable access to such information as place of birth, date of death, and the like. Unfortunately, this handy resource has been deprecated.[4] The good news is that this is part of an attempt to improve the categorization of biographical information by giving it a dedicated space in Wikidata (*https://www.wikidata.org/wiki/Wikidata:Main_Page*), Wikipedia's central storage for its structured data.

```
</table>
<table id="persondata" class="persondata noprint" style="border:1px solid #a
<tr>
<th colspan="2"><a href="/wiki/Wikipedia:Persondata" title="Wikipedia:Person
</tr>
<tr>
<td class="persondata-label" style="color:#aaa;">Name</td>
<td>Röntgen, Wilhelm</td>
</tr>
<tr>
<td class="persondata-label" style="color:#aaa;">Alternative names</td>
<td>Conrad</td>
</tr>
```

Figure 6-4. A Nobel Prize winner's hidden persondata table

Examining Wikipedia's biography pages with Chrome's Elements tab shows a link to the relevant Wikidata item (see Figure 6-5), which takes you to the biographical data held at *https://www.wikidata.org*. By following this link, we can scrape whatever we find there, which we hope will be the bulk of our target data—significant dates and places (see Example 6-1).

---

3 The author got stung by this removal.

4 See here (*http://bit.ly/1Pynkws*) for an insight into Wikipedia dispute management.

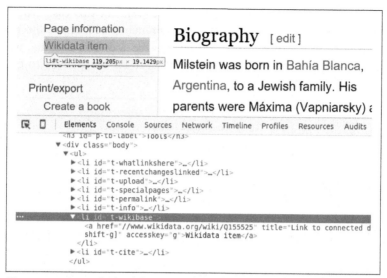

Figure 6-5. Hyperlink to the winner's Wikidata

Following the link to Wikidata shows a page containing fields for the data we are looking for, such as the date of birth of our prize winner. As Figure 6-6 shows, the properties are embedded in a nest of computer-generated HTML, with related codes, which we can use as a scraping identifier (e.g., date of birth has the code P569).

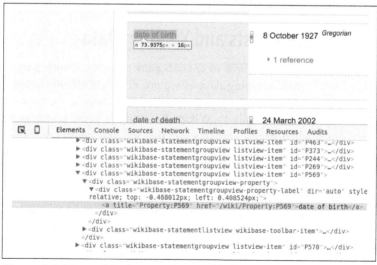

Figure 6-6. Biographical properties at Wikidata

As Figure 6-7 shows, the actual data we want, in this case a date string, is contained in a further nested branch of HTML, within its respective property tag. By selecting the div and right-clicking, we can store the element's xpath and use that to tell Scrapy how to get the data it contains.

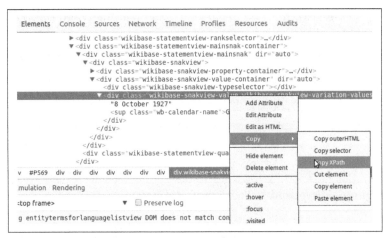

Figure 6-7. Getting the xpath for a Wikidata property

Now that we have the xpaths necessary to find our scraping targets, let's put it all together and see how Scrapy chains requests, allowing for complex, multipage scraping operations.

Chaining Requests and Yielding Data

In this section we'll see how to chain Scrapy requests, allowing us to follow hyperlinks, scraping data as we go. First let's enable Scrapy's page caching. While experimenting with xpath targets, we want to limit the number of calls to Wikipedia, and it's good manners to store our fetched pages. Unlike some datasets out there, our Nobel Prize winners change but once a year.[5]

Caching Pages

As you might expect, Scrapy has a sophisticated caching system (*http://bit.ly/1UAqGVp*) that gives you fine-grained control over

---

[5] Strictly speaking, there are edits being made continually by the Wikipedia community, but the fundamental details should be stable until the next set of prizes.

your page caching (e.g., allowing you to choose between database or filesystem storage backends, how long before your pages are expired, etc.). It is implemented as middleware (*http://bit.ly/ 261ClhH*) enabled in our project's settings.py module. There are various options available but for the purposes of our Nobel scraping, simply setting HTTPCACHE_ENABLED to True will suffice:

```
# -*- coding: utf-8 -*-

# Scrapy settings for nobel_winners project
#
# This file contains only the most important settings by
# default. All the other settings are documented here:
#
#     http://doc.scrapy.org/en/latest/topics/settings.html
#

BOT_NAME = 'nobel_winners'

SPIDER_MODULES = ['nobel_winners.spiders']
NEWSPIDER_MODULE = 'nobel_winners.spiders'

# Crawl responsibly by identifying yourself
# (and your website) on the user-agent
#USER_AGENT = 'nobel_winners (+http://www.yourdomain.com)'

HTTPCACHE_ENABLED = True
```

Check out the full range of Scrapy middleware in Scrapy's documentation (*http://bit.ly/1PypUlU*).

Having ticked the caching box, let's see how to chain Scrapy requests.

Yielding Requests

Our existing spider's parse method cycles through the Nobel winners, using the process_winner_li method to scrape the country, name, year, category, and biography-hyperlink fields. We now want to use the biography hyperlinks to generate a Scrapy request that will fetch the bio-pages and send them to a custom method for scraping.

Scrapy implements a Pythonic pattern for chaining requests, using Python's `yield` statement to create a generator,[6] allowing Scrapy to easily consume any extra page requests we make. Example 6-4 shows the pattern in action.

Example 6-4. Yielding a request with Scrapy

```python
class NWinnerSpider(scrapy.Spider):
    name = 'nwinners_full'
    allowed_domains = ['en.wikipedia.org']
    start_urls = [
        "https://en.wikipedia.org/wiki/List_of_Nobel_laureates" \
        "_by_country"
    ]

    def parse(self, response):
        filename = response.url.split('/')[-1]

        h2s = response.xpath('//h2')
        for h2 in list(h2s)[:2]:
            country = h2.xpath('span[@class="mw-headline"]/text()')
                      .extract()
            if country:
                winners = h2.xpath('following-sibling::ol[1]')
                for w in winners.xpath('li'):
                    wdata = process_winner_li(w, country[0])
                    request = scrapy.Request(    ❶
                        wdata['link'],
                        callback=self.parse_bio,    ❷
                        dont_filter=True)
                    request.meta['item'] = NWinnerItem(**wdata)    ❸
                    yield request    ❹

    def parse_bio(self, response):
        item = response.meta['item']    ❺
        ...
```

❶ Makes a request to the winner's biography page, using the link (`wdata[link]`) scraped from `process_winner_li`.

❷ Sets the callback function to handle the response.

---

6 See Jeff Knupp's blog, "Everything I Know About Python" (*https://www.jeffknupp.com/blog/2013/04/07/improve-your-python-yield-and-generators-explained/*), for a nice rundown of Python generators and the use of `yield`.

❸ Creates a Scrapy `Item` to hold our Nobel data and initializes it with the data just scraped from `process_winner_li`. This `Item` data is attached to the metadata of the request to allow any response access to it.

❹ By yielding the request, we make the `parse` method a generator of consumable requests.

❺ This method handles the callback from our bio-link request. In order to add scraped data to our Scrapy `Item`, we first retrieve it from the `response` metadata.

Our investigation of the Wikipedia pages in "Scraping the Individual Biography Pages" on page 177 showed that we need to locate a winner's Wikidata link from their biography page and use it to generate a request. We will then scrape the date, place, and gender data from the response.

Example 6-5 shows `parse_bio` and `parse_wikidata`, the two methods used to scrape our winners' biographical data. `parse_bio` uses the scraped Wikidata link to request the Wikidata page, yielding the `request` as it in turn was yielded in the `parse` method. At the end of the request chain, `parse_wikidata` retrieves the item and fills in any of the fields available from Wikidata, eventually yielding the item to Scrapy.

Example 6-5. Parsing the winners' biography data

```
# ...

    def parse_bio(self, response):
        item = response.meta['item']
        href = response.xpath("//li[@id='t-wikibase']/a/@href") ❶
            .extract()
        if href:
            request = scrapy.Request('https:' + href[0],\
                        callback=self.parse_wikidata,\ ❷
                        dont_filter=True)
            request.meta['item'] = item
            yield request


    def parse_wikidata(self, response):
```

```
item = response.meta['item']
property_codes = [  ❸
    {'name':'date_of_birth', 'code':'P569'},
    {'name':'date_of_death', 'code':'P570'},
    {'name':'place_of_birth', 'code':'P19', 'link':True},
    {'name':'place_of_death', 'code':'P20', 'link':True},
    {'name':'gender', 'code':'P21', 'link':True}
]

p_template = '//*[@id="{code}"]/div[2]/div/div/div[2]' \
             '/div[1]/div/div[2]/div[2]{link_html}/text()'  ❹

for prop in property_codes:

    link_html = ''
    if prop.get('link'):
        link_html = '/a'
    sel = response.xpath(p_template.format(\  ❺
        code=prop['code'], link_html=link_html))
    if sel:
        item[prop['name']] = sel[0].extract()

    yield item  ❻
```

❶ Extracts the link to Wikidata identified in Figure 6-5.

❷ Uses the Wikidata link to generate a request with our spider's parse_wikidata as a callback to deal with the response.

❸ These are the property codes we found earlier (see Figure 6-6), with names corresponding to fields in our Scrapy item, NWinner Item. Those with a True link attribute are contained in <a> tags.

❹ The nasty, nested xpath for the Wikidata properties used to create this template comes straight from Chrome's Elements tab (see Figure 6-7). Here we create a Python string template, with the named variables code and link_html in curly brackets. We can supply the code and link_html strings using this string's format method.

❺ We use the string template's format method (https://docs.python.org/2/library/string.html#format-string-syntax) to create the xpath based on the required property codes, appending an <a> tag if the property is a link.

❻ Finally we yield the item, which at this point should have all the target data available from Wikipedia.

With our request chain in place, let's check that the spider is scraping our required data:

```
$ scrapy crawl nwinners_full
2015-... [scrapy] ... started (bot: nobel_winners)
...
2015-... [nwinners_full] DEBUG: Scraped from
        <200 https://www.wikidata.org/wiki/Q155525>
  {'born_in': '',
   'category': u'Physiology or Medicine',
   'date_of_birth': u'8 October 1927',
   'date_of_death': u'24 March 2002',
   'gender': u'male',
   'link': u'http://en.wikipedia.org/wiki/C%C3%A9sar_Milstein',
   'name': u'C\xe9sar Milstein',
   'country': u'Argentina',
   'place_of_birth': u'Bah\xeda Blanca',
   'place_of_death': u'Cambridge',
   'text': u'C\xe9sar Milstein , Physiology or Medicine, 1984',
   'year': 1984}
2015-... [nwinners_full] DEBUG: Scraped from
        <200 https://www.wikidata.org/wiki/Q193672>
  {'born_in': '',
   'category': u'Peace',
   'date_of_birth': u'1 November 1878',
   'date_of_death': u'5 May 1959',
   'gender': u'male',
   'link': u'http://en.wikipedia.org/wiki/Carlos_Saavedra_Lamas',
   ...
```

Things are looking good. With the exception of the born_in field, which is dependent on a name in the main Wikipedia Nobel Prize winners list having an asterisk, we're getting all the data we were targeting. This dataset is now ready to be cleaned by Pandas in the coming chapter.

Now that we've scraped our basic biographical data for the Nobel Prize winners, let's go scrape our remaining targets, some biographical body text, and a picture of the great man or woman, where available.

Scrapy Pipelines

In order to add a little personality to our Nobel Prize visualization, it would be good to have a little biographical text and an image of the winner. Wikipedia's biographical pages generally provide these things, so let's go about scraping them.

Up to now, our scraped data has been text strings. In order to scrape images in their various formats, we need to use a Scrapy *pipeline*. Pipelines (*http://doc.scrapy.org/en/latest/topics/item-pipeline.html*) provide a way of post-processing the items we have scraped, and you can define any number of them. You can write your own or take advantage of those already provided by Scrapy, such as the ImagesPipeline we'll be using.

In its simplest form, a pipeline need only define a process_item method. This receives the scraped items and the spider object. Let's write a little pipeline to reject genderless Nobel Prize winners (so we can omit prizes given to organizations rather than individuals) using our existing nwinners_full spider to deliver the items. First we add a DropNonPersons pipeline to the pipelines.py module of our project:

```
# nobel_winners/nobel_winners/settings.py

# Define your item pipelines here
#
# Don't forget to add your pipeline to the ITEM_PIPELINES setting
# See: http://doc.scrapy.org/en/latest/topics/item-pipeline.html

from scrapy.exceptions import import DropItem


class DropNonPersons(object):
    """ Remove non-person winners """

    def process_item(self, item, spider):
        if not item['gender']:                          ❶
            raise DropItem("No gender for %s"%item['name'])
        return item ❷
```

❶ If our scraped item failed to find a gender property at Wikidata, it is probably an organization such as the Red Cross. Our visualization is focused on individual winners, so here we use DropItem to remove the item from our output stream.

❷ We need to return the item to further pipelines or for saving by Scrapy.

As mentioned in the `pipelines.py` header, in order to add this pipeline to the spiders of our project, we need to register it in the `settings.py` module by adding it to a `dict` of pipelines and setting it to active (1):

```
# nobel_winners/nobel_winners/settings.py

BOT_NAME = 'nobel_winners'
SPIDER_MODULES = ['nobel_winners.spiders']
NEWSPIDER_MODULE = 'nobel_winners.spiders'

HTTPCACHE_ENABLED = True
ITEM_PIPELINES = {'nobel_winners.pipelines.DropNonPersons':1}
```

Now that we've got the basic workflow for our pipelines, let's add a useful one to our project.

Scraping Text and Images with a Pipeline

We now want to scrape the winners' biography and photos (see Figure 6-1), where available. We can scrape the biographical text using the same method as our last spider, but the photos are best dealt with by an image pipeline.

We could easily write our own pipeline to take a scraped image URL, request it from Wikipedia, and save to disk, but to do it properly requires a bit of care. For example, we would like to avoid reloading an image that was recently downloaded or hasn't changed in the meantime. Some flexibility in specifying where to store the images is a useful feature. It would also be good to have the option of converting the images into a common format (e.g., JPG or PNG) or of generating thumbnails. Luckily, Scrapy provides an `ImagesPi` `peline` object with all this functionality and more. This is one of its media pipelines (*http://doc.scrapy.org/en/latest/topics/media-pipeline.html*), which includes a `FilesPipeline` for dealing with general files.

We could add the image and biography-text scraping to our existing `nwinners_full` spider, but that's starting to get a little large, and segregating this character data from the more formal categories makes sense. So we'll create a new spider called `nwinners_minibio` that will reuse parts of the previous spider's `parse` method in order to loop through the Nobel winners.

As usual, when creating a Scrapy spider, our first job is to get the xpaths for our scraping targets—in this case, where available that's the first part of the winners' biographical text and a photograph of them. To do this, we fire up Chrome Elements and explore the HTML source of the biography pages looking for the targets shown in Figure 6-8.

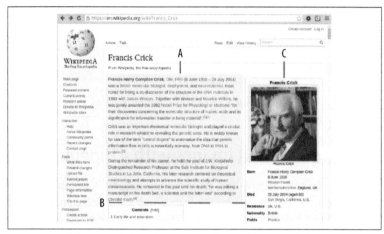

Figure 6-8. The target elements for our biography scraping: the first part of the biography (A) marked by a stop-point (B), and the winner's photograph (C)

Investigating with Chrome Elements shows the biographical text (Figure 6-8 A) is contained in the first paragraphs of the <div> with id mw-content-text, captured by the xpath //*[@id="mw-content-text"]/p. There is an empty paragraph, which signals the stop-point (Figure 6-8 B) of the first section of the biography:

```
<div id="mw-content-text">
...
<p>...</p>
<p>...</p>
<p></p> <---- stop-point -->
...
</div>
```

The exploration shows that the photos (Figure 6-8 C) are contained in a table of class infobox and are the only image tags (<img>) in that table:

```
<table class="infobox vcard">
...
        <img alt="Francis Crick crop.jpg" src="//upload... />
```

```
  ...
</table>
```

The xpath `//table[contains(@class,"infobox")]//img/@src` will get the source address of the image.

As with our first spider, we first need to declare a Scrapy `Item` to hold our scraped data. We'll scrape the bio-link and name of the winner, which we can use as identifiers for the image and text. We also need somewhere to store our `image-urls` (though we will only scrape one bio-image, I'll cover the multiple-image use case), the resultant images references (a file path), and a `bio_image` field to store the particular image we're interested in:

```
import scrapy
import re

BASE_URL = 'http://en.wikipedia.org'


class NWinnerItemBio(scrapy.Item):
    link = scrapy.Field()
    name = scrapy.Field()
    mini_bio = scrapy.Field()
    image_urls = scrapy.Field()
    bio_image = scrapy.Field()
    images = scrapy.Field()
  ...
```

Now we reuse the scraping loop over our Nobel Prize winners (see Example 6-4 for details), this time yielding a request to our new `get_mini_bio` method, which will scrape the image URLs and bio text:

```
class NWinnerSpiderBio(scrapy.Spider):

    name = 'nwinners_minibio'
    allowed_domains = ['en.wikipedia.org']
    start_urls = [
        "https://en.wikipedia.org/wiki/List_of_Nobel_" \
        "laureates_by_country"
    ]

    def parse(self, response):

        filename = response.url.split('/')[-1]
        h2s = response.xpath('//h2')

        for h2 in h2s:
            country = h2.xpath('span[@class="mw-headline"]'\
```

```
'text()').extract()
if country:
    winners = h2.xpath('following-sibling::ol[1]')
    for w in winners.xpath('li'):
        wdata = {}
        wdata['link'] = BASE_URL + \
        w.xpath('a/@href').extract()[0]
        # Process the winner's bio page with
        # the get_mini_bio method
        request = scrapy.Request(wdata['link'],
                        callback=self.get_mini_bio)
        request.meta['item'] = NWinnerItem(**wdata)
        yield request
```

Our get_mini_bio method will add any available photo URLs to the
image_urls list and add all paragraphs of the biography up to the
<p></p> stop-point to the item's mini_bio field:

```
...
def get_mini_bio(self, response):
    """ Get the winner's bio-text and photo """

    BASE_URL_ESCAPED = 'http:\/\/en.wikipedia.org'
    item = response.meta['item']
    item['image_urls'] = []
    img_src = response.xpath(\
        '//table[contains(@class,"infobox")]//img/@src')  ❶
    if img_src:
        item['image_urls'] = ['http:' +\
        img_src[0].extract()]
    mini_bio = ''
    paras = response.xpath(
        '//*[@id="mw-content-text"]/p[text() or' \
        'normalize-space(.)=""]').extract()  ❷

    for p in paras:
        if p == '<p></p>': # the bio-intros stop-point  ❸
            break
        mini_bio += p

    # correct for wiki-links
    mini_bio = mini_bio.replace('href="/wiki', 'href="'
                    + BASE_URL + '/wiki')  ❹
    mini_bio = mini_bio.replace('href="#',\
        item['link'] + '#')
    item['mini_bio'] = mini_bio
    yield item
```

❶ Targets the first (and only) image in the table of class infobox and gets its source (src) attribute (e.g., <img src=// *upload.wikimedia.org/…/Max_Perutz.jpg…*).

❷ This xpath gets all the paragraphs in the <div> with id mw-content-text. If the paragraphs are empty (text() == False), then the normalize-space(.) command is used to force the contents of the paragraph (. represents the p-node in question) to an empty string. This is to make sure any empty paragraph matches the stop-point marking the end of the intro section of the biography.

❸ Iterates through the available paragraphs, breaking on the empty paragraph stop-point.

❹ Replaces Wikipedia's internal hrefs (e.g., */wiki/…*) with the full addresses our visualization will need.

With our bio-scraping spider defined, we need to create its complementary pipeline, which will take the image URLs scraped and convert them into saved images. We'll use Scrapy's images pipeline (*http://bit.ly/1sK2cys*) for this job.

The ImagesPipeline shown in Example 6-6 has two main methods, get_media_requests, which generates the requests for the image URLs, and item_completed, called after the requests have been consumed.

Example 6-6. Scraping images with the image pipeline

```python
import scrapy
from scrapy.contrib.pipeline.images import ImagesPipeline
from scrapy.exceptions import DropItem

class NobelImagesPipeline(ImagesPipeline):

    def get_media_requests(self, item, info):   ❶

        for image_url in item['image_urls']:
            yield scrapy.Request(image_url)

    def item_completed(self, results, item, info):   ❷

        image_paths = [x['path'] for ok, x in results if ok]   ❸
        if image_paths:
```

```
    item['bio_image'] = image_paths[0]

    return item
```

❶ This takes any image URLs scraped by our *nwinners_minibio*
spider and generates an HTTP request for their content.

❷ After the image URL requests have been made, the results are
delivered to the `item_completed` method.

❸ This Python list-comprehension filters the list of result tuples
(of form [(`True`, `Image`), (`False`, `Image`) ...]) for those that
were successful and stores their file paths relative to the directory specified by the `IMAGES_STORE` variable in `settings.py`.

Now that we have the spider and pipeline defined, we just need to
add the pipeline to our `settings.py` module and set the
`IMAGES_STORE` variable to the directory we want to save the images
in:

```
# nobel_winners/nobel_winners/settings.py

...

ITEM_PIPELINES = {'nobel_winners.pipelines'\
                  '.NobelImagesPipeline':1}
IMAGES_STORE = 'images'
```

Let's run our new spider from the *nobel_winners* root directory of
our project, and check its output:

```
$ scrapy crawl nwinners_minibio -o minibios.json
...
2015-... DEBUG: Scraped from <200 http:.../Albert_Claude>
{'image_urls': [],
 'link': u'http://en.wikipedia.org/wiki/Albert_Claude',
 'mini_bio': u'<p><b>Albert Claude</b> (24 August 1899...
    <a href="http://en.wikipedia.org/wiki/Belgium"...>Belgian
    <a href="http://en.wikipedia.org/wiki/Medical_doctor"...>
2015-... DEBUG: Scraped from <200 http:.../Brian_P._Schmidt>
{ 'bio_image': 'full/a5f763b828006e704cb291411b8b643bfb91.jpg',
  'image_urls': [u'http://upload.wiki...Brian_Schmidt.jpg'],
  'link': u'http://en.wikipedia.org/wiki/Brian_P._Schmidt',
  'mini_bio': u'<p><b>Brian Paul Schmidt</b>...
...
```

We can see that scraping Albert Claude's biography page failed to
turn up an image (a quick trip to Wikipedia confirms that it's missing), but Brian Schmidt's page came up just fine. The image was

stored in `image_urls` and successfully processed, loading the JPG file stored in the *images* directory we specified with `IMAGE_STORE` with a relative path (`full/a5f763b828006e704cb291411b8b643bfb1 886c.jpg`). The filename is, conveniently enough, a SHA1 hash (*https://en.wikipedia.org/wiki/Secure_Hash_Algorithm*) of the image's URL, which allows the image pipeline to check for existing images, enabling it to prevent redundant requests.

A quick listing of our images directory shows a nice array of Wikipedia Nobel Prize winner images, ready to be used in our web visualization:

```
$ (nobel_winners) tree images
images
└── full
    ├── 0512ae11141584da1262661992a1b05dfb20dd52.jpg
    ├── 092a92689118c16b15b1613751af422439df2850.jpg
    ├── 0b6a8ca56e6ff115b7d30087df9c21da09684db1.jpg
    ├── 1197aa95299a1fec983b3dbdeaeb97a1f7e545c9.jpg
    ├── 1f6fb8e9e2241733da47328291b25bd1a78fa588.jpg
    ├── 272cf1b089c7a28ea0109ad8655bc3ef1c03fb52.jpg
    ├── 28dcc7978d9d5710f0c29d6dfcf09caa7e13a1d0.jpg
    ...
```

As we'll see in Chapter 15, we will be placing these in the *static* folder of our web app, ready to be accessed via the winner's `bio_image` field.

With our images and biography text to hand, we've successfully scraped all the targets we set ourselves at the beginning of the chapter (see Example 6-1 and Figure 6-1). Now, it's time for a quick summary before moving on to clean this inevitably dirty data with help from Pandas.

Specifying Pipelines with Multiple Spiders

The pipelines enabled in `settings.py` are applied to all spiders in our Scrapy project. Often, if you have a number of spiders, you'll want to be able to specify which pipelines are applied on a spider-by-spider basis. There are a number of ways (*http://bit.ly/28KVdWr*) to achieve this, but the best I've seen is to use the spiders' cus tom_settings class property to set the `ITEM_PIPELINES` dictionary instead of setting it in `settings.py`. In the case of our nwin ners_minibio spider, this means adapting the `NWinnerSpiderBio` class like so:

```
class NWinnerSpiderBio(scrapy.Spider):
    name = 'nwinners_minibio'
    allowed_domains = ['en.wikipedia.org']
    start_urls = [
      "http://en.wikipedia.org/wiki"\
      "List_of_Nobel_laureates_by_country"
    ]

    custom_settings = {
        'ITEM_PIPELINES':\
        {'nobel_winners.pipelines.NobelImagesPipeline':1}
    }

    # ...
```

Now the NobelImagesPipeline pipeline will only be applied while scraping the Nobel Prize winners' biographies.

Summary

In this chapter we produced two Scrapy spiders that managed to grab the simple statistical dataset of our Nobel Prize winners plus some biographical text (and, where available, a photograph, to add some color to the stats). Scrapy is a powerful library that takes care of everything you could need in a full-fledged scraper. Although the workflow requires more effort to implement than doing some hacking with BeautifulSoup, Scrapy has far more power and comes into its own as your scraping ambitions increase. All Scrapy spiders follow the standard recipe demonstrated here, and the workflow should become routine after you program a few.

I hope this chapter has conveyed the rather hacky, iterative nature of scraping, and some of the quiet satisfaction that can be had when producing relatively clean data from the unpromising mound of stuff so often found on the Web. The fact is that now and for the foreseeable future, the large majority of interesting data (the fuel for the art and science of data visualization) is trapped in a form that is unusable for the web-based visualizations that this book focuses on. Scraping is, in this sense, an emancipating endeavor.

The data we scraped, much of it human-edited, will certainly have some errors—from badly formatted dates to categorical anomalies to missing fields. Making that data presentable is the focus of the next Pandas-based chapters. But first, we need a little introduction to Pandas and its building block, NumPy.

## PART III

Cleaning and Exploring Data with Pandas

In this part of the book, in the second phase of our toolchain (see Figure III-1) we take the Nobel Prize dataset we just scraped with Scrapy in Chapter 6 and first clean it up, then explore it for interesting nuggets. The principal tools we'll be using are the large Python libraries Matplotlib and Pandas.

Pandas will be introduced in the next couple of chapters, along with its building block, NumPy. In Chapter 9 we'll use Pandas to clean the Nobel dataset. Then in Chapter 11, in conjunction with Python's plotting library Matplotlib, we'll use it to explore it.

In Part IV we'll see how to deliver the freshly cleaned Nobel Prize dataset to the browser, using Python's Flask web server.

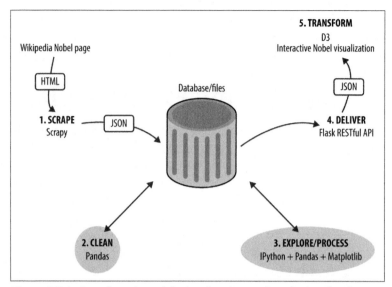

Figure III-1. Our dataviz toolchain: cleaning and exploring the data

## CHAPTER 7

Introduction to NumPy

This chapter aims to introduce the Numeric Python library (NumPy) to those unacquainted. NumPy is the key building block of Pandas, the powerhouse data analysis library that we will be using in the upcoming chapters to clean and explore our recently scraped Nobel Prize dataset (see Chapter 6). A basic understanding of NumPy's core elements and principles is important if you are to get the most out of Pandas. Therefore, the emphasis of the chapter is to provide a foundation for the upcoming introduction to Pandas.

NumPy is a Python module that allows access to very fast, multidimensional array manipulation, implemented by low-level libraries written in C and Fortran.[1] Python's native performance with large quantities of data is relatively slow, but NumPy allows you to perform parallel operations on large arrays all at once, making it very fast. Given that NumPy is the chief building block of most of the heavyweight Python data-processing libraries, Pandas included, it's hard to argue with its status as linchpin of the Python data-processing world.

In addition to Pandas, NumPy's huge ecosystem includes Science Python (SciPy), which supplements NumPy with hardcore science and engineering modules; Scikit-learn, which adds a host of modern machine-learning algorithms in such domains as classification and

---

[1] Python's scripted ease of use comes at the cost of raw speed. By wrapping fast, low-level libraries, initiatives like NumPy aim for simple, cruft-free programming and blinding performance.

feature extraction; and many other specialized libraries that use NumPy's multidimensional arrays as their primary data objects. In this sense, basic NumPy mastery can massively extend your Python range in the data-processing realm.

The key to understanding NumPy is its arrays. If you understand how these work and how to manipulate them, then a lot of other stuff should follow painlessly.[2] The next few sections will cover basic array manipulation with a few examples of NumPy in action, setting the scene for the introduction of Panda's datasets in Chapter 8.

The NumPy Array

Everything in NumPy is built around its homogeneous, multidimensional ndarray object. Operations on these arrays are performed using very fast, compiled libraries, allowing NumPy to massively outperform native Python. Among other things you can perform standard arithmetic on these arrays, much as you would a Python int or float.[3] In the following code, a whole array is added to itself as easily and as quickly as adding two integers:

```
import numpy as np ❶

a = np.array([1, 2, 3]) ❷
a + a
# output array([2, 4, 6])
```

❶ The standard way to use the NumPy library and much preferred to "from numpy import *".[4]

❷ Automatically converts a Python list of numbers.

Behind the scenes, NumPy can leverage the massively parallel computation available to modern CPUs allowing, for example, large matrices (2D arrays) to be crunched in acceptable times.

The key properties of the NumPy ndarray are its number of dimensions (ndim), shape (shape), and numeric type (dtype). The same

---

2 NumPy is used to implement some very advanced math, so don't expect to understand everything you see online—just the building blocks.

3 This assumes the arrays meet shape and type constraints.

4 Importing all module variables into your namespace using * is almost always a bad idea.

---

array of numbers can be reshaped in place, which will sometimes involve changing the array's number of dimensions. Let's demonstrate some reshaping with a little eight-member array. We'll use a print_array_details method to output the key array properties:

```
def print_array_details(a):
    print('Dimensions: %d, shape: %s, dtype: %s'\
        %(a.ndim, a.shape, a.dtype))
```

First we'll create our one-dimensional array. As the printed details show, by default this has a 64-bit integer numeric type (int64):

```
In [1]: a = np.array([1, 2, 3, 4, 5, 6, 7, 8])

In [2]: a
Out[2]: array([1, 2, 3, 4, 5, 6, 7, 8])

In [3]: print_array_details(a)
Dimensions: 1, shape: (8,), dtype: int64
```

Using the reshape method, we can change the shape and number of dimensions of a. Let's reshape a into a two-dimensional array composed of two four-member arrays:

```
In [4]: a = a.reshape([2, 4])
In [5]: a
Out[5]:
array([[1, 2, 3, 4],
       [5, 6, 7, 8]])

In [6]: print_array_details(a)
Dimensions: 2, shape: (2, 4), dtype: int64
```

An eight-member array can also be reshaped into a three-dimensional array:

```
In [7]: a = a.reshape([2, 2, 2])

In [8]: a
Out[8]:
array([[[1, 2],
        [3, 4]],

       [[5, 6],
        [7, 8]]])

In [9]: print_array_details(a)
Dimensions: 3, shape: (2, 2, 2), dtype: int64
```

The shape and numeric type can be specified on creation of the array or later. The easiest way to change an array's numeric type is by using the `astype` method to make a resized copy of the original with the new type.[5]

```
In [0]: x = np.array([[1, 2, 3], [4, 5, 6]], np.int32) ❶
In [1]: x.shape
Out[1]: (2, 3)
In [2]: x.shape = (6,)
In [3]: x
Out[3]: array([1, 2, 3, 4, 5, 6])
In [4]  x = x.astype('int64')
In [5]: x.dtype
Out[5]: dtype('int64')
```

❶ The array will convert a nested list of numbers into a suitably shaped multidimensional form.

Creating Arrays

As well as creating arrays with lists of numbers, NumPy provides some utility functions to create arrays with a specific shape. `zeros` and `ones` are the most common functions used, creating prefilled arrays. Here's a couple of examples. Note that the default `dtype` of these methods is a 64-bit float (`float64`):

```
In [32]: a = np.zeros([2,3])
In [33]: a
Out[33]:
array([[ 0.,  0.,  0.],
       [ 0.,  0.,  0.]])

In [34]: a.dtype
Out[34]: dtype('float64')

In [35]: np.ones([2, 3])
Out[35]:
array([[ 1.,  1.,  1.],
       [ 1.,  1.,  1.]])
```

The faster `empty` method just takes a memory block without the fill overhead, leaving the initialization up to you (use with caution):

---

5 A more memory-efficient and performant way involves manipulating the array's view, but it does involve some extra steps. See this Stack Overflow article (*http://stackover flow.com/questions/4389517/in-place-type-conversion-of-a-numpy-array*) for some examples and a discussion of the pros and cons.

```
empty_array = np.empty((2,3)) # create an uninitialized array

empty_array
Out[3]:
array([[  6.93185732e-310,   2.52008024e-316,   4.71690401e-317],
       [  2.38085057e-316,   6.93185752e-310,   6.93185751e-310]])
```

Another useful utility function is random, found along with some useful siblings in NumPy's random module. This creates a shaped random array:

```
>>> np.random.random((2,3))
>>> Out:
array([[ 0.97519667,  0.94934859,  0.98379541], ❶
       [ 0.10407003,  0.35752882,  0.62971186]])
```

❶ A 2×3 array of random numbers within the range 0 <= x < 1.

The handy linspace creates a specified number of evenly spaced samples over a set interval. arange is similar but uses a step-size argument.

```
np.linspace(2, 10, 5) # 5 numbers in range 2-10
Out: array([2., 4.,6., 8., 10.]) ❶
```

```
np.arange(2, 10, 2) # from 2 to 10 (exlusive) with step-size 2.
Out: array([2, 4, 6, 8])
```

Note that unlike arange, linspace is inclusive of the upper value and that the array's datatype is the default float64.

Array Indexing and Slicing

One-dimensional arrays are indexed and sliced much as Python lists:

```
a = np.array([1, 2, 3, 4, 5, 6])
a[2] # Out: 3
a[3:5] # Out: array([4, 5])
# every second item from 0-4 set to 0
a[:4:2] = 0 # Out: array([0, 2, 0, 4, 5, 6])
a[::-1] # Out: array([6, 5, 4, 3, 2, 1]), reversed
```

Indexing multidimensional arrays is similar to the *1-D* form. Each dimension has its own indexing/slicing operation and these are specified in a comma-separated tuple.[6] Figure 7-1 shows how this works.

```
import numpy as np

a = np.arange(16, dtype='int32')
a = a.reshape([2, 2, 4])
```

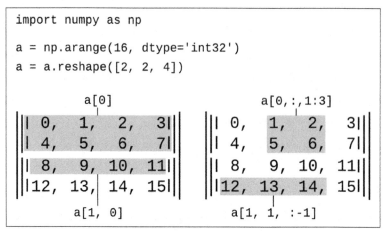

Figure 7-1. Multidimensional indexing with NumPy

Note that if the number of objects in the selection tuple is less than the number of dimensions, the remaining dimensions are assumed to be fully selected (:). Ellipsis can also be used as a shorthand for full selection of all indices, expanding to the required number of : objects:

```
a = np.array(arange(8))
a.shape = (2, 2, 2)
a[1] == a[1,:] == a[1,:,:]
a[...,0] == a[:,:,0]
```

A Few Basic Operations

One of the really cool things about NumPy arrays is that you can perform basic (and not so basic) math operations in much the same way that you would with normal numeric variables. Figure 7-2 shows the use of some overloaded arithmetic operators on a two-dimensional array. The simple mathematical operations are applied to all members of the array. Note that where the array is divided by a floating-point value (2.0), the result is automatically converted to a float type (float64). Being able to manipulate arrays as easily as

---

6 There is a shorthand dot notation (e.g., [..1:3]) to select all indices.

single numbers is a huge strength of NumPy and a large part of its expressive power.

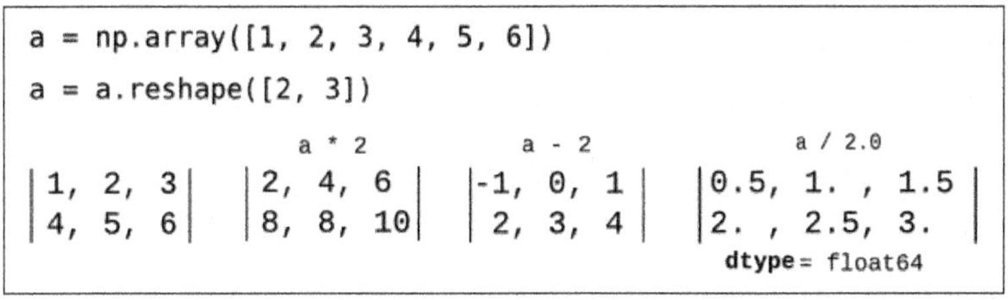

```
a = np.array([1, 2, 3, 4, 5, 6])
a = a.reshape([2, 3])
```

a * 2	a - 2	a / 2.0
	1, 2, 3	2, 4, 6	-1, 0, 1	0.5, 1. , 1.5
	4, 5, 6	8, 8, 10	2, 3, 4	2. , 2.5, 3.

dtype= float64

Figure 7-2. A few basic math operations on a two-dimensional NumPy array

Boolean operators work in a similar way to the arithmetic ones. As we'll see in the next chapter, this is a very useful way to create the boolean masks often used in Pandas. Here's a little example:

```
a = array([45, 65, 76, 32, 99, 22])
a < 50
Out[69]: array([ True, False, False,  True, False,  True]
            , dtype=bool)
```

Arrays also have a number of useful methods, a selection of which is demonstrated in Example 7-1. You can get a comprehensive run-down in the official NumPy docs (*http://docs.scipy.org/doc/numpy/reference/arrays.ndarray.html*).

Example 7-1. Some array methods

```
a = np.arange(8).reshape((2,4))
# array([[0, 1, 2, 3],
#        [4, 5, 6, 7]])

a.min(axis=1)
# array([0, 4])
a.sum(axis=0)
# array([4, 6, 8, 10])
a.mean(axis=1) ❶
# array([ 1.5, 5.5 ])
a.std(axis=1) ❷
# array([ 1.11803399,  1.11803399])
```

❶ Average along second axis.

❷ The standard deviation of [0, 1, 2, 3],...

There are also a large number of built-in array functions. Example 7-2 demonstrates a selection of these, and you will find a comprehensive list of NumPy's built-in mathematical routines at the official NumPy site (*http://docs.scipy.org/doc/numpy/reference/routines.math.html*).

Example 7-2. Some NumPy array math functions

```
# Trigonometric functions
pi = np.pi
a = np.array([pi, pi/2, pi/4, pi/6])

np.degrees(a) # radians to degrees
# Out: array([ 180., 90., 45., 30.,])

sin_a = np.sin(a)
# Out: array([ 1.22464680e-16,   1.00000000e+00,  ❶
                7.07106781e-01,   5.00000000e-01])
# Rounding
np.round(sin_a, 7) # round to 7 decimal places
# Out: array([ 0.,   1.,   0.7071068,   0.5 ])

# Sums, products, differences
a = np.arange(8).reshape((2,4))
# array([[0, 1, 2, 3],
#        [4, 5, 6, 7]])

np.cumsum(a, axis=1) # cumulative sum along second axis
# array([[ 0,   1,   3,   6],
#        [ 4,   9, 15, 22]])

np.cumsum(a) # without axis argument, array is flattened
# array([ 0,   1,   3,   6, 10, 15, 21, 28])
```

❶ Note the floating-point rounding error for sin(pi).

Creating Array Functions

Whether you're using Pandas or one of the many Python data-processing libraries, such as Scipy, scikit-learn, or PyBrain, chances are the core data structure being used is the NumPy `array`. The ability to craft little `array` processing functions is therefore a great addition to your data-processing toolkit and the data visualization toolchain. Often a short Internet search will turn up a community solution, but there's a lot of satisfaction to be gained from crafting your own, besides being a great way to learn. Let's see how we can harness the NumPy `array` to calculate a moving average (*https:// en.wikipedia.org/wiki/Moving_average*). A moving average is a series of averages based on a moving window of the last *n* values, where *n* is variable, also known as a *moving mean* or *rolling mean*.

Calculating a Moving Average

Example 7-3 shows the few lines needed to calculate a moving average on a one-dimensional NumPy `array`.[7] As you can see, it's nice and concise, but there's a fair amount going on in those few lines. Let's break it down a bit.

Example 7-3. A moving average with NumPy

```
def moving_average(a, n=3):
    ret = np.cumsum(a, dtype=float)
    ret[n:] = ret[n:] - ret[:-n]
    return ret[n - 1:] / n
```

The function receives an `array` *a* and number *n* specifying the size of the moving window.

We first calculate the cumulative sum of the array using NumPy's built-in method.

```
a = np.arange(6)
# array([0, 1, 2, 3, 4, 5])
csum = np.cumsum(a)
csum
Out: array([0, 1, 3, 6, 10, 15])
```

Starting at the *n*th index of the cumulative sum `array`, we subtract the *i*–*n*th value for all *i*, which means *i* now has the sum of the last *n* values of *a*, inclusive. Here's an example with a window of size three:

```
# a = array([0, 1, 2, 3, 4 , 5])
# csum = array([0, 1, 3, 6, 10, 15])
csum[3:] = csum[3:] - csum[:-3]
# csum = array([0, 1, 3, 6, 9, 12])
```

Comparing the array `a` with the final array `csum`, index 5 is now the sum of the window [3, 4, 5].

---

7 NumPy has a `convolve` method, which is the easiest way to calculate a simple moving average but less instructive. Also, Pandas has a number of specialized methods for this.

Because a moving average only makes sense for index (*n*–1) onward, it only remains to return these values, divided by the window size *n* to give the average.

The `moving_average` function takes a bit of time to get but is a good example of the concision and expressiveness that can be achieved with NumPy arrays and `array` slicing. You could easily write the function in vanilla Python, but it would likely be a fair bit more involved and, crucially, be much slower for arrays of significant size.

Putting the function to work:

```
a = arange(10)
moving_average(a, 4)
Out[98]: array([ 1.5,  2.5,  3.5,  4.5,  5.5,  6.5,  7.5])
```

Summary

This chapter laid the foundations of NumPy, focusing on its building block, the NumPy array or `ndarray`. Being proficient with NumPy is a core skill for any Pythonista working with data. It underpins most of Python's hardcore data-processing stack, so for this reason alone, you should be comfortable with its array manipulations.

Being comfortable with NumPy will make Pandas work that much easier and open up the rich NumPy ecosystem of scientific, engineering, machine learning, and statistical algorithmics to your Pandas workflow. Although Pandas hides its NumPy arrays behind data containers such as its `DataFrame` and `Series`, which are adapted to deal with heterogeneous data, these containers behave for the most part like NumPy arrays and will generally do the right thing when asked. Knowing that `ndarrays` are at its core also helps when you are trying to frame problems for Pandas—ultimately the requested data manipulation has to play nicely with NumPy. Now that we've got its building blocks in place, let's see how Pandas extends the homogeneous NumPy array into the realm of heterogeneous data, where much of data visualization work takes place.

## CHAPTER 8

Introduction to Pandas

Pandas is a key element in our dataviz toolchain, as we will use it for both cleaning and exploring our recently scraped dataset (see Chapter 6). The last chapter introduced NumPy, the Python array processing library that is the foundation of Pandas. Before we move on to applying Pandas, this chapter will introduce its key concepts and show how it interacts with existing data files and database tables. The rest of your Pandas learning will be on the job over the next couple of chapters.

Why Pandas Is Tailor-Made for Dataviz

Take any dataviz, whether web-based or in print, and chances are that the data visualized was at one point stored in row-columnar form in a spreadsheet like Excel, a CSV file, or HDF5. There are certainly visualizations, like network graphs, for which row-columnar data is not the best form, but they are in the minority. Pandas is tailor-made to manipulate row-columnar data tables with its core datatype, the DataFrame, which is best thought of as a very fast, programmatic spreadsheet.

Why Pandas Was Developed

First revealed by Wes Kinney in 2008, Pandas was built to solve a particular problem—namely, that while Python was great for manipulating data, munging it, and preparing it, it was weak in the area of data analysis and modeling, certainly compared with big hitters like R.

Pandas is designed to work with heterogeneous data like that found in row-columnar spreadsheets, but cleverly manages to leverage some of the speed of Python's NumPy, originally intended for the sort of homogeneous numeric arrays used by mathematicians, physicists, computer graphics, and the like. Combined with the IPython interpreter-on-steroids and the Matplotlib plotting library (and family), Pandas represents a first-class interactive data analysis tool. Because it's part of the NumPy ecosystem, its data modeling is easily enhanced by such libraries as SciPy, Statsmodel, and Scikit-learn, to name but a few.

Heterogeneous Data and Categorizing Measurements

I'll cover the core concepts of Pandas in the next section, focusing on the DataFrame and how to get your data into and out of it via the common datastores, CSV files and SQL databases. But first let's take a little diversion to consider what we really mean by the heterogeneous datasets that Pandas was designed to work with and that are the mainstay of data visualizers.

Chances are that a visualization, maybe a bar chart or line graph used to illustrate an article or a modern web dashboard, presents the results of measurements in the real world, the price of commodities as they change over time, changes in rainfall over a year, voting intentions by ethnic group, and so forth. These measurements can be broadly broken into two groups, numerical and categorical. Numerical values can be divided into interval and ratio scales, and categorical values can in turn be divided into nominal and ordinal measurements. This gives four broad categories of observation available to the data visualizer.

Let's take a set of tweets as an example in order to draw out these measurement categories. Each tweet has various data fields:

```
{
    "text": "#Python and #JavaScript sitting in a tree...", ❶
    "id": 2103303030333004303, ❶
    "favorited": true, ❷
    "filter_level":"medium", ❸
    "created_at": "Wed Mar 23 14:07:43 +0000 2015", ❹
```

```
    "retweet_count":23, ❺
    "coordinates":[-97.5, 45.3] ❻
    ...
}
```

❶ The text and id fields are unique indicators. The former might
   contain categorical information (e.g., the category of tweets
   containing the #Python hashtag), and the latter might be used to
   create a category (e.g., the set of all users retweeting this tweet),
   but they are not per se visualizable fields.

❷ favorited is Boolean, categorical information, dividing the
   tweets into two sets. This would count as a *nominal* category, as
   it can be counted but not ordered.

❸ filter_level is also categorical information, but it is ordinal.
   There is an order, low→medium→high, to the filter levels.

❹ The created_at field is a timestamp, a numerical value on an
   interval scale. We would probably want to order the tweets on
   this scale, something Pandas does automatically, and then
   maybe box into broader intervals, say by the day or week.
   Again, Pandas makes this trivial.

❺ retweet_count is likewise on a numerical scale, but it is a ratio
   one. A ratio scale, as opposed to an interval scale, has a meaningful concept of zero—in this case, no retweets. Our cre
   ated_at timestamp, on the other hand, can have an arbitrary
   baseline (e.g., unix-time or Gregorian year 0), much in the same
   way as temperature scales, with 0 degrees Celsius being the
   same as 173 degrees Kelvin.

❻ coordinates, if available, has two numerical scales for longitude
   and latitude. Whereas longitude is taken arbitrarily from the
   Greenwich Meridian, a historical artifact of the British Empire,
   the line of latitude from the equator is nonarbitrary in as much
   as the earth's pole disambiguates. Both are interval scales,
   though, as it doesn't make much sense to speak of ratios of
   degrees.

So a small subset of our humble tweet's fields contains heterogeneous information covering all the generally accepted divisions of
measurement. Whereas the NumPy array is generally used for

homogeneous, numerical number crunching, Pandas is designed to deal with categorical data, time series, and items that reflect the heterogeneous nature of real-world data. This makes it a great fit for the data visualization.

Now that we know the type of data Pandas is designed to deal with, let's look at the data structures it uses.

The DataFrame

The first step in a Pandas session is usually to load some data into a DataFrame. We'll cover the various ways we can do this in a later section. For now, let's read our *nobel_winners.json* JSON data from a file. read_json returns a DataFrame, parsed from the JSON file specified. By convention, DataFrame variables start with df:

```
df = pd.read_json('data/nobel_winners.json')
```

With our DataFrame in hand, let's inspect its content. A quick way to get the row-columnar structure of the DataFrame is to use its head method to show (by default) the top five items. Figure 8-1 shows the output from an IPython (or Jupyter (*http://jupyter.org/*)) Notebook, with key elements of the DataFrame highlighted.

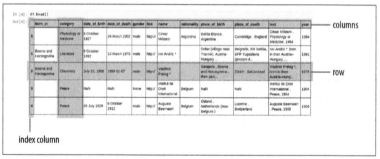

Figure 8-1. The key elements of a Pandas DataFrame

Indices

The DataFrame's columns are indexed by a columns property, which is a Pandas index instance. Let's select the columns in Figure 8-1:

```
In [0]: df.columns
Out[0]: Index([u'born_in', u'category', ... , dtype='object')
```

Initially, Pandas rows have a single numeric index (Pandas can handle multiple indexes if necessary) that can be accessed by the index property:

```
In [1]: df.index
Out[1]: Int64Index([0, 1, 2, 3, 4, 5, 6, 7, ...], dtype='int64')
```

As well as integers, row indices can be strings, DatetimeIndices, or PeriodIndices for time-based data, and so on. Often, to aid selections, a column of the DataFrame will be set to the index via the set_index method. In the following code, we first use the set_index method to set our Nobel DataFrame's index to the name column and then use the loc method to select a row by the index label (name in this case):

```
In [2] df = df.set_index('name')  ❶
In [3] df.loc('Albert Einstein')  ❷
Out[3]:
award_age                             42
category                         Physics
...
year                                1921
Name: Albert Einstein, dtype: object

df = df.reset_index()  ❸
```

❶ Set the index to the name column.

❷ You can now select a row by the name label.

❸ Return the index to original integer-based state.

Rows and Columns

The rows and columns of a DataFrame are stored as Pandas Series (*http://bit.ly/1UT76Cl*), a heterogeneous counterpart to NumPy's array. These are essentially a labeled one-dimensional array that can contain any datatype from integers, strings, and floats to Python objects and lists.

There are three ways to select a row from the DataFrame. We've seen the loc method, which selects by label. There's also an iloc method, which selects by position. So to select the row in Figure 8-1, we grab row number two:

```
In [4] df.iloc[2]
Out[4]:
born_in                          Bosnia and Herzegovina
category                                      Chemistry
...
name                                 Vladimir Prelog *
year                                              1975
Name: 2, dtype: object
```

There is also an `ix` convenience method, which combines label access by `loc` with access by position `iloc`. `ix` prioritizes access by label, with a fallback to access by integer position if you use it with an integer and the axis (e.g., our Nobel Prize names column) is not an integer. Here are a few examples:

```
In [5] df.ix[2] # equivalent to df.iloc[2]
Out[5]:
...
name                                 Vladimir Prelog *
...
In [6] df = df.set_index('name') # index is now a name string
In [7] df.ix['Albert Einstein'] # == df.loc['Albert Einstein']
Out[7]:
...
Name: Albert Einstein, dtype: object
In [8] df.ix[2] # numeric access defaults to +iloc+
Out[8]:
...
name                                 Vladimir Prelog *
```

`ix` is a convenient method, but there is scope for confusion when it's used with integer axes. If in doubt, it's best to be explicit and use either `loc` or `iloc`.

You can grab a column of your `DataFrame` using dot notation[1] or conventional array access by keyword string. This returns a Pandas `Series` with all the column fields with their `DataFrame` indices preserved:

```
In [9] gender_col = df.gender # or df['gender']
In [10] type(gender_col)
Out[10] pandas.core.series.Series
In [11] gender_col.head() # grab the Series' first five items
Out[11]:
0    male #index, object
1    male
```

---

1 Only if the column name is a string without spaces.

```
2    male
3    male
4    male
Name: gender, dtype: object
```

Selecting Groups

There are various ways we can select groups (or subsets of rows) of
our DataFrame, returning a new, filtered DataFrame. Often we want
to select all rows with a specific column value (e.g., all rows with category Physics). One way to do this is to use the DataFrame's groupby
method to group a column (or list of columns) and then use the
get_group method to select the required group. Let's use these two
methods to select all Nobel Physics Prize winners:

```
In [12] df = df.groupby('category')
In [13] df.groups.keys()
Out[13]:
[u'Physiology or Medicine',
 u'Literature',
 u'Economics',
 ...

In [14] phy_group = df.get_group('Physics')
In [15] phy_group.head()
Out[15]:
    born_in category    date_of_birth      date_of_death gender  \
13          Physics   6 November 1932                     male
19          Physics    7 October 1885  18 November 1962   male
23          Physics     July 9, 1926                      male
24          Physics     19 June 1922   8 September 2009   male
47          Physics       3 May 1902    7 January 1984    male
...
```

Another way to select row subsets is to use a Boolean mask to create
a new DataFrame. You can apply Boolean operators to all rows in a
DataFrame in much the same way as you can to all members of a
NumPy array:

```
In [16] df.category == 'Physics'
Out[16]:
0     False
1     False
...
10     True
11    False
...
```

The resulting Boolean mask can then be applied to the original Data Frame to select a subset of its rows:

```
In [17]: df[df.category == 'Physics']
Out[17]:
         born_in category      date_of_birth  ... gender  \
13               Physics    6 November 1932    ...   male
19               Physics    7 October 1885     ...   male
23               Physics      July 9, 1926     ...   male
...
```

We'll cover a lot more examples of data selections in the coming chapters. For now, let's take a quick look at Pandas Panels, which are containers for multiple DataFrames, before moving on to see how to create DataFrames from existing data and how to save the results of our DataFrame manipulations.

Creating and Saving DataFrames

The easiest way to create a DataFrame is to use a Python dictionary. It's also a way you won't be using very often, as you will likely be accessing your data from files or databases. Nevertheless, it has its use cases.

By default, we specify the columns separately, in the following example creating three rows with name and category columns.

```
df = DataFrame({
    'name': ['Albert Einstein', 'Marie Curie',\
    'William Faulkner'],
    'category': ['Physics', 'Chemistry', 'Literature']
    })
```

We can use the from_dict method to allow us to use our preferred record-based object arrays. from_dict has an orient argument to allow us to specify record-like data, but Pandas is smart enough to work out the data form:

```
df = DataFrame.from_dict([ ❶
    {'name': 'Albert Einstein', 'category':'Physics'},
    {'name': 'Marie Curie', 'category':'Chemistry'},
    {'name': 'William Faulkner', 'category':'Literature'}
    ])
```

❶ Here we pass in an array of objects, each corresponding to a row in our DataFrame.

The methods just shown produce an identical DataFrame:

```
df.head()
Out:
     category              name
0     Physics   Albert Einstein
1   Chemistry       Marie Curie
2  Literature  William Faulkner
```

As mentioned, you probably won't be creating DataFrames from Python containers directly. Instead, you will probably use one of the Pandas data reading methods.

Pandas has an impressive array of read_[format]/to_[format] methods, covering most conceivable data-loading use cases, from CSV through binary HDF5 to SQL databases. We'll cover the subset most relevant to dataviz work. For a full list, see the Pandas documentation (*http://pandas.pydata.org/pandas-docs/dev/io.html*).

Note that by default Pandas will try to convert the loaded data sensibly. The convert_axes (try to convert the axes to the proper dtypes), dtype (guess datatype), and convert_dates arguments to the read methods are all True by default. See here (*http://pandas.pydata.org/pandas-docs/stable/io.html#reading-json*) for a full list of options.

Let's cover file-based DataFrames first, then see how to interact with (No)SQL databases.

JSON

Loading data from our preferred JSON format is trivial in Pandas:

```
df = pd.read_json('file.json')
```

There are various forms the JSON file can take, specified by an optional orient argument, one of [split, records, index, columns, values]. An array of records, our standard form, will be detected:

```
[{"name":"Albert Einstein", "category":"Physics", ...},
 {"name":"Marie Curie", "category":"Chemistry", ... } ... ]
```

The default for a JSON object is columns, in the form:

```
{"name":{"0":"Albert Einstein","1":"Marie Curie" ... },
 "category":{"1","Physics","2":"Chemistry" ... }}
```

As discussed, for web-based visualization work, particularly D3, record-based JSON is the most common way of passing row-columnar data to the browser.

Note that you will need valid JSON files to work with Pandas because the `read_json` method and Python JSON parsers in general tend to be fairly unforgiving, and exceptions not as informative as they might be.[2] A common JSON error is failing to enclose keys in double-quote marks or using single quotes where double quotes are expected. The latter is particularly common for those coming from languages where single- and double-string quotes are essentially interchangeable and one reason why you should never build JSON documents yourself—always use an official or well-respected library.

There are various ways to store `DataFrames` in JSON, but the format that will play most nicely with any dataviz work is the array of records. This is the most common form of D3 data and the one I recommend outputting from Pandas.[3] Writing a `DataFrame` as records to JSON is then simply a case of specifying the `orient` field in the `to_json` method.

```
df = pd.read_json('data.json')
# ... Perform data-cleaning operations
json = df.to_json('data_cleaned.json', orient='records') ❶
Out:
[{"name":"Albert Einstein", "category":"Physics", ...},
 {"name":"Marie Curie", "category":"Chemistry", ... } ... ]
```

❶ Override the default save to store the JSON as dataviz-friendly records.

We also have the parameters `date_format`(*epoch* timestamp, *iso* for ISO8601, etc.), `double_precision`, and `default_handler` to call if the object cannot be converted into JSON using Pandas' parser. Check the Pandas documentation (*http://pandas.pydata.org/pandas-docs/dev/io.html#writing-json*) for more details.

---

2 If you have problems, you might try a subset of your data here (*http://jsonlint.com*) for better feedback.

3 D3 takes a number of other data formats, such as hierarchical (tree type) data or node and link graph formats. Here is a pretty comprehensive list (*http://wiki.cfcl.com/Projects/D3/DF_DS*).

CSV

As befits Pandas' data-table ethos, its handling of CSV files is sophisticated enough to cope with pretty much all conceivable data. Conventional CSV files, which is the large majority, will load without parameters.

```
# data.csv:
# name,category
# "Albert Einstein",Physics
# "Marie Curie",Chemistry

df = pd.read_csv('data.csv')
df
Out:
             name    category
0  Albert Einstein    Physics
1      Marie Curie  Chemistry
```

But there is a lot of CSV type data out there that is not comma-separated or that uses idiosyncratic quoting for strings containing spaces or special characters. In this case, we can specify any non-standard elements in our read request. We'll use Python's handy StringIO module to emulate reading from a file:[4]

```
from StringIO import StringIO

data = "  `Albert Einstein`| Physics \n`Marie Curie`|  Chemistry"

df = pd.read_csv(StringIO(data),
    sep='|', ❶
    names=['name', 'category'], ❷
    skipinitialspace=True, quotechar="`")

df
Out:
             name    category
0  Albert Einstein    Physics
1      Marie Curie  Chemistry
```

❶ The fields are pipe-separated, not the default comma-separated.

❷ Here we provide the missing column headers.

---

[4] I recommend using this approach if you want to get a feel for the CSV or JSON parsers. It's much more convenient than managing local files.

We have the same degree of flexibility when saving CSV files, here setting the encoding to Unicode utf-8.

```
df.to_csv('data.csv', encoding='utf-8')
```

For full coverage of the CSV options, see here (*http://pandas.pydata.org/pandas-docs/dev/io.html#csv-text-files*).

Excel Files

Pandas uses Python's xlrd module to read Excel 2003 (*.xls*) and Excel 2007 (*.xlsx*) files. Excel documents have multiple named sheets, each of which can be passed to a `DataFrame`. There are two ways to read a datasheet into a `DataFrame`. The first is by creating and then parsing an `ExcelFile` object.

```
dfs = {}
xls = pd.ExcelFile('nobel_winners.xls') # load Excel file
dfs['WSheet1'] = xls.parse('WinnersSheet1', na_values=['NA']) ❶
dfs['WSheet2'] = xls.parse('WinnersSheet2',
    index_col=1, ❷
    na_values=['-'], ❸
    skiprows=3 ❹
    )
```

❶ Grab a sheet by name and save to a dictionary.

❷ Specify the column, by position, to use as `DataFrame`'s row labels.

❸ A list of additional strings to recognize as NaN.

❹ The number of rows (e.g., metadata) to skip before processing.

Alternatively you can use the `read_excel` method, which is a convenience method for loading multiple spreadsheets.

```
data = read_excel('nobel_winners.xls', ['WSheet1','WSheet2'],
                  index_col=None, na_values=['NA'])
```

The only reason not to use `read_excel` is if you need different arguments for reading each Excel sheet.

You can specify sheets by index or name using the second (`sheet name`) parameter. `sheetname` can be a single name-string or index (beginning at 0) or a mixed list. By default `sheetname` is 0, returning the first sheet. Example 8-1 shows some variations. Setting sheet name to None returns a sheetname-keyed dictionary of DataFrames.

Example 8-1. Loading Excel sheets

```
# return the first datasheet
df = read_excel('nobel_winners.xls')


# return a named sheet
df = read_excel('nobel_winners.xls', 'WSheet3')

# first sheet and sheet named 'WSheet3'
df = read_excel('nobel_winners.xls', [0, 'WSheet3'])

# all sheets loaded into a name-keyed dictionary
dfs = read_excel('nobel_winners.xls', sheetname=None)
```

The parse_cols parameter lets you select the sheet columns to be parsed. Setting parse_cols to an integer value selects all columns up to that ordinal. Setting parse_cols to a list of integers allows you to select specific columns.

```
# parse up to the fifth column
read_excel('nobel_winners.xls', 'WSheet1', parse_cols=4)

# parse the second and fourth columns
read_excel('nobel_winners.xls', 'WSheet1', parse_cols=[1, 3])
```

For more information on read_excel, see here (*http://bit.ly/ 1tAISErl*).

You can save a DataFrame to the sheet of an Excel file with the to_excel method, giving the Excel filename and a sheetname, 'nobel_winners' and 'WSheet1', respectively, in this example:

```
df.to_excel('nobel_winners', sheet_name='WSheet1')
```

There are various options similar to to_csv and covered here (*http://bit.ly/1W3YPxO*). Because Pandas Panels and Excel files can store multiple DataFrames, there is a Panel to_excel method to write all its DataFrames to an Excel file.

If you need to select multiple DataFrames to write to a shared Excel file, you can use an ExcelWriter object.

```
with pd.ExcelWriter('nobel_winners.xlsx') as writer:
    df1.to_excel(writer, sheet_name='WSheet1')
    df2.to_excel(writer, sheet_name='WSheet2')
```

SQL

If available, and I'd highly recommend that it is, Pandas uses Python's SQLAlchemy module to do the database abstraction; otherwise, there is an sqlite fallback using Python's standard database library. If using SQLAlchemy, you'll also need the driver library for your database.

The easiest way to load a database table or the results of an SQL query is with the read_sql method.

```
import sqlalchemy

engine = sqlalchemy.create_engine(
                'mysql://USER:PASSWORD@localhost/db') ❶
df = pd.read_sql('nobel_winners', engine) ❷
```

❶ Here, we use a MySQL database. SQLAlchemy can create engines for all the commonly used databases.

❷ Read the contents of the 'nobel_winners' SQL table into a DataFrame.

read_sql is a convenience wrapper around the read_sql_table and read_sql_query methods and will do the right thing depending on its first argument.

Writing DataFrames to an SQL database is simple enough. Using the engine we just created:

```
# save DataFrame df to nobel_winners SQL table
df.to_sql('nobel_winners', engine)
```

If you encounter errors due to packet-size limitations, the chunk size parameter can set the number of rows to be written at a time.

```
# write 500 rows at a time
df.to_sql('nobel_winners', engine, chunksize=500)
```

Pandas will do the sensible thing and try to map your data to a suitable SQL type, inferring the datatype of objects. If necessary, the default type can be overridden in the load call:

```
from sqlalchemy.types import String
df.to_sql('nobel_winners', engine, dtype={'year': String}) ❶
```

❶ Override Pandas' inference, and specify year as a String column.

Further details of Pandas-SQL interaction can be found in the Pandas documentation (*http://pandas.pydata.org/pandas-docs/dev/io.html#sql-queries*).

MongoDB

For dataviz work, there's a lot to be said for the convenience of document-based NoSQL databases like MongoDB. In MongoDB's case, things are even better, as it uses a binary form of JSON for its datastore—namely BSON, short for binary JSON. Since JSON is our data glue of choice, as it connects our web dataviz with its backend server, there's a good reason to consider storing your datasets in Mongo. It also plays nicely with Pandas.

As we've seen, Pandas DataFrames convert nicely to and from JSON format, so getting a Mongo document collection into a Pandas Data Frame is a pretty easy affair:

```
import pandas as pd
from pymongo import MongoClient

client = MongoClient() ❶

db = client.nobel_prize ❷
cursor = db.winners.find() ❸
df = pd.DataFrame(list(cursor)) ❹
```

❶ Create a Mongo client, using the default host and ports.

❷ Get the nobel_prize database.

❸ Find all documents in the winner collection.

❹ Load all documents from the cursor into a list and use to create a DataFrame.

It's just as easy to insert a DataFrame's records into a MongoDB database. Here, we use the get_mongo_database method we defined in Example 3-5 to get our nobel_prize database and save the Data Frame to its winners collection:

```
db = get_mongo_database('nobel_prize')

records = df.to_dict('records') ❶
db[collection].insert(records) ❷
```

❶ Converts the DataFrame to a dict, using the records argument to convert the rows into individual objects.

❷ For PyMongo version 3 and later, use the faster insert_many method.

Let's write a couple of convenience functions to read and write a DataFrame to a MongoDB database; we'll use these in the next data cleaning chapter:

```python
def mongo_to_dataframe(db_name, collection, query={},\
                       host='localhost', port=27017,\
                       username=none, password=none,\
                       no_id=true):
    """ create a dataframe from mongodb collection """

    db = get_mongo_database(db_name, host, port, username,\
    password)

    cursor = db[collection].find(query)

    df =  pd.dataframe(list(cursor))

    if no_id: ❶
        del df['_id']

    return df

def dataframe_to_mongo(df, db_name, collection,\
                       host='localhost', port=27017,\
                       username=none, password=none):
    """ save a dataframe to mongodb collection """
    db = get_mongo_database(db_name, host, port, username,\
    password)

    records = df.to_dict('records')
    db[collection].insert(records)
```

❶ Mongo's _id field will be included in the DataFrame. By default, remove the column.

Another way to create DataFrames is to build them from a collection of Series. Let's have a look at that, taking the opportunity to explore Series in more detail.

Series into DataFrames

The key idea with Pandas `Series` is the index. These indices function as labels for the heterogeneous data contained in, say, a row of data. When Pandas operates on more than one data object, these indices are used to align the fields.

`Series` can be created in one of three ways. The first is from a Python list or NumPy array:

```
s = Series([1, 2, 3, 4]) # Series(np.arange(4))
Out:
0    1 # index, value
1    2
2    3
3    4
dtype: int64
```

Note that integer indices are automatically created for our `Series`. If we were adding a row of data to a `DataFrame` (table), we would want to specify the column indices by passing them as a list of integers or labels.

```
s = Series([1, 2, 3, 4], index=['a', 'b', 'c', 'd'])
s
Out:
a    1
b    2
c    3
d    4
dtype: int64
```

Note that the length of the index array should match the length of the data array.

We can specify both data and index using a Python `dict`:

```
s = Series({'a':1, 'b':2, 'c':3})
Out:
a    1
b    2
c    3
dtype: int64
```

If we pass an index array along with the `dict`, Pandas will do the sensible thing, matching the indices to the data array. Any unmatched indices will be set to `NaN` (not a number), and any unmatched data discarded.

```
s = Series({'a':1, 'b':2}, index=['a', 'b', 'c'])
Out:
a 1
b 2
c NaN

s = Series({'a':1, 'b':2, 'c':3}, index=['a', 'b'])
Out:
a 1
b 2
```

Finally, we can pass a single, scalar value as data to the `Series`, provided we also specify an index. The scalar value is then applied to all indices.

```
Series(9, {'a', 'b', 'c'})
Out:
a    9
b    9
c    9
```

`Series` are like NumPy arrays (`ndarray`), which means they can be passed to most NumPy functions:

```
s = pd.Series([1, 2, 3, 4], ['a', 'b', 'c', 'd'])
np.sqrt(s)
Out:
a    1.000000
b    1.414214
c    1.732051
d    2.000000
dtype: float64
```

Slicing operations work as they would with Python lists or `ndarrays`, but note that the index labels are preserved:

```
s[1:3]
Out:
b    2
c    3
```

And of course, unlike `ndarrays`, multiple datatypes are handled sensibly:

```
pd.Series([1, 2.1, 'foo']) + pd.Series([2, 3, 'bar'])
Out:
0         3 # 1 + 2
1       5.1 # 2.1 + 3
2    foobar # strings correctly concatenated
dtype: object
```

The ability to create and manipulate individual Series is particularly important when you are interacting with the NumPy ecosystem, manipulating data from a DataFrame, or creating visualizations outside of Pandas' Matplotlib wrapper.

As Series are the building block of DataFrames, it's easy to join them together to create a DataFrame, using Pandas' concat method:

```
names = pd.Series(['Albert Einstein', 'Marie Curie'],\
  name='name') ❶
categories = pd.Series(['Physics', 'Chemistry'],\
  name='category')

df = pd.concat([names, categories], axis=1) ❷

df.head()
Out:
               name     category
0   Albert Einstein      Physics
1       Marie Curie    Chemistry
2  William Faulkner   Literature
```

❶ Create our DataFrame columns, using the name argument, to provide a header label.

❷ Concatenate the two Series using the axis argument of 1 to indicate that the Series are columns.

Along with the many ways to create DataFrames from files and databases just discussed, you should now have a solid grounding in getting data into and out of DataFrames.

Panels

Pandas provides a Panel (*http://pandas.pydata.org/pandas-docs/ stable/generated/pandas.Panel.html*) class, which is essentially a container for multiple DataFrames. In the same way that DataFrames function as dictionaries of Series, the Panel functions as a dictionary of DataFrames.

The Panel adds another dimension to the DataFrame, making it a three-dimensional container. So in addition to the index and columns of a DataFrame, it has an extra axis used to specify one of its DataFrames.

We can create a `Panel` by providing it with a dictionary of `Data Frames`:

```
In [0]: df1 = pd.DataFrame({'foo': [1, 2, 3],
'bar':['a', 'b', 'c']})

In [1]: df2 = pd.DataFrame({'baz': [7, 8, 9, 11],
'qux':['p', 'q', 'r', 't']})

In [2]: pn = pd.Panel({'item1':df1, 'item2':df2})
In [3]: pn
Out[3]:
<class 'pandas.core.panel.Panel'>
Dimensions: 2 (items) x 4 (major_axis) x 4 (minor_axis) ❶
Items axis: item1 to item2
Major_axis axis: 0 to 3
Minor_axis axis: bar to qux
```

❶ The `Panel`'s major and minor axes (rows and columns) have expanded to accommodate the two `DataFrames`.

The `Panel` items are expanded where necessary to accommodate missing rows or columns, with `NaN` added as padding. You can select them by name using square brackets:

```
panel['item1']
Out[66]:
   bar  baz  foo  qux
0    a  NaN    1  NaN
1    b  NaN    2  NaN
2    c  NaN    3  NaN
3  NaN  NaN  NaN  NaN
```

I think it's fair to say `Panel`s are a less used aspect of Pandas, but you may well run into them when dealing with Excel, where the multiple sheets in a workbook map nicely to multiple `DataFrames` in a `Panel`.

Summary

This chapter laid a foundation for the two Pandas-based chapters to come. The core concepts of Pandas—the `DataFrame`, `Index`, and `Ser ies`—were discussed and we saw why Pandas is such a good fit with the type of real-world data that data visualizers deal with, extending the NumPy `ndarray` by allowing the storage of heterogeneous data and adding a powerful indexing system.

With Pandas' core data structures under our belts, the next few chapters will show you how to use them to clean and process your dataset of Nobel Prize winners, extending your knowledge of the Pandas toolkit and showing you how to go about applying it in a data visualization context.

Now that we know how to get data into and out of a DataFrame, it's time to see what Pandas can do with it. We'll first see how to give your data a clean bill of health, discovering and fixing anomalies such as duplicate rows, missing fields, and corrupted data.

## CHAPTER 9

Cleaning Data with Pandas

The previous two chapters introduced Pandas and NumPy, the Numeric Python library it extends. Armed with basic Pandas know-how, we're ready to start the cleaning stage of our toolchain, aiming to find and eliminate the dirty data in our scraped dataset (see Chapter 6). This chapter will also extend your Pandas knowledge, introducing new methods in a working context.

In Chapter 8, we covered the core components of Pandas: the Data Frame, a programmatic spreadsheet capable of dealing with the many different datatypes found in the real world, and its building block, the Series, a heterogeneous extension of NumPy's homogeneous ndarray. We also covered how to read from and write to different datastores, including JSON, CSV files, MongoDB, and SQL databases. Now we'll start to put Pandas through its paces showing how it can be used to clean dirty data. I'll introduce the key elements of data cleaning using our dirty Nobel Prize dataset as an example.

I'll take it slowly, introducing key Pandas concepts in a working environment. Let's first establish why cleaning data is such an important part of a data visualizer's work.

Coming Clean About Dirty Data

I think it's fair to say that most people entering the field of data visualization underestimate, often by a fairly large factor, the amount of time they're going to spend trying to make their data presentable. The fact is that getting clean datasets that are a pleasure to transform into cool visualizations could well take over half your time. Data in the wild is very rarely pristine, often bearing the sticky paw prints of mistaken manual data entry, missing whole fields due to oversight or parsing errors and/or mixed datetime formats.

For this book, and to pose a properly meaty challenge, our Nobel Prize dataset has been scraped from Wikipedia, a manually edited website with fairly informal guidelines. In this sense, the data is bound to be dirty—humans make mistakes even when the environment is a good deal more forgiving. But even data from the official APIs of—for example, large social media sites—is often flawed, with missing or incomplete fields, scar tissue from countless changes to the data schemas, deliberate misentry, and the like.

So cleaning data is a fundamental part of the job of a data visualizer, stealing time from all the cool stuff you'd rather be doing—which is an excellent reason to get really good at it and free up that drudge time for more meaningful pursuits. And a large part of getting good at cleaning data is choosing the right toolset, which is where Pandas comes in. It's a great way to slice and dice even fairly large datasets,[1] and being comfortable with it could save you a lot of time. That is where this chapter comes in.

To recap, scraping the Nobel data from Wikipedia using Python's Scrapy library (see Chapter 6) produced an array of JSON objects of the form:

```
{
  "category": "Physics",
  "name": "Albert Einstein",
  "gender": "male",
  "place_of_birth": "Ulm , Baden-W\u00fcrttemberg ,
    German Empire",
  "date_of_death": "1955-04-18",
  ...
}
```

The job of this chapter is to turn that array into as clean a data source as possible before we explore it with Pandas in the next chapter.

---

[1] *Large* is a very relative term, but Pandas will take pretty much whatever will fit in your computer's RAM memory, which is where DataFrames live.

There are many forms of dirty data, most commonly:

- Duplicate entries/rows
- Missing fields
- Misaligned rows
- Corrupted fields
- Mixed datatypes in a column

We'll now probe our Nobel Prize data for these kinds of anomalies.

First we need to load our JSON data into a DataFrame, as shown in the previous chapter (see "Creating and Saving DataFrames" on page 214). We can open the JSON data file directly:

```
import pandas as pd

df = pd.read_json(open('data/nobel_winners_full.json'))
```

But, by preference, using our MongoDB database is cleaner and cuts down on the file management. Let's use the utility function we defined in "MongoDB" on page 221 to load our freshly scraped collection of Nobel Prize winners into a DataFrame:

```
df = mongo_to_dataframe('nobel_prize', 'winners')  ❶
```

❶ Create a DataFrame with the entire collection of winners from our nobel_prize database.

Now that we've got our dirty scraped data into a DataFrame, let's get a broad overview of what we have.

Inspecting the Data

The Pandas DataFrame has a number of methods and properties that give a quick overview of the data contained within. The most general is info, which gives a neat summary of the number of data entries by column:

```
df.info()
<class 'pandas.core.frame.DataFrame'>
Int64Index: 1052 entries, 0 to 1051
Data columns (total 12 columns):
born_in          1052 non-null object
category         1052 non-null object
date_of_birth    1044 non-null object
date_of_death    1044 non-null object
```

```
gender            1040 non-null object # missing fields
link              1052 non-null object
name              1052 non-null object
country           1052 non-null object
place_of_birth    1044 non-null object
place_of_death    1044 non-null object
text              1052 non-null object
year              1052 non-null int64
dtypes: int64(1), object(11)
memory usage: 106.8 KB
```

You can see that some fields are missing entries. For example, although there are 1,052 rows in our `DataFrame`, there are only 1,040 gender attributes. Note also the handy `memory_usage`—Pandas `Data Frames` are held in RAM so as datasets increase in size, this number gives a nice indication of how close we are to our machine-specific memory limits.

`DataFrame`'s `describe` method gives a handy statistical summary of relevant columns.

```
df.describe()
Out:
             year
count  1052.000000
mean   1968.729087
std      33.155829
min    1809.000000
25%    1947.000000
50%    1975.000000
75%    1996.000000
max    2014.000000
```

As you can see, by default only numerical columns are described. Already we can see an error in the data, the minimum year being 1809, which is impossible when the first Nobel was awarded in 1901.

`describe` takes an `include` parameter that allows us to specify the column datatypes (`dtypes`) to be assessed. Other than year, the columns in our Nobel Prize dataset are all objects, which are Pandas' default, catch-all `dtype`, capable of representing any numbers, strings, data times, and more. Example 9-1 shows how to get their stats.

Example 9-1. Describing the DataFrame

```
In [140]: df.describe(include=['object']) ❶
Out[140]:
          born_in  category date_of_birth date_of_death gender  \
count        1052      1052          1044          1044   1040
unique         40         7           853           563      2
top               Physio..    9 May 1947                  male
freq          910       250             4           362    983

                         link           name  \
count                    1052           1052
unique                    893            998
top      http://eg/wiki/...     Daniel Kahneman
freq                        4              2

           country place_of_birth place_of_death  \
count         1052           1044           1044
unique          59            735            410
top    United States
freq           350             29            409
...
```

❶ The `include` argument is a list (or single item) of columnar
   dtypes to summarize.

There's quite a lot of useful information to be gleaned from the output of Example 9-1, such as that there are 59 unique nationalities
with the United States, at 350, being the largest group.

One interesting tidbit is that of 1,044 recorded dates of birth, only
853 are unique, which could mean any number of things. Possibly
some auspicious days saw the birth of more than one laureate or,
wearing our data-cleaning hats, it's more likely that there are some
duplicated winners or that some dates are wrong or have only recorded the year. The duplicated winners hypothesis is confirmed by the
observation that of 1,052 name counts, only 998 are unique. Now
there have been a few multiple winners but not enough to account
for 54 duplicates.

DataFrame's head and tail methods provide another easy way to get
a quick feel for the data. By default, they display the top or bottom
five rows, but we can set that number by passing an integer as the
first argument. Example 9-2 shows the result of using head with our
Nobel DataFrame.

Example 9-2. Sampling the first five DataFrame rows

```
df.head()
Out:
                        born_in                   category   date_of_bi..
0                                  Physiology or Medicine  8 October 1..
1  Bosnia and Herzegovina                     Literature  9 October 1..❶
2  Bosnia and Herzegovina                      Chemistry     July 23, 1..
3                                                   Peace              ..
4                                                   Peace     26 July 1..


      date_of_death gender                                              ..
0   24 March 2002   male   http://en.wikipedia.org/wiki/C%C3%A..
1   13 March 1975   male         http://en.wikipedia.org/wi..
2      1998-01-07   male       http://en.wikipedia.org/wiki/Vl..❷
3            NaN   None   http://en.wikipedia.org/wiki/Institu..
4  6 October 1912   male   http://en.wikipedia.org/wiki/Auguste..


                                name country  \
0                    César Milstein   Argentina
1                       Ivo Andric *                    ❶
2                    Vladimir Prelog *
3  Institut de Droit International     Belgium
4               Auguste Beernaert     Belgium
```

❶   These rows have an entry for the `born_in` field and an asterisk by their name.

❷   The `date_of_death` field has a different time format than the other rows.

The first five winners in Example 9-2 show a couple of useful things. First we see the names in rows 1 and 2 are marked by an asterisk and have an entry in the `born_in` field ❶. Second, note that row 2 has a different time format for `date_of_death` than the others, and that there are both month-day and day-month time formats in the `date_of_birth` field ❷. This kind of inconsistency is a perennial problem for human-edited data, particularly dates and times. We'll see how to fix it with Pandas later.

Example 9-1 gives an object count of 1,052 for the `born_in` field, indicating no empty fields, but `head` shows only rows 1 and 2 have content. This suggests that the missing fields are an empty string or space, both of which count as data to Pandas. Let's change them to a noncounted `NaN`, which will make more sense of the numbers. But first we're going to need a little primer in Pandas data selection.

Indices and Pandas Data Selection

Before beginning to clean our data, let's do a quick recap of basic Pandas data selection, using the Nobel Prize dataset as an example.

Pandas indexes by rows and columns. Usually column indices are specified by the data file, SQL table, and so on, but, as shown in the last chapter, we can set or override these when the `DataFrame` is created by using the `names` argument to pass a list of column names. The columns index is accessible as a `DataFrame` property:

```
# Our Nobel dataset's columns
df.columns
Out: Index([u'born_in', u'category', u'date_of_birth',
...
          u'place_of_death', u'text', u'year'], dtype='object')
```

By default, Pandas specifies a zero-base integer index for the rows, but we can override this by passing a list in the `index` parameter on creation of the `DataFrame` or afterward by setting the `index` property directly. More often we want to use one or more[2] of the `DataFrame`'s columns as an index. We can do this using the `set_index` method. If you want to return to the default index, you can use the `reset_index` method, as shown in Example 9-3.

Example 9-3. Setting the DataFrame's index

```
# set the name field as index
df = df.set_index('name') ❶
df.head(2)
Out:
                              born_in                 category  \
name ❷
César Milstein                               Physiology or Medicine
Ivo Andric *    Bosnia and Herzegovina                  Literature
...

df.reset_index(inplace=True) ❸

df.head(2)
Out:
              name              born_in                 category  \
```

---

2 Pandas supports multiple indices using the `MultiIndex` object. This provides a very powerful way of refining higher-dimensional data. Check out the details in the Pandas documentation (*http://pandas.pydata.org/pandas-docs/stable/advanced.html#advanced*).

```
0   César Milstein                Physiology or Medicine  ❹
1    Ivo Andric *  Bosnia and Herzegovina        Literature
```

❶ Sets the frame's index to its name column. Set the result back to df.

❷ The rows are now indexed by name.

❸ Resets the index to its integer. Note that we change it in place this time.

❹ The index is now by integer position.

 There are two ways to change a Pandas Data Frame or Series: by altering the data in place or by assigning a copy. There is no guarantee that in place is faster, plus method-chaining requires that the operation return a changed object. Generally, I use the df = df.foo(…) form, but most mutating methods have an inplace argument df.foo(…, inplace=True).

Now that we understand the row-columnar indexing system, let's start selecting slices of the DataFrame.

We can select a column of the DataFrame by dot notation (where no spaces or special characters are in the name) or square-bracket notation. Let's take a look at that born_in column:

```
bi_col = df.born_in # or bi = df['born_in']
bi_col
Out:
0
1       Bosnia and Herzegovina
2       Bosnia and Herzegovina
3
...
1051
Name: born_in, Length: 1052, dtype: object

type(bi_col)
Out: pandas.core.series.Series
```

Note that the column selection returns a Pandas Series, with the DataFrame indexing preserved.

DataFrames and Series share the same methods for accessing rows/ members. iloc selects by integer position, loc selects by label, and ix selects by label with an positional integer fallback. One gotcha with ix happens if we use an alternative integer index. In this case, only label-based access is supported and explicit use of iloc is needed to specify position.

```
# access the first row
df.iloc[0] # or df.ix[0]
Out:
name                          César Milstein
born_in
category                      Physiology or Medicine
...

# set the index to 'name' and access by name-label
df.set_index('name', inplace=True)
df.loc['Albert Einstein'] # or df.ix['Albert Einstein']
Out:
                 born_in category date_of_birth date_of_death...
Albert Einstein          Physics  1879-03-14    1955-04-18...
...
```

Selecting Multiple Rows

Standard Python array slicing can be used with a DataFrame to select multiple rows:

```
# select the first 10 rows
df[0:10]
Out:
                      born_in              category   date_of_b..
0                             Physiology or Medicine  8 October ..
1  Bosnia and Herzegovina                 Literature  9 October ..
...
9                                             Peace      1910-0..
# select the last four rows
df[-4:]
Out:
       born_in            category     date_of_birth date_..
1048                         Peace    November 1, 1878  May..
1049   Physiology or Medicine         1887-04-10        19..
1050                     Chemistry    1906-9-6          1..
1051                         Peace    November 26, 1931     ..
```

The standard way to select multiple rows based on a conditional expression (e.g., is the value of the column value greater than x) is to create a Boolean mask and use it in a selector. Let's find all the

Nobel Prize winners after the year 2000. First we create a mask by performing a Boolean expression on each of the rows:

```
mask = df.year > 2000 ❶
mask
Out:
0       False
1       False
...
13      True
...
1047    True
1048    False
...
Name: year, Length: 1052, dtype: bool
```

❶ `True` for all rows where the `year` field is greater than 2000.

The resulting Boolean mask shares our `DataFrame`'s index and can be used to select all `True` rows:

```
mask = df.year > 2000
winners_since_2000 = df[mask] ❶
winners_since_2000.count()
Out:
...
year                202 # number of winners since 2000
dtype: int64

winners_since_2000.head()
Out:
...
                                                   text  year
13                    François Englert , Physics, 2013  2013
32         Christopher A. Pissarides , Economics, 2010  2010
66                         Kofi Annan , Peace, 2001     2001
87                 Riccardo Giacconi *, Physics, 2002  2002
88    Mario Capecchi *, Physiology or Medicine, 2007  2007
```

❶ This will return a `DataFrame` containing only those rows where the Boolean `mask` array is `True`.

Boolean masking is a very powerful technique capable of selecting any subset of the data you need. I recommend setting a few targets to practice constructing the right Boolean expressions. Generally, we dispense with the intermediate mask creation:

```
winners_since_2000 = df[df.year > 2000]
```

Now that we can select individual and multiple rows by slicing or using a Boolean mask, in the next sections we'll see how we can change our DataFrame, purging it of dirty data as we go.

Cleaning the Data

Now that we know how to access our data, let's see how we can change it for the better, starting with what looks like empty born_in fields we saw in Example 9-2. If we look at the count of the born_in columns, it doesn't show any missing rows, which it would were any fields missing or NaN (not a number):

```
In [0]: df.born_in.describe()
Out[0]:
count     1052
unique      40
top
freq       910
Name: born_in, dtype: object
```

Finding Mixed Types

Note that Pandas stores all string-like data using the dtype object. A cursory inspection suggests that the column is a mixture of empty and country-name strings. We can quickly check that all the column members are Unicode by mapping the Python type (*https:// docs.python.org/2/library/functions.html#type*) function to all members using the apply method and then making a set of the resulting list of column members by type:

```
In [1]: set(df.born_in.apply(type))
Out[1]: {unicode}
```

This shows that all of the born_in column members are of type uni code. Now let's replace any empty strings with an empty field.

Replacing Strings

We want to replace these empty strings with a NaN, to prevent them being counted.[3] The Pandas replace method is tailor-made for this and can be applied to the whole DataFrame or individual Series:

---

3 By default, Pandas uses NumPy's NaN (not a number) float to designate missing values.

```
bi_col.replace('', np.nan, inplace=True)
bi_col
Out:
0                          NaN ❶
1      Bosnia and Herzegovina
2      Bosnia and Herzegovina
3                          NaN
...

bi_col.count()
Out: 142 ❷
```

❶ Our empty ' ' strings have been replaced with NumPy's NaN.

❷ Unlike the empty strings, the NaN fields are discounted.

After replacing the empty strings with NaNs, we get a true count of 142 for the born_in field.

Let's replace all empty strings in our DataFrame with discounted NaNs:

```
df.replace('', np.nan, inplace=True)
```

Pandas allows sophisticated replacement of strings (and other objects) in columns (e.g., allowing you to craft regex expressions (*https://en.wikipedia.org/wiki/Regular_expression*), which are applied to whole Series, typically DataFrame columns). Let's look at a little example, using the asterisk-marked names in our Nobel Prize Data Frame.

Example 9-2 showed that some of our Nobel Prize names are marked with an asterisk, denoting that these winners are recorded by country of birth, not country at the time of winning the prize:

```
df.head()
Out:
...

                                  name country  \
0                      César Milstein    Argentina
1                         Ivo Andric *
2                     Vladimir Prelog *
3  Institut de Droit International       Belgium
4                    Auguste Beernaert    Belgium
```

Let's set ourselves the task of cleaning up those names by removing the asterisks and stripping any remaining whitespace.

Pandas Series have a handy str member, which provides a number of useful string methods to be performed on the array. Let's use it to check how many asterisked names we have:

```
df[df.name.str.contains('\*')]['name'] ❶
Out:
1               Ivo Andric *
2           Vladimir Prelog *
...
1041        John Warcup Cornforth *
1046        Elizabeth H. Blackburn *
Name: name, Length: 142, dtype: object ❷
```

❶ We use str's contains method on the name column. Note that we have to escape the asterisk ('*') as this is a regex string. The Boolean mask is then applied to our Nobel Prize DataFrame and the resulting names listed.

❷ 142 of our 1,052 rows have a name containing *.

To clean up the names, let's replace the asterisks with an empty string and strip any whitespace from the resulting names:

```
df.name = df.name.str.replace('*', '') ❶
# strip the whitespace from the names
df.name = df.name.str.strip()
```

❶ Removes all asterisks in the name fields and return the result to the DataFrame.

A quick check shows that the names are now clean:

```
df[df.name.str.contains('\*')]
Out:
Empty DataFrame
```

Pandas Series have an impressive number of string-handling functions, enabling you to search and adapt your string columns. You can find a full list of these in the API docs (*http://pandas.pydata.org/pandas-docs/stable/api.html#string-handling*).

Removing Rows

To recap, the 142 winners with born_in fields are duplicates, having an entry in the Wikipedia by both the country they were born in and their country when given the prize. Although the former could form the basis of an interesting visualization,[4] for our visualization we want each individual prize represented once only and so need to remove these from our DataFrame.

We want to create a new DataFrame using only those rows with a NaN born_in field. You might naively assume that a conditional expression comparing the born_in field to NaN would work here, but by definition[5] NaN boolean comparisons always return False:

```
np.nan == np.nan
Out: False
```

As a result, Pandas provides the dedicated isnull method to check for discounted (null) fields:

```
df = df[df.born_in.isnull()] ❶
df.count()
Out:
born_in          0 # all entries now empty
category       910
...
dtype: int64
```

❶ isnull produces a Boolean mask with True for all rows with an empty born_in field.

The born_in column is no longer of use, so let's remove it:[6]

```
df = df.drop('born_in', axis=1) ❶
```

❶ drop takes a single label or index (or list of same) as a first argument and an axis argument to indicate row (0 and default) or column (1) index.

Finding Duplicates

Now, a quick Internet search shows that 889 people and organizations have received the Nobel Prize up to 2014. With 910 remaining rows, we still have a few duplicates or anomalies to account for.

---

4 One interesting visualization might be charting the migration of Nobel Prize winners from their homeland.

5 See IEEE 754 and *http://en.wikipedia.org/wiki/NaN*.

6 As you'll see in the next chapter, the born_in fields contain some interesting information about the movements of Nobel Prize winners. We'll keep a copy of them for that purpose.

Pandas has a handy `duplicated` method for finding matching rows. This matches by column name or list of column names. Let's get the list of all duplicates by name:

```
dupes_by_name = df[df.duplicated('name')]  ❶
dupes_by_name.count()
Out:
...
year               46
dtype: int64
```

❶ `duplicated` returns a Boolean array with `True` for the first occurrence of any rows with the same `name` field.

Now, a few people have won the Nobel Prize more than once but not 46, which means 40-odd winners are duplicated. Given that the Wikipedia page we scraped listed prize winners by country, the best bet is winners being "claimed" by more than one country.

Let's look at some of the ways we can find duplicates by name in our Nobel Prize `DataFrame`. Some of these are pretty inefficient, but it's a nice way to demonstrate a few Pandas functions.

By default, `duplicated` indicates all duplicates after the first occurrence, but it has a `take_last` option to prioritize the last occurrence. By combining these two using a Boolean *or* (|), we can get the full list of duplicates.

```
all_dupes = df[df.duplicated('name')\
                | df.duplicated('name', keep='last')]
all_dupes.count()
Out:
...
year               92
dtype: int64
```

We could also get all the duplicates by testing whether our `Data Frame` rows have a name in the list of duplicate names. Pandas has a handy `isin` method for this.

```
all_dupes = df[df.name.isin(dupes_by_name.name)]  ❶
all_dupes.count()
Out:
...
year               92
dtype: int64
```

❶ `dupes_by_name.name` is a column `Series` containing all the duplicated names.

We can also find all duplicates by using Pandas' powerful `groupby` method, which groups our `DataFrame`'s rows by column or list of columns. It returns a list of key-value pairs with the column value(s) as key and list of rows as values:

```
for name, rows in df.groupby('name'): ❶
    print('name: %s, number of rows: %d'%(name, len(rows)))

name: A. Michael Spence, number of rows: 1
name: Aage Bohr, number of rows: 1
name: Aaron Ciechanover, number of rows: 1
...
```

❶ `groupby` returns an iterator of (group name, group) tuples.

In order to get all duplicate rows, we merely need to check the length of the list of rows returned by key. Anything greater than one has name duplicates. Here we use Pandas' `concat` method, which takes a list of row lists and creates a `DataFrame` with all the duplicated rows. A Python list constructor is used to filter for groups with more than one row:

```
pd.concat([g for _,g in df.groupby('name')\ ❶
                if len(g) > 1])['name']

Out:
121          Aaron Klug
131          Aaron Klug
615       Albert Einstein
844       Albert Einstein
...
489       Yoichiro Nambu
773       Yoichiro Nambu
Name: name, Length: 92, dtype: object
```

❶ Create a Python list by filtering the `name` row groups for those with more than one row (i.e., duplicated names).

Different paths to the same goal

With a large library like Pandas, there are usually a number of ways to achieve the same thing. With small datasets like our Nobel Prize winners, any one will do, but for large datasets there could be significant performance implications. Just because Pandas will do what you ask doesn't mean it's necessarily efficient. With a lot of complex data manipulation going on behind the scenes, it's a good idea to be prepared to be flexible and alert to inefficient approaches.

Sorting Data

Now that we have our `all_dupes` DataFrame, with all duplicated rows by name, let's use it to demonstrate Pandas' sort method.

Pandas provides a sophisticated `sort` method for the `DataFrame` and `Series` classes, capable of sorting on multiple column names.

```
df2 = pd.DataFrame(\
    {'name':['zak', 'alice', 'bob', 'mike', 'bob', 'bob'],\
     'score':[4, 3, 5, 2, 3, 7]})
df2.sort_values(['name', 'score'],\  ❶
    ascending=[1,0])  ❷
```

```
Out:
     name  score
1    alice     3
5      bob     7
2      bob     5
4      bob     3
3     mike     2
0      zak     4
```

❶ Sorts the `DataFrame` first by name, then by score within those subgroups. Older Pandas versions use `sort`, now deprecated.

❷ Sorts the names in alphabetical ascending order; sorts scores from high to low.

Let's sort the DataFrame of all_dupes by name and then look at the name, country, and year columns:

```
In [306]: all_dupes.sort_values('name')\
    [['name', 'country', 'year']]
Out[306]:
                          name          country  year
121                  Aaron Klug     South Africa  1982
131                  Aaron Klug   United Kingdom  1982
615             Albert Einstein      Switzerland  1921
844             Albert Einstein          Germany  1921
...
910                 Marie Curie           France  1903
919                 Marie Curie           France  1911
706     Marie Skłodowska-Curie           Poland  1903
709     Marie Skłodowska-Curie           Poland  1911
...
650               Ragnar Granit           Sweden  1967
960               Ragnar Granit          Finland  1809
...
396               Sidney Altman    United States  1990
995               Sidney Altman           Canada  1989
...
[92 rows x 3 columns]
```

This output shows that, as expected, some winners have been attributed twice for the same year with different countries. It also reveals a few other anomalies. Although Marie Curie did win a Nobel Prize twice, she's included here with both French and Polish nationalities.[7] The fairest thing here is to split the spoils between Poland and France while settling on the single compound surname. We have also found our anomalous year of 1809 at row 960. Sidney Altman is both duplicated and given the wrong year of 1990.

Removing Duplicates

Let's go about removing the duplicates we just identified and start compiling a little cleaning function.

---

7 While France was Curie's adopted country, she retained Polish citizenship and named her first discovered radioactive isotope *polonium* after her home country.

Views Versus Copies

It's very important when working with Pandas to be clear whether you are altering a view or copy of your DataFrame, Series, and so on. The following seems like a natural way to change the country field of a row (Marie Curie's) but gives a potentially confusing warning:

```
df['country'][709] = 'France' ❶
-c:1: SettingWithCopyWarning:
A value is trying to be set on a copy of a slice from a
DataFrame

See the caveats in the documentation:
    http://pandas.pydata.org/pandas-docs/stable/...
```

❶ Set the country of row 709, Marie Curie, from Poland to France.

This is all the more confusing when you find that it has worked as expected:

```
df['country'][709]
Out: 'France'
```

It turns out that such *chained* operations are discouraged by the Pandas devs because it's easy to unintentionally alter a copy of the datatype, not the original (view).[8]

These warnings[9] are there to encourage best practice, which is to use the ix (or the more specific loc and iloc) method:

```
df.ix[709, 'country'] = 'France'
```

---

8 Some users dismiss such warnings as nannying paranoia. See the discussion on Stack Overflow (*http://stackoverflow.com/questions/20625582/how-to-deal-with-this-pandas-warning*).

9 They can be turned off with pd.options.mode.chained_assignment = None # default=*warn*.

Changing rows by numeric index is fine if you know your dataset is stable and don't anticipate running any of your cleaning scripts again. But if, as in the case of our scraped Nobel Prize data, you may want to run the same cleaning script on an updated dataset, it's much better to use stable indicators (i.e., grab the row with name Marie Curie and year 1911, not index 919).

A more robust way of changing the country of a specific row is to use stable column values to select the row rather than its index. So to change Marie Curie's 1911 prize country to France, we can use a Boolean mask with the loc method to select a row and then set its country column to France. Note that we need to specify the Unicode to include the Polish ł.

```
df.loc[(df.name == u'Marie Sk\u0142odowska-Curie') &\
    (df.year == 1911), 'country'] = 'France'
```

As well as changing Marie Curie's country, we want to remove or drop some rows from our DataFrame, based on column values. There are two ways we can do this, firstly by using the DataFrame's drop method, which takes a list of index labels, or by creating a new DataFrame with a Boolean mask that filters the rows we want to drop. If we use drop, we can use the inplace argument to change the existing DataFrame.

In the following code, we drop our duplicate Sidney Altman row by creating a DataFrame with the single row we want (remember, index labels are preserved) and passing that index to the drop method and changing the DataFrame in place:

```
df.drop(df[(df.name == 'Sidney Altman') &\
    (df.year == 1990)].index,
    inplace=True)
```

Another way to remove the row is to use the same Boolean mask with a logical not (~) to create a new DataFrame with all rows except the one(s) we're selecting:

```
df = df[~((df.name == 'Sidney Altman') & (df.year == 1990))]
```

Let's add this change and all current modifications to a clean_data method:

```
def clean_data(df):
    df = df.replace('', np.nan)
```

```
df = df[df.born_in.isnull()]
df = df.drop('born_in', axis=1)
df.drop(df[df.year == 1809].index, inplace=True)
df = df[~(df.name == 'Marie Curie')]
df.loc[(df.name == u'Marie Sk\u0142odowska-Curie') &\
       (df.year == 1911), 'country'] = 'France'
df = df[~((df.name == 'Sidney Altman') &\
  (df.year == 1990))]
return df
```

We now have a mix of valid duplicates (those few multiple Nobel Prize winners) and those with dual country. For the purposes of our visualization, we want each prize to count only once so have to discard half the dual-country prizes. The easiest way is to use the `dupli cated` method, but because we collected the winners alphabetically by country, this would favor those nationalities with first letters earlier in the alphabet. Short of a fair amount of research and debate, the fairest way seems to pick one out at random and discard it. There are various ways to do this, but the simplest is to randomize the order of the rows before using `drop_duplicates`, a Pandas method that drops all duplicated rows after the first encountered or, with the `take_last` argument set to `True`, all before the last.

NumPy has a number of very useful methods in its `random` module, of which `permutation` is perfect for randomizing the row index. This method takes an array (or Pandas index) of values and shuffles them. We can then use the `DataFrame` `reindex` method to apply the shuffled result. Note that we drop those rows sharing both name and year, which will preserve the legitimate double winners with different years for their prizes.

```
df = df.reindex(np.random.permutation(df.index))   ❶
df = df.drop_duplicates(['name', 'year'])           ❷
df = df.sort_index()                                ❸
df.count()
Out:
...
year               865
dtype: int64
```

❶   Create a shuffled version of df's index and reindex df with it.

❷   Drop all duplicates sharing name and year.

❸   Return the index to sorted-by-integer position.

If our data wrangling has been successful, we should have only valid duplicates left, those vaunted double-prize winners. Let's list the remaining duplicates to check:

```
In : df[df.duplicated('name') |
         df.duplicated('name', keep='last')]\ ❶
     .sort_values(by='name')\
     [['name', 'country', 'year', 'category']]
Out:
                      name       country  year  category
548      Frederick Sanger  United Kingdom  1958  Chemistry
580      Frederick Sanger  United Kingdom  1980  Chemistry
292          John Bardeen   United States  1956    Physics
326          John Bardeen   United States  1972    Physics
285       Linus C. Pauling  United States  1954  Chemistry
309       Linus C. Pauling  United States  1962      Peace
706  Marie Skłodowska-Curie          Poland  1903    Physics
709  Marie Skłodowska-Curie          France  1911  Chemistry
```

❶ We combine duplicates from the first with the last to get them all. If using an older version of Pandas, you may need to use the argument take_last=True.

A quick Internet check shows that we have the correct four double-prize winners.

Assuming we've caught the unwanted duplicates,[10] let's move on to other "dirty" aspects of the data.

Dealing with Missing Fields

Let's see where we stand as far as *null* fields are concerned by counting our DataFrame:

```
df.count()
Out:
category        864  # missing field
date_of_birth   857
date_of_death   566
gender          858  # seven missing genders
link            865
name            865
country         865
place_of_birth  831
place_of_death  524
text            865
```

---

10 Depending on the dataset, the cleaning phase is unlikely to catch all transgressors.

```
year                 865
dtype: int64
```

We appear to be missing a `category` field, which suggests a data entry mistake. If you remember, while scraping our Nobel Prize data we checked the category against a valid list (see Example 6-3). One of them appears to have failed this check. Let's find out which one it is by grabbing the row where the category field is null and showing its name and text columns:

```
df[df.category.isnull()][['name', 'text']]
Out:
                name                          text
922  Alexis Carrel    Alexis Carrel , Medicine, 1912
```

We saved the original link text for our winners and, as you can see, Alexis Carrel was listed as winning the Nobel prize for `Medicine`, when it should have been `Physiology or Medicine`. Let's correct that now:

```
...
df.ix[df.name == 'Alexis Carrel', 'category'] =\
  'Physiology or Medicine'
```

We are also missing `gender` for seven winners. Let's list them:

```
df[df.gender.isnull()]['name']
Out:
3                      Institut de Droit International
156                       Friends Service Council
574                       Amnesty International
650                              Ragnar Granit
947                       Médecins Sans Frontières
1000   Pugwash Conferences on Science and World Affairs
1033              International Atomic Energy Agency
Name: name, dtype: object
```

With the exception of Ragnar Granit, all these are genderless (missing person data) institutions. The focus of our visualization is on individual winners, so we'll remove these while establishing Ragnar Granit's gender:

```
...
def clean_data(df):
    ...
    df.ix[df.name == 'Ragnar Granit', 'gender'] = 'male'
    df = df[df.gender.notnull()] # remove genderless entries
```

Let's see where those changes leave us by performing another count on our `DataFrame`:

```
df.count()
Out:
category        858
date_of_birth   857 # missing field
...
year            858
dtype: int64
```

Having removed all the institutions, all entries should have at least a
date of birth. Let's find the missing entry and fix it:

```
df[df.date_of_birth.isnull()]['name']
Out:
782   Hiroshi Amano
Name: name, dtype: object
```

Probably because Hiroshi Amano is a very recent (2014) winner, his
date of birth was not available to be scraped. A quick web search
establishes Amano's date of birth, which we add to the DataFrame by
hand:

```
...
    df.ix[df.name == 'Hiroshi Amano', 'date_of_birth'] =\
    '11 September 1960'
```

We now have 858 individual winners. Let's do a final count to see
where we stand:

```
df.count()
Out:
category        858
date_of_birth   858
date_of_death   566
gender          858
link            858
name            858
country         858
place_of_birth  831
place_of_death  524
text            858
year            858
dtype: int64
```

The key fields of category, date_of_birth, gender, country, and
year are all filled and there's a healthy amount of data in the remaining stats. All in all, there's enough clean data to form the basis for a
rich visualization.

Now let's put on the finishing touches by making our temporal fields
more usable.

Dealing with Times and Dates

Currently the `date_of_birth` and `date_of_death` fields are represented by strings. As we've seen, Wikipedia's informal editing guidelines have led to a number of different time formats. Our original `DataFrame` shows an impressive variety of formats in the first 10 entries:

```
df[['name', 'date_of_birth']]
Out[14]:
                        name        date_of_birth
0            César Milstein        8 October 1927
...
2          Vladimir Prelog *        July 23, 1906
...
9             Georges Pire          1910-02-10
...
```

In order to compare the date fields (for example, subtracting the prize *year* from *date of birth* to give the winners' ages), we need to get them into a format that allows such operations. Unsurprisingly, Pandas is good with parsing messy dates and times, converting them by default into the NumPy `datetime64` object, which has a slew of useful methods and operators.

Converting a time column to `datetime64`, we use Pandas' `to_date time` method:

```
pd.to_datetime(df.date_of_birth, errors='raise') ❶
Out:
0     1927-10-08
4     1829-07-26
...
1050    1906-09-06
1051    1931-11-26
Name: date_of_birth, Length: 858, dtype: datetime64[ns]
```

❶ errors' default is `ignore`, but we want them flagged.

By default `to_datetime` ignores errors, but here we want to know if Pandas has been unable to parse a `date_of_birth`, giving us the opportunity to fix it manually. Thankfully, the conversion passes without error.

Running `to_datetime` on the `date_of_birth` field raises a `ValueError` and an unhelpful one at that, giving no indication of the entry that triggered it.

```
In [143]: pd.to_datetime(df.date_of_death, errors='raise')
-----------------------------------------------------------------
ValueError                        Traceback (most recent call last)
...
   301     if arg is None:

ValueError: month must be in 1..12
```

One naive way to find the bad dates would be to iterate through our rows of data, and catch and display any errors. Pandas has a handy iterrows method that provides a row iterator. Combined with a Python try-except block, this successfully finds our problem date fields.

```
for i,row in df.iterrows():
    try:
        pd.to_datetime(row.date_of_death, errors='raise') ❶
    except:
        print '%s(%s, %d)'%(row.date_of_death.ljust(30) ❷
                            row['name'], i) ❸
```

❶ Run to_datetime on the individual row and catch any errors.

❷ We left-justify the date of death in a text column of width 30.

❸ Pandas rows have a masking Name property, so we use string-key access with [name].

This lists the offending rows:

```
1968-23-07              (Henry Hallett Dale, 150)
May 30, 2011 (aged 89)  (Rosalyn Yalow, 349)
living                  (David Trimble, 581)
Diederik Korteweg       (Johannes Diderik van der Waals, 746)
living                  (Shirin Ebadi, 809)
living                  (Rigoberta Menchú, 833)
1 February 1976, age 74 (Werner Karl Heisenberg, 858)
```

which is a good demonstration of the kind of data errors you get with collaborative editing.

Although the last method works, whenever you find yourself iterating through rows of a Pandas DataFrame, you should pause for a second and try to find a better way, one that exploits the multirow array handling that is a fundamental aspect of Pandas' efficiency.

A better way to find the bad dates exploits the fact that Pandas' to_datetime method has a coerce argument, which, if True, converts any date exceptions to NaT (not a time), the temporal equivalent of NaN. We can then create a Boolean mask out of the resulting DataFrame based on the NaT date rows, producing Figure 9-1.

```
with_death_dates = df[df.date_of_death.notnull()] ❶
bad_dates = pd.isnull(pd.to_datetime(\
            with_death_dates.date_of_death, errors='coerce')) ❷
with_death_dates[bad_dates][['category', 'date_of_death',\
'name']]
```

❶ Gets all rows with non-null date fields.

❷ Creates a Boolean mask for all bad dates in with_death_dates by checking against null (NaT) after coercing failed conversions to NaT. For older Pandas versions, you may need to use coerce=True.

	category	date_of_death	name
150	Physiology or Medicine	1968-23-07	Henry Hallett Dale
349	Physiology or Medicine	May 30, 2011 (aged 89)	Rosalyn Yalow
581	Peace	living	David Trimble
746	Physics	Diederik Korteweg	Johannes Diderik van der Waals
809	Peace	living	Shirin Ebadi
833	Peace	living	Rigoberta Menchú
858	Physics	1 February 1976, age 74	Werner Karl Heisenberg

Figure 9-1. The unparseable date fields

Depending on how fastidious you want to be, these can be corrected by hand or coerced to NumPy's time equivalent of NaN, NaT. We've got more than 500 valid dates of death, which is enough to get some interesting time stats, so we'll run to_datetime again and force errors to null:

```
df.date_of_death = pd.to_datetime(df.date_of_death,\
errors='coerce')
```

Now that we have our time fields in a usable format, let's add a field for the age of the winner on receiving his/her Nobel Prize. In order to get the year value of our new dates, we need to tell Pandas that it's dealing with a date column, using the DatetimeIndex method.

```
df['award_age'] = df.year - pd.DatetimeIndex(df.date_of_birth)\
.year ❶
```

❶ Convert the column to a `DatetimeIndex`, an `ndarray` of date time64 data, and use the `year` property.

Let's use our new `award_age` field to see the youngest recipients of the Nobel Prize:

```
# use +sort+ for older Pandas
df.sort_values('award_age').iloc[:10]\
        [['name', 'award_age', 'category', 'year']]
Out:
                     name  award_age       category  year
725       Malala Yousafzai         17          Peace  2014 ❶
525  William Lawrence Bragg         25        Physics  1915
626       Georges J. F. Köhler     30  P...Medicine  1976
247           Carl Anderson         31        Physics  1936
858   Werner Karl Heisenberg        31        Physics  1932
294           Tsung-Dao Lee         31        Physics  1957
146             Paul Dirac         31        Physics  1933
226         Tawakkol Karman         32          Peace  2011
986    Frederick G. Banting        32  P...Medicine  1923
877        Rudolf Mössbauer        32        Physics  1961
```

❶ For activism for female education, I'd recommend reading more about Malala's inspirational story (*http://en.wikipedia.org/wiki/ Malala_Yousafzai*).

Now we have our date fields in a manipulable form, let's have a look at the full `clean_data` function, which summarizes this chapter's cleaning efforts.

The Full clean_data Function

For manually edited data like scraped Wikipedia datasets, it's unlikely that you'll catch all the errors on a first pass. So expect to pick up a few during the data exploration phase. Nevertheless, our Nobel Prize dataset is looking very usable. We'll declare it clean enough and the job of this chapter done. Example 9-4 shows the steps we used to achieve this cleaning feat.

Example 9-4. The full Nobel Prize dataset cleaning function

```
def clean_data(df):
    df = df.replace('', np.nan)
    df_born_in = df[df.born_in.notnull()] ❶
    df = df[df.born_in.isnull()]
    df = df.drop('born_in', axis=1)
    df.drop(df[df.year == 1809].index, inplace=True)
```

```
df = df[~(df.name == 'Marie Curie')]
df.loc[(df.name == u'Marie Sk\u0142odowska-Curie') &\
       (df.year == 1911), 'country'] = 'France'
df = df[~((df.name == 'Sidney Altman') & (df.year == 1990))]
df = df.reindex(np.random.permutation(df.index)) ❷
df = df.drop_duplicates(['name', 'year'])
df = df.sort_index()
df.ix[df.name == 'Alexis Carrel', 'category'] =\
    'Physiology or Medicine'
df.ix[df.name == 'Ragnar Granit', 'gender'] = 'male'
df = df[df.gender.notnull()] # remove institutional prizes
df.ix[df.name == 'Hiroshi Amano', 'date_of_birth'] =\
'11 September 1960'
df.date_of_birth = pd.to_datetime(df.date_of_birth) ❸
df.date_of_death = pd.to_datetime(df.date_of_death,\
errors='coerce')
df['award_age'] = df.year - pd.DatetimeIndex(df.date_of_birth)\
.year
return df, df_born_in
```

❶ Makes a DataFrame containing the rows with born_in fields.

❷ Removes duplicates from the DataFrame after randomizing the row order.

❸ Converts the date columns to the practical datetime64 data-type.

Saving the Cleaned Dataset

Now let's save the results of our cleaning function to our Mongo database using the utility method we wrote in the last chapter (see "MongoDB" on page 221).

```
df_clean, df_born_in = clean_data()

dataframe_to_mongo(df_clean, 'nobel_prize', 'winners') ❶
dataframe_to_mongo(df_born_in, 'nobel_prize', 'winners_born_in')
```

❶ Save the cleaned DataFrame to the nobel_prize database, collection name winners_cleaned.

Let's also save a copy of our df_clean DataFrame to an SQLite nobel_prize database in a local *data* directory. We'll use this to demonstrate the Flask-Restless SQL web API in "RESTful SQL with Flask-Restless" on page 361. Three lines of Python and the data frame's `to_sql` method do the job succinctly (see "SQL" on page 220 for more details):

```
import sqlalchemy

engine = sqlalchemy.create_engine(\
'sqlite:///data/nobel_prize.db')
df_clean.to_sql('winners', engine)
```

Merging DataFrames

At this point, we can also create a merged database of our clean `win` `ners` data and the image and biography dataset we scraped in "Scraping Text and Images with a Pipeline" on page 187. This will provide a good opportunity to demonstrate Pandas' ability to merge `DataFrames`. The following code shows how to merge `df_clean` and the bio dataset:

```
# Read the Scrapy bio-data into a DataFrame
df_winners_bios = pd.read_json(\
open('data/scrapy_nwinners_minibio.json'))

df_winners_all = pd.merge(df_clean, df_winners_bios,\
how='outer', on='link') ❶
```

❶ Panda's `merge` (*http://bit.ly/1UT8fd7*) takes two `DataFrames` and merges them based on shared column name(s) (`link`, in this case). The `how` (*http://bit.ly/1UdUSC2*) argument specifies how to determine which keys are to be included in the resulting table and works in the same way as SQL joins. In this case, `outer` specifies a `FULL_OUTER_JOIN`.

Merging the two `DataFrames` results in redundancies in our merged dataset, with more than the 858 winning rows:

```
df_winners_all.count()
Out:
award_age      1023
category       1023
...
bio_image       978
mini_bio       1086
```

We can easily remove these by using `drop_duplicates` to remove any rows that share a `link` and `year` field after removing any rows without a `name` field:

```
df_winners_all = df_winners_all[~df_winners_all.name.isnull()]\
.drop_duplicates(subset=['link', 'year'])
```

A quick count shows that we now have the right number of winners with images for 770 and a `mini_bio` for all but one:

```
df_winners_all.count()
award_age        858
category         858
. . .
bio_image        770
mini_bio         857
dtype: int64
```

While we're cleaning our dataset, let's see which winner is missing a `mini_bio` field:

```
df_winners_all[df_winners_all.mini_bio.isnull()]
Out:
. . .
                                        link         name  \
229  http://en.wikipedia.org/wiki/L%C3%AA_%C3...   Lê Đức Thọ
. . .
```

It turns out to be a Unicode error in creating the Wikipedia link for Lê Đức Thọ, the Vietnamese Peace Prize winner. This can be corrected by hand.

It only remains to save our merged dataset to MongoDB:

```
dataframe_to_mongo(df_winners_all, 'nobel_prize', 'winners_all')
```

With our cleaned data in the database, we're ready to start exploring it in the next chapter.

Summary

In this chapter, you learned how to clean a fairly messy dataset, producing data that will be much nicer to explore and generally work with. Along the way, a number of new Pandas methods and techniques were introduced to extend the last chapter's introduction to basic Pandas.

In the next chapter, we will use our newly minted dataset to start getting a feel for the Nobel Prize recipients, their country, gender, age, and any interesting correlations (or lack thereof) we can find.

## CHAPTER 10

Visualizing Data with Matplotlib

As a data visualizer, one of the best ways to come to grips with your data is to visualize it interactively, using the full range of charts and plots that have evolved to summarize and refine datasets. Conventionally, the fruits of this exploratory phase are then presented as static figures, but increasingly they are used to construct more engaging interactive web-based charts, such as the cool D3 visualizations you have probably seen (one of which we'll be building in Part V).

Python's Matplotlib and its family of extensions (such as the statistically focused Seaborn) form a mature and very customizable plotting ecosystem. Matplotlib plots can be used interactively by IPython (the Qt and Notebook versions), providing a very powerful and intuitive way of finding interesting nuggets in your data. In this chapter we'll introduce Matplotlib and one of its great extensions, Seaborn.

Pyplot and Object-Oriented Matplotlib

Matplotlib can be more than a little confusing, especially if you start randomly sampling examples online. The main complicating factor is that there are two main ways to create plots, which are similar enough to be confused but different enough to lead to a lot of frustrating errors. The first way uses a global state machine to interact directly with Matplotlib's `pyplot` module. The second, object-oriented approach uses the more familiar notion of figure and axes classes to provide a programmatic alternative. I'll clarify their differences in the sections ahead, but as a rough rule of thumb, if you're working interactively with single plots, pyplot's global state is a convenient shortcut. For all other occasions, it makes sense to explicitly declare your figures and axes using the object-oriented approach.

Starting an Interactive Session

Within an IPython session, Matplotlib has two modes of operation: inline and as a standalone window (Qt). IPython's Qt console (*http://bit.ly/1S9Kadw*) supports both modes; the Notebook (*http:// bit.ly/1rtACUU*) supports inline graphics, whereas IPython started from the command line only supports a standalone window.

First start an IPython session from the command line with an optional notebook or qt flag:

```
$ ipython [notebook | qt]
```

If using the Jupyter notebook (*http://jupyter.org*), use the following command to start a session:

```
$ jupyter notebook
```

You can then use one of the Matplotlib magic commands (*http:// bit.ly/1UAH8on*) within the IPython session to enable interactive Matplotlib. On its own, %matplotlib will use the default GUI backend to create a plotting window, but you can specify the backend directly. The following should work on standard and Qt console IPython:[1]

```
%matplotlib [qt | osx | wx ...]
```

To get inline graphics in the Notebook or Qt console, you can use the inline directive. Note that with inline plots, you can't amend them after creation, unlike the standalone Matplotlib window:

```
%matplotlib inline
```

Whether you are using Matplotlib interactively or in Python programs, you'll use similar imports:

---

[1] If you have errors trying to start a GUI session, try changing the backend setting (e.g., if using OS X and %matplotlib qt doesn't work, try %matplotlib osx).

```
import numpy as np
import pandas as pd
import matplotlib.pyplot as plt
```

You will find many examples of Matplotlib using pylab. Pylab is a convenience module that bulk-imports matplotlib.pyplot (for plotting) and NumPy in a single namespace. Pylab is pretty much deprecated now, but even were it not, I'd still recommend avoiding this namespace and merging and importing pyplot and numpy explicitly.

While NumPy and Pandas are not mandatory, Matplotlib is designed to play well with them, handling NumPy arrays and, by association, Pandas Series.

The ability to create inline plots is key to enjoyable interaction with Matplotlib, and we achieve this in IPython with the following "magic"[2] injunction:

```
In [0]: %matplotlib inline
```

Your Matplotlib plots will now be inserted into your IPython work-flow. This works with Qt and Notebook versions. In the Notebooks, the plots are incorporated into the active cell.

Amending plots

In inline mode, after an IPython cell or (multi-line) input has been run, the drawing context is flushed. This means you cannot change the plot from a previous cell or input using the gcf (get current figure) method but have to repeat all the plot commands with any additions or amendments in a new input/cell.

---

2 IPython has a large number of such functions to enable a whole slew of useful extras to the vanilla Python interpreter. Check them out on the IPython website (*https:// ipython.org/ipython-doc/dev/interactive/tutorial.html*).

Interactive Plotting with Pyplot's Global State

The pyplot module provides a global state that you can manipulate interactively.[3] This is intended for use in interactive data exploration and is best when you are creating simple plots, usually containing single figures. pyplot is convenient and many of the examples you'll see use it, but for more complex plotting Matplotlib's object-oriented API (which we'll see shortly) comes into its own. Before demoing use of the global plot, let's create some random data to display, courtesy of Panda's useful period_range method:

```
x = pd.period_range(pd.datetime.now(), periods=200, freq='d')❶
x = x.to_timestamp().to_pydatetime() ❷
y = np.random.randn(200, 3).cumsum(0) ❸
```

❶ Creates a Pandas datetime index with 200 day (d) elements, starting from the current time (datetime.now()).

❷ Converts datetime index to Python datetimes.

❸ Creates three 200-element random arrays summed along the 0 axis.

We now have a y-axis with 200 time slots and three random arrays for the complementary x values. These are provided as separate arguments to the (line)plot method:

```
plt.plot(x, y)
```

This gives us the not particularly inspiring chart shown in Figure 10-1. Note how Matplotlib deals naturally with a multidimensional NumPy line array.

---

3 This was inspired by Matlab (*http://uk.mathworks.com/products/matlab/*).

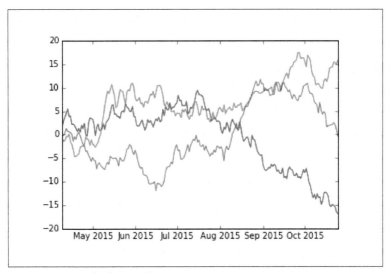

Figure 10-1. Default line plot

Although Matplotlib's defaults are, by general consensus, less than ideal, one of its strengths is the sheer amount of customization you can perform. This is why there is a rich ecosystem of chart libraries that wrap Matplotlib with better defaults, more attractive color schemes, and more. Let's see some of this customization in action by using vanilla Matplotlib to tailor our default plot.

Configuring Matplotlib

Matplotlib provides a wide range of configurations (*http://bit.ly/1ZWSMKA*), which can be specified in a matplotlibrc file (*http://bit.ly/1UTaxJ1*) or dynamically, through the dictionary-like rcPar ams variable. Here we change the width and default color of our plot lines:

```
import matplotlib as mpl
mpl.rcParams['lines.linewidth'] = 2
mpl.rcParams['lines.color'] = 'r' # red
```

You can find a sample matplotlibrc file at the main site (*http://bit.ly/21r1YHF*).

As well as using the rcParams variable, you can use the gcf (get current figure) method to grab the currently active figure and manipulate it directly.

Let's see a little example of configuration, setting the current figure's size.

Setting the Figure's Size

If your plot's default readability is poor or the width-to-height ratio suboptimal, you will want to change its size. By default, Matplotlib uses inches for its plotting size. This makes sense when you consider the many backends (often vector-graphic-based) that Matplotlib can save to. Here we use pyplot to set the figure size to eight by four inches, using rcParams and gcf:

```
# set figure size to 8 by 4 inches
plt.rcParams['figure.figsize'] = (8,4)
plt.gcf().set_size_inches(8, 4)
```

Points, Not Pixels

Matplotlib uses points, not pixels, to measure the size of its figures. This is the accepted measure for print-quality publications, and Matplotlib is used to deliver publication-quality images.

By default a point is approximately 1/72 of an inch wide, but Matplotlib allows you to adjust this by changing the dots-per-inch (dpi) for any figures generated. The higher this number, the better the quality of the image. For the purpose of the inline figures shown interactively during IPython sessions, the resolution is usually a product of the backend engine being used to generate the plots (e.g., Qt, WXAgg, tkinter). See here (*http://matplotlib.org/faq/usage_faq.html#what-is-a-backend*) for an explanation of backends.

Labels and Legends

Figure 10-1 needs, among other things, to tell us what the lines mean. Matplotlib has a handy legend box for line labeling, which, like most things Matplotlib, is heavily configurable. Labeling our three lines involves a little indirection as the plot method only takes one label, which it applies to all lines generated. Usefully, the plot command returns all Line2D objects created. These can be used by the legend method to set individual labels.

```
plots = plt.plot(x,y)
plots
Out:
[<matplotlib.lines.Line2D at 0x9b31a90>,
```

```
<matplotlib.lines.Line2D at 0x9b4da90>,
<matplotlib.lines.Line2D at 0x9b4dcd0>]
```

The legend (*http://bit.ly/1ZWTIPb*) method can set labels, suggest a location for the legend box, and configure a number of other things (*http://bit.ly/1rtCY69*):

```
plt.legend(plots, ('foo', 'bar', 'baz'), ❶
           loc='best', ❷
           framealpha=0.5, ❸
           prop={'size':'small', 'family':'monospace'}) ❹
```

❶ Sets the labels for our three plots.

❷ Using the best location should avoid obscuring lines.

❸ Sets the legend's transparency.

❹ Here we adjust the font properties of the legend.[4]

Titles and Axes Labels

Adding a title and label for your axes is as easy as can be:

```
plt.title('Random trends')
plt.xlabel('Date')
plt.ylabel('Cum. sum')
```

You can add some text with the figtext method:[5]

```
plt.figtext(0.995, 0.01, ❶
            u'© Acme designs 2015',
            ha='right', va='bottom') ❷
```

❶ The location of the text proportionate to figure size.

❷ Horizontal (ha) and vertical (va) alignment.

The complete code is shown in Example 10-1 and the resulting chart in Figure 10-2.

---

4 See the docs (*http://bit.ly/1ZWTG9X*) for more details.

5 See the Matplotlib website (*http://bit.ly/1YyaMMr*) for details.

Example 10-1. Customized line chart

```
plots = plt.plot(x, y)
plt.legend(plots, ('foo', 'bar', 'baz'), loc='best,
                   framealpha=0.25,
                   prop={'size':'small', 'family':'monospace'})
plt.gcf().set_size_inches(8, 4)
plt.title('Random trends')
plt.xlabel('Date')
plt.ylabel('Cum. sum')
plt.grid(True) ❶
plt.figtext(0.995, 0.01, u'\u00a9 Acme Designs 2015',
ha='right', va='bottom')
plt.tight_layout() ❷
```

❶ This will add a dotted grid to the figure, marking the axis ticks.

❷ The `tight_layout` method (*http://bit.ly/1Qc75KX*) should guarantee that all your plot elements are within the figure box.
   Otherwise, you might find tick-labels or legends truncated.

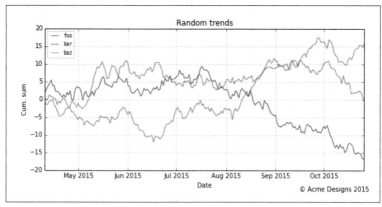

Figure 10-2. Customized line chart

We used the `tight_layout` method in Example 10-1 to prevent plot
elements from being obscured or truncated. `tight_layout` has been
known to cause problems with some systems, particularly OS X. If
you have any problems, this issue thread (*https://github.com/matplot
lib/matplotlib/issues/1852*) may help. As of now, the best advice is to
use the `set_tight_layout` method on the current figure:

```
plt.gcf().set_tight_layout(True)
```

Saving Your Charts

One area where Matplotlib shines is in saving your plots, providing many output formats.[6] The available formats depend on the backends available, but generally PNG, PDF, PS, EPS, and SVG are supported.

Saving is as simple as this:

```
plt.tight_layout() # force plot into figure dimensions
plt.savefig('mpl_3lines_custom.svg')
```

You can set the format explicitly using `format="svg"`, but Matplotlib understands the *.svg* suffix. To avoid truncated labels, use the `tight_layout` method.[7]

Figures and Object-Oriented Matplotlib

As just shown, interactively manipulating Pyplot's global state works fine for quick data sketching and single-plot work. However, if you want to have more control over your charts, Matplotlib's `figure` and `axes` OOP approach is the way to go. Most of the more advanced plotting demos you see will be done this way.

In essence, with OOP Matplotlib we are dealing with a `figure`, which you can think of as a drawing area with one or more axes (or plots) embedded in it. Both `figures` and `axes` have properties that can be independently specified. In this sense, the interactive `pyplot` route discussed earlier was plotting to a single axis of a global figure.

We can create a figure by using Pyplot's `figure` method:

```
fig = plt.figure(
        figsize=(8, 4), # figure size in inches
        dpi=200, # dots per inch
        tight_layout=True, # fit axes, labels, etc. to canvas
        linewidth=1, edgecolor='r' # 1 pixel wide, red border
        )
```

---

6 As well as providing many formats, it also understands LaTex (*https://www.latex-project.org/*) math mode, which means you can use mathematical symbols in the titles, legends, and the like. This is one of the reasons Matplotlib is much beloved by academics, as it is quite capable of journal-quality images.

7 More details are available on the Matplotlib website (*http://matplotlib.org/users/tight_layout_guide.html*).

As you can see, figures share a subset of properties with the global pyplot module. These can be set on creation of the figure or through similar methods (i.e., fig.text() as opposed to plt.fig_text()). Each figure can have multiple axes, each of which is analogous to the single, global plot state but with the considerable advantage that multiple axes can exist on one figure, each with independent properties.

Axes and Subplots

The figure.add_axes method allows precise control over the position of axes within a figure (e.g., enabling you to embed a smaller plot within the main). Positioning of plot elements uses a 0 → 1 coordinate system, where 1 is the width or height of the figure. You can specify the position using a four-element list or tuple to set bottom-left and top-right bounds [bottom(h*0.2), left(w*0.2), top(h*0.8), right(w*0.8)]:

```
fig.add_axes([0.2, 0.2, 0.8, 0.8])
```

Example 10-2 shows the code needed to insert smaller axes into larger ones, using our random test data. The result is shown in Figure 10-3.

Example 10-2. A plot insert with figure.axes

```
fig = plt.figure(figsize=(8,4))
# --- Main Axes
ax = fig.add_axes([0.1, 0.1, 0.8, 0.8])
ax.set_title('Main Axes with Insert Child Axes')
ax.plot(x, y[:,0]) ❶
ax.set_xlabel('Date')
ax.set_ylabel('Cum. sum')
# --- Inserted Axes
ax = fig.add_axes([0.15, 0.15, 0.3, 0.3])
ax.plot(x, y[:,1], color='g') # 'g' for green
ax.set_xticks([]); ❷
```

❶ This selects the first column of our random NumPy y-data.

❷ Removes the x ticks and labels from our embedded plot.

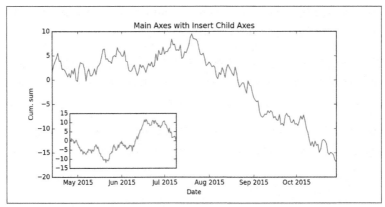

Figure 10-3. Inserted plot with figure.add_axes

Although `add_axes` gives us a lot of scope for fine-tuning the appearance of our charts, most of the time Matplotlib's built-in grid-layout system makes life much easier.[8] The simplest option is to use `figure.subplots`, which allows you to specify row-column layouts of equal-sized plots. If you want a grid with different-sized plots, the `gridspec` module is your go-to.

Calling `subplots` without arguments returns a figure with single axes. This is closest in use to using the Pyplot state machine. Example 10-3 shows the figure and axes equivalent to the `pyplot` demo in Example 10-1, producing the chart in Figure 10-2. Note the use of "setter" methods for `figure` and `axes`.

Example 10-3. Plotting with single figure and axes

```
figure, ax = plt.subplots()
plots = ax.plot(x, y, label='')
figure.set_size_inches(8, 4)
ax.legend(plots, ('foo', 'bar', 'baz'), loc='best', framealpha=0.25,
prop={'size':'small', 'family':'monospace'})
ax.set_title('Random trends')
ax.set_xlabel('Date')
ax.set_ylabel('Cum. sum')
ax.grid(True)
figure.text(0.995, 0.01, u'\u00a9 Acme Designs 2015',
ha='right', va='bottom')
figure.tight_layout()
```

---

8 The handy `tight_layout` option assumes grid-layout subplots.

Calling `subplots` with arguments for number of rows (`nrows`) and columns (`ncols`) (as shown in Example 10-4) allows multiple plots to be placed on a grid layout (see the results in Figure 10-4). The call to `subplots` returns the figure and an array of axes, in row-column order. In the example, we specify one column so `axes` is a single array of three stacked axes. We make use of Python's handy `zip` method to produce three dictionaries with line data. `zip` (*https:// docs.python.org/2/library/functions.html#zip*) takes lists or tuples of length *n* and returns *n* lists, formed by matching the elements by order:

```
letters = ['a', 'b']
numbers = [1, 2]
zip(letters, numbers)
Out:
[('a', 1), ('b', 2)]
```

In the `for` loop, we use `enumerate` to supply an index i, which we use to select an axis by row, using our zipped `labelled_data` to provide the plot properties.

Note the shared x- and y-axes specified in the `subplots` call. This allows easy comparison of the three charts, particularly on the now normalized y-axis. To avoid redundant x labels, we only call `set_xla bel` on the last row, using Python's handy negative indexing.

Example 10-4. Using subplots

```
fig, axes = plt.subplots(
                nrows=3, ncols=1, ❶
                sharex=True, sharey=True, ❷
                figsize=(8, 8))
labelled_data = zip(y.transpose(), ❸
                ('foo', 'bar', 'baz'), ('b', 'g', 'r'))
fig.suptitle('Three Random Trends', fontsize=16)
for i, ld in enumerate(labelled_data):
    ax = axes[i]
    ax.plot(x, ld[0], label=ld[1], color=ld[2])
    ax.set_ylabel('Cum. sum')
    ax.legend(loc='upper left', framealpha=0.5,
            prop={'size':'small'})
axes[-1].set_xlabel('Date') ❹
```

❶ Specifies a subplot grid of three rows by one column.

❷ We want to share x- and y-axes, automatically adjusting limits for easy comparison.

❸ Switch y to row-column and zip the line data, labels, and line colors together.

❹ Labels the last of the shared x-axes.

Now that we've covered the two ways in which IPython and Matplotlib engage interactively, using the global state (accessed through plt) and the object-oriented API, let's look at a few of the common plot types you'll use to explore your datasets.

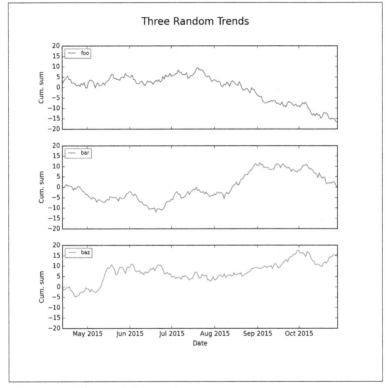

Figure 10-4. Three subplots

Plot Types

As well as the line plot just demonstrated, Matplotlib has a number of plot types available. I'll now demonstrate a few of the ones commonly used in exploratory data visualization.

Bar Charts

The humble bar chart is a staple for a lot of visual data exploration. As with most of Matplotlib charts, there's a good deal of customization possible. We'll now run through a few variants to give you the gist.

The code in Example 10-5 produces the bar chart in Figure 10-5. Note that you have to specify your own bar and label locations. This kind of flexibility is beloved by hardcore Matplotlibbers and is pretty easy to get the hang of. Nevertheless, it's the sort of thing that can get tedious. It's trivial to write some helper methods here, and there are many libraries that wrap Matplotlib and make things a little more user-friendly. As we'll see in Chapter 11, Panda's built-in Matplotlib-based plots are quite a bit simpler to use.

Example 10-5. A simple bar chart

```
labels = ["Physics", "Chemistry", "Literature", "Peace"]
foo_data =   [3, 6, 10, 4]

bar_width = 0.5
xlocations = np.array(range(len(foo_data))) + bar_width  ❶
plt.bar(xlocations, foo_data, width=bar_width)
plt.yticks(range(0, 12))
plt.xticks(xlocations+bar_width/2, labels)  ❷
plt.xlim(0, xlocations[-1]+bar_width*2)  ❸
plt.title("Prizes won by Fooland")
plt.gca().get_xaxis().tick_bottom()
plt.gca().get_yaxis().tick_left()
plt.gcf().set_size_inches((8, 4))
```

❶ Here we create the left-edge bar locations, starting a bar_width points.

❷ This places tick labels at the middle of the bars.

❸ We set the x limits to allow for right and left padding of one bar-width.

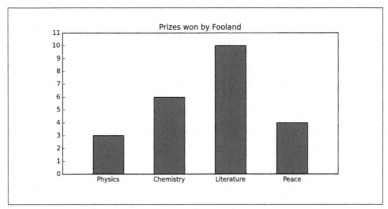

Figure 10-5. A simple bar chart

Bar charts with multiple groups are particularly useful. In Example 10-6, we add some more country data (for a mythical Barland) and use the subplots method to produce grouped bar charts (see Figure 10-6). Once again we specify the bar locations manually, adding two bar groups—this time with ax.bar. Note that our axes' x-limits are automatically rescaled in a sensible fashion, at increments of 0.5:

```
ax.get_xlim()
# Out: (-0.5, 3.5)
```

Use the respective setter methods (set_xlim, in this case) if autoscaling doesn't achieve the desired look.

Example 10-6. Creating a grouped bar chart

```
labels = ["Physics", "Chemistry", "Literature", "Peace"]
foo_data =   [3, 6, 10, 4]
bar_data = [8, 3, 6, 1]

fig, ax = plt.subplots(figsize=(8, 4))
bar_width = 0.4 ❶
xlocs = np.arange(len(foo_data))
ax.bar(xlocs-bar_width, foo_data, bar_width,
       color='#fde0bc', label='Fooland') ❷
ax.bar(xlocs, bar_data, bar_width, color='peru', label='Barland')
#--- ticks, labels, grids, and title
ax.set_yticks(range(12))
ax.set_xticks(ticks=range(len(foo_data)))
ax.set_xticklabels(labels)
ax.yaxis.grid(True)
ax.legend(loc='best')
```

```
ax.set_ylabel('Number of prizes')
fig.suptitle('Prizes by country')
fig.tight_layout(pad=2) ❸
fig.savefig('mpl_barchart_multi.png', dpi=200) ❹
```

❶ With a width of 1 for our two-bar groups, this bar width gives
0.1 bar padding.

❷ Matplotlib supports standard HTML colors, taking hex values
or a name.

❸ We use the pad argument to specify padding around the figure
as a fraction of the font size.

❹ This saves the figure at the high resolution of 200 dots per inch.

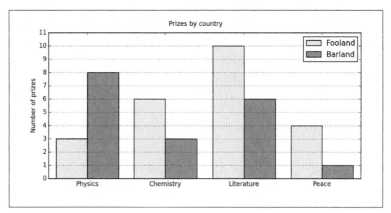

Figure 10-6. Grouped bar charts

It's often useful to use horizontal bars, particularly if there are a lot
of them and/or you are using tick labels, which are likely to run into
one another if placed on the same line. Turning Figure 10-6 on its
side is easy enough, requiring only that we replace the bar method
with its horizontal counterpart barh and switch the axis labels and
limits (see Figure 10-7).

Example 10-7. Converting Example 10-6 to horizontal bars

```
# ...
ylocs = np.arange(len(foo_data))
ax.barh(ylocs-width, foo_data, width, color='#fde0bc',
        label='Fooland') ❶
ax.barh(ylocs, bar_data, width, color='peru', label='Barland')
```

```
# --- labels, grids, and title, then save
ax.set_xticks(range(12)) ❷
ax.set_yticks(ticks=range(len(foo_data)))
ax.set_yticklabels(labels)
ax.xaxis.grid(True)
ax.legend(loc='best')
ax.set_xlabel('Number of prizes')
# ...
```

❶ To create a horizontal bar chart, we use `barh` in place of `bar`.

❷ A horizontal chart necessitates swapping the horizontal and vertical axes.

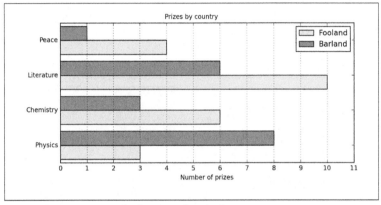

Figure 10-7. Turning the bars on their side

Stacked bars are easy to achieve in Matplotlib.[9] Example 10-8 converts Figure 10-6 to a stacked form; Figure 10-8 shows the result. The trick is to use the bottom argument to `bar` to set the bottom of the raised bars as the top of the previous group.

Example 10-8. Converting Example 10-6 to stacked bars

```
# ...
bar_width = 0.8 # bar width
xlocs = np.arange(len(foo_data))
ax.bar(xlocs, foo_data, bar_width, color='#fde0bc', ❶
       label='Fooland')
```

---

9 It's questionable whether stacked bar charts are a particularly good way of appreciating groups of data. See Solomon Messing's blog (*http://bit.ly/1V2dG6B*) for a nice discussion and one example of "good" use.

```
ax.bar(xlocs, bar_data, bar_width, color='peru',        ❷
       label='Barland', bottom=foo_data)
# --- labels, grids and title, then save
ax.set_yticks(range(18))
ax.set_xticks(ticks=np.array(range(len(foo_data))) + bar_width/2)
ax.set_xticklabels(labels)
ax.set_xlim(-(1-bar_width), xlocs[-1]+1) ❸
# ...
```

❶ The foo_data and bar_data bar groups share the same x-
  locations.

❷ The bottom of the bar_data group is the top of the foo_data,
  providing stacked bars.

❸ Sets the x-limits manually, allowing a padding of 1-bar_width.

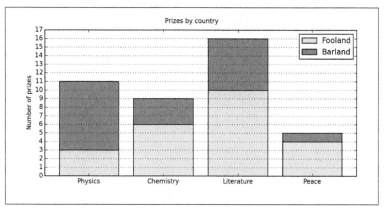

Figure 10-8. Stacked bar chart

Scatter Plots

Another useful chart is the scatter plot, which takes 2D arrays of
points with options for point size, color, and more.

Example 10-9 shows the code for a quick scatter plot, using Matplotlib autoscaling for x and y limits. We create a noisy line by adding
normally distributed random numbers (sigma of 10). Figure 10-9
shows the resulting chart.

Example 10-9. A simple scatter plot

```
num_points = 100
gradient = 0.5
```

```
x = np.array(range(num_points))
y = np.random.randn(num_points) * 10 + x*gradient ❶
fig, ax = plt.subplots(figsize=(8, 4))
ax.scatter(x, y) ❷

fig.suptitle('A Simple Scatterplot')
```

❶ randn gives normally distributed random numbers, which we
    scale to be within 0 and 10 and to which we then add an x-
    dependent value.

❷ The equally sized x and y arrays provide the point coordinates.

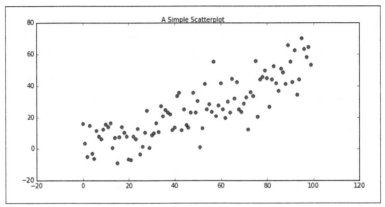

Figure 10-9. A simple scatter plot

We can adjust the size and color of individual points by passing an
array of marker sizes and color indices to the current default colormap. One thing to note, which can be confusing, is that we are specifying the area of the markers' bounding boxes, not the circles'
diameters. This means if we want points to double the diameter of
the circles, we must increase the size by a factor of four.[10] In
Example 10-10, we add size and color information to our simple
scatter plot, producing Figure 10-10.

---

10 Setting marker size, rather than width or radius, is actually a good default, making it
   proportional to whatever value we are trying to reflect.

Example 10-10. Adjusting point size and color

```
num_points = 100
gradient = 0.5
x = np.array(range(num_points))
y = np.random.randn(num_points) * 10 + x*gradient
fig, ax = plt.subplots(figsize=(8, 4))
colors = np.random.rand(num_points) ❶
size = (2 + np.random.rand(num_points) * 8) ** 2 ❷
ax.scatter(x, y, s=size, c=colors, alpha=0.5) ❸
fig.suptitle('Scatterplot with Color and Size Specified')
```

❶ This produces 100 random color values between 0 and 1 for the default colormap.

❷ We use the power notation ** to square values between 2 and 10, the width range for our markers.

❸ We use the alpha argument to make our markers half-transparent.

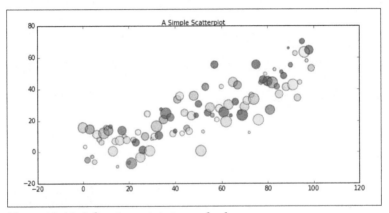

Figure 10-10. Adjusting point size and color

 Matplotlib colormaps

Matplotlib has a huge variety of colormaps available, the choice of which can significantly improve the quality of your visualization. See the colormap docs (*http://matplotlib.org/users/colormaps.html*) for details.

Adding a regression line

A regression line is a simple predictive model of the correlation between two variables, in this case the x and y coordinates of our scatter plot. The line is essentially a best fit through the points of the plot, and adding one to a scatter plot is a useful dataviz technique and a good way to demo Matplotlib, NumPy interaction.

In Example 10-11 NumPy's very useful `polyfit` function is used to generate the gradient and constant of a best-fit line for the points defined by the x and y arrays. We then plot this line on the same axes as the scatter plot (see Figure 10-11).

Example 10-11. Scatter plot with regression line

```
num_points = 100
gradient = 0.5
x = np.array(range(num_points))
y = np.random.randn(num_points) * 10 + x*gradient
fig, ax = plt.subplots(figsize=(8, 4))
ax.scatter(x, y)
m, c = np.polyfit(x, y ,1) ❶
ax.plot(x, m*x + c) ❷
fig.suptitle('Scatterplot With Regression-line')
```

❶ We use NumPy's `polyfit` in 1D to get a line gradient (m) and constant (c) for a best-fit line through our random points.

❷ Use the gradient and constant to plot a line on the scatter plot's axes (y = mx + c).

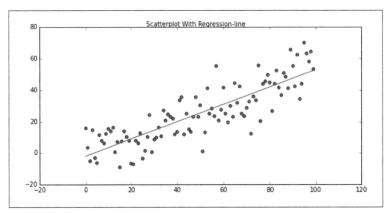

Figure 10-11. Scatter plot with regression line

It's generally a good idea to plot confidence intervals when doing line regression. This gives an idea of how reliable the line fit is, based on the number and distribution of the points. Confidence intervals can be achieved with Matplotlib and NumPy, but it is a little awkward. Luckily, there is a library built on Matplotlib that has extra, specialized functions for statistical analysis and data visualization and, in the opinion of many, looks a lot better than Matplotlib's defaults. That library is Seaborn, which we are going to take a quick look at now.

Seaborn

There are a number of libraries that wrap the powerful plotting abilities of Matplotlib in a more user-friendly guise[11] and, as important for us data visualizers, play nicely with Pandas:

- *ggplot* (*https://github.com/yhat/ggplot*) is a Python port of R's highly rated *ggplot2*. While it's a very good stab, replicating a lot of the functionality of *ggplot2*, its development seems quite intermittent.
- *Bokeh* (*http://bokeh.pydata.org/en/latest/*) is an interactive visualization library with the Web in mind, producing browser-rendered output and therefore playing very nicely with IPython Notebook. It's a great achievement, with a design philosophy similar to D3's.[12]

But for the kind of interactive, exploratory dataviz necessary to get a feel for your data and suggest visualizations, I recommend Seaborn (*http://stanford.edu/~mwaskom/software/seaborn/index.html*). Seaborn extends Matplotlib with some powerful statistical plots and is well integrated with the PyData stack, playing nicely with NumPy, Pandas, and the statistical routines found in Scipy and Statsmodels (*http://statsmodels.sourceforge.net/stable/*).

One of the nice things about Seaborn is that it doesn't hide the Matplotlib API, allowing you to tweak your charts with Matplotlib's

---

11 It's generally agreed that Matplotlib's defaults aren't that great and making them better is an easy win for any wrapper.

12 Both D3 and Bokeh tip their hats to the classic visualization text, Leland Wilkinson's *The Grammar of Graphics* (Springer).

extensive tools. In this sense, it's not a replacement for Matplotlib and the relevant skills, but a very impressive extension.

To work with Seaborn, simply extend your standard Matplotlib imports:

```
import numpy as np
import pandas as pd
import seaborn as sns # relies on matplotlib
import matplotlib as mpl
import matplotlib.pyplot as plt
```

Many of Seaborn's functions are designed to accept a Pandas Data Frame, allowing you to specify, for example, the column values describing 2D scattered points. Let's take our existing x and y arrays from Example 10-9 and use them to make some dummy data.

```
data = pd.DataFrame({'dummy x':x, 'dummy y':y})
```

We now have some data with columns of x ('dummy_x') and y ('dummy_y') values. Example 10-12 demonstrates the use of Seaborn's dedicated linear regression plot lmplot, which produces the chart in Figure 10-12. Note that for some Seaborn plots, to adjust figure size we pass a size (height) in inches and an aspect ratio (width/height). Note also that Seaborn shares pyplot's global context.

Example 10-12. Linear regression plot with Seaborn

```
data = pd.DataFrame({'dummy x':x, 'dummy y':y})
sns.lmplot('dummy x', 'dummy y', data, ❶
           size=4, aspect=2) ❷
plt.tight_layout() ❸
plt.savefig('mpl_scatter_seaborn.png') ❸
```

❶ The first two arguments specify the column names of Data Frame data, which define the coordinates of the plot points.

❷ To set figure size, we provide the height in inches and an aspect ratio of width/height.

❸ Seaborn shares the pyplot global context, allowing you to save its plots as you would Matplotlib's.

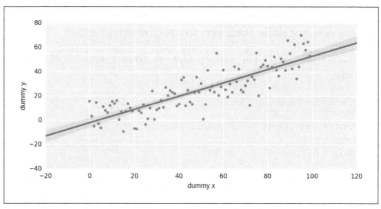

Figure 10-12. Linear regression plot with Seaborn

As you would expect from a library that places an emphasis on attractive-looking plots, Seaborn allows a lot of visual customization. Let's make a few changes to the look of Figure 10-12 and adjust the confidence interval to the standard error (*https://en.wikipe dia.org/wiki/Standard_error*) estimate of 68% (see Figure 10-13 for the result):

```
sns.lmplot('dummy x', 'dummy y', data, size=4, aspect=2,
           scatter_kws={"color": "slategray"}, ❶
           line_kws={"linewidth": 2, "linestyle":'--', ❷
                     "color": "seagreen"},
           markers='D', ❸
           ci=68) ❹
```

❶ Provide the scatter plot component's keyword arguments, setting our points' color to slate gray.

❷ Provide the line plot component's keyword arguments, setting line width and style.

❸ Sets the plot markers to diamonds using Matplotlib marker code *D*.

❹ We set a confidence interval of 68%, the standard error estimate.

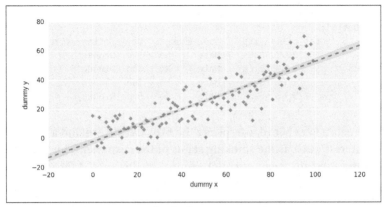

Figure 10-13. Customizing the Seaborn scatter plot

Seaborn offers a number of useful plots beyond Matplotlib's basic set. Let's take a look at one of the most interesting, using Seaborn's `FacetGrid` to plot reflections of multidimensional data.

FacetGrids

Often referred to as "lattice" or "trellis" plotting, the ability to draw multiple instances of the same plot on different subsets of your dataset is a good way to get a bird's-eye view of your data. Large amounts of information can be presented in one plot, and relationships between the different dimensions can be quickly apprehended. This technique is related to the small multiples (*https://en.wikipedia.org/wiki/Small_multiple*) popularized by Edward Tufte.

`FacetGrids` require the data to be in the form of a Pandas `DataFrame` (see "The DataFrame" on page 210) and in a form referred to by Hadley Whickam, creator of ggplot, as "tidy," meaning each column in the `DataFrame` should be a variable and each row an observation.

Let's use Tips, one of Seaborn's test datasets,[13] to show a `FacetGrid` in action. Tips is a small set of data showing the distribution of tips by various dimensions, such as day of the week or whether the customer was a smoker. First let's load our Tips dataset into a Pandas `DataFrame` using the `load_dataset` method:

---

13 Seaborn has a number of handy datasets, which you can find on GitHub (*https://github.com/mwaskom/seaborn-data*).

```
In [0]: tips = sns.load_dataset('tips')
Out[0]:
   total_bill   tip     sex smoker  day    time  size
0       16.99  1.01  Female     No  Sun  Dinner     2
1       10.34  1.66    Male     No  Sun  Dinner     3
2       21.01  3.50    Male     No  Sun  Dinner     3
3       23.68  3.31    Male     No  Sun  Dinner     2
...
```

To create a FacetGrid, we specify the tips DataFrame and a column of interest, such as the smoking status of the customer. This column will be used to create our plot groups; in this case, 'smoker=Yes' and 'smoker=No'. We then use the grid's map method to create multiple scatter plots of tip size against total bill.

```
g = sns.FacetGrid(tips, col="sex")
g.map(plt.scatter, "total_bill", "tip") ❶
```

❶ map takes a plot class, in this case scatter, and two (tips) dimensions required for this scatter plot.

This produces the two scatter plots shown in Figure 10-14, one for each smoker status, with tips and total bills correlated.

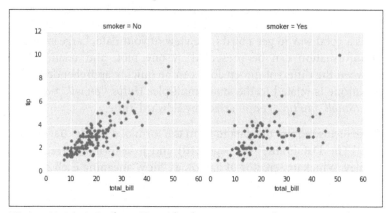

Figure 10-14. A Seaborn FacetGrid using scatter plots

We can include another dimension of the tips data by specifying the marker to be used in our scatter plots. Let's make it a red diamond for females and a blue square for males:

```
pal = dict(Female='red', Male='blue')
g = sns.FacetGrid(tips, col="smoker",
                  hue="sex", hue_kws={"marker": ["D", "s"]}, ❶
                  palette=pal, size=4, aspect=1, )
```

```
g.map(plt.scatter, "total_bill", "tip", alpha=.4)
g.add_legend();
```

❶ Adds a marker color (hue) for the sex dimension with diamond (D) and square (s) shapes, and uses our color palette (pal) to make them red and blue.

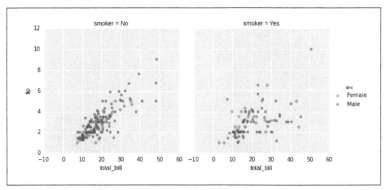

Figure 10-15. Scatter plot with diamond and square markers for sex

We can use rows as well as columns to create subsets of the data by dimension. Combining the two allows, with the help of a regplot,[14] five dimensions to be explored:

```
pal = dict(Female='red', Male='blue')
g = sns.FacetGrid(tips, col="smoker", row="time",  ❶
                  hue="sex", hue_kws={"marker": ["D", "s"]},
                  palette=pal, size=4, aspect=1, )
g.map(plt.regplot, "total_bill", "tip", alpha=.4)
g.add_legend();
```

❶ Adds a time row to separate tips by lunch and dinner.

Figure 10-16 shows four regplots producing a linear-regression model fit with confidence intervals for Female and Male hue-groups. The plot titles show the data subset being used, each row having the same time and smoker status.

---

14 regplot is equivalent to lmplot, used in Example 10-12. The latter combines regplot and FacetGrid for convenience.

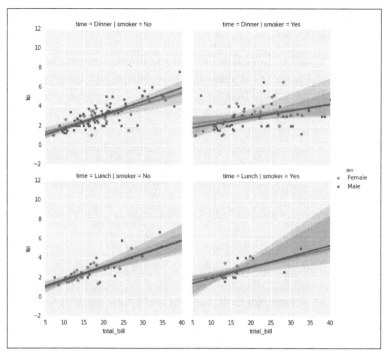

Figure 10-16. Visualizing five dimensions

We can achieve the same effect using the `lmplot` we saw in Example 10-12, which wraps the functionality of `FacetGrid` and `regplot` for convenience. The following code produces Figure 10-16.

```
pal = dict(Female='red', Male='blue')
sns.lmplot(x="total_bill", y="tip", hue="sex",\
markers=["D", "s"], ❶
         col="smoker", row="time", data=tips, palette=pal,
         size=4, aspect=1
         );
```

❶ Note the use of a `markers` keyword as opposed to the `kws_hue` dictionary we used with the `FacetGrid` plot.

`lmplot` offers a nice shortcut to producing `FacetGrid regplots`, but `FacetGrid`'s `map` allows you to use the full panoply of Seaborn and Matplotlib charts to create plots on dimensional subsets. It's a very powerful technique and a great way to drill down into your data.

Pairgrids

Pairgrids are another rather cool Seaborn plot type that provide a way to quickly assess multidimensional data. Unlike with Face tGrids, you don't divide the dataset into subsets that are then compared by designated dimensions. With Pairgrids, the dataset's dimensions are all compared pair-wise in a square grid. By default all dimensions are compared, but you can specify which ones get plotted by providing a list to the vars parameter when declaring the Pairgrid.[15]

Let's demonstrate the utility of this pair-wise comparison by using the classic Iris dataset, showing some vital statistics for a set containing members of three Iris species. First we'll load the example dataset:

```
In [0]: iris = sns.load_dataset('iris')
In [1]: iris
Out[1]:
    sepal_length sepal_width petal_length petal_width species
0          5.1         3.5          1.4         0.2  setosa
1          4.9         3.0          1.4         0.2  setosa
2          4.7         3.2          1.3         0.2  setosa
...
```

To capture the relationship between petal and sepal dimensions by species, we first create a PairGrid object, set its hue to species, and then use its mapping methods to create plots on and off the diagonal of the pair-wise grid, producing the charts in Figure 10-17.

```
sns.set(font_scale=1.5) ❶
g = sns.PairGrid(iris, hue="species") ❷
g.map_diag(plt.hist) ❸
g.map_offdiag(plt.scatter) ❹
g.add_legend();
```

❶ Tweaks the font size using Seaborn's set method (see here (*http://stanford.io/1V2gP6m*) to see the full list of available tweaks.)

❷ Sets the markers and subbars to be colored by species.

---

15 There are also x_vars and y_vars parameters enabling you to specify nonsquare grids.

❸ Places histograms of the species' dimensions on the grid's diagonal.

❹ Uses standard scatter plots to compare the dimensions of the diagonal.

As you can see in Figure 10-17, a few lines of Seaborn goes a long way in creating a richly informative set of plots correlating the different Iris metrics. This plot is known as a scatter-plot matrix (*http://bit.ly/1XuexDu*) and is a great way of finding linear correlations between pairs of variables in a multivariate set. As it stands, there is redundancy in the grid: for example, plots for `sepal_width`-`petal_length` and `petal_length`-`septal_width`. `PairGrid` gives you the opportunity to use the redundant plots above or below the main diagonal to provide a different reflection of the data. Check out some of the examples at the Seaborn docs (*http://stanford.io/1YydS2V*) for more info.[16]

I've covered a few of the Seaborn plots in this section, and you'll be seeing a few more when we explore our Nobel Prize dataset in the next chapter. But Seaborn has a lot of other very handy and very powerful plotting tools, mainly of a statistical nature. For further investigation, I'd recommend starting with the main Seaborn documentation (*http://stanford.io/28L8ezk*). There are some nice examples, a well-documented API, and some good tutorials that should complement what you've learned in this chapter.

---

16 There are some nice D3 examples of scatter-plot matrices at the bl.ocks.org site (*https://bl.ocks.org/mbostock/3213173*).

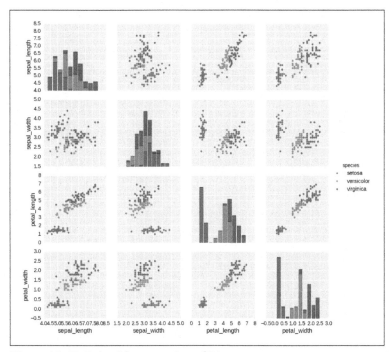

Figure 10-17. Pairgrid summation of Iris measures

Summary

This chapter introduced Matplotlib, Python's plotting powerhouse. It's a big, mature library with lots of documentation and an active community. If you have a particular customization in mind, chances are there's an example out there somewhere. I'd recommend firing up IPython Qt or Notebook (now called Jupyter Notebook (*http://jupyter.org*)) and playing around with a dataset.

We saw how Seaborn extends Matplotlib with some useful statistical methods and that it has what many consider to be superior aesthetics. It also allows access to the Matplotlib figure and axes internals, allowing full customization if required.

In the next chapter we'll use Matplotlib along with Pandas to explore our freshly scraped and cleaned Nobel dataset. We'll use some of the plot types demonstrated in this chapter and see a few useful new ones.

## CHAPTER 11

Exploring Data with Pandas

In the previous chapter, we cleaned the Nobel Prize dataset that we scraped from Wikipedia in Chapter 6. Now it's time to start exploring our shiny new dataset, looking for interesting patterns, stories to tell, and anything else that could form the basis for an interesting visualization.

First off, let's try to clear our minds and take a long, hard look at the data to hand to get a broad idea of the visualizations suggested. Example 11-1 shows the form of the Nobel dataset, with categorical, temporal, and geographical data.

Example 11-1. Our cleaned Nobel Prize dataset

```
[{
  'category': u'Physiology or Medicine',
  'date_of_birth': u'8 October 1927',
  'date_of_death': u'24 March 2002',
  'gender': 'male',
  'link': u'http://en.wikipedia.org/wiki/C%C3%A9sar_Milstein',
  'name': u'C\xe9sar Milstein',
  'country': u'Argentina',
  'place_of_birth': u'Bah\xeda Blanca , Argentina',
  'place_of_death': u'Cambridge , England',
  'year': 1984
},
  ...
}]
```

The data in Example 11-1 suggests a number of *stories* we might want to investigate, among them:

- Gender disparities among the prize winners
- National trends (e.g., which country has most prizes in Economics)
- Details about individual winners, such as their average age on receiving the prize or life expectancy
- Geographical journey from place of birth to adopted country using the born_in and country fields

These investigative lines form the basis for the coming sections, which will probe the dataset by asking questions of it, such as "How many women other than Marie Curie have won the Nobel Prize for Physics?", "Which countries have the most prizes per capita rather than absolute?", and "Is there a historical trend to prizes by nation, a changing of the guard from old (science) world (big European nations) to new (US and upcoming Asians)?" Before beginning our explorations, let's set up IPython and load our Nobel Prize dataset.

Starting to Explore

Before starting our exploration, we need to set up our IPython environment. First fire up an IPython Notebook or Qt console session from the Nobel work directory:

```
$ ipython [notebook | qt]
```

If using the latest IPython Jupyter Notebook, you'll need to run this:

```
$ jupyter notebook
```

In your IPython Qt console or Notebook, use the *magic* matplotlib command to enable inline plotting:

```
%matplotlib inline
```

Then import the standard set of data exploration modules:

```
import pandas as pd
import numpy as np
import matplotlib.pyplot as plt
import json
import seaborn as sb ❶

plt.rcParams['figure.figsize'] = 8, 4 ❷
```

❶ Importing Seaborn will apply its arguably superior looks to all the plots, not just the Seaborn-specific.

❷ Sets the default plotting size to eight inches by four.

At the end of Chapter 9, we saved our clean dataset to MongoDB using a utility function (see "MongoDB" on page 221). Let's load the clean data into a Pandas DataFrame, ready to begin exploring.

```
df = mongo_to_dataframe('nobel_prize', 'winners_clean')
```

Let's get some basic information about our dataset's structure:

```
df.info()
```

```
<class 'pandas.core.frame.DataFrame'>
Int64Index: 858 entries, 0 to 857
Data columns (total 12 columns):
award_age        858 non-null int64
category         858 non-null object
country          858 non-null object
date_of_birth    858 non-null object
date_of_death    559 non-null object
gender           858 non-null object
link             858 non-null object
name             858 non-null object
place_of_birth   831 non-null object
place_of_death   524 non-null object
text             858 non-null object
year             858 non-null int64
dtypes: int64(2), object(10)
memory usage: 87.1+ KB
```

Note that our dates of birth and death columns have the standard Pandas datatype of object. In order to make date comparisons, we'll need to convert those to the datetime type, datetime64. We can use Pandas' to_datetime (*http://pandas.pydata.org/pandas-docs/stable/generated/pandas.to_datetime.html*) method to achieve this conversion:

```
df.date_of_birth = pd.to_datetime(df.date_of_birth)
df.date_of_death = pd.to_datetime(df.date_of_death)
```

Running df.info() should now show two datetime columns:

```
df.info()

...
date_of_birth    858 non-null datetime64[ns]
```

```
date_of_death      559 non-null datetime64[ns]
...
```

to_datetime usually works without needing extra arguments, but it's worth checking the converted columns to make sure. In the case of our Nobel Prize dataset, everything checks out.

Plotting with Pandas

Both Pandas Series and DataFrames have integrated plotting, which wraps the most common Matplotlib charts, a few of which we explored in the last chapter. This makes it easy to get quick visual feedback as you interact with your DataFrame. And if you want to visualize something a little more complicated, the Pandas containers will play nicely with vanilla Matplotlib. You can also adapt the plots produced by Pandas using standard Matplotlib customizations.

Let's look at an example of Pandas' integrated plotting, starting with a basic plot of gender disparity in Nobel Prize wins. Notoriously, the Nobel Prize has been distributed unequally among the sexes. Let's get a quick feel for that disparity by using a bar plot on the *gender* category. Example 11-2 produces Figure 11-1, showing the huge difference, with men receiving 811 of the 858 prizes in our dataset.

Example 11-2. Using Pandas' integrated plotting to see gender disparities

```
by_gender = df.groupby('gender')
by_gender.size().plot(kind='bar')
```

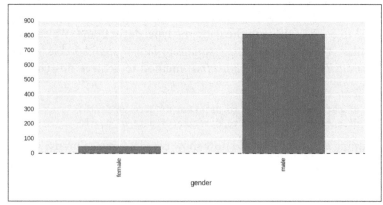

Figure 11-1. Prize counts by gender

In Example 11-2, the Series produced by the gender group's size method has its own integrated plot method, which turns the raw numbers into a chart:

```
by_gender.size()
Out:
gender
female    47
male      811
dtype: int64
```

In addition to the default line plot, the Pandas plot method takes a kind argument to select among other possible plots. Among the more commonly used are:

- bar or barh (*h* for horizontal) for bar plots
- hist for a histogram
- box for a box plot
- scatter for scatter plots

You can find a full list of Panda's integrated plots in the docs (*http:// pandas.pydata.org/pandas-docs/stable/visualization.html#other-plots*) as well as some Pandas plotting functions that take DataFrames and Series as arguments.

Let's extend our investigation into gender disparities and start extending our plotting know-how.

Gender Disparities

Let's break down the gender numbers shown in Figure 11-1 by category of prize. Pandas' groupby method can take a list of columns to group by, with each group being accessed by multiple keys.

```
by_cat_gen = df.groupby(['category','gender'])

by_cat_gen.get_group(('Physics', 'female'))[['name', 'year']] ❶
Out:
                name  year
268    Maria Goeppert-Mayer  1963
613  Marie Skłodowska-Curie  1903
```

❶ Gets a group using a category and gender key.

Using the `size` method to get the size of these groups returns a `Ser`
`ies` with a `MultiIndex` that labels the values by both category and
gender:

```
by_cat_gen.size()
Out:
category                gender
Chemistry               female      4
                        male      167
Economics               female      1
                        male       74

...

Physiology or Medicine  female     11
                        male      191
dtype: int64
```

We can plot this multi-indexed `Series` directly, using `hbar` as the
`kind` argument to produce a horizontal bar chart. This code produces Figure 11-2:

```
by_cat_gen.size().plot(kind='barh')
```

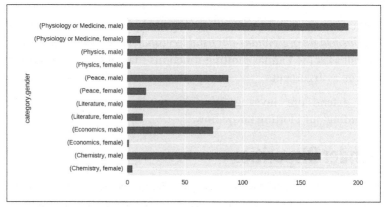

Figure 11-2. Plotting multikey groups

Figure 11-2 is a little crude and makes comparing gender disparities
harder than it should be. Let's go about refining our charts to make
those disparities clearer.

Unstacking Groups

Figure 11-2 isn't the easiest chart to read, even were we to improve the sorting of the bars. Handily, Pandas `Series` have a cool `unstack` method that takes the multiple indices—in this case, gender and category—and uses them as columns and indices, respectively, to create a new `DataFrame`. Plotting this `DataFrame` gives a much more usable plot, as it compares prize wins by gender. The following code produces Figure 11-3:

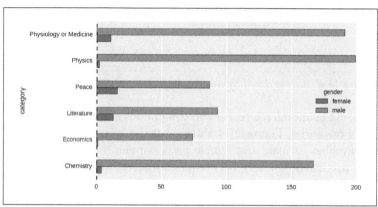

Figure 11-3. Unstacked Series of group sizes

Let's improve Figure 11-3 by ordering the bar groups by number of female winners (low to high) and adding a total winners bar group for comparison. Example 11-3 produces the chart in Figure 11-4.

Example 11-3. Sorting and summing our gender groups

```
cat_gen_sz = by_cat_gen.size().unstack()
cat_gen_sz['total'] = cat_gen_sz.sum(axis=1) ❶
cat_gen_sz = cat_gen_sz.sort_values(by='female', ascending=True) ❷
cat_gen_sz[['female', 'total', 'male']].plot(kind='barh')
```

❶ Sums the male and female totals. The `axis` argument is `0` for index sum, `1` for columns.

❷ Sorts the rows using the `female` field, from low to high.

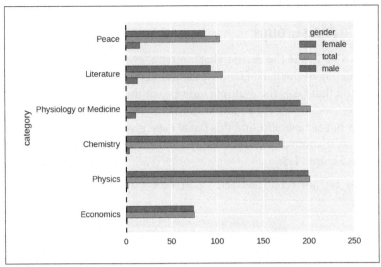

Figure 11-4. Bars ordered by number of female winners

Ignoring Economics, a recent and contentious addition to the Nobel Prize categories, Figure 11-4 shows that the largest discrepancy in the number of male and female prize winners is in Physics, with only two female winners. Let's remind ourselves who they are:

```
df[(df.category == 'Physics') & (df.gender == 'female')]\
    [['name', 'country','year']]

Out:
                      name    country  year
267      Maria Goeppert-Mayer  United States  1963
611  Marie Skłodowska-Curie         Poland  1903
```

While most people will have heard of Marie Curie, who is actually one of the four illustrious winners of two Nobel Prizes, few have heard of Maria Goeppert-Mayer.[1] This ignorance is surprising, given the drive to encourage women into science. I would want my visualization to enable people to discover and learn a little about Maria Goeppert-Mayer.

---

[1] Anecdotally, no one I have asked in person or in talk audiences has known the name of the *other* female Nobel Prize winner for Physics.

Historical Trends

It would be interesting to see if there has been any increase in female prize allocation in recent years. One way to visualize this would be as grouped bars over time. Let's run up a quick plot, using unstack as in Figure 11-3 but using the year and gender columns.

```
by_year_gender = df.groupby(['year','gender'])
year_gen_sz = by_year_gender.size().unstack()
year_gen_sz.plot(kind='bar', figsize=(16,4))
```

Figure 11-5, the hard-to-read plot produced, is only functional. The trend of female prize distributions can be observed, but the plot has many problems. Let's use Matplotlib's and Pandas' eminent flexibility to fix them.

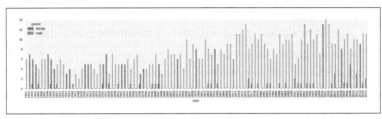

Figure 11-5. Prizes by year and gender

The first thing we need to do is reduce the number of x-axis labels. By default, Matplotlib will label each bar or bar group of a bar plot, which in the case of our hundred years of prizes creates a mess of labels. What we need is the ability to thin out the number of axis labels as desired. There are various ways to do this in Matplotlib; I'll demonstrate the one I've found to be most reliable. It's the sort of thing you're going to want to reuse, so it makes sense to stick it in a dedicated function. Example 11-4 shows a function to reduce the number of ticks on our x-axis.

Example 11-4. Reducing the number of x-axis labels

```
def thin_xticks(ax, tick_gap=10, rotation=45):
    """ Thin x-ticks and adjust rotation """
    ticks = ax.xaxis.get_ticklocs() ❶
    ticklabels = [l.get_text()\
                for l in ax.xaxis.get_ticklabels()] ❶
    ax.xaxis.set_ticks(ticks[::tick_gap]) ❷
    ax.xaxis.set_ticklabels(ticklabels[::tick_gap],\ ❷
                        rotation=rotation) ❸
    ax.figure.show()
```

❶ Gets the existing locations and labels of the x-ticks, currently one per bar.

❷ Sets the new tick locations and labels at an interval of `tick_gap` (default 10).

❸ Rotates the labels for readability, by default on an upward diagonal.

As well as needing to reduce the number of ticks, the x-axis in Figure 11-5 has a discontinuous range, missing the years 1939–1945 of WWII, during which no Nobel Prizes were presented. We want to see such gaps, so we need to set the x-axis range manually to include all years from the start of the Nobel Prize to the current day.

The current unstacked group sizes use an automatic year index:

```
by_year_gender = df.groupby(['year', 'gender'])
by_year_gender.size().unstack()
Out:
gender  female  male
year
1901       NaN    6
1902       NaN    7
...
2014         2   11
[111 rows x 2 columns]
```

In order to see any gaps in the prize distribution, all we have to do is reindex this `Series` with one containing the full range of years:

```
new_index = pd.Index(np.arange(1901, 2015), name='year')   ❶
by_year_gender = df.groupby(['year','gender'])
year_gen_sz = by_year_gender.size().unstack()
    .reindex(new_index)   ❷
```

❶ Here we create a full-range index named `year`, covering all the Nobel Prize years.

❷ We replace our discontinuous index with the new continuous one.

Another problem with Figure 11-5 is the excessive number of bars. Although we do get male and female bars side by side, it looks messy and has aliasing artifacts too. It's better to have dedicated male and female plots but stacked so as to allow easy comparison. We can achieve this using the subplotting method we saw in "Axes and Subplots" on page 270, using the Pandas data but customizing the plot using our Matplotlib know-how. Example 11-5 shows how to do this, producing the plot in Figure 11-6.

Example 11-5. Stacked gender prizes by year

```
new_index = pd.Index(np.arange(1901, 2015), name='year')
by_year_gender = df.groupby(['year','gender'])

year_gen_sz = by_year_gender.size().unstack().reindex(new_index)

fig, axes = plt.subplots(nrows=2, ncols=1, ❶
            sharex=True, sharey=True) ❷

ax_f = axes[0]
ax_m = axes[1]

fig.suptitle('Nobel Prize-winners by gender', fontsize=16)

ax_f.bar(year_gen_sz.index, year_gen_sz.female) ❸
ax_f.set_ylabel('Female winners')

ax_m.bar(year_gen_sz.index, year_gen_sz.male)
ax_m.set_ylabel('Male winners')

ax_m.set_xlabel('Year')
```

❶ Creates two axes, on a two (row) by one (column) grid.

❷ We'll share the x- and y-axes, which will make comparisons between the two plots sensible.

❸ We provide the axis's bar chart (bar) method with the continuous year index and the unstacked gender columns.

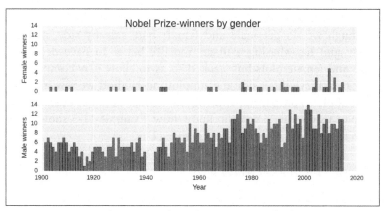

Figure 11-6. Prizes by year and gender, on two stacked axes

So the take-home from our investigation into gender distributions is that there is a huge discrepancy but, as shown by Figure 11-6, a slight improvement in recent years. Moreover, with Economics being an outlier, the difference is greatest in the sciences. Given the fairly small number of female prize winners, there's not a lot more to be seen here.

Let's now take a look at national trends in prize wins and see if there are any interesting nuggets for visualization.

National Trends

The obvious starting point in looking at national trends is to plot the absolute number of prize winners. This is easily done in one line of Pandas, broken up here for ease of reading:

```
df.groupby('country').size().order(ascending=False)\
    .plot(kind='bar', figsize=(12,4))
```

This produces Figure 11-7, showing the United States with the lion's share of prizes.

The absolute number of prizes will be bound to favor countries with large populations. Let's look at a fairer comparison, visualizing prizes per capita.

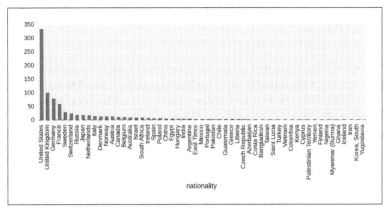

Figure 11-7. Absolute prize wins by country

Prize Winners per Capita

The absolute number of prize winners is bound to favor larger countries, which raises the question, how do the numbers stack up if we account for population sizes? In order to test prize haul per capita, we need to divide the absolute prize numbers by population size. In "Getting Country Data for the Nobel Dataviz" on page 138, we downloaded some country data from the Web and stored it to MongoDB. Let's retrieve it now and use it to produce a plot of prizes relative to population size.

First let's get the national group sizes, with country names as index labels:

```
nat_group = df.groupby('country')
ngsz = nat_group.size()
ngsz.index
Out:
Index([u'Argentina', u'Australia', u'Austria', u'Azerbaijan',...
```

Now let's load our country data into a DataFrame using our utility function mongo_to_dataframe and remind ourselves of the data it contains:

```
df_countries = mongo_to_dataframe('nobel_prize', 'countries')
df_countries.ix[0] # selects the first row by position
Out:
alpha3Code            ARG
area            2.7804e+06
capital       Buenos Aires
gini                  44.5
latlng       [-34.0, -64.0]
```

```
name              Argentina
population         42669500
Name: Argentina, dtype: object
```

If we set the index of our country dataset to its `name` column and add the `ngsz` national group-size `Series`, which also has a country name index, the two will combine on the shared indices, giving our country data a new `nobel_wins` column. We can then use this new column to create a `nobel_wins_per_capita` by dividing it by population size:

```
df_countries = df_nat.set_index('name')
df_countries['nobel_wins'] = ngsz
df_countries['nobel_wins_per_capita'] =\
    df_countries.nobel_wins / df_countries.population
```

We now need only sort the `df_countries DataFrame` by its new `nobel_wins_per_cap` column and plot the Nobel Prize wins per capita, producing Figure 11-8.

```
df_nat.sort('nobel_per_capita', ascending=False)\
    .nobel_per_capita.plot(kind='bar')
```

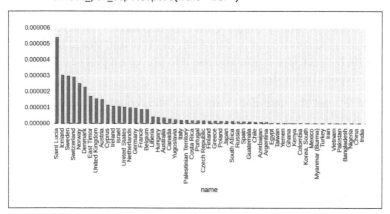

Figure 11-8. National prize numbers per capita

This shows the Caribbean Island of Saint Lucia taking top place. Home to the Nobel Prize–winning poet Derek Walcott (*https:// en.wikipedia.org/wiki/Derek_Walcott*), its small population of 175,000 gives it a high Nobel Prizes per capita.

Let's see how things stack up with the larger countries by filtering the results for countries that have won more than two Nobel Prizes:

```
df_nat[df_nat.nobel_wins > 2]
    .sort('nobel_per_capita', ascending=False)\
    .nobel_per_capita.plot(kind='bar')
```

The results in Figure 11-9 show the Scandinavian countries and Switzerland punching above their weight.

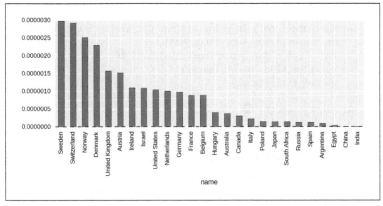

Figure 11-9. National prize numbers per capita, filtered for three or more wins

Changing the metric for national prize counts from absolute to per capita makes a big difference. Let's now refine our search a little and focus on the prize categories, looking for interesting nuggets there.

Prizes by Category

Let's drill down a bit into the absolute prize data and look at wins by category. This will require grouping by country and category columns, getting the size of those groups, unstacking the resulting Ser ies and then plotting the columns of the resulting DataFrame. First we get our categories with country group sizes:

```
nat_cat_sz = df.groupby(['country', 'category']).size()
.unstack()
nat_cat_sz
Out:
category    Chemistry Economics Literature  Peace  \...
country
Argentina           2       NaN        NaN      4
Australia         NaN         2          2    NaN
Austria             6       NaN          2      4
Azerbaijan        NaN       NaN        NaN    NaN
Bangladesh        NaN       NaN        NaN      2
```

We then use the `nat_cat_sz` DataFrame to produce subplots for the six Nobel Prize categories:

```
COL_NUM = 2
ROW_NUM = 3

fig, axes = plt.subplots(ROW_NUM, COL_NUM, figsize=(12,12))

for i, (label, col) in enumerate(nat_cat_sz.iteritems()): ❶
    ax = axes[i/COL_NUM, i%COL_NUM]
    col = col.order(ascending=False)[:10] ❷
    col.plot(kind='barh', ax=ax)
    ax.set_title(label)

plt.tight_layout() ❸
```

❶   `iteritems` returns an iterator for the DataFrames columns in form of (column_label, column) tuples.

❷   `order` orders the column's Series by first making a copy. It is the equivalent of `sort(inplace=False)`.

❸   `tight_layout` should prevent label overlaps among the subplots. If you have any problems with `tight_layout`, see the end of "Titles and Axes Labels" on page 267.

This produces the plots in Figure 11-10.

A couple of interesting nuggets from Figure 11-10 are the United States' overwhelming dominance of the Economics prize, reflecting a post-WWII economic consensus, and France's leadership of the Literature prize.

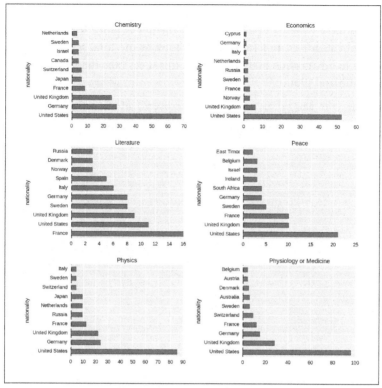

Figure 11-10. Prizes by country and category

Historical Trends in Prize Distribution

Now that we know the aggregate prize stats by country, are there any interesting historical trends to the prize distribution? Let's explore this with some line plots.

First, let's increase the default font size to 20 points to make the plot labels more legible:

```
plt.rcParams['font.size'] = 20
```

We're going to be looking at prize distribution by year and country, so we'll need a new unstacked DataFrame based on these two columns. As previously, we add a new_index to give continuous years:

```
new_index = pd.Index(np.arange(1901, 2015), name='year')

by_year_nat_sz = df.groupby(['year', 'country'])\
    .size().unstack().reindex(new_index)
```

The trend we're interested in is the cumulative sum of Nobel Prizes by country over its history. We can further explore trends in individual categories, but for now we'll look at the total for all. Pandas has a handy cumsum method for just this. Let's take the United States column and plot it:

```
by_year_nat_sz['United States'].cumsum().plot()
```

This produces the chart in Figure 11-11.

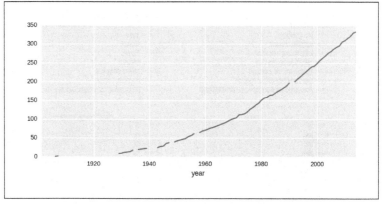

Figure 11-11. Cumulative sum of US prize winners over time

The gaps in the line plot are where the fields are NaN, years when the US won no prizes. The cumsum algorithm returns NaN here. Let's fill those in with a zero to remove the gaps:

```
by_year_nat_sz['United States'].fillna(0)
    .cumsum().plot()
```

This produces the cleaner chart shown in Figure 11-12.

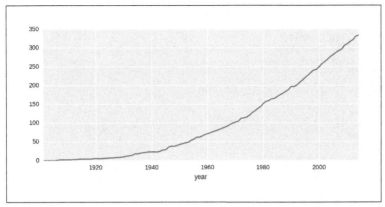

Figure 11-12. Cumulative sum of US prize winners over time

Let's compare the US prize rate with that of the rest of the world:

```python
by_year_nat_sz = df.groupby(['year', 'country'])
    .size().unstack().fillna(0)

not_US = by_year_nat_sz.columns.tolist() ❶
not_US.remove('United States')

by_year_nat_sz['Not US'] = by_year_nat_sz[not_US].sum(axis=1) ❷
ax = by_year_nat_sz[['United States', 'Not US']]\
    .cumsum().plot()
```

❶ Gets the list of country column names and removes United States.

❷ Uses our list of non-US country names to create a 'Not_US' column, the sum of all the prizes for countries in the not_US list.

This code produces the chart shown in Figure 11-13.

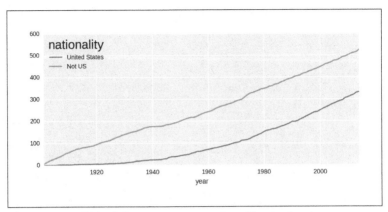

Figure 11-13. United States versus rest of world prize hauls

Where the 'Not_US' haul shows a steady increase over the years of
the prize, the US shows a rapid increase around the end of World
War II. Let's investigate that further, looking at regional differences.
We'll focus on the two or three largest winners for North America,
Europe, and Asia:

```
by_year_nat_sz = df.groupby(['year', 'country'])\
    .size().unstack().reindex(new_index).fillna(0)

regions = [ ❶
    {'label':'N. America',
     'countries':['United States', 'Canada']},
    {'label':'Europe',
     'countries':['United Kingdom', 'Germany', 'France']},
    {'label':'Asia',
     'countries':['Japan', 'Russia', 'India']}
]

for region in regions: ❷
    by_year_nat_sz[region['label']] =\
        by_year_nat_sz[region['countries']].sum(axis=1)

by_year_nat_sz[[r['label'] for r in regions]].cumsum()\
    .plot() ❸
```

❶ Our continental country list created by selecting the biggest two
    or three winners in the three continents compared.

❷ Creates a new column with a region label for each dict in the
    regions list, summing its countries members.

❸ Plots the cumulative sum of all the new region columns.

This gives us the plot in Figure 11-14. The rate of Asia's prize haul has increased slightly over the years, but the main point of note is North America's huge increase in prizes around the mid-1940s, overtaking a declining Europe in total prizes around the mid-1980s.

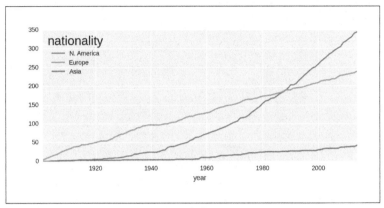

Figure 11-14. Historical prize trends by region

Let's improve the resolution of the previous national plots by summarizing the prize rates for the 16 biggest winners, excluding the outlying United States:

```
COL_NUM = 4
ROW_NUM = 4

by_nat_sz = df.groupby('country').size()
by_nat_sz.sort_values(ascending=False,\
    inplace=True)  ❶

fig, axes = plt.subplots(COL_NUM, ROW_NUM,\  ❷
    sharex=True, sharey=True,  ❷
    figsize=(12,12))

for i, nat in enumerate(by_nat.index[1:17]):  ❸
    ax = axes[i/COL_NUM, i%ROW_NUM]
    by_year_nat_sz[nat].cumsum().plot(ax=ax)  ❹
    ax.set_title(nat)
```

❶ Sorts our country groups from highest to lowest win hauls.

❷ Gets a 4×4 grid of axes with shared x- and y-axes for normalized comparison.

❸ Enumerates over the sorted index from second row (1), excluding the US (0).

❹ Selects the `nat` country name column and plots its cumulative sum of prizes on the grid axis `ax`.

This produces Figure 11-15, which shows some nations like Japan, Australia, and Israel on the rise historically, while others flatten off.

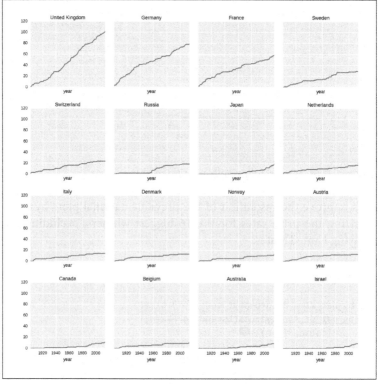

Figure 11-15. Prize rates for the 16 largest national winners after the US

Another good way to summarize national prize rates over time is by using a heatmap and dividing the totals by decade. This division is also known as *binning* (*https://en.wikipedia.org/wiki/Data_binning*), as it creates *bins* of data. Pandas has a handy cut method for just this job, taking a column of continuous values—in our case, Nobel Prize years—and returning ranges of a specified size. You can supply the DataFrame's groupby method with the result of cut and it will group by the range of indexed values. The following code produces Figure 11-16.

```
bins = np.arange(df.year.min(), df.year.max(), 10) ❶

by_year_nat_binned = df.groupby(
    [pd.cut(df.year, bins, precision=0), 'country'])\ ❷
    .size().unstack().fillna(0)

plt.figure(figsize=(8, 8))

sns.heatmap(\
    by_year_nat_binned[by_year_nat_binned.sum(axis=1) > 2]) ❸
```

❶ Gets our bin ranges for the decades from 1901 (1901, 1911, 1921…).

❷ Cuts our Nobel Prize years into decades using the bins ranges with precision set to 0, to give integer years.

❸ Before heatmapping, we filter for those countries with over two Nobel Prizes.

Figure 11-16 captures some interesting trends, such as Russia's brief flourishing in the 1950s, which petered out around the 1980s.

Now that we've investigated the Nobel Prize nations, let's turn our attention to the individual winners. Are there any interesting things we can discover about them using the data at hand?

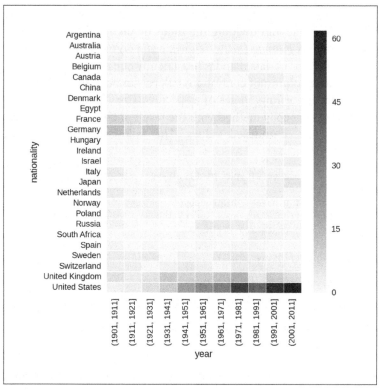

Figure 11-16. Nations' Nobel Prize hauls by decade

Age and Life Expectancy of Winners

We have the date of birth for all our winners and the date of death for 559 of them. Combined with the year in which they won their prizes, we have a fair amount of individual data to mine. Let's investigate the age distribution of winners and try to glean some idea of the winners' longevity.

Age at Time of Award

In Chapter 9 we added an `'award_age'` column to our Nobel Prize dataset by subtracting the winners' ages from their prize years. A quick and easy win is to use Pandas' histogram plot to assess this distribution:

```
df['award_age'].hist(bins=20)
```

Here we require that the age data be divided into 20 bins. This produces Figure 11-17, showing that the early 60s is a sweet spot for the prize and if you haven't achieved it by 100, it probably isn't going to happen. Note the outlier around 20, which is the recently awarded 17-year-old recipient of the Peace Prize, Malala Yousafzai (*https://en.wikipedia.org/wiki/Malala_Yousafzai*).

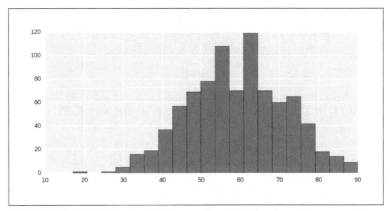

Figure 11-17. Distribution of ages at time of award

We can use Seaborn's `distplot` to get a better feel for the distribution, adding a kernel density estimate (KDE)[2] to the histogram. The following one-liner produces Figure 11-18, showing that our sweet spot is around 60 years of age:

```
sns.distplot(df['award_age'])
```

---

2 See Wikipedia (*https://en.wikipedia.org/wiki/Kernel_density_estimation*) for details. Essentially the data is smoothed and a probability density function derived.

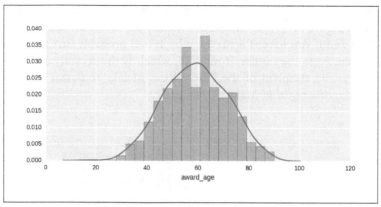

Figure 11-18. Distribution of ages at time of award with KDE super-imposed

A box plot (*https://en.wikipedia.org/wiki/Box_plot*) is a good way of visualizing continuous data, showing the quartiles, the first and third marking the edges of the box and the second quartile (or median average) marking the line in the box. Generally, as in Figure 11-19, the horizontal end lines (known as the whisker ends) indicate the max and min of the data. Let's use a Seaborn box plot and divide the prizes by gender:

```
sns.boxplot(df.gender, df.award_age)
```

This produces Figure 11-19, which shows that the distributions by gender are similar, with women having a slightly lower average age. Note that with far fewer female prize winners, their statistics are subject to a good deal more uncertainty.

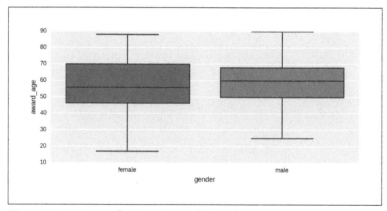

Figure 11-19. Ages of prize winners by gender

Seaborn's rather nice violinplot combines the conventional box plot with a kernel density estimation to give a more refined view of the breakdown by age and gender. The following code produces Figure 11-20.

```
sns.violinplot(df.gender, df.award_age)
```

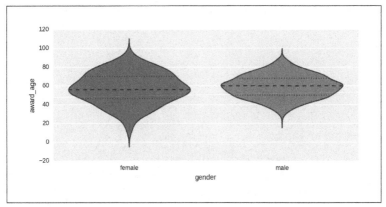

Figure 11-20. Violinplots of prize-age distribution by gender

Life Expectancy of Winners

Now let's look at the longevity of Nobel Prize winners, by subtracting the available dates of death from their respective dates of birth. We'll store this data in a new `'age_at_death'` column:

```
df['age_at_death'] = (df.date_of_death - df.date_of_birth)\
                     .dt.days/365  ❶
```

❶ `datetime64` data can be added and subtracted in a sensible fashion, producing a Pandas `timedelta` column. We can use its `dt` method to get the interval in days, dividing this by 365 to get the age at death as a float.

We make a copy of the `'age_at_death'` column,[3] removing all empty `NaN` rows. This can then be used to make the histogram and KDE shown in Figure 11-21.

---

3 We are ignoring leap years and other subtle, complicating factors in deriving years from days.

```
age_at_death = df[df.age_at_death.notnull()].age_at_death ❶

sns.distplot(age_at_death, bins=40)
```

❶ Removes all `NaNs` to clean the data and reduce plotting errors (e.g., `distplot` fails with `NaNs`).

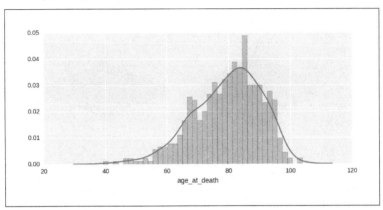

Figure 11-21. Life expectancy of the Nobel Prize winners

Figure 11-21 shows the Nobel Prize winners to be a remarkably long-lived bunch, with an average age in the early 80s. This is all the more impressive given that the large majority of winners are men, who have considerably lower average life expectancies in the general population than women. One contributary factor to this longevity is the selection bias we saw earlier. Nobel Prize winners aren't generally honored until they're in their late 50s and 60s, which removes the subpopulation who died before having the chance to be acknowledged, pushing up the longevity figures.

Figure 11-21 shows some centenarians among the prize winners. Let's find them:

```
df[df.age_at_death > 100][['name', 'category', 'year']]
Out:
                     name           category    year
68   Rita Levi-Montalcini  Physiology or Medicine  1986
103         Ronald Coase              Economics  1991
```

Now let's superimpose a couple of KDEs to show differences in mortality for male and female recipients:

```
df2 = df[df.age_at_death.notnull()] ❶
sns.kdeplot(df2[df2.gender == 'male']
    .age_at_death, shade=True, label='male')
```

```
sns.kdeplot(df2[df2.gender == 'female']
    .age_at_death, shade=True, label='female')

plt.legend()
```

❶ Creates a DataFrame with only valid 'age_at_death' fields.

This produces Figure 11-22, which, allowing for the small number of female winners and flatter distribution, shows the male and female averages to be close. Female Nobel Prize winners seem to live relatively shorter lives than their counterparts in the general population.

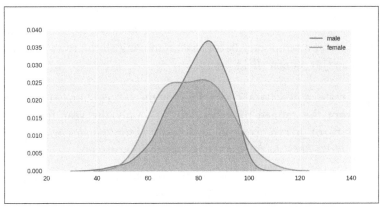

Figure 11-22. Nobel Prize winner life expectancies by gender

A violinplot provides another perspective, shown in Figure 11-23.

```
sns.violinplot(df.gender, age_at_death)
```

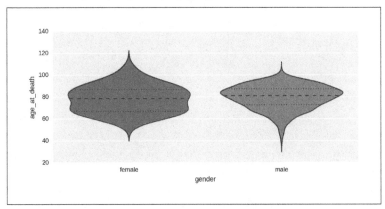

Figure 11-23. Winner life expectancies by gender

Increasing Life Expectancies over Time

Let's do a little historical demographic analysis by seeing if there's a correlation between the date of birth of our Nobel Prize winners and their life expectancy. We'll use one of Seaborn's `lmplot`s to provide a scatter plot and line-fitting with confidence intervals (see "Seaborn" on page 282).

```
df_temp=df[df.age_at_death.notnull()] ❶
data = pd.DataFrame( ❷
    {'age at death':df_temp.age_at_death,
     'date of birth':df_temp.date_of_birth.dt.year})
sns.lmplot('date of birth', 'age at death', data,\
    size=6, aspect=1.5)
```

❶ Creates a temporary `DataFrame`, removing all the rows with no `'age_at_death'` field.

❷ Creates a new `DataFrame` with only the two columns of interest from the refined `df_temp`. We grab only the year from the `date_of_birth`, using its `dt` accessor (*http://pandas.pydata.org/pandas-docs/stable/basics.html#basics-dt-accessors*).

This produces Figure 11-24, showing an increase in life expectancy of a decade or so over the prize's duration.

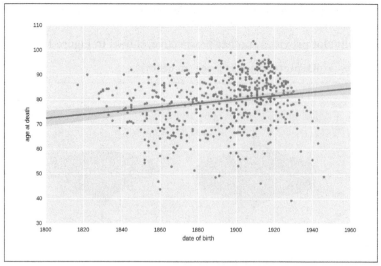

Figure 11-24. Correlating date of birth with age at death

The Nobel Diaspora

While cleaning our Nobel Prize dataset in Chapter 9, we found duplicate entries recording the winner's place of birth and country at time of winning. We preserved these, giving us 104 winners whose country at time of winning was different from their country of birth. Is there a story to tell here?

A good way to visualize the movement patterns from the winners' country of birth to their adopted country is by using a heatmap to show all born_in/country pairs. The following code produces the heatmap in Figure 11-25:

```
by_bornin_nat = df[df.born_in.notnull()].groupby(\ ❶
    ['born_in', 'country']).size().unstack()
by_bornin_nat.index.name = 'Born in' ❷
by_bornin_nat.columns.name = 'Moved to'
plt.figure(figsize=(8, 8))

ax = sns.heatmap(by_bornin_nat, vmin=0, vmax=8) ❸
ax.set_title('The Nobel Diaspora')
```

❶ Selects all rows with a 'born_in' field, and forms groups on this and the country column.

❷ We rename the row index and column names to make them more descriptive.

❸ Seaborn's heatmap attempts to set the correct bounds for the data, but in this case, we must manually adjust the limits (vmin and vmax) to see all the cells.

Figure 11-25 shows some interesting patterns, which tell a tale of persecution and sanctuary. First, the United States is the overwhelming recipient of relocated Nobel winners, followed by the United Kingdom. Note that the biggest contingents for both (except cross-border traffic from Canada) are from Germany. Italy, Hungary, and Austria are the next largest groups. Examining the individuals in these groups shows that the majority were displaced as a result of the rise of antisemitic fascist regimes in the run-up to World War II and the increasing persecution of Jewish minorities.

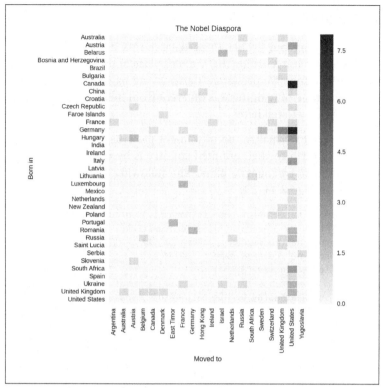

Figure 11-25. The Nobel Prize diaspora

To take an example, all four of the Nobel winners who moved from Germany to the United Kingdom were German research scientists with Jewish ancestry who moved in response to the Nazis' rise to power:

```
df[(df.born_in == 'Germany') & (df.country == 'United Kingdom')]
    [['name', 'date_of_birth', 'category']]
```

```
Out:
                  name date_of_birth             category
976    Ernst Boris Chain   1906-06-19  Physiology or Medicine
1342    Hans Adolf Krebs   1900-08-25  Physiology or Medicine
1344            Max Born   1882-12-11                 Physics
1360        Bernard Katz   1911-03-26  Physiology or Medicine
```

Ernst Chain pioneered the industrial production of penicillin. Hans Krebs discovered the Krebs cycle, one of the most important discoveries in biochemistry, which regulates the energy production of cells. Max Born was one of the pioneers of quantum mechanics, and Bernard Katz uncovered the fundamental properties of synaptic junctions in neurons.

There are many such illustrious names among the winning emigrants. One interesting discovery is the number of prize winners who were part of the famous Kindertransport (*https://en.wikipedia.org/wiki/Kindertransport*), an organized rescue effort that took place nine months before the outbreak of WWII and saw 10,000 Jewish children from Germany, Austria, Czechoslovakia, and Poland transported to the United Kingdom. Of these children, four went on to win a Nobel Prize.

Summary

In this chapter, we explored our Nobel Prize dataset, probing the key fields of gender, category, country, and year (of prize) looking for interesting trends and stories we can tell or enable visually. We used a fair number of Matplotlib (by way of Pandas) and Seaborn's plots, from basic bar charts to more complicated statistical summaries like violinplots and heatmaps. Mastery of these tools and the others in the Python chart armory will allow you to quickly get the feel of your datasets, which is a prerequisite to building a visualization around them. We found more than enough stories in the data to suggest a web visualization. In the next chapter we will imagine and design just such a Nobel Prize winner visualization, cherry-picking the nuggets gained in this chapter.

## PART IV

Delivering the Data

In this part of the book, we'll see how to deliver our select Nobel Prize dataset, recently cleaned and explored, to the browser, wherein JavaScript and D3 will turn it into an engaging, interactive visualization (see Figure IV-1).

The great thing about using a general-purpose library like Python is that you can as easily roll a web server in a few, impressively succinct lines, as mine your data with powerful data-processing libraries.

The key server tool in our toolchain is Flask, Python's powerful but lightweight web framework. In Chapter 12 we'll see how to serve your data statically (serving system files) and dynamically, usually as a database selection specified in the request. In Chapter 13 we'll see how two Flask-based libraries make creating a RESTful web API the work of a few lines of Python.

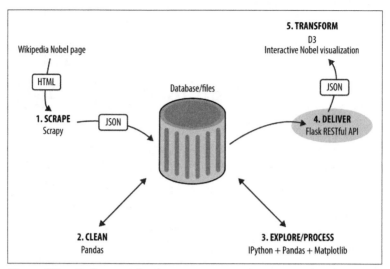

Figure IV-1. Delivering the data

## CHAPTER 12

Delivering the Data

Chapter 6 showed how to grab your data of interest from the Web with a web scraper. We used Scrapy to fetch a dataset of Nobel Prize winners and then in Chapters 9 and 11 we cleaned and explored the Nobel Prize dataset using Pandas.

This chapter will show you how to deliver data statically or dynamically from a Python server to JavaScript on the client/browser, using our Nobel Prize dataset as an example. This data is stored in the JSON format and consists of a list of Nobel Prize–winner objects like the one shown in Example 12-1.

Example 12-1. Our Nobel Prize JSON data, scraped and then cleaned

```
[
  {
    "category": "Physiology or Medicine",
    "country": "Argentina",
    "date_of_birth": "1927-10-08T00:00:00.000Z",
    "date_of_death": "2002-03-24T00:00:00.000Z",
    "gender": "male",
    "link": "http:\/\/en.wikipedia.org\/wiki\/C%C3%A9sar_Milstein",
    "name": "C\u00e9sar Milstein",
    "place_of_birth": "Bah\u00e9da Blanca , Argentina",
    "place_of_death": "Cambridge , England",
    "text": "C\u00e9sar Milstein , Physiology or Medicine, 1984",
    "year": 1984,
    "award_age": 57
  }
  ...
]
```

As with the rest of this book, the emphasis will be on minimizing the amount of web development so you can get down to the business of building the web visualization in JavaScript.

 A good rule of thumb is to aim to do as much data manipulation as possible with Python—it's much less painful than equivalent operations in JavaScript. Following from this, the data delivered should be as close as possible to the form it will be consumed in (i.e., for D3 this will usually be a JSON array of objects, such as the one we produced in Chapter 9).

Serving the Data

You'll need a web server to process HTTP requests from the browser, for the initial static HTML and CSS files used to build the web page, and for any subsequent AJAX requests for data. During development, this server will typically be running on a port of localhost (on most systems this has an IP address of 127.0.0.1). Conventionally, an *index.html* HTML file is used to initialize the website or, in our case, the single-page application (SPA) (*http://bit.ly/1Yyc364*) constituting our web visualization.

The Single-Line Servers

While developing or running demos that depend on static content, it is often handy to have a little web server that just delivers the HTML, CSS, JavaScript, and JSON files to a browser running locally, usually on port 8000 or 8080. The classic Python solution is SimpleHTTPServer, which can be fired up from the root directory of your project with:

```
viz $ python -m SimpleHTTPServer
Serving HTTP on 0.0.0.0 port 8000 ...
```

SimpleHTTPServer works pretty well most of the time but is getting a little long in the tooth. For example, it fails over quite reasonable hurdles like streaming video. And the nature of web data visualization is that you are often close to those edge cases. If you have node.js (see here (*http://bit.ly/23gGEWT*) for installation details) installed, I recommend the even more succinct and more capable

---

`http-server`. Install with `npm install -g http-server` and run from your project root like so:

```
viz $ http-server
Starting up http-server, serving ./ on port: 8080
Hit CTRL-C to stop the server
```

Serving your SPA with a single-line server can be fine for visualization prototyping and sketching out ideas but gives you no control over even basic server functionality, such as URL routing or the use of dynamic templates. Thankfully, Python has a great little web server that provides all the functionality a web visualizer could need without sacrificing our aim to minimize the boilerplate and cruft standing between our Python-processed data and JavaScripted visualization masterwork. Flask is the mini web server in question and a worthy addition to our best-of-breed toolchain.

Most people, if they've heard of a Python web server, have heard of Django. It's a great, full-featured web framework with all sorts of bells and whistles that make the job of creating a *proper* website a breeze. It's also huge and opinionated—for example, using its own object-relational mapping (ORM) to access backend databases, rather than allowing you to choose, for example, SQLAlchemy (in my opinion Python's best SQL library; see "SQL" on page 69). But creating a full-featured website is beyond the scope of this book, and Flask is a better tool for creating a simple API to serve data to a modern web-based visualization and smoothing learning curves. It's considerably more lightweight than Django, allows the use of best-of-breed components (only as many as you need), and can scale to most conceivable dataviz tasks. It's also mature, very well-written,[1] has an active open source community, and has a slew of useful plugins, such as the RESTful libraries we'll be seeing in the next chapter.

Organizing Your Flask Files

How to organize your project files is one of those really useful bits of information that is often neglected in tutorials and the like, possibly

---

1 Flask builds on the much respected Werkzeug (*http://werkzeug.pocoo.org/*), a WSGI (*https://en.wikipedia.org/wiki/Web_Server_Gateway_Interface*) utility library for Python.

because things can get opinionated fast and at the end of the day, it's a personal preference. Nevertheless, good file organization can really pay off, especially when you start collaborating.

Figure 12-1 gives a rough idea of where your files should go as you move from the basic dataviz JavaScript prototype using a one-line server labeled (a), through a more complex project labeled (b), to a typical, simple Flask setup labeled (c).

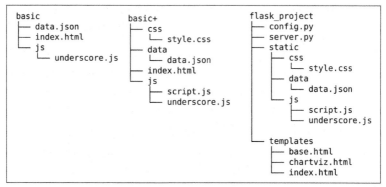

Figure 12-1. Organizing your server project files

The key thing with file organization is consistency. It helps enormously to have the position of files in your procedural memory.

Serving Data with Flask

If, as advised, you're using Python's Anaconda packages (see Chapter 1), then Flask is already available to you. Otherwise, a simple `pip` install should make it available:

```
$ pip install Flask
```

With the Flask modules in hand, we can set up a server with a few lines to serve the universal programming greeting:

```
# nobel_viz.py
from flask import Flask
app = Flask(__name__)

@app.route("/") ❶
def hello():
    return "Hello World!"

if __name__ == "__main__":
    app.run(port=8000, debug=True) ❷
```

❶ Flask routes allow you to direct your web traffic. This is the root route (i.e., *http://localhost:8000*).

❷ Sets the localhost port the server will run on (default 5000). In debug mode, Flask will provide useful logging to screen and in the event of an error, a browser-based report.

Now, just go to the directory containing *nobel_viz.py* and run the module:

```
$ python nobel_viz.py
 * Running on http://127.0.0.1:8000/ (Press CTRL+C to quit)
 * Restarting with stat
 * Debugger is active!
 * Debugger pin code: 231-942-935 ❶
 ...
```

❶ This pin code was recently added for security reasons. See here (*http://bit.ly/1tAL3b1*) for more details.

You can now go to your web browser of choice and see the emphatic result shown in Figure 12-2.

Figure 12-2. A simple message served to the browser

Templating with Jinja2

By default, Flask uses the powerful and fairly intuitive Jinja2 templating library (*http://jinja.pocoo.org/docs/dev/*), which can use Python variables to configure an HTML page. The following code shows a little template that loops through an array of winners to create an unordered list:

```
<!-- testj2.html -->
<!DOCTYPE html>
<meta charset="utf-8">

<body>
  <h2>\{{ heading \}}</h2>
  <ul>
    {% for winner in winners %}
    <li><a href="{{ 'http://wikipedia.com/wiki/'
        + winner.name }}">
```

```
            {{ winner.name }}</a>
            {{ ', category: ' + winner.category }}
        </li>
        {% endfor %}
    </ul>
</body>
```

When using Jinja2 with Flask you will typically use the render_tem
plate method to produce an HTML response from a template in
the project's *templates* (by default) directory. Any arguments made
to render_template after its first template file reference are made
available to the template. So with *testj2.html* in our project's template directory, the following code will render the template when
the user visits the /demolist address, producing the list shown in
Figure 12-3.

```
# ...
app = Flask(__name__)
# ...

winners = [
    {'name': 'Albert Einstein', 'category':'Physics'},
    {'name': 'V.S. Naipaul', 'category':'Literature'},
    {'name': 'Dorothy Hodgkin', 'category':'Chemistry'}
]

@app.route('/demolist')
def demo_list():
    return render_template('testj2.html',
                            heading="A little winners'  list",
                            winners=winners
                            )
```

Jinja2 is a powerful and mature templating language with comprehensive docs (*http://jinja.pocoo.org/docs/dev/*), which makes it a
cinch to use data to render HTML pages server-side.

Figure 12-3. A winners' list rendered from the testj2.html template

As we'll see in "Dynamic Data with Flask" on page 340, pattern matching with Flask routing makes it trivial to roll out a simple web API. It's also easy to use templates to generate dynamic web pages as shown in Figure 12-4. Templates can be useful in visualizations for composing essentially static HTML pages server-side, but generally you'll be delivering a simple HTML backbone on which to build a visualization with JavaScript. With the visualization being configured in JavaScript, the chief job of the server (aside from delivering the static files needed to seed the process) is to dynamically negotiate data (usually providing it) with the browser's and JavaScript AJAX requests.

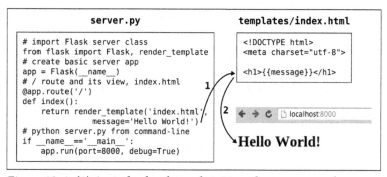

Figure 12-4. (1) An index.html template is used to create a web page using a message variable, which is then (2) served to the browser

Flask is perfectly capable of delivering full websites, with powerful HTML templating, blueprints (*http://bit.ly/1WRJnpp*) for modularizing large sites and supporting common usage patterns, and a slew of useful plugins and extensions. Here (*http://flask.pocoo.org/docs/0.10/*) is a good starting point for learning more, and the API specifics can be found here (*http://bit.ly/1rtEO6U*). The single-page apps that characterize most web visualizations don't need a lot of bells and whistles server-side to deliver the necessary static files. Our key interest in Flask is its ability to provide simple, efficient data servers, with robust RESTful web APIs available in a few lines of Python. We'll demonstrate this in "Dynamic Data with Flask" on page 340 and Chapter 13, but first let's deal with the slower-paced delivery of static data.

Delivering Static Files

Many websites that don't need the overhead of dynamically configured data choose to deliver their data in a *static* form, which essentially means that all the HTML files and, crucially, data (usually in
JSON or CSV format), exist as files on the server's filesystem, ready
to be delivered without, for example, making calls to a database.

Static pages are easy to cache, meaning their delivery can be much
faster. It can also be more secure, as those database calls can be a
common attack vector for nefarious hackers (e.g., injection attacks
(*https://en.wikipedia.org/wiki/SQL_injection*)). The price paid for
this increased speed and security is a loss of flexibility. Being limited
to a set of preassembled pages means prohibiting user interactions
that might demand multivariate combinations of data.

For the budding data visualizer, there is an attraction in supplying
static data. You can easily create a standalone project without needing a web API and are able to deliver your work (in progress) as a
single folder of HTML, CSS, and JSON files.

The simplest example of data-driven web visualizations with static
files is probably that seen in the many cool D3 examples at *http://
bl.ocks.org/mbostock*.[2] They follow a similar structure to the basic
page we discussed in "A Basic Page with Placeholders" on page 105.
Although the examples use <script> and <style> tags to embed
JavaScript and CSS in the HTML page, I'd recommend keeping your
CSS and JavaScript in separate files, where you get the advantages of
a decent format-aware editor and easier debugging.

Example 12-2 shows such an *index.html* basic page with <h2> and
<div> data placeholders and a <script> tag that loads a local
script.js file. As we're only setting the font-family style, we'll inline
the CSS in the page. With our *nobel_winners.json* dataset in a *data*
subdirectory, this gives us the following file structure:

```
viz
├── data
│   └── nobel_winners.json
├── index.html
└── script.js
```

---

2 Mike Bostock, D3's creator, is a big advocate of examples. Here's (*http://bit.ly/1tuhZBp*)
a great talk where he emphasizes the role examples have played in the success of D3.

Example 12-2. A basic HTML page with data placeholders

```html
<!DOCTYPE html>
<meta charset="utf-8">

<style>
  body{ font-family: sans-serif; }
</style>

<h2 id='data-title'></h2>
<div id='data'>
    <pre></pre>
</div>

<script src="http://d3js.org/d3.v3.min.js"></script>
<script src="script.js"></script>
```

The static data file for these examples consists of a single JSON file (*nobel_winners.json*) sitting in a *data* subdirectory. Consuming this data requires a JavaScript AJAX (*https://en.wikipedia.org/wiki/Ajax_%28programming%29*) call to our server. Both jQuery and D3 provide convenient libraries for making AJAX calls, with D3's format-specific `json`, `csv`, and `tsv` methods being handier for web visualizers.[3] Example 12-3 shows how to load data with D3's `json` method using a callback function.

Example 12-3. Using D3's json method to load data

```javascript
d3.json('data/nobel_winners.json', function(error, data){

    if(error){
        console.log(error);
    }

    d3.select('h2#data-title').text('All the Nobel-winners');
    d3.select('div#data pre')
      .html(JSON.stringify(data, null, 4)); ❶

});
```

---

3 For those more familiar with jQuery's AJAX methods, D3's are equally as capable and more convenient for the budding data visualizer. Check out this handy article (*http://blog.webkid.io/replacing-jQuery-with-d3/*) showing how to replace jQuery with D3.

❶ JavaScript's `JSON.stringify` (*https://mzl.la/1WRMJZu*) method is a handy way to prettify a JavaScript object for output. Here we insert some whitespace to indent the output by four spaces.

If you run a one-line server (e.g., `http-server`) in your *viz* directory and open the localhost page in your web browser, you should see something similar to Figure 12-5, indicating the data has been successfully delivered to JavaScript, ready to be visualized.

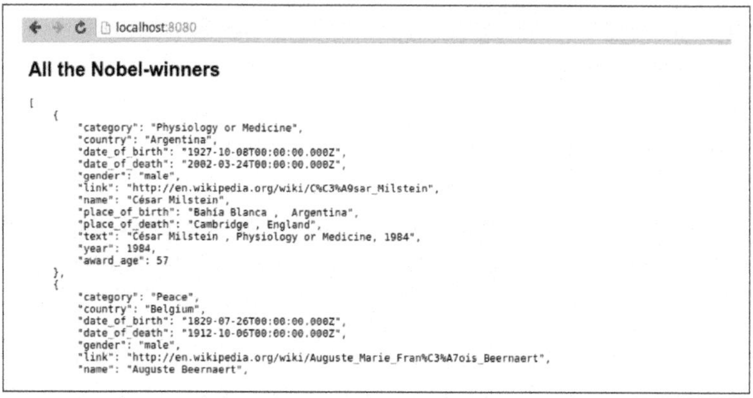

Figure 12-5. Delivering JSON to the browser

The `nobel_winners.json` dataset we're using isn't particularly large, but if we were to start adding biographical body text or other textual data, it could easily grow to a size that strains available browser bandwidth and starts to make the user wait uncomfortably. One strategy to limit loading times is to break the data down into subsets based on one of the dimensions. An obvious way to do this with our data is to store the winners by country. A few lines of Pandas does the job of creating a suitable *data* directory:

```
import pandas as pd

df_winners = pd.read_json('data/nobel_winners.json')

for name, group in df_winners.groupby('country'): ❶
    group.to_json('data/winners_by_country' + name + '.json',\
                  orient='records')
```

❶ Groups the winners `DataFrame` by `country` and iterates over the group name and members.

This should give us a `winners_by_country` *data* subdirectory:

```
$ ls data/winners_by_country
Argentina.json  Azerbaijan.json   Canada.json
Colombia.json   Czech Republic.json  Egypt.json  ...
```

We can now consume our data by country using a little tailor-made function:

```
var loadCountryWinnersJSON = function(country){
    d3.json('data/winners_by_country/' + country + '.json',
      function(error, data) {

        if(error){ console.log(error); }

        d3.select('h2#data-title')
          .text('All the Nobel-winners from ' + country);
        d3.select('div#data pre')
          .html(JSON.stringify(data, null, 4));
    });
};
```

The following function call will select all the Australian Nobel Prize winners, producing Figure 12-6:

```
loadCountryWinnersJSON('Australia');
```

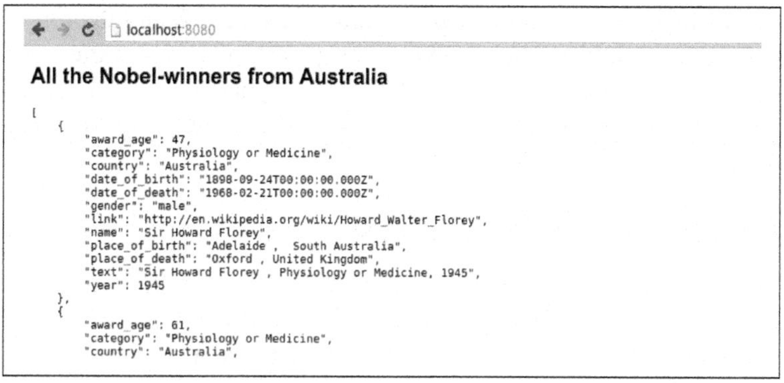

Figure 12-6. Selecting winners by country

For the right visualization, the ability to select winners by country could reduce the data bandwidth and subsequent lag, but what if we wanted winners by year or gender? Each division by dimension (categorical, temporal, etc.) would require its own subdirectory, creating a mess of files and all the bookkeeping that entails. What if we wanted to make fine-grained requests for data (e.g., all US prize winners since 2000)? At this point we need a data server that can respond dynamically to such requests, usually driven by user interaction. The next section will show you how to start crafting such a server with Flask.

Dynamic Data with Flask

Static data delivery has its place, for the reasons just mentioned, and is perfect for small demos and prototypes. But it is an inflexible form of delivery and means all possible required transformations of the data have to be created as files beforehand. Authentication and session management to control user access to data are also more than a little awkward with static files. If you want to restrict certain data to certain people, it's far better to negotiate this through an API call. If the data is changing in size or scope, then an API can inform the client JavaScript, the alternative being increasingly awkward bookkeeping with JSON config files and the like. In short, there is a reason why databases exist and why you probably want a server API to negotiate access to them when your data requirements hit a certain size and/or complexity.

If we're delivering data dynamically, we're going to need some kind of API to enable our JavaScript to request data. In "Using Python to Consume Data from a Web API" on page 134, we covered the types of web API and why RESTful[4] APIs are acquiring a well-deserved prominence. Let's see how easy it is to lay the foundations of a very simple RESTful API with Flask.

A Simple RESTful API with Flask

Example 12-4 shows the beginnings of a very simple Flask-based RESTful server (`server_nosql.py`) using MongoDB. This only implements HTTP GET requests for consuming data.

Example 12-4. A simple RESTful Flask API

```
# server_nosql.py
from flask import Flask, request, abort
from pymongo import MongoClient
from bson.json_util import dumps, default
```

---

4 Essentially, RESTful means resources being identified by a stateless, cacheable URI/URL and manipulated by HTTP verbs such as GET or POST. See here (*http:// bit.ly/1a1kVX5*) for Wikipedia's take and here (*http://bit.ly/1OuMAso*) for a little debate.

```
app = Flask(__name__)

db = MongoClient().nobel_prize

@app.route('/api/winners')
def get_country_data():

    query_dict = {}
    for key in ['country', 'category', 'year']: ❶
        arg = request.args.get(key) ❷
        if arg:
            query_dict[key] = arg

    winners = db.winners_clean.find(query_dict)
    if winners:
        return dumps(winners) ❸
    abort(404) # resource not found

if __name__=='__main__':
    app.run(port=8000, debug=True)
```

❶ Restricts our database queries to keys in this list.

❷ request.args gives us access to the arguments of the request
   (e.g., '?country=Australia&category=Chemistry').

❸ Unlike Python's native json.dumps, bson.dumps can serialize
   date objects and the like to JSON.

In addition to our Flask app, we also make a db reference to the
MongoDB 'winners_clean' table we scraped from the Web and
cleaned. A single route on our app[5] returns some winners from the
table. After checking for valid keys, we use the arguments[6] from the
request as a direct query to the Mongo database, first converting
them to a conventional Python dict. PyMongo's use of a dict-
specified query makes this trivial. If the db request returns data, we

---

5 On our localhost development server, this route would be http://localhost:
  8000/api/winners.

6 This is a dictionary of the key-value pairs specified following the ? on a web call (e.g.,
  http://nobelviz/api/winners?country=USA&category=Physics gives a requests
  dictionary of {'country':'USA', 'category':'Physics'}).

send it back to the client, otherwise throwing an HTTP 404 Not Found error.[7]

Let's set our API running:

```
viz $ python server_nosql_basic.py
 * Running on http://127.0.0.1:8000/ (Press CTRL+C to quit)
 ...
```

Now let's use `requests` from the Python interpreter to test our new web API, getting all Australian winners:

```python
import requests

response = requests.get('http://localhost:8000/api/winners',\
                        params={'country':'Australia'})

response.json()
Out:
[{u'_id': {u'$oid': u'56e068e126a71108192d8534'},
  u'award_age': 47,
  u'category': u'Physiology or Medicine',
  u'country': u'Australia',
  u'date_of_birth': u'1898-09-24T00:00:00.000Z',
  u'date_of_death': u'1968-02-21T00:00:00.000Z',
  u'gender': u'male',
  u'link': u'http://en.wikipedia.org/wiki/
Howard_Walter_Florey',
  u'name': u'Sir Howard Florey',
  u'place_of_birth': u'Adelaide ,  South Australia',
  u'place_of_death': u'Oxford , United Kingdom',
  u'text': u'Sir Howard Florey , Physiology or Medicine, 1945',
  u'year': 1945},
  ...
]
```

Because we're using Flask in debug mode, we can see details of the request at the console:

```
127.0.0.1 [...] "GET /api/winners?country=Australia HTTP" 200
```

Unlike our static country files in the previous section, we're not restricted to dividing our data on one dimension. We can, for example, request all the United States' Physics winners:

---

7 You'll want to use the correct HTTP status codes as your APIs become more interesting. See "Getting Web Data with the requests Library" on page 129 for a rundown of them.

```
response = requests.get('http://localhost:8000/api/winners',\
                        params={'country':'United States',\
                                'category':'Physics'})

response.json()
Out:
[{u'_id': {u'$oid': u'56e068e126a71108192d8262'},
 u'award_age': 42,
 u'category': u'Physics',
 u'country': u'United States',
 u'date_of_birth': u'1969-12-16T00:00:00.000Z',
 u'date_of_death': None,
 u'gender': u'male',
 u'link': u'http://en.wikipedia.org/wiki/Adam_G._Riess',
 u'name': u'Adam G. Riess',
 u'place_of_birth': u'Washington, D.C., United States',
 u'place_of_death': None,
 u'text': u'Adam G. Riess , Physics, 2011',
 u'year': 2011},
  ...
```

Using dataset (see "Easier SQL with Dataset" on page 77), we can
easily adapt Example 12-4 for an SQL database:

```
from flask import Flask, request, abort
import dataset
...
db = dataset.connect('sqlite:///data/nobel_winners.db')
...
@app.route('/api/winners')
def get_country_data():
    print 'Request args: ' + str(dict(request.args))
    query_dict = {}
    for key in ['country', 'category', 'year']:
        arg = request.args.get(key)
        if arg:
            query_dict[key] = arg

    winners = db['winners'].find(**query_dict) ❶
    if winners:
        return dumps(winners)
    abort(404) # resource not found
...
```

❶ dataset's find method requires our argument dictionary to be
  unpacked with ** (i.e., find(country='Australia', cate
  gory='Literature')).

You've now seen how easy it is to start creating a simple API. There are lots of ways one can extend it, but for fast and dirty prototyping, this is a handy little form.

But what if you want pagination, authentication, and a host of other things a sophisticated RESTful API would provide? At this point your Python spidey sense should be tingling along with a strong disinclination to reinvent the wheel. Flask is a very popular framework and RESTful APIs are fast becoming the web standard—somebody somewhere has probably done your job for you. In the next chapter, we'll see two Flask RESTful plugins in action, an SQL and a MongoDB-based NoSQL example. These libraries allow you to roll a full-featured RESTful API in a few lines of Python, providing all the data cutting and slicing a budding web visualizer could possibly need.

Using Static or Dynamic Delivery

When to use static or dynamic delivery is highly dependent on context and is an inevitable compromise. Bandwidths vary regionally and with devices. For example, if you're developing a visualization that should be accessible from a smartphone in a rural context, the data constraints are very different from those of an in-house data app running on a local network.

The ultimate guide is user experience. If a little wait at the beginning while the data caches leads to a lightning-fast JavaScript dataviz, then purely static delivery may well be the answer. If you are allowing the user to cut and slice a large, multivariate dataset, then this probably won't be possible without an annoyingly long wait time. As a rough rule of thumb, any dataset less than 200 KB should be fine with purely static delivery. As you move into the megabytes of data and beyond, you'll probably need a database-driven API from which to fetch your data.

Summary

This chapter explained the rudiments of static data delivery of files on the web server, and dynamic delivery of data, sketching the basis of a simple Flask-based RESTful web server. Although Flask makes rolling a basic data API pretty trivial, adding such bells and whistles as pagination, selective data queries, and the full complement of

HTTP verbs requires a deal more work. For such a full-featured RESTful server, it's best to turn, where possible, to established libraries, and Flask happens to have a number of robust, well-supported libraries catering to the two most common use cases: SQL-based and NoSQL-based databases. In the next chapter, we'll see how two of the most popular Flask RESTful libraries make creating a solid, featureful data API a snap.

## CHAPTER 13

RESTful Data with Flask

In Chapter 12 we saw how to begin building a basic RESTful web server with Flask, limited to GET requests. This allowed retrieval of a dataset and some of its subsets. For most visualizations, the constraint that data be passively consumed, not altered, is acceptable,[1] but even allowing for this, a lot of fairly basic stuff was missing (e.g., the ability to paginate retrieved data, allowing you to control the size of responses from the server). In this chapter, we'll see two Flask RESTful plugins that add this functionality and a whole lot more for the price of a few lines of Python. I think you'll be impressed by how much web API can be rolled with so little.

We'll deal with the two major use cases: serving data from SQL and NoSQL (in the shape of MongoDB) databases with Flask-Restless and Flask Eve, respectively.

Although there are some Flask RESTful plugins that can be adapted to work with both SQL and NoSQL database backends (e.g., Flask-RESTful), in my experience adapting them is a little awkward and, given the shallow learning curve and limited boilerplate code involved, it's easier to stick with the specialist solutions like the two we're about to put through their paces. First off we'll examine Python Eve, a fairly recent Flask RESTful library that is impressively full-featured and succinct.

---

[1] That still leaves a lot of visualizations, such as dashboards, where user-driven changes to data via HTTP POST, PUT, and DELETE are very much required.

A RESTful, MongoDB API with Eve

Python Eve is a plugin for the Flask framework that makes implementing a MongoDB-based RESTful API a relatively painless affair. It's full-featured, with a huge array of options, and has been well thought through. If MongoDB is your database of choice, this is a great way to deliver data to the browser with support for pagination, authentication, and a whole load of things that should cover pretty much every eventuality. If anything's missing, it's a healthy, open source framework with a responsive development team and a large GitHub following (*https://github.com/nicolaiarocci/eve*).

Eve isn't part of the Anaconda Python package recommended for this book but can easily be installed with `pip`:

```
$ pip install eve
```

Once Eve is installed, we can turn our existing MongoDB 'nobel_prize' database into a fully fledged RESTful API with the addition of a couple of lines to a *settings.py* file. We'll be putting our Eve files in an *api* subdirectory of our root *nobel_viz* directory:

```
nobel_viz
├── index.html
├── nobel_viz.py
├── api
│   ├── server_eve.py
│   └── settings.py
...
```

In *settings.py* we specify our preferred URL prefix for the API (`api`), the name of the database we're serving (`nobel_prize`), and the table we're exposing (`winners`) in the DOMAIN dictionary. It's sensible to add a schema providing at least the type of the fields we're exposing:

```
# api/settings.py

# Optional MONGO variables
#MONGO_HOST = 'localhost'
#MONGO_PORT = 27017
#MONGO_USERNAME = 'user'
#MONGO_PASSWORD = 'user'

URL_PREFIX = 'api'
MONGO_DBNAME = 'nobel_prize'
DOMAIN = {'winners':{
    'schema':{                    ❶
        'country':{'type':'string'},
```

```
        'category':{'type':'string'},
        'name':{'type':'string'},
        'year':{'type': 'integer'},
        'gender':{'type':'string'}
    }
}}
```

❶ The schema allows us to expose fields in our winners data that we want delivered with the item data. It is also used for proper data validation. The schema definition is based on the Cerberus grammar (*https://github.com/nicolaiarocci/cerberus*).

There are a huge number of Eve-specific parameters (*http://bit.ly/1tui8VC*) you can add to the settings. There's also a comprehensive section on DOMAIN configuration (*http://bit.ly/261YMZA*). With the settings specified, we need only create a tiny server module in the same directory:

```
# api/server_eve.py
from eve import Eve

app = Eve()

if __name__=='__main__':
    app.run(debug=True)
```

You can now go to the *api* directory and start the server, like so:

```
$ python server_eve.py
 * Running on http://127.0.0.1:5000/ (Press CTRL+C to quit)
 * Restarting with stat
```

Testing APIs with curl

curl is a handy command-line tool for transferring data using various protocols. It's pretty easy to do the same using Python's requests module, but sometimes curl is just that little bit more convenient and a useful way of demonstrating the general-purpose nature of your RESTful API, being language-agnostic. Unlike requests, with curl you don't have to quiz a response object to get the output. Basic retrieval is as easy as:

```
curl www.example.com
```

curl can handle posted data, HTTP headers, and all the other aspects of an HTTP request. See here (*http://curl.haxx.se/docs/manpage.html*) for more details.

Let's get all the French Nobel Prize winners using a where clause to specify our query. Note that we use curl's -g flag to switch off its URL globbing parser (*http://ec.haxx.se/cmdline-globbing.html*). The globbing parser interprets the brackets ({} and []). By turning it off, we can use them to construct our Eve query:

```
curl -g http://127.0.0.1:5000/api/winners\?where\=
\{\"country\":\"France\"\}
{
  "_items": [
    {
      "category": "Chemistry",
      "_updated": "Thu, 01 Jan 1970 00:00:00 GMT",
      "name": "Ir\u00e8ne Joliot-Curie",
      "gender": "female",
      "year": 1935,
      "_links": { ❶
        "self": {
          "href": "winners\/568d03a826a7113f2cc0a86a",
          "title": "Winner"
        }
      },
      "country": "France",
      "_created": "Thu, 01 Jan 1970 00:00:00 GMT",
      "_id": "568d03a826a7113f2cc0a86a",
      "_etag": "dcaff67c8e9ab22a6830fec9313ed61c8a1c8ffc"
    },
    ...
    "_meta": {
    "max_results": 25, ❷
    "total": 60,
    "page": 1
  }
}
```

❶ Eve has *Hypermedia as the Engine of Application State* (HATEOAS (*https://en.wikipedia.org/wiki/HATEOAS*)) enabled by default (set the domain's hateoas variable to False in *settings.py* to turn it off). This allows clients to dynamically navigate the API without knowing its structure beforehand (see the Python Eve site (*http://python-eve.org/features.html#hateoas*) for details).

❷ Pagination is on by default, delivering a maximum of 25 items from the 60 French winners available. The PAGINATION_DEFAULT setting allows you to specify how large you want the item pages to be.

Eve supports the full MongoDB query document (*https://docs.mongodb.org/manual/tutorial/query-documents/*) and operators (*https://docs.mongodb.org/manual/reference/operator/query/*), allowing fine-grained access to the dataset. For example, let's request all female winners since the year 2000:[2]

```
curl -g http://127.0.0.1:5000/api/winners\?
          where\=\{\"year\"\:\{\"\$gt\"\:2000\},
          \"gender\":\"female\"\}
{
  "_items": [
    {
      "category": "Peace",
      "_updated": "Thu, 01 Jan 1970 00:00:00 GMT",
      "name": "Leymah Gbowee",
      "gender": "female",
      "year": 2011,
      "_links": {
        "self": {
          "href": "winners\/568d03a826a7113f2cc0a8a2",
          "title": "Winner"
        }
      },
      "country": "Liberia",
      "_created": "Thu, 01 Jan 1970 00:00:00 GMT",
      "_id": "568d03a826a7113f2cc0a8a2",
      "_etag": "78126885f22a973af96e39f293df16f270a13c1e"
    },
    ...
      "_meta": {
      "max_results": 25,
      "total": 17,
      "page": 1
    }
  }
}
```

Eve is extremely configurable, with a huge range of options (*http://python-eve.org/config.html*) with which to craft a RESTful API fitting your exact requirements. For example, you can change the query keynames (where, sort, etc.), specify date formatting for Python datetime values, fix the HTTP methods allowed at resource endpoints (default is ['GET']), rate-limit requests, and set the value of the Cache-Control header field used when serving GET requests.

---

2 When using MongoDB's mathematical operators such as $gt (greater than), it's important to specify the right field type (integer in the case of years) for your schema declaration in *settings.py*.

Using AJAX to Access the API

Now that we've used curl to verify that our Eve API is working, let's see how to access it from a browser using a JavaScript AJAX call. To demonstrate good practice, the JavaScript consuming the data will be run from a different server than the one running the API.

We'll make the AJAX request from a page served by a basic Flask web server that just delivers an *index.html* in the root directory. The following code sets up that server, running on port 8080 (our API is on port 5000) and serving a little HTML index file:

```python
# nobel_viz.py
from flask import Flask, send_from_directory

app = Flask(__name__)

@app.route('/')
def root():
    return send_from_directory('.', 'index.html')  ❶

if __name__ == '__main__':
    app.run(port=8080)
```

❶ Serves a file from the directory—in this case, the local directory (.)]—specified in the first argument.

The *index.html* file we're serving has a couple of placeholders for the request and response data, and adds the jQuery and D3 libraries along with the *script.js* file containing the AJAX call:

```html
<!-- index.html -->
<!DOCTYPE html>
<meta charset="utf-8">

<style>
  body{ font-family: sans-serif;}
</style>

<h3>Request</h3>
<div id='query'>
    <pre></pre>
</div>

<h3>Response</h3>
<div id='data'>
    <pre></pre>
</div>
```

```
<script src="//code.jQuery.com/jQuery-1.11.0.min.js"></script>
<script src="http://d3js.org/d3.v3.min.js"></script>

<script src="static/js/script.js"></script>
```

To make the AJAX GET request, we'll use one of D3's request methods (*https://github.com/mbostock/d3/wiki/Requests*) to make an XMLHttpRequest, or XHR (*http://en.wikipedia.org/wiki/XMLHttpRequest*). D3's convenience method `json` is built on the main `xhr` method but is specialized for getting JSON data. If the request is successful, the data is delivered as fully parsed JSON, ready to use.

Example 13-1 shows the code required to make an AJAX call for JSON data to our Eve API. The `displayJSON` method takes a query string (e.g., `'/winners?where={"gender":"female}'`) and uses it to make a request for JSON data to the API.

Example 13-1. Making an AJAX call to the Eve API with D3

```
// static/js/script.js
var API_URL = 'http://localhost:5000/api';

var displayJSON = function(query) {

    d3.json(API_URL + query, function(error, data) {

        // log any error to the console as a warning
        if(error){
            return console.warn(error);
        }

        d3.select('#query pre').html(query); ❶
        d3.select('#data pre').html(JSON.stringify(data, null, 4));
        console.log(data);
    });
};

var query = '/winners?where=' + JSON.stringify({ ❷
    "year": {"$gt":2000},
    "gender": "female"
});

displayJSON(query);
```

❶ We use D3 to select our content `pre` tags and fill them with the query string and the JSON data returned from the server, using `JSON.stringify` to turn the JavaScript object into a formatted JSON string.

❷ Here we construct the query string to our API, with a `where` argument containing the MongoDB query dictionary.

Now that our data flow is in place, let's start the `nobel_viz` server running, serving our simple *index.html* file:

```
$ python nobel_viz.py
 * Running on http://127.0.0.1:8080/ (Press CTRL+C to quit)
```

With the server running, if you open your browser and navigate to *http://localhost:8080*, you'll see that the AJAX call has failed. Opening the browser's console (Ctrl-Shift-I on Chrome) will show something like Figure 13-1 indicating that the API request has been denied because of the CORS constraint. You can also see the `XMLHttpRequest` logged-on error by the `d3.json` method in Example 13-1.

Figure 13-1. Cross-origin error on request

Cross-Origin Resource Sharing

Although you can serve your data web API from the same server as all your other HTML, that's not a very flexible approach and it's often better to have the API stand alone. This means it can be used by multiple sites and placed wherever you want (e.g., if large datasets are involved, somewhere cheap and reliable). If you want to call down data from a different server to the one generating the Java-Script AJAX call, you'll run into *cross-origin resource sharing* (CORS).

CORS (*http://en.wikipedia.org/wiki/Cross-origin_resource_sharing*) is a mechanism that allows restricted resources on a web page to be requested from a domain other than that from which the resource originated. In other words, it allows your JavaScript to request data from another website—in our case, the RESTful data server. These types of requests are forbidden by default for security purposes (they would make it trivial to *emulate* another site, for example, possibly fooling the user into giving away sensitive information). CORS lets us get around this constraint by allowing the data server (in our example) to specify whitelisted sites through its `Access-Control-Allow-Origin` header. Setting this to * allows all sites to access the data; setting it to `http://foo.com` allows only requests from *foo.com*. Figure 13-2 shows a request loop being mediated by CORS.

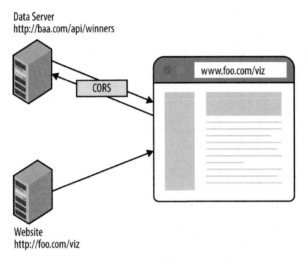

Figure 13-2. Getting data from a RESTful web API

CORS should be mediated by the HTTP server (e.g., Apache or Nginx), but it's useful during development to specify it at the application level in order to easily test your APIs.

With regard to CORS restrictions, Eve has a number of variables that allow you to expose a standalone API to selected sites. For example, the `X_DOMAINS` variable allows a list of domains that are allowed to perform a CORS request (the default is `None`). `X_DOMAINS` can take a string or list of strings specifying the domains from which calls to the API are allowed (a whitelist). We are running our `nobel_viz` server from `http:localhost:8080`, so adding the following to *settings.py* will allow the API call and stop the CORS error:

```
# ...
X_DOMAINS = 'http://localhost:8080'
```

If you wanted to allow all sites to access the API (only advisable during development and then with caution), you could use an asterisk wildcard for `X_DOMAINS`:

```
# ...
X_DOMAINS = '*'
```

If you add our `X_DOMAIN` whitelist to *settings.py*, restart the `nobel_viz`, and navigate to `http:localhost:8080`, you should see something like Figure 13-3 showing that our request for all female Nobel Prize winners since the year 2000 has been successful.

Figure 13-3. Displaying the data retrieved by AJAX to the browser window

Now that we know how to roll a MongoDB RESTful API with Eve and a few lines of Python, let's see how we extend it to deliver the Nobel Prize dataset to our Nobel Prize web visualization.

Delivering Data to the Nobel Prize Visualization

At this point along our toolchain, we have three datasets that will be needed for our visualization:

1. The `winners` dataset of basic Nobel Prize winner information, which we cleaned in Chapter 9.

2. The `winners_bios` dataset of winners' images and mini-biographies, which we scraped in "Scrapy Pipelines" on page 185.

3. The country data we downloaded in "Getting Country Data for the Nobel Dataviz" on page 138, with useful national statistics.

The winners and country datasets are fairly small and will be required to initialize the visualization. It makes sense to download them in their entirety. The winners_bios dataset is considerably larger than the others, containing a few paragraphs of body text for each winner. As the biographies will only be used one at a time, it is better that they be downloaded as required, driven by user interaction. As datasets become nontrivial, downloading the whole set and caching in JavaScript becomes impractical. It's likely the user will only be interested in a tiny fraction of the data available and it's better to supply that on demand with AJAX than risk a lengthy start-up.

We'll use MongoDB and Eve to deliver the winners' data for our Nobel Prize visualization. While we could keep the winners and winners_bios datasets separate (in an SQL database such tabular decomposition into, say, users and biographies is usual), in a document-based database it seems more natural to store all the data on an individual in one document. This also simplifies our API to one exposed domain/table. Given this, we'll be using the merged dataset winners_all we created in "Saving the Cleaned Dataset" on page 257, which contains all the Nobel Prize data we scraped (with the filepaths for our Nobel photos).

First we adapt Eve's *settings.py* file with our new DOMAIN and the X_DOMAINS variable set to allow all CORS requests (for all domains, during development). We'll also set the HATEOAS variable to False as we won't be using those links, and turn off pagination so we can get the set of Nobel Prize winners on our first initializing request:

```
# api/settings.py
URL_PREFIX = 'api'
DOMAIN = {'winners_full':{
    'item_title': 'winners',
    'schema':{
        'country':{'type':'string'},
        'category':{'type':'string'},
        'name':{'type':'string'},
        'year':{'type': 'integer'},
        'gender':{'type':'string'},
        'mini_bio':{'type':'string'}, ❶
        'bio_image':{'type':'string'}
    },
```

```
        'url':'winners'  ❷
}}
. . .
X_DOMAINS = '*'
HATEOAS = False
PAGINATION = False
```

❶ Adds fields for our biographical data.

❷ The url key allows us to change from the winners_full default
    for the domain to the preferable winners (i.e., /api/winners?
    \where...).

We'll use the same server setup we saw in "Using AJAX to Access the
API" on page 352 to test our API, using the displayJSON method
from Example 13-1 to send a URL and some query data to an AJAX
GET request. If the request is successful, we'll see the results on the
web page.

Within the visualization, we'll be making two types of requests for
data:

1. Get the basic data for all the Nobel Prize winners without
   including the large mini_bio field.
2. Get all the data for a single individual.

In order to make request 1, we need to tell our API to withhold the
mini_bio field. We can achieve this by using a cool feature of Eve,
projections (http://python-eve.org/features.html#projections). Projections allow us to selectively turn fields on (to the exclusion of all
others) or off (sending everything else).[3] So to get all the winners
data without the mini-bios, we just add a projection argument to
our API request. In the following code, we use the displayJSON
method from Example 13-1 to display the request string and JSON
response data in the browser window:

```
var query = '/winners?projection=' + JSON.stringify({  ❶
    "mini_bio":0
});

displayJSON(query);
```

---

3 Note that one limitation of MongoDB is that you can't mix inclusive and exclusive
  projections.

❶ The `projection` argument is an exclusive dictionary that removes the `mini_bio` field from the Nobel Prize winner items returned on a request to the `winners` resource of our API.

This should produce Figure 13-4, showing that the items are missing the `mini_bio` field.

```
← → ⟳  🗋 localhost:8080

Request

{
    "projection": "{\"mini_bio\":0}"
}

Response

{
    "_items": [
        {
            "category": "Physiology or Medicine",
            "_updated": "Thu, 01 Jan 1970 00:00:00 GMT",
            "name": "César Milstein",
            "country": "Argentina",
            "year": 1984,
            "gender": "male",
            "bio_image": "full/6bf65058d573e07b72231407842018afc98fd3ea.jpg",
            "_id": "5693be6c26a7113f2cc0b33a",
            "_etag": "73ffa45d17210944b49516b14097e04905b496ce",
            "_created": "Thu, 01 Jan 1970 00:00:00 GMT"
        },
        {
            "category": "Peace",
            "_updated": "Thu, 01 Jan 1970 00:00:00 GMT",
            "name": "Auguste Beernaert",
            "country": "Belgium",
            "year": 1909,
            "gender": "male",
```

Figure 13-4. Requesting all the winners, without the biographical text

As part of the visualization, we want the user to be able to select one of the filtered winners from a list and then display any available photograph and biographical text we scraped from Wikipedia. With the dataset we're using, the size of the biographical text is much greater than the other fields combined, so we don't really need to use a projection to select it exclusively. But as a demonstration, let's select a certain famous Nobel Prize winner based on his name and include the biographical data we scraped in "Scraping Text and Images with a Pipeline" on page 187:

```
...

var query = '/winners?where=' + JSON.stringify({
    "name":"Albert Einstein"});

displayJSON(query);
```

Although for demonstration we queried for Albert Einstein by name on the `winners` collection, the items in Figure 13-4 provide their MongoDB ids with an `_id` field. We can use this id to request an individual winner resource directly, providing a cleaner data response:

```
// on selection of Albert Einstein (albert_item):

// http://localhost:5000/api/winners/5693be6c26a7113f2cc0b601
var query = '/winners/' + albert_item._id;

displayJSON(query);
```

This produces a nice, clean data object shown in Figure 13-5, with which to build a little biographical window.

Figure 13-5. Requesting the biographical data for a single Nobel Prize winner

We now have the RESTful API needed for the Nobel Prize visualization and the queries required to get the data we need. In the coming chapters, we'll see how that data is turned into a modern, interactive web visualization.

Eve comes with MongoDB support out of the box and, in terms of documentation, community support, and so on, is currently a NoSQL specialist. It was envisaged that Eve would provide support for SQL databases, and there is a recent eve-sqlalchemy (*https://github.com/RedTurtle/eve-sqlalchemy*) extension that does just this. It is currently at version 0.1 and has a small (but growing) GitHub following. For now, if you need to use an SQL database, I'd recommend using a library dedicated to the job. Flask-Restless (*https://flask-restless.readthedocs.org/en/latest/*) is a good choice and is particularly easy to get up and running. Let's now see how it works.

RESTful SQL with Flask-Restless

There are a number of SQL-capable Flask RESTful plugins, including the powerful and well-specced Flask RESTful,[4] but Flask-Restless is quite a bit easier to get up and running and for most data visualization work (primarily about consuming data) does the job nicely.

Flask-Restless is not part of the Anaconda Python package so will need a `pip` install:

```
$ pip install flask-restless
```

For this section, you will also need the Flask-SQLAlchemy plugin, once again installed with `pip`:

```
$ pip install flask-sqlalchemy
```

Creating the API

With our modules installed, let's create an API based on our stored SQLite *nobel_prize.db* database (see "Saving the Cleaned Dataset" on page 257). The `winners` table contains the scraped and cleaned winners data so we'll expose that, using an SQLAlchemy schema to specify the data we require.

Example 13-2 shows the code required to turn our *winners* table into a RESTful resource.

Example 13-2. Nobel Prize winners Flask-Restless API

```python
# server_flask_restless.py
import flask
import flask.ext.sqlalchemy
import flask.ext.restless


# Create the Flask application and the Flask-SQLAlchemy object.
app = flask.Flask(__name__)
app.config['DEBUG'] = True
```

---

4 Flask RESTful wins the GitHub stars award by a comfortable margin and is a very good library.

```
app.config['SQLALCHEMY_DATABASE_URI'] = \
'sqlite:///data/nobel_prize.db'

db = flask.ext.sqlalchemy.SQLAlchemy(app)

# Create your Flask-SQLALchemy models as usual but with the
# following two (reasonable) restrictions:
#   1. They must have a primary key column of type
#      sqlalchemy.Integer or type sqlalchemy.Unicode.
#   2. They must have an __init__ method which accepts keyword
#      arguments for all columns (the constructor in
#      flask.ext.sqlalchemy.SQLAlchemy.Model supplies such a
#      method, so you don't need to declare a new one).
class Winners(db.Model):
    __tablename__ = 'winners' # optional, default being class-name
    index = db.Column(db.Integer, primary_key=True) ❶
    name = db.Column(db.Unicode, unique=True)
    category = db.Column(db.Unicode)
    year = db.Column(db.Unicode)
    country = db.Column(db.Unicode)
    gender = db.Column(db.Unicode)


# Create the database tables.
db.create_all()

# Create the Flask-Restless API manager.
manager = flask.ext.restless.APIManager(app, flask_sqlalchemy_db=db)

# Create API endpoints, which will be available at
# /api/<tablename> by default.
# Allowed HTTP methods can be specified as well.
manager.create_api(Winners,
                   methods=['GET'], # optional POST, DELETE etc..
                   max_results_per_page=1000)

# start the flask loop
app.run()
```

❶ The index of our saved Pandas `DataFrame` (see "Saving the Cleaned Dataset" on page 257).

Flask-Restless is doing some introspective magic behind the scenes, simplifying the boilerplate. Note that by default the name of our db.Model (Winners) is the capitalized name of the table we're exposing, which we can set explicitly by declaring the class __table name__ variable. The Flask app is first used to create an SQLAlchemy database db, which in turn creates the Winners model. The database and app are then used to configure a Flask-Restless `APIManager`. Finally, the `create_api` method is used to make a resource point for the `winners` table. We restrict HTTP methods to GET and increase the maximum results per page to 1,000.

Adding CORS Support

While CORS is best handled in production servers by the likes of Apache (*http://bit.ly/1Ue2eWa*) or Nginx (*http://bit.ly/23gK63y*), in order to test standalone API, it's useful to be able to regulate access during development. Flask has a handy plugin (*http://bit.ly/23gJH1d*) for just this need, which works well with Flask-Restless. A `pip` install will make it available:

```
$ pip install flask-cors
```

We can then add a few lines to our RESTful server (see Example 13-2) to add CORS support.

```
...
from flask.ext.cors import CORS

app = flask.Flask(__name__)
...
app.config['CORS_ALLOW_HEADERS'] = "Content-Type"
app.config['CORS_RESOURCES'] = {r"/api/*": {"origins": "*"}}  ❶

...
cors = CORS(app)
...

app.run()
```

❶ For development, we'll expose the URL route `/api/` to requests from any origin.

With our API established and CORS support in place, let's start the RESTful server running:

```
$ python server_flask_restless.py
 * Running on http://127.0.0.1:5000/ (Press CTRL+C to quit)
```

With our server up and running, let's start requesting some data.

Querying the API

The Flask-Restless API provides a wide range of query operators (*http://bit.ly/1UEwBEM*), allowing you full control over the data you want returned. The Flask-Restless query engine is pretty fine-grained, essentially emulating the standard SQL operation set. The operator strings recognized by the API include:

- ==, eq, equals, equals_to
- !=, neq, does_not_equal, not_equal_to
- >, gt, <, lt
- >=, ge, gte, geq, \<=, le, lte, leq
- in, not_in
- is_null, is_not_null
- like, has, any

These correspond to the SQLAlchemy column operators (*http://bit.ly/1UEz7uA*).

Let's use the displayJSON method from Example 13-1 to request some JSON data from our API using a query string. We'll use a couple of filters to specify all female winners since the year 2000 and order them by ascending year. These filters take a column name, SQL operation (e.g., not_in), and value. The following code should produce the browser output shown in Figure 13-6 if you navigate to http://localhost:8080:

```
// ...
var filters = [ {"name":"year", "op":"gte", "val":2000},
                {"name":"gender", "op":"==", "val":"female"} ];

var order_by = [ {"field":"year", "direction":"asc"} ];

var query = '/winners?' +
    'q=' + JSON.stringify({'filters':filters,
                           'order_by': order_by
                          });

displayJSON(query);
```

As you can see from Figure 13-6, by default the output of Flask-Restless is a good deal less sophisticated than that of Eve. The metadata and HATEOS (*https://en.wikipedia.org/wiki/HATEOAS*) links are missing and only the item data specified in the SQLAlchemy model is included. This would be a drawback for certain applications, but most visualization work only really needs these object fields.

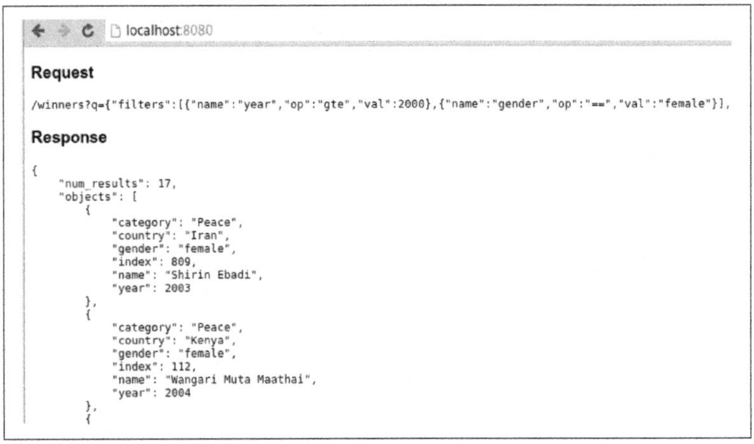

Figure 13-6. Querying the Nobel Prize winners API

Flask-Restless gives you all the fine-grained queries you're likely to need and, in conjunction with SQLite, is a very lightweight solution to a data API.

Summary

This chapter showed how Python and Flask can combine with ease to deliver your data to the web browser with a flexible, RESTful API. This ability really opens up the possibilities of web dataviz. Although you can do some amazing things with your data delivered in static files, being able to negotiate fine-grained access to a server-side database extends the realm of web dataviz enormously. Depending on the bandwidth available, for datasets beyond a few hundred kilobytes, caching all the data on initialization is likely to make for a slow, frustrating user experience.

We also saw how we'll use Flask Eve to deliver the winners' data our visualization will need, using projections to dictate which data fields are needed. In the next chapter we'll see how that data is used to initialize our Nobel Prize visualization.

Visualizing Your Data with D3

In this part of the book, we take our hard-won Nobel Prize dataset, scraped from the web in Chapter 6 and cleaned in Chapter 9, and turn it into a modern, engaging, interactive web visualization using primarily the fantastic D3 library (see Figure V-1). We'll deliver the main Nobel Prize dataset using the RESTful API we built in "Delivering Data to the Nobel Prize Visualization" on page 356, and the other data statically, as shown in "Delivering Static Files" on page 336.

We'll cover the realization of the Nobel Prize dataviz in some detail, acquiring D3 and JavaScript knowledge as we go. First, let's imagine what our visualization should be, using insights gained in Chapter 11.

You can find the Python and JavaScript source code for this visualization in the *nobel_viz* directory of the book's GitHub repo (see "The Accompanying Code" on page 1 for details).

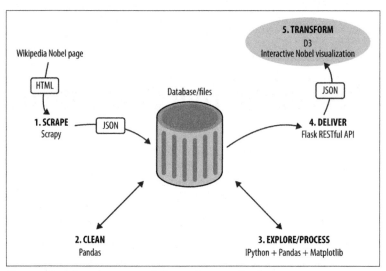

Figure V-1. Our dataviz toolchain: Getting the data

Imagining a Nobel Visualization

In Chapter 13, we explored the Nobel Prize dataset, looking for interesting stories to tell based on aspects of the data that should engage and educate. We found some interesting nuggets, among them:

- Maria Goeppert, the only female physicist other than Marie Curie to win a Physics Nobel

- The post-WWII surge of American Nobels, passing the declining tallies of the three biggest European winners, the UK, Germany, and France

- The difference in continental prize distributions

- The dominance of the Scandinavian countries when prize tallies are adjusted for population size

These and a number of other narratives require particular types of visualization. Comparison of Nobel Prize numbers by nation is probably best achieved by means of a conventional bar chart, whereas geographic prize distributions demand a map. In this chapter we will try to design a modern, interactive visualization that incorporates some of the key stories we discovered while exploring the dataset.

Who Is It For?

The first consideration when imagining a visualization is its target audience. A visualization intended for display in a gallery or museum will likely be very different from one intended for an in-house dashboard, even though they could use the same dataset. The Nobel Prize visualization anticipated for this book has as its chief constraint that it teach a key subset of D3 and the JavaScript needed to create a modern interactive web visualization. It is a fairly informal dataviz and should entertain and inform. It does not require a specialist audience.

Choosing Visual Elements

The first constraint on our Nobel Prize visualization is that it be simple enough to teach and provide a set of the key D3 skills. But even if that constraint was not in place, it is probably sensible to limit the scope of any visualization. This scope depends very much on the context,[1] but, as in many learning contexts, less is often more. Too much interactivity risks overwhelming the user and diluting the impact of any stories we might wish to tell.

With this in mind, let's look at the key elements we want to include and how these are to be visually arranged.

A menu bar of some sort is a must, allowing the user to engage with the visualization and manipulate the data. Its functionality will depend on the stories we choose to tell, but it will certainly provide some way to explore or filter the dataset.

Ideally, the visualization should display each prize by year and this display should update itself as the user refines the data through the menu bar. Given that national and regional trends are of interest, a map should be included, highlighting the prize-winning countries selected and giving some indication of their tally. A bar chart is the best way to compare the number of prizes by country, and this too should adapt dynamically to any data changes. There should also be a choice of measuring the absolute number of prizes by country or per capita, taking into account the respective population sizes.

In order to personalize the visualization, we should be able to select individual winners, showing any available picture and the short biography we scraped from Wikipedia. This requires a list of cur-

---

1 A specialized dashboard, designed for experts, could tolerate more functionality than a general-purpose educational visualization.

rently selected winners and a window in which to display the selected individual.

The aforementioned elements provide enough scope to tell the key stories we discovered in the last chapter and with a bit of finessing should fit into a standard form factor.[2]

Our Nobel Prize visualization uses a fixed size for all devices, which means compromising larger devices with higher resolutions in order to accommodate smaller ones, such as last-generation smartphones or tablets. I find that for a lot of visualization work, a fixed size gives you much-needed control over specific placement of visual content blocks, information boxes, labels, and so on. For some visualizations, particularly multi-element dashboards, a different approach may be required. Responsive web design (RWD) (*http://bit.ly/1rtE9CE*) attempts to adapt the look and feel of your visualization to optimize for the specific device. Some popular CSS libraries such as Bootstrap (*http://getbootstrap.com/*) detect the device size (e.g., a tablet with resolution of 1,280×800 pixels) and change the stylesheet applied in order to get the most out of the available screen real estate. Specifying a fixed size for your visualization and using absolute positioning within it is the way to go if you require pinpoint control of the placement of your visual elements. However, you should be aware of the challenges of RWD, particularly when required to build multicomponent dashboards and the like.

Now let's aim to pin down the look, feel, and requirements of the individual elements of our Nobel Prize visualization, beginning with the main user control, the menu bar.

Menu Bar

An interactive visualization is driven by the user selecting from options, clicking on things, manipulating sliders, and so on. These allow the user to define the scope of the visualization, which is why we'll deal with them first. Our user controls will appear as a toolbar at the top of the visualization.

A standard way to drive interesting discoveries is to allow the user to filter the data in key dimensions. The obvious options for our

---

2 With a pixel measure, it's worth keeping track of changing device resolutions. As of May 2015, pretty much all devices will accommodate a 1,000×800 pixel visualization.

Nobel Prize visualization are category, gender, and country, the focus of our exploration in the last chapter. These filters should be cumulative, so, for example, selecting gender female and category Physics should return the two winning female physicists. In addition to those filters, we should have a radio button to choose between absolute and per capita numbers of national prize winners.

Figure 14-1 shows a menu bar that meets our requirements. Placed at the top of our visualization, it has selectors to filter our required dimensions and a radio button to select our national winner metric, either absolute or per capita.

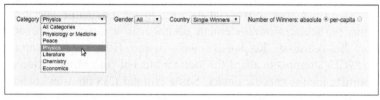

Figure 14-1. The user's controls

The menu bar will sit atop the key component of our visualization, a chart showing all the Nobel Prizes over time. Let's describe that next.

Prizes by Year

The last chapter showed a lot of interesting historical trends in the Nobel Prizes by country. We also saw that although female recipients have increased recently, they are way behind in the sciences. One way of allowing these trends to be discovered is to show all the Nobel Prizes on a timeline and provide a filter to select the prizes by gender, country, and category (using the menu bar just discussed).

If we make our visualization 1,000 pixels wide then, with 114 years of prizes to cover, we are allowed around 8 pixels per prize, enough to differentiate them. The highest number of prizes awarded in any one year is 14, in the year 2000, giving a minimal height for this element of 8×14 pixels, around 120. A circle, color-coded by category, seems a good way to represent the individual prizes, giving us a chart something like the one shown in Figure 14-2.

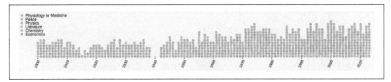

Figure 14-2. A timeline of Nobel Prizes by year, color-coded by category

The individual prizes are the essence of the visualization, so we'll place this timeline prominently at the top above our central element, which should be a map, reflecting the international nature of the prize and allowing the user to see any global trends.

A Map Showing Selected Nobel Countries

Mapping is one of D3's strengths, with many global projections available, from the classic Mercator to 3D spherical presentations.[3] Though maps are obviously engaging, they are also often overused and inappropriate when presenting nongeographical data. For example, unless you're careful, large geographical areas, such as countries in Europe or states of the US, tend to outweigh smaller ones even when the latter have far larger populations. When you are presenting demographic information, this skew is hard to avoid and a misrepresentation can result.[4]

But the Nobel Prize is an international one and the distribution of prizes by continent is of interest, making a global map a good way to depict the filtered data. If we superimpose a filled circle at the center of each country to reflect the prize measure (absolute or per capita), then we avoid skewing in favor of the larger land masses. In Europe, with many relatively small countries by land mass, these circles will intersect. By making them slightly transparent,[5] we can still see the superimposed circles and, by adding the opacities, give a sense of prize density. Figure 14-3 demonstrates this.

---

3 These 3D orthographic projections are "fake" in the sense that they do not use a 3D graphics context, such as WebGL. There are some nice examples from Jason Davies (*https://www.jasondavies.com/maps/rotate/*), bl.ocks.org (*http://bl.ocks.org/dwtkns/4686432*), and nullschool (*http://earth.nullschool.net/*).

4 See xkcd (*http://xkcd.com/1138/*) for an example.

5 By adjusting the alpha channel in the RGBA code with the CSS property opacity, from 0 (none) to 1 (full).

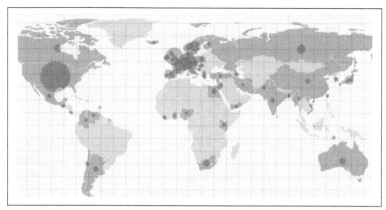

Figure 14-3. Global distribution of prizes

We'll provide a little tooltip for the map, both as a way of demon-strating how to build this handy visual component and also to help a little with naming the countries. Figure 14-4 shows what we're aim-ing for.

Figure 14-4. A simple tooltip for our Nobel Prize map

The last of the larger elements will be placed below the map: a bar chart allowing the user to make clear comparisons of the number of Nobel Prizes by country.

A Bar Chart Showing Number of Winners by Country

There is a lot of evidence that bar charts are great for making numeric comparisons.[6] A reconfigurable bar chart gives our visualization a lot of flexibility, allowing it to present the results of user-directed data filtering, choice of metric (i.e., absolute versus per capita counts), and more.

Figure 14-5 shows the bar chart we'll use to compare the prize hauls of chosen countries. Both the axes ticks and bars should respond dynamically to user interaction, driven by the menu bar (see Figure 14-1). An animated transition between bar chart states would be good and (as we'll see in "Transitions" on page 442) pretty much comes free with D3. As well as being attractive, there's reason to think such transitions are also effective communicators. See this Stanford University (*http://stanford.io/1Ue3cBR*) paper on the effectiveness of animated transitions in data visualization for some insights.

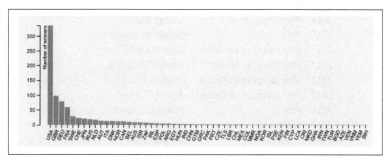

Figure 14-5. A bar chart component

To the side of the map and bar chart, we'll place a list of currently selected winners and a biography box, allowing the user to discover something about individual winners.

A List of the Selected Winners

We want the user to be able to select individual winners, displaying a mini-biography and picture when available. The easiest way to

---

6 See Stephen Few's insightful blog post (*http://www.perceptualedge.com/blog/?p=1492*).

achieve this is to have a list box, showing the currently selected winners, filtered from the full dataset using the menu bar selectors. Ordering these by year, in descending order, is a sensible default. And although we could allow the list to be sorted by column, it seems an unnecessary complication.

A simple HTML table with column headers should do the job here. It will look something like Figure 14-6.

Year	Category	Name
Selected winners		
2014	Chemistry	Eric Betzig
2014	Physiology or Medicine	May-Britt Moser
2014	Physics	Isamu Akasaki
2014	Chemistry	William E. Moerner
2014	Economics	Jean Tirole
2014	Literature	Patrick Modiano
2014	Physics	Hiroshi Amano
2014	Peace	Kailash Satyarthi
2014	Physics	Shuji Nakamura
2014	Chemistry	Stefan Hell
2014	Physiology or Medicine	Edvard Moser
2014	Peace	Malala Yousafzai
2014	Physiology or Medicine	John O'Keefe
2013	Physiology or Medicine	Randy Schekman
2013	Physiology or Medicine	Thomas C. Südhof
2013	Physiology or Medicine	James Rothman
2013	Physics	François Englert
2013	Chemistry	Arieh Warshel
2013	Chemistry	Michael Levitt
2013	Economics	Robert J. Shiller

Figure 14-6. A list of selected winners

The list will have clickable rows, allowing the user to select an individual winner to be displayed in our last element, a small biography box.

A Mini-Biography Box with Picture

The Nobel Prize is given to individuals, each with a story to tell. To both humanize and enrich our visualization, we should use the individual mini-biographies and images we scraped from Wikipedia (see

Chapter 6) to display the result of selecting an individual from our list element.

Figure 14-7 shows a biography box with a colored top border indicating the category of prize, with colors shared by our time chart (Figure 14-2), a top-right photograph (when available), and the first few paragraphs of Wikipedia's biographic entry.

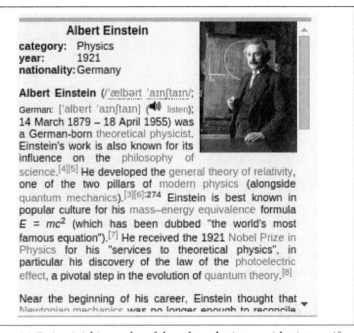

Figure 14-7. A mini-biography of the selected winner with picture, if available

The bio-box completes our set of visual components. We can now put them together in our specified 1,000×800 pixel frame.

The Complete Visualization

Figure 14-8 shows our complete Nobel Prize visualization with the five key elements plus the topmost user controls arranged to fit in a 1,000×800 pixel frame. Because we decided our timeline should take pride of place and the global map rather demanded the center, the other elements order themselves. The bar chart needs extra width to accommodate the labeled bars of all 58 countries, while the list of selected winners and mini-bio fit nicely to the right.

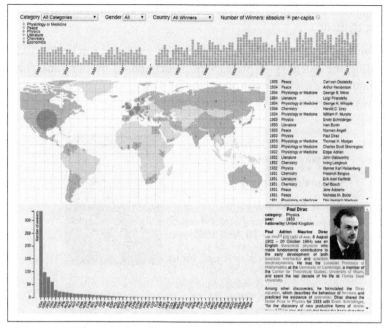

Figure 14-8. The complete Nobel Prize visualization

Let's summarize our imaginings before proceeding to the next chapter, where we'll see how to realize them.

Summary

In this chapter, we imagined our Nobel visualization, establishing a minimal set of visual elements necessary to tell the key stories discovered during our explorations of the last chapter. These fit neatly into our complete creation, shown in Figure 14-8. In the next chapters, I will show you how to build the individual elements and how to stitch them together to form a modern, interactive web visualization. We start with a gentle introduction to D3, by way of the simple story of a bar chart.

Building a Visualization

In Chapter 14 we used the results of our Pandas exploration of the Nobel Prize dataset (see Chapter 11) to imagine a visualization. Figure 15-1 shows the visualization we imagined, and in this chapter we'll see how to go about building it, leveraging the power of JavaScript and D3.

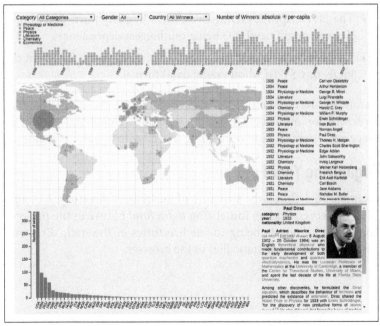

Figure 15-1. Our target, a Nobel Prize visualization

I'll show how the visual elements we conceived combine to transform our freshly cleaned and processed Nobel dataset into an interactive web visualization, deployable to billions of devices at the flick of a switch. But before going into the details, let's have a look at the core components of a modern web visualization.

Preliminaries

Before beginning to build the Nobel visualization, let's consider the core components that will be used and how we will organize our files.

Core Components

As we saw in "A Basic Page with Placeholders" on page 105, building a modern web visualization requires four key components:

- An HTML skeleton upon which to hang our JavaScripted creation
- One or more CSS stylesheets to govern the look and feel of the dataviz
- The JavaScript files themselves, including any third-party libraries you might need (D3 being our biggest dependency)
- And last but not least, the data to be transformed, ideally in the JSON or CSV (if wholly static data) format

Before we start looking at our dataviz components, let's get the file-structure for our Nobel Prize visualization (Nobel-viz) project in place and establish how we're going to feed data to our visualization.

Organizing Your Files

Example 15-1 shows the structure of our project directory. A couple of Flask servers and an initializing *index.html* file are in the project's root, all other assets being in subdirectories of the *static* directory, ready to be served as static files to the browser.

Example 15-1. Our Nobel-viz project's file structure

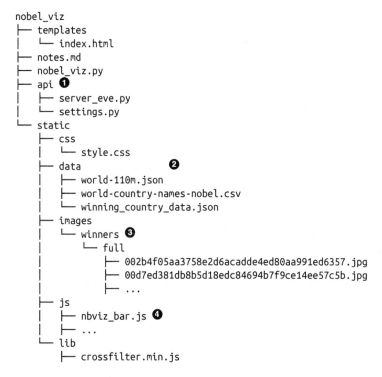

```
nobel_viz
├── templates
│   └── index.html
├── notes.md
├── nobel_viz.py
├── api ❶
│   ├── server_eve.py
│   └── settings.py
└── static
    ├── css
    │   └── style.css
    ├── data               ❷
    │   ├── world-110m.json
    │   ├── world-country-names-nobel.csv
    │   └── winning_country_data.json
    ├── images
    │   └── winners ❸
    │       └── full
    │           ├── 002b4f05aa3758e2d6acadde4ed80aa991ed6357.jpg
    │           ├── 00d7ed381db8b5d18edc84694b7f9ce14ee57c5b.jpg
    │           ├── ...
    ├── js
    │   ├── nbviz_bar.js ❹
    │   ├── ...
    └── lib
        ├── crossfilter.min.js
```

❶ The *api* directory containing the Python Eve server we coded in "Delivering Data to the Nobel Prize Visualization" on page 356.

❷ The static data files we'll be using, including a TopoJSON world map (see Chapter 18) and the country data we grabbed from the Web (see "Getting Country Data for the Nobel Dataviz" on page 138).

❸ The Nobel Prize winners' photos we scraped using Scrapy in "Scraping Text and Images with a Pipeline" on page 187.

❹ The *js* subdirectory contains our Nobel-viz JavaScript files, separated into core elements and starting with *nbviz_*.

Serving the Data

We're going to use a mixture of static and dynamic data delivery for our app, as presented in "Delivering Static Files" on page 336 and "Delivering Data to the Nobel Prize Visualization" on page 356. The static data files will be stored in a static data directory (Example 15-1, #2) and the data to be delivered dynamically stored in a MongoDB database and served by a Python Eve RESTful API.

The use of a RESTful API for our Nobel Prize dataset is slightly contrived, as the dataset, with biographical data, is not particularly large (just over 3 MB uncompressed). But add a few more winners and make the biographies snippets bigger, and we could easily start hitting the 10 MB mark, at which point caching the whole dataset is going to lead to a potentially frustrating wait for the user while the app initializes.

More to the point, being able to deliver fine-grained data from a backend database means you can really take the gloves off as far as creating ambitious visualizations is concerned. Any visualization where a user is encouraged to drill down into a large dataset for items of interest (e.g., a dashboard with stock inventories or a geographical dataset of house prices) will probably require returning to the server to meet the individual data demand. Being able to roll a robust RESTful MongoDB API in a few lines is a huge win here. The dynamic data flow demonstrated in our Nobel Prize visualization is eminently scalable and very flexible and, to reiterate, really takes off the static data handcuffs.

The HTML Skeleton

Although our Nobel visualization has a number of dynamic components, the HTML skeleton required is surprisingly simple. This demonstrates a core theme of the book, that you need very little conventional *web development* to set the stage for programming data visualizations.

The *index.html* file, which creates the visualization on loading, is shown in Example 15-2. The three components are:

1. A CSS stylesheet *style.css*, setting fonts, content-block positions, and the like, is imported.

2. HTML placeholders for our visual elements with ids of the form `nobel-[foo]`.

3. The JavaScript; first third-party libraries, then our original scripts.

We'll cover the individual HTML sections in detail in the coming chapters, but I wanted you to see what is essentially the entire non-programmatic element of the Nobel Prize visualization. With this skeleton in place, you can then turn to the job of creative programming, something D3 encourages and excels at. As you get used to defining your content blocks in HTML, fixing dimensions and positioning with CSS, you'll find you spend more and more time doing what you love best: manipulating data with code.

 I find it helpful to treat the identified placeholders, such as the map holder `<div id="nobel-map"></div>`, as panels *owned* by their respective elements. We set the dimension and relative positioning of these frames in the main CSS or JS[1] file and the elements, such as our dynamic map, adapt themselves to the size of their frame. This allows a nonprogramming designer to change the look and feel or the visualization through CSS styling.

Example 15-2. The index.html access file to our single-page visualization

```
<!DOCTYPE html>
<meta charset="utf-8">
<title>{{config.APP_TITLE}}</title>
<!-- 1. IMPORT THE visualization'S CSS STYLING -->
<link rel="stylesheet" href="static/css/style.css"
media="screen" />
<body>
  <div id='chart'>
    <!-- 2. A HEADER WITH TITLE AND SOME EXPLANATORY INFO -->
```

---

1 I would advise saving JavaScripted styling for special occasions, doing as much as possible with vanilla CSS.

```html
<div id='title'>Visualizing the Nobel Prize</div>
<div id="info">
  This is a companion piece to the book <a href='http://'>
  Data visualization with Python and JavaScript</a>, in which
  its construction is detailed. The data used was scraped
  Wikipedia using the <a href=
  'https://en.wikipedia.org/wiki
  /List_of_Nobel_laureates_by_country'>
  list of winners by country</a> as a starting point. The
  accompanying Github repo is <a href=
  'http://github.com/Kyrand/dataviz-with-python-and-js'>
  here</a>.
</div>
<!-- 3. THE PLACEHOLDERS FOR OUR VISUAL COMPONENTS  -->
<div id="nbviz">
  <!-- BEGIN MENU BAR -->
  <div id="nobel-menu">
    <div id="cat-select">
      Category
      <select></select>
    </div>
    <div id="gender-select">
      Gender
      <select>
        <option value="All">All</option>
        <option value="female">Female</option>
        <option value="male">Male</option>
      </select>
    </div>
    <div id="country-select">
      Country
      <select></select>
    </div>
    <div id='metric-radio'>
      Number of Winners: 
      <form>
        <label>absolute
          <input type="radio" name="mode" value="0" checked>
        </label>
        <label>per-capita
          <input type="radio" name="mode" value="1">
        </label>
      </form>
    </div>
  </div>
  <!-- END MENU BAR -->
  <!-- BEGIN NOBEL-VIZ COMPONENTS -->
  <div id='chart-holder' class='_dev'>
    <!-- TIME LINE OF PRIZES -->
    <div id="nobel-time"></div>
    <!-- MAP AND TOOLTIP -->
```

```
<div id="nobel-map">
  <div id="map-tooltip">
    <h2></h2>
    <p></p>
  </div>
</div>
<!-- LIST OF WINNERS -->
<div id="nobel-list">
  <h2>Selected winners</h2>
  <table>
    <thead>
      <tr>
        <th id='year'>Year</th>
        <th id='category'>Category</th>
        <th id='name'>Name</th>
      </tr>
    </thead>
    <tbody>
    </tbody>
  </table>
</div>
<!-- BIOGRAPHY BOX -->
<div id="nobel-winner">
  <div id="picbox"></div>
  <div id='winner-title'></div>
  <div id='infobox'>
    <div class='property'>
      <div class='label'>Category</div>
      <span name='category'></span>
    </div>
    <div class='property'>
      <div class='label'>Year</div>
      <span name='year'></span>
    </div>
    <div class='property'>
      <div class='label'>Country</div>
      <span name='country'></span>
    </div>
  </div>
  <div id='biobox'></div>
  <div id='readmore'>
    <a href='#'>Read more at Wikipedia</a>
  </div>
</div>
<!-- NOBEL BAR CHART -->
<div id="nobel-bar"></div>
</div>
<!-- END NOBEL-VIZ COMPONENTS -->
</div>
</div>
<!-- 4. THE JAVASCRIPT FILES -->
```

```
<!-- THIRD-PARTY JAVASCRIPT LIBRARIES, MAINLY D3  -->
<script ... </script>
<!-- THE JAVASCRIPT FOR OUR NOBEL ELEMENTS -->
<script ... </script>
</body>
```

The HTML skeleton (Example 15-2, #3) defines the hierarchical structure of our Nobel-viz components, but their visual sizing and positioning are set in the *style.css* file. In the next section, we'll see how this is done and look at the general styling of our visualization.

CSS Styling

We'll deal with the styling of the individual chart components of our chart (Figure 15-1) in their respective chapters. This section will cover the remaining nonspecific CSS, most importantly the sizing and positioning of our elements' content blocks (*panels*).

The size of a visualization can be a tricky choice. There are many more device formats out there these days, with smartphones, tablets, mobile devices, etc. having a variety of different resolutions, such as "retina,"[2] and full HD (1,920×1,080). Most mobile devices can pinch-and-zoom to fit visualizations, but it's best to target a size that will fit without such manipulation. A reasonable expectation these days is that a device has at least 1,280×800 pixels. Using this as our constraint, we will make our Nobel-viz 1,000 pixels wide and 800 pixels high, including our 50-pixels-high topmost user controls.

First we set some general styles we want applied to the whole document using the body selector; a sans-serif font, an off-white background, and some link detailing are specified. We also set the width of the visualization and its margins:

```
body {
    font-family: "Helvetica Neue", Helvetica, Arial, sans-serif;
    background: #fefefe;
    width: 1000px;
    margin: 0 auto; /* top and bottom 0, left and right auto */
}

a:link {
    color: royalblue;
    text-decoration: none; ❶
```

---

2 Currently around 2,560×1,600 pixels.

```
    }

a:hover {
    text-decoration: underline;
}
```

❶ The default underlined hyperlinks look a bit fussy in my opinion, so we remove decoration.

There are three main div content blocks to our Nobel-viz, which we
position absolutely within the #chart div (their relative parent).
These are the main title (#title) , some information on the visualization (#info), and the main container (#nbviz). The title and info
are placed by eye and the main container is placed 90 pixels from
the page top to allow them room, and given a width of 100% to
make it expand to the available space. The following CSS achieves
this:

```
#nbviz {
    position: absolute;
    top: 90px;
    width: 100%;
}

#title {
    position: absolute;
    font-size: 30px;
    font-weight: 100;
    top: 20px;
}

#info {
    position: absolute;
    font-size: 11px;
    top: 18px;
    width: 300px;
    right: 0px;
}
```

The chart-holder is given a height of 750 px, a width of 100% its
parent, and a position property of relative, meaning the absolute
positioning of its child *panels* will be relative to its top-left corner:

```
#chart-holder {
    width: 100%;
    height:750px;
    position: relative;
}
```

```
#chart-holder svg { ❶
    width: 100%;
    height: 100%;
}
```

❶ We want the SVG contexts for our components to expand to fit their containers.

Allowing for the Nobel-viz's height constraint of 750 pixels, the width/height ratio of two for our equirectangular map,[3] and the need to fit over 100 years' worth of Nobel Prize circular indicators into our time chart, playing with the dimensions suggests Figure 15-2 as a good compromise for the size of our visual elements.

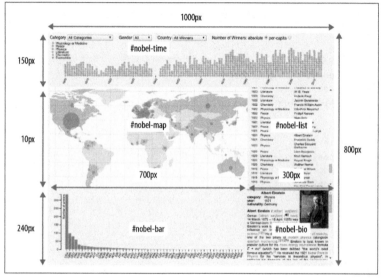

Figure 15-2. The Nobel-viz's dimensions

This CSS positions and sizes the components as shown in Figure 15-2:

```
#nobel-map, #nobel-winner, #nobel-bar, #nobel-time, #nobel-list{
    position:absolute; ❶
}
```

---

3 See "Projections" on page 473 for a comparison of the different geometric projections. Given the constraint of showing all Nobel Prize–winning countries, the equirectangular projection proved most effective.

```
#nobel-time {
    top: 0;
    height: 150px;
    width: 100%; ❷
}

#nobel-map {
    background: azure;
    top: 160px;
    width: 700px;
    height: 350px;
}

#nobel-winner {
    top: 510px;
    left: 700px;
    height: 240px;
    width: 300px;
}

#nobel-bar {
    top: 510px;
    height: 240px;
    width: 700px;
}

#nobel-list {
    top: 160px;
    height: 340px;
    width: 290px;
    left: 700px;
    padding-left: 10px; ❸
}
```

❶ We want absolute, manually adjusted positioning, relative to the `chart-holder` parent container.

❷ The timeline runs the full width of the visualization.

❸ You can use padding to let the components "breathe."

The other CSS styles are specific to the individual components and will be covered in their respective chapters. With the preceding CSS, we have an HTML skeleton on which to flesh out our visualization with JavaScript.

The JavaScript Engine

With a visualization of any size, it's good to start imposing some modularity early on. Many of the D3 examples on the Web[4] are one-page solutions, combining HTML, CSS, JS, and even data on one page. Though this is great for teaching by example, as the code base increases, things will degenerate fast, making changes a slog and increasing the chance of namespace collisions and the like.

Importing the Scripts

Although there are a number of more or less successful attempts to develop a mature import/include system for JavaScript libraries, it's not there yet.[5] For now I would advise most JavaScripters, certainly beginners, to live with including scripts in the right order. It's reliable, doesn't require complicated build scripts or shims, and is good for most small- to medium-sized projects.[6]

We include the JavaScript files for our visualization using `<script>` tags placed at the bottom of the `<body>` tag in our entry *index.html* file, as shown in Example 15-2:

```
<!DOCTYPE html>
<meta charset="utf-8">
...
<body>
...
    <!-- THIRD-PARTY JAVASCRIPT LIBRARIES, MAINLY D3 BASED  --> ❶
    <script
      src="https://cdnjs.cloudflare.com/ajax/libs/d3/3.5.16
      /d3.js">
    </script>
    <script
      src="https://cdnjs.cloudflare.com/ajax/libs/topojson/
      1.6.20/topojson.min.js">
    </script>
```

---

4 See the collection at D3's GitHub (*https://github.com/mbostock/d3/wiki/Gallery*) and the huge collection of 11,000 examples at blockbuilder.org (*http://bit.ly/1ZWYnAC*).

5 ES2015 (aka EcmaScript 6), the new JavaScript specification, is almost here and will go a long way to solving this problem. D3 v4 use ES2015 along with rollup.js (*http://roll upjs.org*) for module management.

6 Right now there are a number of competing module-loading utilities, the most used being requireJS, browserify, and webpack. They each have pros and cons, but all have a learning curve and require adaptation of existing modules.

```
<script
  src="https://cdnjs.cloudflare.com/ajax/libs/queue-async/
  1.0.7/queue.min.js">
</script>
<script src="static/lib/crossfilter.min.js"></script>

<!-- THE JAVASCRIPT FOR OUR NOBEL ELEMENTS -->
<script src="static/js/nbviz_core.js" ></script> ❷
<script src="static/js/nbviz_menu.js" ></script> ❸
<script src="static/js/nbviz_map.js"></script>
<script src="static/js/nbviz_bar.js"></script>
<script src="static/js/nbviz_time.js"></script>
<script src="static/js/nbviz_details.js"></script>
<script src="static/js/nbviz_main.js"></script> ❹
</body>
```

❶ We use cacheable online content delivery networks (CDNs) (*http://bit.ly/1sKdjr1*) to access most of our third-party Java-Script libraries, in this case D3 specific.

❷ These are the shared core JavaScript utilities, constants, and so on.

❸ A script for each of the visualization's elements.

❹ The main entry point for our Nobel app, where it requests its first datasets and sets the display ball rolling.

We'll use the JS-module pattern described in "Keeping Your Namespaces Clean" on page 21 to establish an nbviz namespace, keeping our global namespace clean and allowing for shared methods, parameters, constants, and the like. Each module will expose any necessary methods to the nbviz object, allowing them to be used in the other scripts. For example, nbviz_map.js exposes the nbviz.initMap and nbviz.updateMap methods. Here is the basic structure of our modules:

```
/* global $, _, crossfilter, d3 */ ❶
(function(nbviz) {
    'use strict'; ❷
    //... MODULES PRIVATE VARS ETC..
    nbviz.foo = function(){ //... ❸
    };
}(window.nbviz = window.nbviz || {})); ❹
```

❶ Defining variables as global will prevent them triggering JSLint (*http://www.jslint.com/*) errors.

❷ Enforces ECMAScript 5's strict mode, a great sanity check.

❸ Exposes this function to other scripts as part of shared nbviz namespace.

❹ Uses the nbviz object if available, and creates it otherwise.

In the coming chapters, the JavaScript/D3 used to produce the visualization's elements will be explained in detail. First we'll deal with the flow of data through the Nobel-viz, from the (data) server to the client browser and within the client, driven by user interaction.

Basic Data Flow

There are many ways to deal with data in a project of any complexity. For interactive apps, and particularly data visualizations, I find the most robust pattern is to have a central data object to cache current data. In addition to the cached data, we also have some active reflections or subsets of this dataset, stored in the main data object. For example, in our Nobel-viz a user can select a number of subsets of the data (e.g., only those winners in the Physics category).

If a different data reflection is triggered by the user, such as by choosing the per capita prize metric, a flag[7] is set (in this case, value PerCapita is set to 0 or 1). We then update all the visual components, and those that depend on valuePerCapita adapt accordingly. The size of the map indicators changes and the bar chart reorganizes.

The key idea is to make sure the visual elements are synchronized to any user-driven data changes. A reliable way to do this is to have a single update method (here called onDataChange) that is called whenever a user does something to change the data. This method alerts all the active visual elements to the changed data and they respond accordingly.

Let's now see how the app's code fits together, starting with the shared core utilities.

---

7 In our app, I'm keeping things as simple as possible; as the number of UI options increases, it's sensible to store flags, ranges, etc. in a dedicated object.

The Core Code

The first JavaScript file loaded is *nbviz_core.js*. This script contains any code we might want to share among the other scripts. For example, we have a `categoryFill` method that returns a specific color for each category. This is used by both the timeline component and as a border in the biography box. This core code includes functions we might want to isolate for testing, or simply to make other modules less cluttered.

Often in programming we use string constants as dictionary keys and comparatives, and in generated labels. It's easy to slip into the bad habit of typing these strings when required, but a much better way is to define a constant variable instead. For example, rather than `'if option === "All Categories"'`, we use `'if option === nbviz.ALL_CATS'`. In the former option, mistyping `'All Categories'` will not flag an error, an accident waiting to happen. Having a const also means only one edit is needed to change all occurrences of the string. Note that unlike some languages JavaScript doesn't have immutable constants (*http://bit.ly/1YxorUj*), but by convention uppercase variables should not be changed.

Example 15-3 shows the code shared between the other modules. Anything intended to be used by other *modules* is attached to the shared `nbviz` namespace.

Example 15-3. Shared code base in nbviz_core.js

```
/* global $, _, crossfilter, d3 */
(function(nbviz) {
    'use strict';

    nbviz.data = {}; // our main data object
    nbviz.valuePerCapita = 0; // metric flag
    nbviz.activeCountry = null;
    nbviz.ALL_CATS = 'All Categories';
    nbviz.TRANS_DURATION = 2000; // length in ms for our transitions
    nbviz.MAX_CENTROID_RADIUS = 30;
    nbviz.MIN_CENTROID_RADIUS = 2;
    nbviz.COLORS = {palegold:'#E6BE8A'}; // any named colors we use
```

```
    $EVE_API = 'http://localhost:5000/api/';

    nbviz.CATEGORIES = [
        "Chemistry", "Economics", "Literature", "Peace",
        "Physics", "Physiology or Medicine"
    ];

    nbviz.categoryFill = function(category){
        var i = nbviz.CATEGORIES.indexOf(category);
        return d3.hcl(i / nbviz.CATEGORIES.length * 360, 60, 70);
    };

    nbviz.getDataFromAPI = function(resource, callback){
        d3.json($EVE_API + resource, function(error, data) {
        //...
        });
    };

    var nestDataByYear = function(entries) {              ❶
    //...
    };

    nbviz.makeFilterAndDimensions = function(winnersData){
    //...
    };

    nbviz.filterByCountries = function(countryNames) {
    //...
    };

    nbviz.filterByCategory = function(cat) {
    //...
    };

    nbviz.getCountryData = function() {
    // ...
    };

    nbviz.onDataChange = function() { ❷
        var data = nbviz.getCountryData();
        nbviz.updateBarChart(data);
        nbviz.updateMap(data);
        nbviz.updateList(nbviz.countryDim.top(Infinity));
        data = nestDataByYear(nbviz.countryDim.top(Infinity));
        nbviz.updateTimeChart(data);
    };

}(window.nbviz = window.nbviz || {}));
```

❶ This and the following empty methods will be explained in detail in the following chapters in a use context.

❷ This function is called when the dataset changes (after initialization of the app, this is user-driven) to update the Nobel-viz elements. See "Basic Data Flow" on page 392 for details.

With the core code at hand, let's see how our app is initialized, by loading some datasets from static files and our dynamic RESTful API.

Initializing the Nobel Prize Visualization

The Nobel Prize app is started by a set of data requests made in the *nbviz_main.js* script. We use D3's queue (*https://github.com/d3/d3-queue*) function, one of Mike Bostock's many helpers, to make simultaneous requests for static data files and the set of all winners (courtesy of our Python Eve API). When all the calls to `queue` have been resolved, a callback function specified by the `await` method is called with the data response and any errors generated:

```
//...
var query_winners = 'winners?projection=' +
    JSON.stringify( {"mini_bio":0, "bio_image":0} );

queue()
    .defer(d3.json, "static/data/world-110m.json") ❶
    .defer(d3.csv, "static/data/world-country-names-nobel.csv")
    .defer(d3.json, "static/data/winning_country_data.json")
    .defer(nbviz.getDataFromAPI, query_winners) ❷
    .await(ready);

function ready(error, world, names, countryData, winnersData) {
    // Do something cool with the data...
}
```

❶ The static files consist of a world map (110m resolution) and some country data we'll be using in the visualization. You can find the commonly used *world-110m.json* data at the topojson GitHub repo (*http://bit.ly/268d0EI*).

❷ This makes a request for dynamic data to our Python Eve API using the `query_winners` arguments to exclude the superfluous biographical details (i.e., `http://localhost:5000/api/winners?projection=%7B%22mini_bio...`).

In the call to queue, we make use of a `nbviz.getDataFromAPI` method (defined in *nbviz_core.js*), which wraps a D3 AJAX call to our Python Eve API (running on localhost, port 5000). Example 15-4 shows code for `getDataFromAPI`.

Example 15-4. A wrapper function to get data from our RESTful API using a resource string and some query data

```
var $EVE_API = 'http://localhost:5000/api/';

nbviz.getDataFromAPI = function(resource, callback){ ❶
    d3.json($EVE_API + resource, function(error, data) {
        if(error){
            return callback(error);
        }
        if('_items' in data){ ❷
            callback(null, data._items); ❸
        }
        else{
            callback(null, data);
        }
    });
```

❶ Accepts a resource (e.g., `winners?projection={'mini_bio':0,'bio_image':0})` and a callback to be invoked when the request to our Python Eve API has resolved.

❷ If the response data has an `items` field, then we're dealing with a set of MongoDB items; otherwise, we have an individual resource (i.e., the data for a single Nobel prize winner).

❸ The callback accepts an error argument (null here) and some response data.

If our data requests are successful, the `ready` function receives the requested data and we're ready to start sending data to the visual elements.

Ready to Go

After the deferred requests for data made by the `queue` method are resolved, it calls the specified `ready` function, passing the datasets as arguments in the order in which they were added.

The `ready` function is shown in Example 15-5. If the data has downloaded without error, we use the winners' data to create the active filter (courtesy of the Crossfilter library) we will use to allow the user to select subsets of the Nobel winners based on category, gender, and country. We then call some initializer methods, and finally use the `onDataChange` method to trigger a drawing of the visual elements of dataviz, updating bar chart, map, timeline, and so on. The schematic in Figure 15-3 shows the way in which data changes propagate.

Example 15-5. The ready function is called when the initial data requests have resolved

```
//...
    function ready(error, worldMap, countryNames, countryData,
                    winnersData) {
        // LOG ANY ERROR TO CONSOLE
        if(error){
            return console.warn(error);
        }
        // STORE OUR COUNTRY-DATA DATASET
        nbviz.data.countryData = countryData;
        // MAKE OUR FILTER AND ITS DIMENSIONS
        nbviz.makeFilterAndDimensions(winnersData); ❶
        // INITIALIZE MENU AND MAP
        nbviz.initMenu();
        nbviz.initMap(worldMap, countryNames);
        // TRIGGER UPDATE WITH FULL WINNERS' DATASET
        nbviz.onDataChange();
    }
}(window.nbviz = window.nbviz || {}));
```

❶ This method uses the freshly loaded Nobel Prize dataset to create the filter we will use to allow the user to select subsets of the data to visualize. See "Filtering Data with Crossfilter" on page 400 for details.

We'll see how the `makeFilterAndDimensions` method (Example 15-5, ❶) works when we cover the Crossfilter library in "Filtering Data with Crossfilter" on page 400. For now, we'll assume we have a means of getting the data currently selected by the user via some menu selectors (e.g., selecting all female winners).

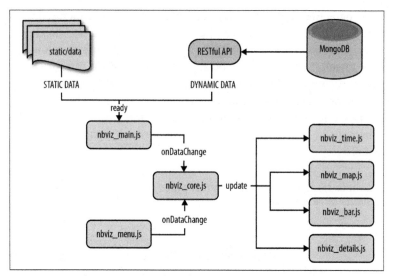

Figure 15-3. The app's main data flow

Data-Driven Updates

After the menu and map have been initialized in the `ready` function (we'll see how that works in their respective chapters: Chapter 18 for the map and Chapter 20 for the menu), we trigger an update of the visual elements with the `onDataChange` method defined in *nbviz_core.js*. `onDataChange` (see Example 15-6) is a shared function that is called whenever the set of displayed data changes in response to user interaction, or when the user chooses a different country prize metric (e.g., measuring per capita rather than absolute numbers).

Example 15-6. Function called to update the visual elements when selected data is changed

```
// nbviz_core.js
nbviz.onDataChange = function() {
    var data = nbviz.getCountryData(); ❶
    nbviz.updateBarChart(data);
    nbviz.updateMap(data);
    nbviz.updateList(nbviz.countryDim.top(Infinity)); ❷
    data = nestDataByYear(nbviz.countryDim.top(Infinity)); ❸
    nbviz.updateTimeChart(data);
};
```

❶ getCountryData returns a tailored data array, based on grouping the winners by country and adding some data from our country dataset. See Example 15-7 for details.

❷ Passes an array of all selected winners to the updateList method (see Chapter 19 for details).

❸ Our time chart needs a nested dataset. We'll cover the construction of this in Chapter 17.

The main dataset, consumed by the timeline, map, and bar chart, is produced by the getCountryData method, which groups the prize winners by country and adds some national information, namely population size and international alphacode. Example 15-7 breaks this method down.

Example 15-7. Creating the main country dataset

```
nbviz.getCountryData = function() {
    var countryGroups = nbviz.countryDim.group().all(); ❶

    // make main data-ball
    var data = countryGroups.map( function(c) { ❷
        var cData = nbviz.data.countryData[c.key]; ❸
        var value = c.value;
        // if per capita value then divide by pop. size
        if(nbviz.valuePerCapita){
            value = value / cData.population; ❹
        }
        return {
            key: c.key, // e.g., Japan
            value: value, // e.g., 19 (prizes)
            code: cData.alpha3Code, // e.g., JPN
        };
    })
        .sort(function(a, b) { ❺
            return b.value - a.value; // descending
        });

    return data;
};
```

❶ countryDim is one of our Crossfilter dimensions (see "Filtering Data with Crossfilter" on page 400), here providing group key, value counts (e.g., {key:Argentina, value:5}).

❷ We use the array's map method to create a new array with added components from our country dataset.

❸ Fetches country data using our group key (e.g., Australia).

❹ Makes the country prize rate a per capita one if valuePerCapita integer is 1.

❺ Uses Array's sort method to make the array descending by value.

The update methods of our Nobel-viz elements all make use of data filtered by the Crossfilter library. Let's see how that's done now.

Filtering Data with Crossfilter

Developed by D3's creators, Mike Bostock and Jason Davies, Crossfilter[8] is a highly optimized library for exploring large, multivariate datasets using JavaScript. It's very fast and can easily handle datasets far larger than our Nobel Prize dataset. We'll be using it to filter our dataset of winners by the dimensions of category, gender, and country.

The choice of Crossfilter is slightly ambitious, but I wanted to show it in action as I've found it to be so useful personally. It's also the basis of dc.js (*https://dc-js.github.io/dc.js/*), the very popular D3 charting library, which testifies to its usefulness. Although Crossfilter can be a little difficult to grasp, especially when we start intersecting dimensional filters, most use cases follow a basic pattern that is quickly absorbed. If you ever find yourself trying to cut and slice large datasets, Crossfilter's optimizations will prove a boon.

Creating the filter

On initializing the Nobel-viz, the makeFilterAndDimensions method defined in *nbviz_core.js* is called from the ready method in *nbviz_main.js* (see "Ready to Go" on page 396). makeFilterAndDimensions uses the freshly loaded Nobel Prize dataset to create a Crossfilter filter and some dimensions (e.g., prize category) based on it.

---

8 See *http://square.github.io/crossfilter/* for an impressive example.

We first create our filter using the dataset of Nobel Prize winners returned by our Python Eve API. Let's remind ourselves what that looks like:

```
// winners =
[{
  name:"C\u00e9sar Milstein",
  category:"Physiology or Medicine",
  gender:"male",
  country:"Argentina",
  year: 1984
},
{
  name:"Auguste Beernaert",
  category:"Peace",
  gender:"male",
  country:"Belgium",
  year: 1909
},
...
}];
```

To create our filter, call the `crossfilter` function with the array of winner objects:

```
nbviz.makeFilterAndDimensions = function(winnersData){
    // ADD OUR FILTER AND CREATE CATEGORY DIMENSIONS
    nbviz.filter = crossfilter(winnersData);
    //...
};
```

Crossfilter works by allowing you to create dimensional filters on your data. You do so by applying a function to the objects. At its simplest, this creates a dimension based on a single category—for example, by gender. Here we create the gender dimension we'll use to filter Nobel Prizes by sex:

```
nbviz.makeFilterAndDimensions = function(winnersData){
//...
    nbviz.genderDim = nbviz.filter.dimension(function(o) {
        return o.gender;
    });
//...
```

This dimension now has an efficient ordering of our dataset by the gender field. We can use it like this, to return all objects with gender female:

```
nbviz.genderDim.filter('female'); ❶
var femaleWinners = nbviz.genderDim.top(Infinity); ❷
femaleWinners.length // 47
```

❶ `filter` takes a single value or, where appropriate, a range (e.g., [5, 21]—all values between 5 and 21). It can also take a Boolean function of the values.

❷ Once the filter is applied, `top` returns the specified number of ordered objects. Specifying `Infinity`[9] returns all the filtered data objects.

Crossfilter really comes into its own when we start applying multiple dimensional filters, allowing us to slice and dice the data into any subsets we require, all achieved with impressive speed.[10]

Let's clear the gender dimension and add a new one, filtering by prize-winning category. To reset a dimension,[11] apply the `filter` method without arguments:

```
nbviz.genderDim.filter();
nbviz.genderDim.top(Infinity) // the full Array[858] of objects
```

We'll now create a new prize category dimension:

```
nbviz.categoryDim = nbviz.filter.dimension(function(o) {
    return o.category;
});
```

We can now filter the gender and category dimensions in sequence, allowing us to find, for example, all female Physics prize winners:

```
nbviz.genderDim.filter('female');
nbviz.categoryDim.filter('Physics');
nbviz.genderDim.top(Infinity);
// Out:
// [
//   {name:"Marie Sklodowska-Curie", category:"Physics",...
//   {name:"Maria Goeppert-Mayer", category:"Physics",...
// ]
```

---

9 JavaScript's `Infinity` (*https://mzl.la/1OuMLUG*) is a numeric value representing infinity.

10 Crossfilter was designed to update millions of records in real time, in response to user input.

11 This will clear all the filters on this dimension.

Note that we can turn the filters on and off selectively. So, for example, we can remove the Physics category filter, meaning the gender dimension now contains all the female Nobel Prize winners.

```
nbviz.categoryDim.filter();
nbviz.genderDim.top(Infinity); // Array[47] of objects
```

In our Nobel-viz, these filter operations will be driven by the user making selections from the topmost menu bar.

As well as returning the filtered subsets, Crossfilter can perform grouping operations on the data. We use this to get the national prize aggregates for the bar chart and map indicators.

```
nbviz.genderDim.filter(); // reset gender dimension
var countryGroup = nbviz.countryDim.group(); ❶
countryGroup.all(); ❷

// Out:
// [
//  {key:"Argentina", value:5}, ❸
//  {key:"Australia", value:9},
//  {key:"Austria", value:14},
//  ...]
```

❶ Group takes an optional function as an argument, but the default is generally what you want.

❷ Returns all groups by key and value. Do not modify the returned array.[12]

❸ value is the total number of Nobel Prize winners for Argentina.

To create our Crossfilter filter and dimensions, we use the makeFil terAndDimensions method, defined in *nbviz_core.js*. Example 15-8 shows the whole method. See "Testing JavaScript Apps" on page 536, which uses makeFilterAndDimensions to demonstrate some JavaScript testing.

---

12 See the Crossfilter GitHub page (*https://github.com/square/crossfilter/wiki/API-Reference#group_all*).

Example 15-8. Making our Crossfilter filter and dimensions

```
nbviz.makeFilterAndDimensions = function(winnersData){
    // ADD OUR FILTER AND CREATE CATEGORY DIMENSIONS
    nbviz.filter = crossfilter(winnersData);
    nbviz.countryDim = nbviz.filter.dimension(function(o){
        return o.country;
    });

    nbviz.categoryDim = nbviz.filter.dimension(function(o) {
        return o.category;
    });

    nbviz.genderDim = nbviz.filter.dimension(function(o) {
        return o.gender;
    });
};
```

Running the Nobel Prize Visualization App

To run the Nobel-viz app, go to the *api* subdirectory of the root *nobel_viz* directory and start the Python Eve RESTful API server on port 5000 (by default):

```
$nobel_viz/api  python server_eve.py
 * Running on http://127.0.0.1:5000/ (Press CTRL+C to quit)
 ...
```

In the project's root directory, set the Nobel-viz server running on port 8000:

```
$nobel_viz  python nobel_viz.py
 * Running on http://127.0.0.1:8000/ (Press CTRL+C to quit)
 ...
```

With these two servers running locally, navigate your browser to http:localhost:8000 and you should see Figure 15-4.

In "Deploying Flask Apps" on page 541, we'll see how to deploy a Flask app on a production machine, using the Apache web server.

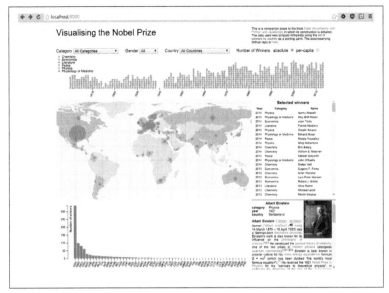

Figure 15-4. The finished Nobel-viz app

Summary

In this chapter, we sketched out how to implement the visualization we imagined in Chapter 14. The backbone was assembled from HTML, CSS, and JavaScript building blocks and the data feed to the app and data flow within it described. In the following chapters, we'll see how the individual components of our Nobel-viz use the data sent to them to create our interactive visualization. We'll start with a big chapter, which will introduce the fundamentals of D3 while showing how to build the bar chart component of our app. This should set you up for the subsequent D3-focused chapters.

## CHAPTER 16

Introducing D3—The Story of a Bar Chart

In Chapter 15 we imagined our Nobel Prize visualization by breaking it into component elements. In this chapter, I will gently introduce you to D3 by showing you how to build the bar chart we need (Figure 16-1).

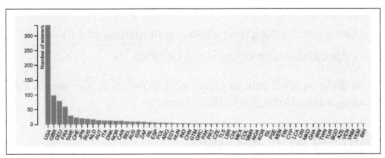

Figure 16-1. This chapter's target bar chart

D3 is much more than a charting library. It's a library you use to build charting libraries, among other things. So why am I introducing you to D3 by way of that ultra-conventional visualization, the bar chart? First, because there should be a little thrill in crafting one from scratch for the first time, having total control over the look and feel of the chart and being unconstrained by whatever prejudices a particular charting library has. And second, because it just happens to be a great way to cover the fundamental elements of D3, particularly data binding and the enter-exit-remove update pattern. If you get those fundamentals in place, you're well on your way to employing the full power and expressivity D3 offers, and producing something more novel than a bar chart.

We'll be using some of the webdev covered in Chapter 4, particularly the SVG graphics that are D3's specialty (see "Scalable Vector Graphics" on page 109). I recommend using the fantastic, purpose-built D3 site blockbuilder.org to try out some of the code snippets.

Before we begin building the bar chart, let's consider its elements.

Framing the Problem

A bar chart has three key components: the axes, legends and labels, and, of course, the bars. As we're producing a modern, interactive bar chart component, we'll need the axes and bars to transform in response to user interaction—namely, filtering the set of prize winners via the top selectors (see Figure 14-1).

We'll build the chart one step at a time, ending with D3 transitions, which can make your D3 creations more engaging and attractive. But first we'll cover the basics of D3:

- Selecting DOM elements in your web page
- Getting and setting their attributes, properties, and styles
- Appending and inserting DOM elements

With these basics firmly in place, we'll move on to the joys of data binding, where D3 begins to flex its muscles.

Working with Selections

Selections are the backbone of D3. Using jQuery-like CSS selectors, D3 can select and manipulate individual and grouped DOM elements. All D3 chained operations begin by selecting a DOM element or set of elements using the `select` and `selectAll` methods. `select` returns the first matching element; `selectAll` returns the set of matching elements.

Figure 16-2 shows some example of D3 selections, using the `select` and `selectAll` methods. These selections are used to change the `height` attribute of one or more bars. The `select` method returns the first `rect` (id `barL`) with class `bar`, whereas `selectAll` can return any combination of the rects depending on the query provided.

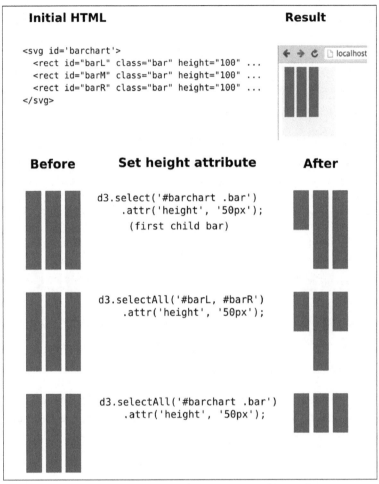

Figure 16-2. Selecting elements and changing attributes: three rectangles are built with the initial HTML. Selections are then made and the height attributes of one or more bar adjusted.

In addition to setting attributes (the named strings on the DOM elements; e.g., id or class), D3 allows you to set elements' CSS styles, properties (e.g., whether a checkbox is checked), text, and HTML.

Figure 16-3 shows all the ways in which a DOM element can be changed with D3. With these few methods, you can achieve pretty much any look and feel you want.

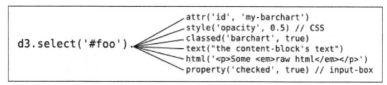

Figure 16-3. Changing a DOM element with D3

Figure 16-4 shows how we can apply CSS styling by adding a class to the element or directly setting a style. We first select the middle bar using its id barM. The `classed` method is then used to apply a yellow highlight (see the CSS) and the `height` attribute set to 50 px. The `style` method is then used to apply a red fill to the bar directly.

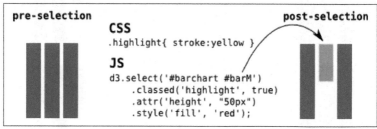

Figure 16-4. Setting attributes and style

D3's `text` method sets the text content of applicable DOM tags, such as `div`, `p`, `h*` headers, and SVG text elements. To see the `text` method in action, let's create a little title placeholder with some HTML:

```
<!DOCTYPE html>
<meta charset="utf-8">

<body>
  <h2>title holder</h2>
</body>
```

Figure 16-5 (before) shows the resulting browser page.

Now let's create a `fancy-title` CSS class with a large, bold font:

```
.fancy-title {
    font-size: 24px;
    font-weight: bold;
}
```

We can now use D3 to select the title header, add the `fancy-title` class to it, and then set its text to My Bar Chart:

```
d3.select('#title#')
  .classed('fancy-title', true)
  .text('My Bar Chart');
```

Figure 16-5 (after) shows the resulting enlarged and emboldened title.

Figure 16-5. Setting text and style with D3

In addition to setting the properties of DOM elements, we can use selections to get those properties. Leaving out the second argument to one of the methods listed in Figure 16-3 allows you to get information about the web page's setup.

Figure 16-6 shows how to get the key properties from an SVG rectangle. As we'll see, getting attributes like width and height from an SVG element can be very useful for programmatic adaptation and adjustment.

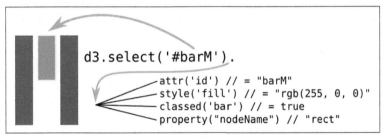

Figure 16-6. Getting a rect bar's details

Figure 16-7 demonstrates the html and text getter methods. After creating a little list (id silly-list), we use D3 to select it and get various properties. The `html` method returns the HTML of the list's child `<li>` tags, while the `text` method returns the text contained in the list, with the HTML tags stripped. Note that for parent tags, the formatting of any text returned is a little messy, but maybe good enough for a string search or two.

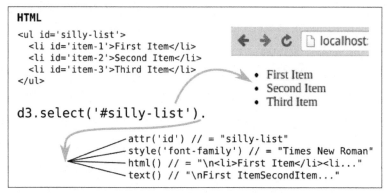

Figure 16-7. Getting HTML and text from a list tag

So far we've been manipulating the attributes, styles, and properties of existing DOM elements. This is a useful skill, but D3 comes into its own when we start creating DOM elements programmatically using its `append` and `insert` methods. Let's look at these now.

Adding DOM Elements

We've seen how to select and manipulate the attributes, styles, and properties of DOM elements. Now we'll see how D3 allows us to append and insert elements, programmatically adapting the DOM tree.

We'll start with a little HTML skeleton containing a `nobel-bar` placeholder:

```
<!DOCTYPE html>
<meta charset="utf-8">
<link rel="stylesheet" href="style.css" />

<body>
  <div id='nobel-bar'></div>

  <script
    src="https://cdnjs.cloudflare.com/ajax/libs/d3/3.5.16
    /d3.js">
  </script>
```

```
<script type="text/javascript" src="script.js"></script> ❶
</body>
```

❶ The *script.js* file is where we'll add our bar chart's JavaScript code.

Let's set the size of the nobel-bar element with a little CSS, placed in *style.css*:

```
#nobel-bar {
  width: 600px;
  height: 400px;
}
```

Usually the first thing one does when creating a chart with D3 is to provide an SVG frame for it. This involves appending an <svg> canvas element to a div chartholder and then appending a <g> group to the <svg> to hold specific chart elements (in our case, the chart bars). This group has margins to accommodate axes, axes labels, and titles.

Getting the Dimensions of an Element

It's very common when programming in D3, or any other JavaScript visualization library, to require the width and height of an SVG or HTML element to use as the basis for setting the size of component elements. One way of doing this is to use D3's style component to grab the CSS dimensions and then use the parseInt function to get an integer value:

```
/* CSS: #nobel-bar { width: 600px }; */

var width = parseInt(d3.select('#nobel-bar')
                    .style('width'), 10); ❶
```

❶ The result of calling the style method is the string '600px', which we can convert to the number 600 using the parseInt function.

This method works pretty well as a rule, although the parseInt feels a bit hacky, turning the string '600px' into the number 600.

Arguably, a better, more robust approach is to get the dimensions of the bounding box of the HTML or SVG element in question. These give both the width, height, and relative position of the element, using the node method to get the DOM element.

```
// For an HTML element, starting with the D3 +ele+ selection
var bRect = ele.node().getBoundingClientRect();
// e.g., bRect is {width: 600, height: 400, ... }
// For an SVG element use the getBBox method:
var bBox = eleSVG.node().getBBox();
// e.g., bBox is {width: 600, height: 400, x: 100, y: 100}
```

Conventionally, you will specify the margin of your chart in a `margin` object and then use that and the CSS-specified width and height of the chart container to derive the width and height of your chart group. The required JavaScript looks like Example 16-1.

Example 16-1. Getting our bar chart's dimensions

```
var chartHolder = d3.select("#nobel-bar");

var margin = {top:20, right:20, bottom:30, left:40};

var boundingRect = chartHolder.node()
    .getBoundingClientRect(); ❶
var width = boundingRect.width - margin.left - margin.right,
height = boundingRect.height - margin.top - margin.bottom;
```

❶ Gets the bounding rectangle for our Nobel bar chart's panel, using it to set the width and height of its bar container group.

With the width and height of our bar group in hand, we use D3 to build our chart's frame, appending the required <svg> and <g> tags and specifying the size of the SVG canvas and translation of the bar group:

```
d3.select('#nobel-bar').append("svg")
    .attr("width", width + margin.left + margin.right)
    .attr("height", height + margin.top + margin.bottom)
    .append("g").classed('chart', true)
    .attr("transform", "translate(" + margin.left + ","
                            + margin.top + ")");
```

This changes the HTML of the nobel-bar content block:

```
...
<div id="nobel-bar">
  <svg width="600" height="400">
    <g class="chart" transform="translate(40, 20)"></g>
  </svg>
```

```
    </div>
    ...
```

The resulting SVG framework is shown in Figure 16-8. The `<svg>` element's width and height are the sum of its child group and the surrounding margins. The child group is offset using `transform` to translate it `margin.left` pixels to the right and `margin.top` pixels down (by SVG convention, in the positive y direction).

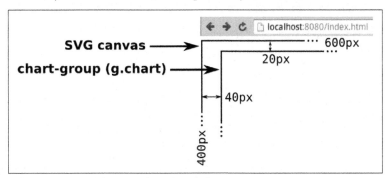

Figure 16-8. Building our bar chart's frame

With our frame in place, let's use `append` to add a few bars. We'll use a little dummy data: an array of objects with the top slice of Nobel Prize–winning countries by prize number.

```
var nobelData = [
    {key:'United States', value:336},
    {key:'United Kingdom', value:98},
    {key:'Germany', value:79},
    {key:'France', value:60},
    {key:'Sweden', value:29},
    {key:'Switzerland', value:23},
    {key:'Japan', value:21},
    {key:'Russia', value:19},
    {key:'Netherlands', value:17},
    {key:'Austria', value:14}
];
```

To build a crude bar chart,[1] we can iterate through the `nobelData` array, appending a bar to the chart group as we go. Example 16-2 demonstrates this. After building a basic frame for our chart, we iterate through the `nobelData` array, using the `value` fields to set the

---

1 We'll be dealing with axes, labels, and the like later in the chapter when we put D3 into top gear and start binding data.

bar's height and y-position. Figure 16-9 shows how the object values are used to append bars to our chart group. Note that because SVG uses a downward y-axis, you have to displace the bars by the height of the bar chart minus that of the bar in order to put the bar chart the right way up. As we'll see later, by using D3's scales, we can limit such geometric bookkeeping.

Example 16-2. Building a crude bar chart with append

```
var buildCrudeBarchart = function() {

    var chartHolder = d3.select("#nobel-bar");

    var margin = {top:20, right:20, bottom:30, left:40};
    var boundingRect = chartHolder.node().getBoundingClientRect();
    var width = boundingRect.width - margin.left - margin.right,
    height = boundingRect.height - margin.top - margin.bottom;
    var barWidth = width/nobelData.length;

    var svg = d3.select('#nobel-bar').append("svg")
        .attr("width", width + margin.left + margin.right)
        .attr("height", height + margin.top + margin.bottom)
        .append("g").classed('chart', true)
        .attr("transform", "translate(" + margin.left + ","
        + margin.top + ")");

    nobelData.forEach(function(d, i) { ❶
        svg.append('rect').classed('bar', true)
            .attr('height', d.value)
            .attr('width', barWidth)
            .attr('y', height-d.value)
            .attr('x', i*(barWidth)));
    });
};
```

❶ Iterates through each of the objects in nobelData, the forEach method providing object and array index to an anonymous function.

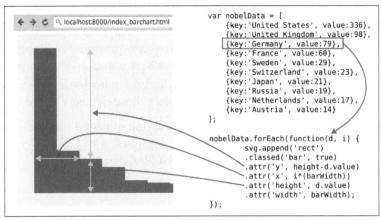

Figure 16-9. Programming a basic bar chart with D3

The other way in which D3 can add elements to the DOM tree is with its `insert` method. `insert` works like `append` but adds a second selector argument to allow you to place elements before a particular position in an sequence of tags, such as at the beginning of an ordered list. Figure 16-10 demonstrates the use of `insert`: list items in the `silly-list` are selected just like `append` and then a second argument (e.g., `':first-child'`) specifies the element to insert before.

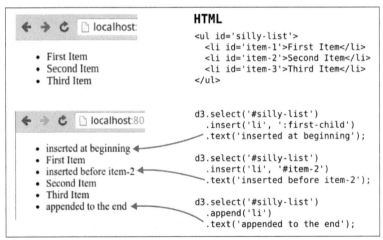

Figure 16-10. Using D3's insert method to add list items

For SVG elements, positioned directly within their parent group using x and y coordinates, `insert` might seem redundant. But, as discussed in "Layering and Transparency" on page 122, DOM ordering is important in SVG as elements are layered, meaning that the last element in the DOM tree overlays any previous. We'll see an example of this in Chapter 18 where we have a grid overlay (or gra ticule) for our world map. We want this grid to be drawn above all other map elements so use insert to place those elements before it.

Our crude bar chart in Figure 16-9 is crying out for a little refinement. Let's see how we can improve things, first with D3's powerful scale objects and then with D3's biggest idea, data binding.

Leveraging D3

In Example 16-2, we built a basic, no-frills bar chart with D3. This chart had a number of problems. First, looping through the data array is a bit clunky. What if we wanted to adapt the dataset for our chart? We'd need some way of adding or removing bars in response and then updating the resulting bars with the new data and redrawing everything. We'd also need to keep scaling the bar dimensions in x and y to reflect the different number of bars and a different maximum bar value. That's quite a lot of bookkeeping already and things could get messy fast. Also, where do we keep the changing datasets? Every data-driven change to our chart would require passing the dataset around and then constructing a loop to iterate over elements. It feels as if the data exists outside the chained D3 workflow when it really needs to be integral to it.

The solution to elegantly integrating our dataset with D3 lies in the concept of data binding, D3's biggest idea. The scaling problems are sorted by one of D3's most useful utility libraries: scale. We'll take a look at these now and then unleash the power of D3 with some data binding.

Measuring Up with D3's Scales

The fundamental idea behind D3's scales is a mapping from an input domain to an output range. This simple procedure can remove a lot of the persnickety aspects of building charts, visualizations, and the like. As you get more comfortable with scales, you'll find more and more situations where you can apply them. Mastering them is a key component to relaxed, effortless D3.

D3 provides a lot of scales, dividing them into three main categories: quantitative, ordinal, and time[2] scales. There are exotic mappings to suit most conceivable situations, but you'll probably find yourself using the linear and ordinal scales much of the time, at least while you win your D3 spurs.

In use, D3 scales can appear slightly strange because they are part object, part function. What this means is that after creating your scale, you can call various methods on it to set its properties (e.g., domain to set its domain), but you can also call it as a function with a domain argument to return a range value. The following example should make the distinction clear:

```
var scale = d3.scale.linear(); // create a linear scale
scale.domain([0, 1]).range([0, 100]); ❶
scale(0.5) // returns 50 ❷
```

❶ We use the scale's domain and range methods to map from 0 → 1 to 0 → 100.

❷ We call the scale like a function with a domain argument of 0.5, returning a range value of 50.

Let's look at the two main D3 scales, the quantitative and the ordinal, showing how we use them to build our bar chart as we go.

Quantitative Scales

A D3 quantitative scale you'll usually employ when building line-charts, bar charts, scatter plots, and the like is linear, mapping a continuous domain to a continuous range. For example, we want our bar heights to be a linear function of the nobelData values. The range of values to be mapped to is between the maximum and minimum height of the bars in pixels (400 px to 0 px) and the domain to be mapped from is between the smallest conceivable value (0) and, in our case, the largest value in the array (336 US winners). In the following code, we first use D3's max method to get the largest value in our nobelData array, using that to specify the end of our domain:

```
var maxWinners = d3.max(nobelData, function(d){
                    return +d.value;
```

---

2 See D3's GitHub page (*https://github.com/mbostock/d3/wiki/Scales*) for a comprehensive list.

```
                });
var yScale = d3.scale.linear()
                .domain([0, maxWinners]) /* [0, 336] */
                .range([height, 0]);
```

One little trick to note is that our range decreases from its maximum. This is because we want to use it to specify a positive displacement along the SVG downward y-axis in order to make the bar chart's y-axis point upward (i.e., the smaller the bar height, the larger the y displacement required). Conversely, you can see that the largest bar (the US winners tally) isn't displaced at all (see Figure 16-11).

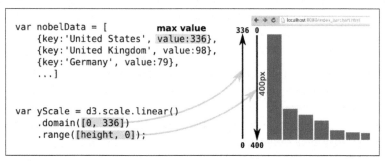

Figure 16-11. Using D3's linear scale to fix the domain and range of our bar chart's y-axis

We're using the simplest possible linear scale for our bar chart's y-axis, mapping from one numeric range to another, but D3's linear scales can do a lot more. The key to understanding this is D3's `inter polate` method.[3] This takes two values and returns an `interpola tor` between them. So, for the range of our yScale in Figure 16-11, `interpolate` returns a numeric `interpolator` for the values 400 and 0:

```
var numInt = d3.interpolate(400, 0);

numInt(0); //    400 ❶
numInt(0.5); // 200
numInt(1); //    0
```

---

3 See the D3 docs (*https://github.com/mbostock/d3/wiki/Transitions#d3_interpolate*) for full details.

❶ Interpolators have a default domain of [0,1].

The `interpolate` method can deal with more than just numbers. Strings, color codes, and even objects are handled sensibly. You can also specify more than two numbers for your domain array—just make sure that domain and range arrays are the same size.[4] We can combine these two facts to create a useful colormap:[5]

```
var color = d3.scale.linear()
    .domain([-1, 0, 1])
    .range(["red", "green", "blue"]);

color(0) // "#008000" green's hex code
color(0.5) // "004080" slate blue
```

D3's linear scales have a lot of useful utility methods and rich functionality. The numeric maps will probably be your workhorse scale, but I recommend reading the D3 docs (*http://bit.ly/1UAO0lI*) to fully appreciate how flexible the linear scales are. On that web page, you'll find D3's other quantitative scales, to suit almost every quantitative occasion:

- Power scales, similar to linear but with exponential transform (e.g., `sqrt`)
- Log scales, similar to linear but with logarithmic transform
- Quantize scales, a variant of linear with a discrete range; that is, although the input is continuous, the output is divided into segments or buckets (e.g., [1, 2, 3, 4, 5])
- Quantile scales, often used for color palettes, are similar to quantize scales but have discrete or bucketed domains as well as ranges
- Identity scales, linear with the same domain and range (fairly esoteric)

Quantitative scales are great for manipulating continuously valued quantities, but often we want to get values based on a discrete

---

4 D3 will truncate whichever is bigger.

5 D3 has many built-in colormaps and sophisticated color handling with RGB, HCL, etc. We'll see a few of these in action in the coming chapters.

domain (e.g., names or categories). D3 has a specialized set of ordinal scales to meet this need.

Ordinal Scales

Ordinal scales take an array of values as their domain and map these to discrete or continuous ranges, producing a single mapped value for each. To explicitly create a one-to-one mapping, we use the scale's range method:

```
var oScale = d3.scale.ordinal()
            .domain(['a', 'b', 'c', 'd', 'e'])
            .range([1, 2, 3, 4, 5]);

oScale('c'); // 3
```

In the case of our bar chart, we want to map an array of indices to a continuous range, to provide our bars' x-coordinates. For this, we can use the rangeBands or the rangeRoundBands methods, the latter snapping output values to individual pixels. Here, we use rangeR oundBands to map an array of numbers to a continuous range:

```
var oScale = d3.scale.ordinal()
            .domain([1, 2, 3, 4, 5])
            .rangeRoundBands([0, 400]);

oScale(3) // 160
oScale(5) // 320
```

In building our original crude bar chart (Example 16-2), we used a barWidth variable to size the bars. Implementing padding between the bars would have required a padding variable and necessary adjustments to barWidth and the bar positions. With our new ordinal scale, we get these things for free, removing the fiddly bookkeeping. Calling the xScale's rangeBand (note the singular form) method provides the calculated bar widths. We can also provide the rangeBands method with a second argument, specifying the padding between the bars as a fraction of the space occupied by each bar. The rangeBand value is adjusted accordingly. Here are some examples of this in action:

```
var oScale = d3.scale.ordinal()
            .domain([1, 2]); ❶

oScale.rangeRoundBands([0, 100]); ❷
oScale(2); // 50
oScale.rangeBand(); // 50
```

```
oScale.rangeRoundBands([0, 100], 0.1); // pBpBp ❸
oScale(1); // 5
oScale(2); // 52
oScale.rangeBand(); // 42, the padded bar width
```

❶ Stores the scale with a fixed domain; useful if we anticipate the range changing.

❷ rangeRoundBands snaps (rounds) the output values to integers.

❸ We specify a padding (p) factor of 0.1 * allocated bar(B)-space.

Figure 16-12 shows our bar chart's ordinal x-scale with a padding factor of 0.1. The continuous range is 600 (pixels), which is the width of the bar chart, and the domain is an array of integers representing the individual bars. As shown, providing xScale with a bar's index number returns its position on the x-axis.

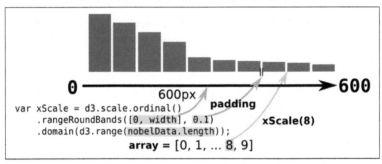

Figure 16-12. Setting the domain and range of our bar chart's x-scale, using a padding factor of 0.1

Armed with our D3 scales, let's turn to D3's central concept, binding data to the DOM in order to drive changes to it.

Unleashing the Power of D3 with Data Binding

D3 stands for *Data-Driven Documents*, and up to now we haven't really been driving with our data. In order to unleash D3, we need to embrace its big idea, which is binding the data in our dataset to its respective DOM elements and updating the web page (document) based on this integration. This small step of binding data to the

DOM enables a huge amount of functionality when combined with the most powerful D3 methods, enter and exit. With enter, we can return any data that is not bound to a DOM element and use it to create a new one (to which it is then bound). exit, the counterpart of enter, allows us to find any DOM elements that are unbound to data and, for example, remove them (with the remove() method). Working in conjunction, enter and exit make updating a bar chart a cinch and are almost certainly at work in the cooler D3 demos you've seen.

In order to demonstrate D3's data binding, let's start with our barless chart, with SVG canvas and chart group in place:

```
...
    <div id="nobel-bar">
      <svg width="600" height="400">
        <g class="chart" transform="translate(40, 20)"></g>
      </svg>
    </div>
...
```

In order to bind data with D3, we first need some data in the right form. Generally that will be an array of objects, like our bar chart's nobelData:

```
var nobelData = [
    {key:'United States', value:336},
    {key:'United Kingdom', value:98},
    {key:'Germany', value:79},
    ...
]
```

With this data in hand, binding it to the DOM is easy. We just make a standard D3 selection and then use the data method to bind the data to it. We'll store the result in a bars variable:

```
var svg = d3.select('#nobel-bar .chart');

var bars = svg.selectAll('.bar')
              .data(nobelData);
```

We now come to a slightly counterintuitive aspect of D3's data method. Our first select returned the chart group in our nobel-bar SVG canvas, but the second selectAll returned all elements with class bars, of which there are none. If there are no bars, what exactly are we binding the data to? The answer is that behind the scenes, D3 is keeping the books and that the bars object returned by data knows which DOM elements have been bound to the `nobel` `Data` and, just as crucially, which haven't. We'll now see how to make use of this fact using the fundamental `enter` method.

The enter Method

D3's `enter` (*https://github.com/mbostock/d3/wiki/Selections#enter*) method (and its sibling, `exit`) is both the basis for D3's superb power and expressiveness and also the root of much confusion. It's worth coming to grips with it at a low level if you really want your D3 skills to grow. Let's introduce it now, with a very simple and slow demonstration.

We'll start with a canonically simple little demonstration, adding a bar rectangle for each member of our Nobel Prize data. We'll use the first six Nobel Prize–winning countries as our bound data:

```
var nobelData = [
    {key:'United States', value:200},
    {key:'United Kingdom', value:80},
    {key:'France', value:47},
    {key:'Switzerland', value:23},
    {key:'Japan', value:21},
    {key:'Austria', value:12}
];
```

With our dataset in hand, let's first use D3 to grab the chart group, saving it to an `svg` variable. We'll use that to make a selection of all elements of class `bar` (none at the moment):

```
var svg = d3.select('#nobel-bar .chart');

var bars = svg.selectAll('.bar')
    .data(nobelData);
```

Now although the `bars` selection is empty, behind the scenes D3 has kept a record of the data we've just bound to it. At this point, we can use that fact and the `enter` method to create a few bars with our data. Calling enter on our `bars` selection returns a subselection of all the data (`nobelData`, in this case) that was not bound to a bar. Since there were no bars in the original selection (our chart being empty), all the data is unbound, so `enter` returns an enter election (essentially placeholder nodes for all the unbound data) of size six:

```
bars = bars.enter(); # returns six placeholder nodes
```

We can use the placeholder nodes in `bars` to create some DOM elements—in our case, a few bars. We won't bother with trying to put them the right way up (the y-axis being down from the top of the screen by convention), but we will use the data values and indexes to set the position and height of the bars:

```
bars.append('rect')
    .classed('bar', true)
    .attr('width', 10)
    .attr('height', function(d){return d.value;}) ❶
    .attr('x', function(d, i) { return i * 12; });
```

❶ If you provide a callback function to D3's setter methods (`attr`, `style`, etc.), then the first and second arguments provided are the value of the individual data object (e.g., `d == {key: 'United States', value: 200}`) and its index (`i`).

Using the callback functions to set height and the x position (allowing a padding of 2 px) of the bars, calling `append` on our six node selection produces Figure 16-13.

Figure 16-13. Producing some bars with D3's enter method

I'd encourage you generally to use Chrome's (or equivalent) Elements tab to investigate the HTML your D3 is producing. Investigating our mini–bar chart with Elements shows Figure 16-14.

```
☐  ☐      Elements   Console   Sources   Network   Timeline   F
  <!DOCTYPE html>
  <html>
  ▶ <head>…</head>
  ▼ <body id="dummybodyid">
    ▼ <div id="nobel-bar">
      ▼ <svg width="600" height="400">
        ▼ <g class="chart" transform="translate(40, 20)">
            <rect width="10" height="200" x="0"></rect>
            <rect width="10" height="80" x="12"></rect>
            <rect width="10" height="47" x="24"></rect>
            <rect width="10" height="23" x="36"></rect>
            <rect width="10" height="21" x="48"></rect>
            <rect width="10" height="12" x="60"></rect>
          </g>
        </svg>
      </div>
  html   body#dummybodyid   div#nobel-bar   svg   g.chart   rect
```

Figure 16-14. Using the Elements tab to see the HTML generated by enter and append

So we've seen what happens when we call enter on an empty selection. But what happens when we already have a few bars, which we would have in an interactive chart with a user-driven, changing dataset?

Let's add a couple of bar class rectangles to our starting HTML:

```
<div id="nobel-bar">
  <svg width="600" height="400">
    <g class="chart" transform="translate(40, 20)">
      <rect class='bar'></rect>
      <rect class='bar'></rect>
    </g>
  </svg>
</div>
```

If we now perform the same data binding and entering as before, on calling data on our selection, the two placeholder rectangles bind to the first two members of our nobelData array (i.e., [{key: 'United States', value: 200}, {key: 'United Kingdom', value:80}]). This means that enter, which returns only unbound data placeholders, now returns only four placeholders, associated with the last four elements of the nobelData array:

```
var svg = d3.select('#nobel-bar .chart');

var bars = svg.selectAll('.bar')
    .data(nobelData);

bars = bars.enter(); # return four placeholder nodes
```

If we now call append on the entered bars, as before, we get the result shown in Figure 16-15, showing the last four bars (note that they preserve their index i, used to set their x positions) rendered.

Figure 16-15. Calling enter and append with existing bars

Figure 16-16 shows the HTML generated for the last four bars. As we'll see, the data from the first two elements is now bound to the two dummy nodes we added to the initial bar group. We just haven't used it yet to adjust those rectangles' attributes. Updating old bars with new data is the one of the key elements of the update pattern we'll see shortly.

```
R  []   Elements  Console  Sources  Network  Timeline  Profiles  F
    <!DOCTYPE html>
    <html>
    ▶ <head>…</head>
    ▼ <body id="dummybodyid">
      ▼ <div id="nobel-bar">
···   ▼ <svg width="600" height="400">
          ▼ <g class="chart" transform="translate(40, 20)">
              <rect class="bar"></rect>
              <rect class="bar"></rect>
              <rect class="bar" width="10" height="47" x="24"></rect>
              <rect class="bar" width="10" height="23" x="36"></rect>
              <rect class="bar" width="10" height="21" x="48"></rect>
              <rect class="bar" width="10" height="12" x="60"></rect>
            </g>
          </svg>
        </div>
    html  body#dummybodyid  div#nobel-bar  svg
```

Figure 16-16. Using the Elements tab to see the HTML generated by enter and append on a partial selection

To emphasize, coming to grips with enter and exit (and remove) is vital to healthy progress with D3. Play around a bit, inspect the HTML you're producing, enter a bit of data, and generally get a bit messy, learning the ins and outs. Let's have a little look at accessing the bound data before moving on to the D3's nexus, the update pattern.

Accessing the Bound Data

A good way to see what's happening to the DOM is to use your browser's HTML inspector and console to track D3's changes. In Figure 16-13, we use Chrome's console to look at the rect element representing the first bar in Figure 16-15, before data has been bound and after the nobelData has been bound to the bars using the data method. As you can see, D3 has added a __data__ object to the rect element with which to store its bound data—in this case, the first member of our nobelData list. The __data__ object is used by D3's internal bookkeeping and, fundamentally, the data in it made available to functions supplied to update methods such as attr.

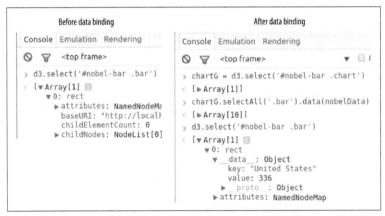

Figure 16-17. Using the Chrome console to show the addition of a __data__ object after data binding using D3's data method

Let's look at a little example of using the data in an element's __data__ object to set its name attribute. The name attribute can be useful for making specific D3 selections. For example, if the user selects a particular country, we can now use D3 to get all its named components and adjust their style if needed. We'll use the bar with bound data in Figure 16-17 and set the name using the key property of its bound data:

```
var bar = d3.select('#nobel-bar .bar');

bar.attr('name', function(d, i){ ❶

    var sane_key = d.key.replace(/ /g, '_'); ❷

    console.log('__data__ is: ' + JSON.stringify(d)
    + ', index is ' + i)

    return 'bar__' + sane_key; ❸
    });
// console out:
// __data__ is: {"key":"United States","value":336}, index is 0
```

❶ All D3 setter methods can take a function as their second argument. This function receives the data (d) bound to the selected element and its position in the data array (i).

❷ We use a regular expression (regex) to replace all spaces in the key with underscores (e.g., United States → United_States).

❸ This will set the bar's id to 'bar__United_States'.

All the setter methods listed in Figure 16-3 (attr, style, text, etc.) can take a function as a second argument, which will receive data bound to the element and the element's array index. The return of this function is used to set the value of the property. As we'll see, with interactive visualizations' changes to the visualized dataset will be reflected when we bind the new data and then use these functional setters to adapt attributes, styles, and properties accordingly.

Now that we've seen how bind data objects to DOM elements and use that data to add and adapt elements, let's look at how to update our visualizations as our data changes. The update pattern we'll learn is the core to using D3 effectively, and it or a close variant will be employed in pretty much all the cool D3 demos you've seen.

The Update Pattern

The previous section showed how we can bind our data to the DOM, use it to append or insert elements, and use data-driven functions to change attributes of the elements. We now want to put these concepts together to fulfill our goal of creating charts or visualizations that can be updated with new data, allowing for user-driven changes and the full scope of interactivity. To do this, we'll employ an update pattern that makes use of one of D3's core concepts, the data-join (*http://bost.ocks.org/mike/join/*). With the enter method, we've already seen one half of the data-join methods at work. Now we'll see how it works in conjunction with its sibling exit to create the update pattern.[6]

 Although you may anticipate building one-off charts, with a single data-binding process, it's good to get into the habit of asking yourself "What if I need to change the data dynamically?" If the answer is not immediately obvious, you have probably implemented a bad D3 design. Catching yourself in the act means you can do a little code audit and make the necessary changes before things start to deteriorate. It's good to kick yourself out of this habit, but also, because D3 is somewhat of a craft skill, constantly reaffirming that best practice will pay off when you need it.

Figure 16-18 shows a D3 update pattern.

1. First we bind the nobelData to a selection of bars (of class bar) containing two existing bars (B_0 and B_1). The first two data objects (O_1 and O_2) are bound to their respective bars, leaving the rest of the objects unbound.

2. Using enter on the bars update selector returns an array with placeholders for all the unbound data objects. These are then used to append new bars to the bar group.

3. We then use chained attribute setters on all the bars in the bars update selector, including the bars we just appended (now freshly bound to their data). We use our x and y scales to get the correct dimensions and positions for the bars. Note that the

---

6 See Mike Bostock's demonstration of the general update pattern at bl.ocks.org (*https://bl.ocks.org/mbostock/3808218*).

code to update the scales' domains given the new data is not shown but will be shortly.

4. Finally we use enter's counterpart in the data-join, exit, to return any bar elements that are not bound to data (in this case an empty list). We then remove any of these.

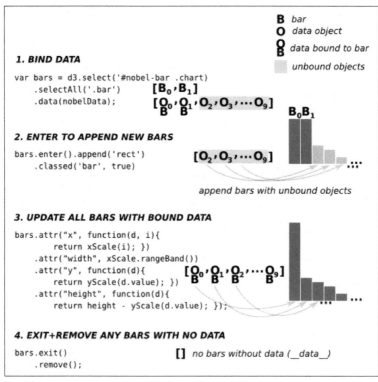

Figure 16-18. D3 update pattern

The update pattern just described is found in some shape or other in almost all interactive D3 charts, and getting your head around it is fundamental to "getting" D3. In fact, I think that if you "get" the update pattern, you "get" D3, so spend some time thinking about it. I'd suggest playing around at Blockbuilder (*http://blockbuilder.org*) (with many thousands of update pattern examples available) and going to the huge collection of D3 examples at *http://bl.ocks.org/mbostock*. Pick an example and see if you can locate and understand its update pattern.

Figure 16-19 shows the update pattern with removal of some unbound dataless bars. Whereas in Figure 16-18 there were more data objects than bars, here the data-join (1) has fewer objects than bars, leaving two bars (B2 and B3) unbound. Entering the data (2) results in an empty array, with no objects unbound to bars. In (3) we update the first two bars with their new data. Note that the bar widths, specified by xScale.rangeBand(), will change as we update our ordinal xScale's domain from [0, 1, 2, 3] to [0, 1], to reflect the change in our size of our dataset. In Figure 16-18, exiting the bars resulted in an empty list, there being no unbound bars. Here, bars B2 and B3 have no data associated with them and are returned by the exit method. A subsequent remove call removes them from the DOM tree, leaving our updated bar chart clutter-free.

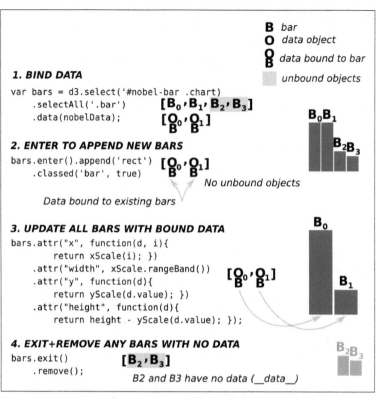

Figure 16-19. D3 update pattern with removal

Example 16-3 shows the complete code for our no-frills bar chart with the update pattern incorporated. Note that the chart details that are independent of the data (our nobelData array) are specified outside of the update function (e.g., the scale ranges), specified by the height and width in pixels of our bar chart, in turn established by the CSS-defined width and height of the #nobel-bar container and the margin variable. Any aspects of the chart that might change with new data are shifted into the update function. So the scale domains, specified by the length of the data array and its maximum value, are set separately from the ranges and updated every time the data changes.

Note also that, once the charts framework is in place, we are only interested in the update method and supplying it with any new data. As we'll see, this allows us to harness JavaScript's closure and create safe, reusable chart objects, hiding the chart's *innards* from the user and reducing possible code conflicts.

Example 16-3. Making a bar chart with the update pattern

```
// GETTING THE CHART DIMENSIONS
var chartHolder = d3.select("#nobel-bar");
var margin = {top:20, right:20, bottom:30, left:40};
var boundingRect = chartHolder.node().getBoundingClientRect();
var width = boundingRect.width - margin.left - margin.right,
height = boundingRect.height - margin.top - margin.bottom;
// SCALES WITH RANGES
var xScale = d3.scale.ordinal()
    .rangeBands([0, width], 0.1);

var yScale = d3.scale.linear()
    .rangeRound([height, 0]);
// CHART-HOLDER GROUP
var svg = d3.select('#nobel-bar').append("svg")
    .attr("width", width + margin.left + margin.right)
    .attr("height", height + margin.top + margin.bottom)
    .append("g").classed('chart', true)
    .attr("transform", "translate(" +
        margin.left + "," + margin.top + ")");
// OUR UPDATE FUNCTION
var update = function(data){
    // UPDATE SCALE DOMAINS FOR CHANGED DATA
    xScale.domain(d3.range(data.length)); ❶
    yScale.domain([0, d3.max(data.map(function(d) { ❷
        return d.value;
    }))]);
    // JOIN DATA TO BAR-GROUP
    var bars = svg.selectAll('.bar')
        .data(data);
    // APPEND BARS FOR UNBOUND DATA
    bars.enter()
        .append('rect').classed('bar', true);
    // UPDATE ALL BARS WITH BOUND DATA
    bars.attr('height', function(d, i){
      return height-yScale(d.value); })
        .attr('width', xScale.rangeBand())
        .attr('y', function(d) {
            return yScale(d.value);
        })
        .attr('x', function(d, i) {
            return xScale(i);
        });
    // REMOVE ANY BARS WITHOUT BOUND DATA
    bars.exit().remove();
};
```

❶ Our x-scale domain is just [0, 1, ... *n*-1], where *n* is the length of our dataset. d3.range is a handy method, which takes an input integer *n* and produces an array [0, ... *n*-1].

❷ Use D3's max method to get the max value in our dataset.

Axes and Labels

Now that we have a working update pattern, we will add the axes and axes labels that any self-respecting bar chart needs.

D3 doesn't offer a lot in the way of high-level chart elements, encouraging you to roll your own. But it does provide a convenient axis object, which takes the sting out of having to craft the SVG elements yourself. It's easy to use and, as you would expect, plays nicely with our data update patterns, allowing for axes ticks and labels that change in response to the data presented.

D3 Axes

D3 axes can be confusing at first, feeling just a little bit magical. It's best to think of them as a plugin[7] that generates the correct axis HTML (lines, ticks, tick labels, etc.) for you and which can respond sensibly to changes in data (i.e., if you change the range of your scales, the axes can change in response using nice, smooth transitions that look pretty cool).

Generally with a D3 axis, you will create an SVG group to hold it and then call the axis on it, having set the scale it will represent. During the call, the axis object will *stamp* the correct HTML on the DOM. So, as a simple demo, the following page describes a simple chart setup with an SVG x-axis group and a D3 axis. Calling the axis on the axis group generates the HTML lines and text needed for an axis.

```
<!DOCTYPE html>
<meta charset="utf-8">
<script
```

---

7 Axes follow a similar pattern to that proposed by Mike Bostock in *Towards Reusable Charts* (*https://bost.ocks.org/mike/chart/*), using the JavaScript objects' call (*https://developer.mozilla.org/en-US/docs/Web/JavaScript/Reference/Global_Objects/Function/call*) method to build HTML on the selected DOM element(s).

```
        src="https://cdnjs.cloudflare.com/ajax/
            libs/d3/3.5.5/d3.min.js">
</script>
<style> svg{width:600px; height:400px} </style>

<body>
  <svg>
    <g id='chart' transform='translate(20,20)'>
      <g id='x-axis'></g>
    </g>
  </svg>
  <script>
    var scale = d3.scale.linear()
                  .domain([0, 10]).range([0,400]); ❶
    var xaxis = d3.svg.axis().scale(scale); ❷
    d3.select('#x-axis').call(xaxis); ❸
  </script>
</body>
```

❶ Creates a scale with a domain of 0 to 10 and a range of 400 (pixels).

❷ Creates a D3 axis, using the scale just defined.

❸ Calling the D3 axis on our x-axis group creates the axis HTML branch shown in Figure 16-21, which looks like Figure 16-20.

0   1   2   3   4   5   6   7   8   9   10

Figure 16-20. A simple D3 axis

```
[⊡ ⬚]   Elements  Console  Sources  Network  Timeline  Profiles  Resources  Security  Audits
        ▼<body>
          ▼<svg>
            ▼<g id="chart" transform="translate(20,20)">
              ▼<g id="x-axis">
                ▼<g class="tick" transform="translate(0,0)" style="opacity: 1;">
                    <line y2="6" x2="0"></line>
                    <text dy=".71em" y="9" x="0" style="text-anchor: middle;">0</text>
                  </g>
                ►<g class="tick" transform="translate(40,0)" style="opacity: 1;">…</g>
                ►<g class="tick" transform="translate(80,0)" style="opacity: 1;">…</g>
                ►<g class="tick" transform="translate(120,0)" style="opacity: 1;">…</g>
                ►<g class="tick" transform="translate(160,0)" style="opacity: 1;">…</g>
```

Figure 16-21. The HTML branch created by a D3 axis instance

Using the call method on a selection is a common D3 technique to create plugins such as tooltips and brushes. There are loads of examples on bl.ocks.org like this one (*http://bl.ocks.org/cpbotha/5073718*) by Charl Botha. I wrote a little blog post (*http://kyrandale.com/blog/building-d3-plugin/*) about extending the technique. The main take-home is that it's not magic and it's certainly important that you understand the basics of what's happening during that call method.

In order to define our x and y axes, we need to know what ranges and domains we want our axes to represent. In our case, it's the same one as the ranges and domains of our x and y scales, so we supply these to the axes' scale method. D3 axes also allow you to specify their orientation, which will fix the relative position of ticks and tick labels. With our bar chart, we want the x-axis on the bottom and the y-axis on the left. Our ordinal x-axis will have a label for each bar, but with our y-axis, the choice of tick numbers is arbitrary. Ten seems like a reasonable number, so we set that using the ticks method. The following code shows how we declare our bar chart's axes:

```
var xAxis = d3.svg.axis()
        .scale(xScale)
        .orient("bottom");

var yAxis = d3.svg.axis()
        .scale(yScale)
        .orient('left')
        .ticks(10)
        .tickFormat(function(d) { ❶
            if(nbviz.valuePerCapita){
                return d.toExponential();
            }
            return d;
        });
```

❶ We want the format of our tick labels to change with our chosen metric, per capita or absolute. Per capita produces a very small number that is best represented in exponential form (e.g., 0.000005 → 5e-6). The tickFormat method allows you to take the data value at each tick and return the desired tick string.

We'll also need a little bit of CSS to style the axes correctly, removing the default fill, setting the stroke color to black, and making the shape render crisply. We'll also specify the font size and family while we're at it:

```
/* style.css */
.axis { font: 10px sans-serif; }
.axis path, .axis line {
    fill: none;
    stroke: #000;
    shape-rendering: crispEdges;
}
```

Up to now, we've been using a numerical domain as placeholder for our ordinal x-axis (see Example 16-3 ❶). Now we need it to contain the bar labels, which will be used to make the x-ticks of our chart. The country data supplied to our `update` method is of the form:

```
[
  {
    code: "USA", // Three-digit country code
    key: "United States",
    population: 319259000,
    value: 336
  },
  // ... 56 more countries
]
```

We want to use those three-digit country codes as handy x-labels, which means updating the domain of our ordinal x-scale. The following code uses the data array's `map` method to return an array of country codes, which are used to set the domain of our x-scale to ["USA", "GBR", "DEU", ...]:

```
xScale.domain( data.map(function(d) { return d.code; }) );
```

Now that we have our `axis` generators, we need a couple of SVG groups to hold the axes they produce. Let's add these to our main `svg` selector as groups with sensible class names:

```
svg.append("g")
    .attr("class", "x axis")
    .attr("transform", "translate(0," + height + ")"); ❶

svg.append("g")
        .attr("class", "y axis");
```

❶ By SVG's convention, y is measured from the top down, so we want our *bottom*-oriented x-axis translated from the chart's top by *height* pixels.

Our bar chart's axes have fixed ranges (the width and height of the chart), but their domains will change as the user filters the dataset. For example, the number of (country) bars will be reduced if the user filters the data by Economics category: this will change the domain of the ordinal x-scale (number of bars) and the quantitative y-scale (maximum number of winners). We want the displayed axes to change with these changing domains, with a nice transition for good measure.

Example 16-4 shows how the axes are updated. First we update our scale domains using the new data (A). These new scale domains are reflected when the axes generators (which are linked to them) are called on their respective axis groups.

Example 16-4. Updating our bar chart's axes

```
update = function(data) {
    // A. Update scale domains with new data
    xScale.domain( data.map(function(d) { return d.code; }) );
    yScale.domain([0, d3.max(data, function(d){
                                    return +d.value; })]);
    // B. Use the axes generators with the new scale domains
    svg.select('.x.axis')
        .call(xAxis) ❶
        .selectAll("text") ❷
        .style("text-anchor", "end")
        .attr("dx", "-.8em")
        .attr("dy", ".15em")
        .attr("transform", "rotate(-65)");

    svg.select('.y.axis')
        .call(yAxis);
    // ...
```

❶ Calling the D3 `axis` on our x-axis group element builds all the necessary axis SVG in it, including ticks and tick labels. D3 `axis` uses an internal update pattern to enable transitions to newly bound data.

❷ After creating the x-axis, we perform some SVG manipulations of the text labels generated. First we select the `text` elements of the axis, the tick labels. We then place their text anchors at the end of the element and shift their position a bit. This is because the text is rotated about its anchor and we want to rotate about the end of the country labels, now positioned under the tick lines. The result of our manipulations is shown in Figure 16-22. Note that without rotating our labels, they would merge into one another.

Figure 16-22. Reoriented tick labels on the x-axis

Now that we have our working axes, let's add a little label to the x-axis and then see how the bar chart copes with our real data:

```
var X_PADDING_LEFT  = 20; ❶
//...
var xScale = d3.scale.ordinal()
    .rangeBands([X_PADDING_LEFT, width], 0.1);
//...
svg.append("g")
    .attr("class", "y axis")
    .append("text")
    .attr('id', 'y-axis-label')
    .attr("transform", "rotate(-90)") ❷
    .attr("y", 6)
    .attr("dy", ".71em") ❸
    .style("text-anchor", "end")
    .text('Number of winners');
```

❶ A left padding constant, in pixels, to make way for the y-axis label.

❷ Rotates the text anticlockwise to the upright position.

❸ dy is a relative coordinate [relative to the *y* coordinate just specified (6)]. By using the em unit (relative to font size), we can make handy adjustments to the text margin and baseline. See the D3 docs (*https://github.com/mbostock/d3/wiki/SVG-Shapes#svg_text*) for a full explanation and examples.

Figure 16-23 shows the result of filtering our Nobel Prize winners' dataset for Chemistry winners, using our category selector filter. The bar widths increase to reflect the reduced number of countries, and both axes adapt to the new dataset.

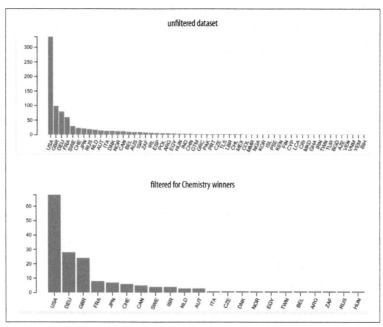

Figure 16-23. The Nobel Prize bar chart before and after we apply the category filter for Chemistry winners

We now have a working bar chart, using the update pattern to adjust itself as the user-driven dataset changes. But although it's functional, the transition in response to data change is visually stark, even jarring. One way to make the change much more engaging and even informative would be to have the chart update continuously over a short time period, with preserved country bars moving from their old to new position while simultaneously adapting their height and width. Such continuous transitions really add life to a visualization and are seen in many of the most impressive D3 pieces. The good news is that transitions are tightly integrated into D3's workflow, which means you can achieve these cool visual effects for the cost of a few lines of code.

Transitions

As it stands, our bar chart is perfectly functional. It responds to data changes by adding or removing bar elements and then updating them using the new data. But the immediate change from one reflection of the data to another feels a little stark and visually jarring.

D3's transitions provide the ability to smooth the visual update of our elements, making them change continuously over a set time period. This can be both aesthetically appealing and, on occasion, informative.[8] The important thing is that D3 transitions can be very engaging for the user, which is reason enough to want to master them.

Figure 16-24 shows the effect we are aiming at. When the bar chart is updated with a newly selected dataset, we want the bars of any countries present before and after the transition to morph smoothly from their old to new positions and dimensions. So in Figure 16-24 the bar for France grows from start to finish over the course of the transition—say, a couple of seconds—with intermediate bars of increasing width and height. The axes ticks and labels will adapt too as the x and y scales change.

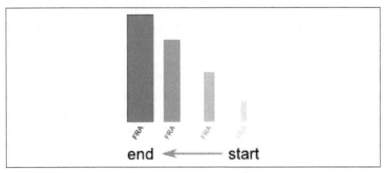

Figure 16-24. Tweened bar transitions on update

The effect shown in Figure 16-24 is surprisingly easy to achieve but involves understanding the precise way data is joined in D3. By default, when new data is bound to existing DOM elements, it is done by array index. Figure 16-25 shows how this works, using our selected bars as an example. The first bar (B0), previously bound to the USA's data, is now bound to France's. It stays in first position and

---

8 For example, when we change our measurement of Nobel Prize wins by country from absolute to per capita, the large amount of movement displayed as the country bars change their order emphasizes the difference between the two metrics.

updates its size and tick label. Essentially, the USA's bar becomes France's.[9]

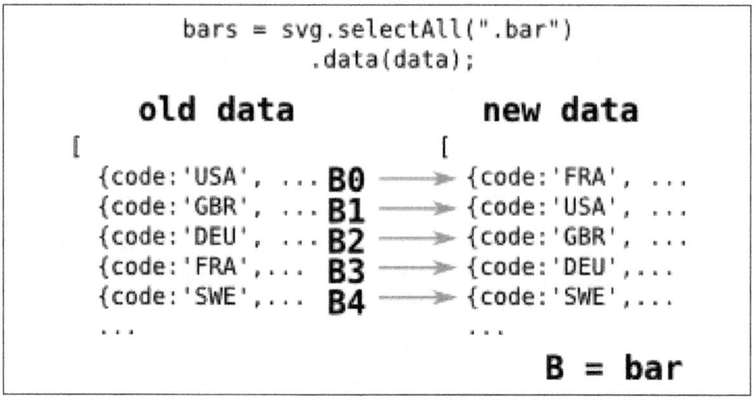

```
bars = svg.selectAll(".bar")
           .data(data);
```

old data   new data
[[
    {code:'USA', ... B0 ─────> {code:'FRA', ...
    {code:'GBR', ... B1 ─────> {code:'USA', ...
    {code:'DEU', ... B2 ─────> {code:'GBR', ...
    {code:'FRA',... B3 ─────> {code:'DEU',...
    {code:'SWE',... B4 ─────> {code:'SWE',...
    . . .   . . .

                                B = bar
```

*Figure 16-25. By default, new data is joined by index*

In order to get continuity during our transitions (i.e., for the USA bar to move to its new position while changing to its new height and width), we need the new data to be bound by a unique key, not the index. D3 allows you to specify a function as a second argument to the data method, which returns a key from the object data to use to bind the new data to the correct respective bars, assuming they still exist. Figure 16-26 shows how this is done. Now, the first bar (0) is bound to the new USA data, changing its position by index as well as its width and height to that of the new American bar.

---

9 See Mike Bostock's nice demonstration of object constancy at his site (*https://bost.ocks.org/mike/constancy/*).
```

```
bars = svg.selectAll(".bar")
        .data(data, function(d) {
            return d.code;
        });
```

old data   **new data**
[[
    {code:'USA', ... **B0** ──→ {code:'FRA', ...
    {code:'GBR', ... **B1**   {code:'USA', ...
    {code:'DEU', ... **B2**   {code:'GBR', ...
    {code:'FRA',... **B3**   {code:'DEU',...
    {code:'SWE',... **B4** ──→ {code:'SWE',...
    ...   ...

                                B = bar

Figure 16-26. Using an object key to join new data

Joining the data by key gives us the correct start and end points for
our national bars. Now all we need is a way to create a smooth tran‐
sition between them. We can do this by using a couple of D3's cool‐
est methods, transition and duration. By calling these before we
change our bar dimension and position attributes, D3 magically
performs a smooth transition between then, as shown in
Figure 16-24. Adding transitions to our bar chart update requires
only a few lines of code:

```
//...
svg.select('.x.axis')
    .transition().duration(nbviz.TRANS_DURATION) ❶
    .call(xAxis) //...
//...
svg.select('.y.axis')
    .transition().duration(nbviz.TRANS_DURATION)
    .call(yAxis);
//...
var bars = svg.selectAll(".bar")
    .data(data, function(d) {
        return d.code; ❷
    });
//...
bars
    .classed('active', function(d) {
        return d.key === nbviz.activeCountry;
    })
    .transition().duration(nbviz.TRANS_DURATION)
    .attr("x", function(d) { return xScale(d.code); }) ❸
    .attr("width", xScale.rangeBand())
```

```

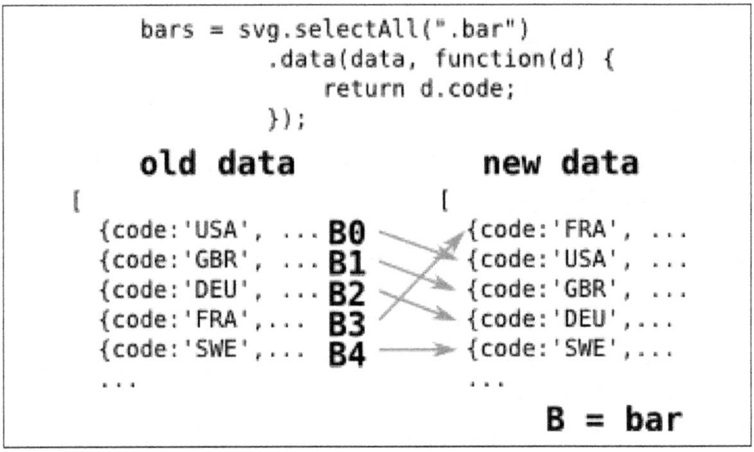
```

```
      .attr("y", function(d) { return yScale(d.value); })
      .attr("height", function(d) {
        return height - yScale(d.value); });
  //...
```

❶ A transition with duration of two seconds, which is our TRANS_DURATION constant of 2000 (ms).

❷ Using the data object's code property to make the continuous data joins.

❸ These attributes will be smoothly morphed from current values to those defined here.

Transitions will work on most obvious attributes and styles of an existing DOM element.[10]

The transitions just shown perform a smooth change of the attributes from starting point to end goal, but D3 allows for a lot of tuning for these effects. You can, for example, use the delay method to specify the time before the transition starts. This delay can also be a function of the data.

Probably the most useful extra transitioning method is ease, which allows you to specify the way in which the elements' attributes are updated over the transition's duration. The default easing function is cubic-in-out (*https://github.com/mbostock/d3/wiki/Transitions#ease*), but you can also specify things like *quad*, which speeds things up as the transition progresses, or *bounce* and *elastic*, which do pretty much what is says on the tin, giving a bouncy feel to the change. There's also *sin*, which speeds up at the beginning and slows down toward the end. See *http://easings.net/* for a nice description of different easing functions and this block (*http://bl.ocks.org/hunzy/ 9929724*) for a cool little demo of most of those available to D3. Gizma (*http://gizma.com/easing/*) has a great little app you can use to visualize the different easing functions.

If the easing functions available to D3 don't suit your needs or you're feeling particularly ambitious, as with most things D3 you can roll

---

10 Transitions only apply to existing elements—you can't fade in the creation of a DOM element, for example. You could, however, fade it in and out using the opacity CSS style.

your own to fit any subtle requirements. The `tween` method provides the fine-grained control you might need.

With a working update pattern and some cool transitions, we have completed our Nobel-viz bar chart. There's always room for refinement, but this bar chart will more than do the job. Let's summarize what we've learned in this rather large chapter before moving on to the other components of our Nobel Prize visualization.

Summary

This has been a large and quite challenging chapter. D3 isn't the easiest library to learn, but I have smoothed the learning curve by breaking things down into digestible chunks. Take your time absorbing the fundamental ideas and, crucially, start setting yourself little objectives to stretch your D3 knowledge. I think D3 is very much an art form and, more than most libraries, one learns while doing.

The key elements to understanding D3 and applying it effectively are the update pattern and the data binding involved. If you understand this at a fundamental level, most of D3's other pyrotechnics slot nicely into place. Focus on the `data`, `enter`, `exit`, and `remove` methods and make sure you really understand what's going on. It's the only way to advance from much of the cut-and-paste style of D3 programming, which is initially productive, there being so many cool examples out there, but will eventually frustrate. Use your browser's developer console (currently Chrome and Chromium have the best tools here) to inspect DOM elements, to see what data is bound to them via the `__data__` variable. If it doesn't match your expectations, you'll learn a lot by finding out why.

You should now have a pretty good grounding in D3's core techniques. In the next chapter we'll aim to challenge those new skills with a rather more ambitious chart, our Nobel Prize timeline.

## CHAPTER 17

Visualizing Individual Prizes

In Chapter 16 you learned the basics of D3, how to select and change DOM elements, how to add new ones, and how to apply the data update pattern, which is the axis around which interactive D3 spins. In this chapter, I will expand on what you've learned so far and show you how to build a fairly novel visual element, showing all the individual Nobel Prizes by year (Figure 17-1). This Nobel timeline will allow us to expand on the knowledge of the last chapter, demonstrating a number of new techniques including more advanced data manipulation.

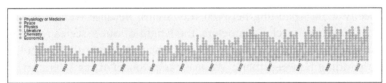

Figure 17-1. This chapter's target chart, a timeline of Nobel Prizes

Let's start by showing how we build the HTML framework for our timeline chart.

Building the Framework

Our target chart's construction is similar to that of our Nobel Prize bar chart, which we covered in detail in the last chapter. We first use D3 to select our <div> container with id nobel-time, then use the width and height of the container, along with our specified margins, to create our svg chart group:

```
/* global $, _, crossfilter, d3 */
(function(nbviz) {
    'use strict';

    var chartHolder = d3.select('#nobel-time');

    var margin = {top:20, right:20, bottom:30, left:40};
    var boundingRect = chartHolder.node()
      .getBoundingClientRect();
    var width = boundingRect.width - margin.left
    - margin.right,
    height = boundingRect.height - margin.top - margin.bottom;

    var svg = chartHolder.append("svg")
            .attr("width", width + margin.left + margin.right)
            .attr("height", height + margin.top
            + margin.bottom)
            .append('g')
            .attr("transform",
                    "translate(" + margin.left + ","
                    + margin.top + ")");
    // ...
```

With our svg chart group in place, let's add the scales and axes.

Scales

To place the circular indicators we use two ordinal scales
(Example 17-1). The x-scale uses the rangeRoundBands method to
specify a 10% padding between the circles. Because we use the x-
scale to set the circles' diameters, the height of our y-scale's range is
manually adjusted to accommodate all the indicators, allowing a little padding between them. We use rangeRoundPoints to round to
integer pixel coordinates.

Example 17-1. The chart's two ordinal scales, for x and y axes

```
var xScale = d3.scale.ordinal()
        .rangeRoundBands([0, width], 0.1) ❶
        .domain(d3.range(1900, 2015)); // years of Nobel Prize

var yScale = d3.scale.ordinal()
            .rangeRoundPoints([height, 0])
            .domain(d3.range(15));// from 0 to max. in any one year
```

❶ We're using a padding factor of 0.1, which is approximately 10%
of an indicator's diameter.

Unlike our bar chart from the last chapter, both ranges and domains of this chart are fixed. The domain of the xScale is the years over which the Nobel Prize has run, and that of the yScale is from zero to the maximum number of prizes in any given year (14 in the year 2000). Neither of these will change in response to user interaction, so we define them outside the update method.

Axes

With a maximum of 14 prizes in any one year and with a circular indicator for each, it is easy to make a prize count by eye if necessary. Given this, the emphasis on providing a relative indicator of prize distribution (e.g., showing the spurt in post-WWII US science prizes), and the long length of the chart, a y-axis is redundant for our chart.

For the x-axis, labeling the decades' starts seems about right. It reduces visual clutter and is also the standard human way of charting historical trends. Example 17-2 shows the construction of our x-axis, using D3's handy axis object. We override the tick values using the tickValues method, filtering the domain range (1900–2015) to return only those dates ending with zero.

Example 17-2. Making the x-axis, with tick labels per decade

```
var xAxis = d3.svg.axis()
            .scale(xScale)
            .orient("bottom");
            .tickValues(xScale.domain().filter(
              function(d,i){
                return !(d%10); ❶
              })
            );
```

❶ Returns true for years ending in 0, giving a tick label at the start of every decade.

As with the scales, we don't anticipate the axes changing,[1] so we can add them before receiving the dataset in the `updateTimeChart` function:

```
svg.append("g") // group to hold the axis
    .attr("class", "x axis")
    .attr("transform", "translate(0," + height + ")")
    .call(xAxis) ❶
    .selectAll("text") ❷
    .style("text-anchor", "end")
    .attr("dx", "-.8em")
    .attr("dy", ".15em")
    .attr("transform", "rotate(-65)");
```

❶ Calls our D3 axis on the `svg` group, with the `axis` object taking care of building the axis elements.

❷ As in "Axes and Labels" on page 436, we rotate the axis tick labels to place them diagonally.

With axes and scales taken care of, we need only add a little legend with our colored category labels before moving on to the cool, interactive elements of the chart.

Category Labels

The last of our *static* components is a legend, containing the category labels shown in Figure 17-2.

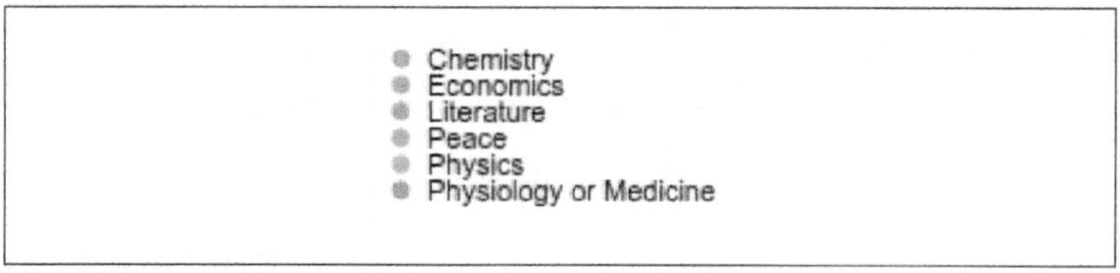

Figure 17-2. Categories legend

To create the legend, we first create a group, class `labels`, to hold the labels. We bind our `nbviz.CATEGORIES` data to a `label` selection

---

1 D3 has some handy brushes that make selecting portions of the x- or y-axis easy. Combined with transitions, this can make for an engaging and intuitive way to increase the resolution of large datasets. See this bl.ocks.org (*http://bl.ocks.org/mbostock/1667367*) for a good example.

on this `labels` group, enter the bound data, and attach a group for each category, displaced on the y-axis by index:

```
var catLabels = chartHolder.select('svg').append('g')
    .attr('transform', "translate(10, 10)")
    .attr('class', 'labels')
    .selectAll('label').data(nbviz.CATEGORIES) ❶
    .enter().append('g')
    .attr('transform', function(d, i) {
        return "translate(0," + i * 10 + ")"; ❷
});
```

❶ Binds our array of categories (`["Chemistry"`, `"Economics"`, ...]) to the `label` group.

❷ Creates a group for each category, spaced vertically 10 pixels apart.

Now that we have our `catLabels` selection, let's add a circular indicator (matching those seen in the timeline) and text label to each of its groups:

```
catLabels.append('circle')
    .attr('fill', (nbviz.categoryFill)) ❶
    .attr('r', xScale.rangeBand()/2); ❷

catLabels.append('text')
    .text(function(d) {
        return d;
    })
    .attr('dy', '0.4em')
    .attr('x', 10);
```

❶ We use our shared `categoryFill` method to return a color based on the bound category.

❷ We use the diameter produced by our `xScale` to make these circles the same size as those in the timeline.

The `categoryFill` function (Example 17-3) is defined in *nbviz_core.js* and is used by the app to provide colors for the categories. It uses D3's `hcl` method to return equally spaced colors in the [0, 360] color hue range.[2] These are converted by D3 to CSS RGB.

---

2 See the D3 GitHub (*https://github.com/mbostock/d3/wiki/Colors#hsl*) for details.

Example 17-3. Setting the category colors

```
nbviz.CATEGORIES = [
    "Physiology or Medicine", "Peace", "Physics",
    "Literature", "Chemistry", "Economics"];

nbviz.categoryFill = function(category){
    var i = nbviz.CATEGORIES.indexOf(category);
    // return equally-spaced color hues
    return d3.hcl(i / cats.length * 360, 60, 70);
};
```

Now that we've covered all static elements to our time chart, let's look at how we knock it into usable form with D3's nest library.

Nesting the Data

In order to create this timeline component, we need to reorganize our flat array of winners objects into a form that will allow us to bind it to the individual Nobel Prizes in our timeline. What we need, to make binding this data with D3 as smooth as possible, is an array of prize objects by year, with the year groups available as arrays. Let's demonstrate the conversion process with our Nobel Prize dataset.

The following is the flat Nobel Prize dataset we begin with, ordered by year:

```
// var data =
[
  {"year":1901,"name":"Wilhelm Conrad R\\u00f6ntgen",...},
  {"year":1901,"name":"Jacobus Henricus van \'t Hoff",...},
  {"year":1901,"name":"Sully Prudhomme",...},
  {"year":1901,"name":"Fr\\u00e9d\\u00e9ric Passy",...},
  {"year":1901,"name":"Henry Dunant",...},
  {"year":1901,"name":"Emil Adolf von Behring",...},
  {"year":1902,"name":"Theodor Mommsen",...},
  {"year":1902,"name":"Hermann Emil Fischer",...},
  ...
];
```

We want to take this data and convert it to the following nested format, an array of objects with year keys and winners-by-year values:

```
// data =
[
  {"key":"1901",
   "values":[
     {"year":1901,"name":"Wilhelm Conrad R\\u00f6ntgen",...},
     {"year":1901,"name":"Jacobus Henricus van \'t Hoff",...},
```

```
    {"year":1901,"name":"Sully Prudhomme",...},
    {"year":1901,"name":"Fr\\u00e9d\\u00e9ric Passy",...},
    {"year":1901,"name":"Henry Dunant",...},
    {"year":1901,"name":"Emil Adolf von Behring",...}
   ]
  },
  {"key":"1902",
   "values":[
    {"year":1902,"name":"Theodor Mommsen",...},
    {"year":1902,"name":"Hermann Emil Fischer",...},
    ...
   ]
  },
  ...
 ];
```

We can iterate through this nested array and bind the year groups in turn, each one represented by a column of indicators in our timeline.

D3 provides a handy nest operator to convert datasets to the desired nested form. Example 17-4 achieves the required conversion of our Nobel Prize dataset.

Example 17-4. Nesting our winners' array by year

```
var nestDataByYear = function(entries) { ❶
    return nbviz.data.years = d3.nest()
        .key(function(w) { ❷
            return w.year;
        })
        .entries(entries);
};
```

❶ Entries is a flat dataset with all the currently selected Nobel Prize winners.

❷ Creates the first key for our nested array. You can use the key method multiple times to create deeper nested data. See this handy bl.ocks.org (*http://bl.ocks.org/phoebebright/raw/3176159/*) for some examples and a tutorial.

As discussed in "Basic Data Flow" on page 392, the onDataChange function uses the nestDataByYear function to convert the array of selected winners into the data needed by this component's updateTimeChartMethod.

Data nesting is the basis for many of the D3 network examples and the creation of the *flare* data structures used by D3's very cool hierarchy layouts (*https://github.com/mbostock/d3/wiki/Hierarchy-Layout*). In the nesting terminology, we want each branch of our simple tree to represent a Nobel Prize year and each leaf one of the prizes won in that year.

Now that we've seen how to turn our dataset into the required nested form, let's see how we use two data entry steps to turn that data into our prize indicators.

Adding the Winners with a Nested Data-Join

The update pattern used in our time chart is similar to that explained in "The Update Pattern" on page 430 but with an added element. Whereas with our bar chart we were creating simple SVG rect rectangles for each country, here we are creating a group of prizes for each year. This requires an extra data-join to our update cycle (using the data, enter, and exit methods).

The nested data is first passed from onDataChange to our time-chart's updateTimeChart method. We then create the year groups using our ordinal xScale to position them horizontally (see Example 17-5).

Example 17-5. Creating the year groups with a data-join

```
nbviz.updateTimeChart = function(data) {

    var years = svg.selectAll(".year")
        .data(data, function(d) {
            return d.key; ❶
        });

    years.enter().append('g')
        .classed('year', true)
        .attr('name', function(d) { return d.key;})
        .attr("transform", function(year) {
            return "translate(" + xScale(+year.key) + ",0)"; ❷
        });

    years.exit().remove(); ❸
    // ...
```

❶ We want to join the year data to its respective column by its year key, not the default array index, which will change if there are year gaps in our nested array, as there often will be for the user-selected datasets.

❷ Position our year column according to its year key. We use +year to convert the string to an integer.

❸ Removes any year columns not bound to the new dataset.

Let's use Chrome's Elements tab to see the changes we've made from this first data-join. Figure 17-3 shows our year groups nestled nicely in their parent chart group.

```
HTML before
▼ <div id="chart-holder" class="_dev">
  ▼ <div id="nobel-time">
    ▼ <svg width="1000" height="150">
      ▼ <g class="chart" transform="translate(40,20)">
        ▶ <g class="x axis" transform="translate(0,100)">.
        </g>
      ▶ <g class="labels" transform="translate(10, 10)">…‹
      </svg>
```

```
HTML after
▼ <div id="nobel-time">
  ▼ <svg width="1000" height="150">
    ▼ <g class="chart" transform="translate(40,20)">
      ▶ <g class="x axis" transform="translate(0,100)">…</g>
        <g class="year" name="1901" transform="translate(18,0)
        <g class="year" name="1902" transform="translate(26,0)
        <g class="year" name="1903" transform="translate(34,0)
        <g class="year" name="1904" transform="translate(42,0)
        <g class="year" name="1905" transform="translate(50,0)
```

Figure 17-3. The result of creating our year groups during the first data-join

Let's also do a sanity check to make sure our nested data has been bound correctly to its respective year groups. In Figure 17-4, we select a group element by its year name and inspect it. As required, the correct data has been bound by year, showing an array of data objects for the six Nobel Prize winners of 1901.

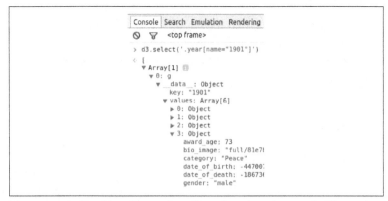

Figure 17-4. Checking the results of our first data-join with Chrome's console

Having bound our year data to their respective groups, we will use a second pass to select the *winner* groups, enter the data, and use it to append the circle indicators.

The full code is shown in Example 17-6. Note that the circles' x-coordinates are fixed relative to their respective year groups and that each circle is bound to its data object by the name field.[3] This means that after a circle indicator is appended to its group, the only dynamic attribute is its y-coordinate. This y-value is set by the index of the circle in its year-group's `values` array (containing its winners), and this can change as the user applies selection filters and the size of `values` changes.

Example 17-6. A second data-join to produce the prizes' circle indicators

```
var winners = years.selectAll(".winner")
        .data(function(d) { ❶
            return d.values;
        }, function(d) {
            return d.name;
        });

winners.enter().append('circle')
    .classed('winner', true)
    .attr('fill', function(d) {
```

---

3 In other words, the Albert Einstein circle indicator will always have the Physics category and be colored green.

```
            return nbviz.categoryFill(d.category); ❷
    })
    .attr('cx', xScale.rangeBand()/2) ❸
    .attr('r', xScale.rangeBand()/2);

winners.attr('cy', function(d, i) {
        return yScale(i); ❹
    });

winners.exit().remove(); ❺
```

❶ This data call first binds the year's prizes (the values array) to
    the year group and then sets the winner's name as a key to his or
    her indicator.

❷ Uses our shared categoryFill method (defined in
    nbviz_core.js) to color the indicators by prize category.

❸ Places the center circle on the group's y-axis by adjusting its x-
    position by half the indicator's radius.

❹ Places the indicator vertically by array index of prize using the
    ordinal yScale.

❺ Removes any indicators (keyed by the winner's name) without
    bound data in the new dataset.

The code in Example 17-6 does the job of building our Prize time
chart, creating new indicator circles if required and placing them,
along with any existing ones, at their correct position, as designated
by their array index (see Figure 17-5).

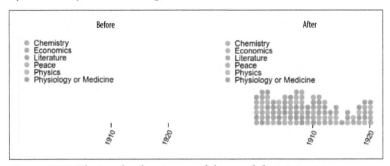

Figure 17-5. The result of our successful second data-join

Although we have produced a perfectly usable timeline, which will respond to user-driven changes in the data, the transition is a little stark and unengaging.[4] Let's now see a great demonstration of D3's power: how the addition of two lines of code can buy a rather cool visual effect as our timeline changes state.

A Little Transitional Sparkle

As things stand, when the user selects a new dataset,[5] the update pattern in Example 17-6 instantly sets the position of the relevant circles. What we now want to do is to animate this repositioning, smoothing it out over a couple of seconds.

Any user-driven filtering will either leave some existing indicators (e.g., when we select only the Chemistry prizes from all categories), add some new ones (e.g., changing our category from Physics to Chemistry), or do both. An edge case is when the filtering leaves nothing (e.g., selecting female Economics winners). This means we need to decide what existing indicators should do and how to animate the positioning of new indicators.

Figure 17-6 shows what we want to happen on selecting a subset of the existing data, in this case filtering all Nobel Prizes to include only those Physics winners. On the user's selection of the Physics category, all indicators except the Physics ones are removed by the exit and remove methods. Meanwhile, the existing Physics indicators begin a two-second transition from their current position to an end position, dictated by their array index.

---

4 As discussed in "Transitions" on page 442, the visual transition from one dataset to another can be both informative and lend a sense of continuity to the visualization, making it more appealing.

5 For example, filtering the prizes by category to show only the Physics winners.

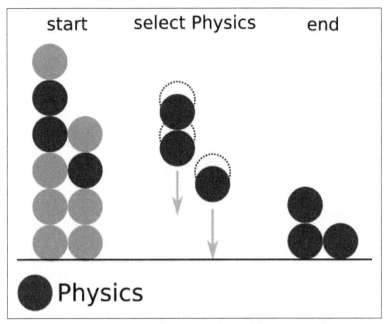

Figure 17-6. Transition on selecting a subset of the existing data

Achieving this effect requires the addition of a single line of code to our update pattern, adding a transition of duration 2,000 ms to our update of the circles' cy attribute:

```
// ...
winners
    .transition().duration(2000) ❶
    .attr('cy', function(d, i) {
      return yScale(i);
    });

winners.exit().remove();
```

❶ Moves the circle from its current position to the new one over a two-second interval.

For newly appended indicators, a nice visual effect is to *grow* them from the bottom of the chart to their index-specified positions. Figure 17-7 shows an example, as the user increases the dataset by selecting All Categories after a Physics selection. The new circles are added to bottom of the chart and then all indicators proceed to their (new) positions over a two-second interval.

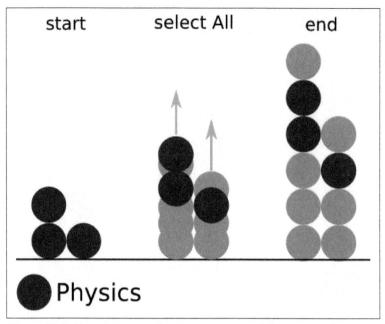

Figure 17-7. Transition on selecting a superset of the existing data

Once again, we can achieve this visual effect by adding a single line of code to our update pattern:

```
// ...

winners.enter().append('circle')
    .classed('winner', true)
    .attr('fill', function(d) {
        return nbviz.categoryFill(d.category);
    })
    .attr('cy', height) ❶
    .attr('cx', xScale.rangeBand()/2)
    .attr('r', xScale.rangeBand()/2);

winners
    .transition().duration(2000)
    .attr('cy', function(d, i) {
    return yScale(i); ❷
    });

winners.exit().remove();
```

❶ We first place the new circles at the bottom of the chart.

❷ Then we move them to their new positions over two seconds.

As you can see, D3 makes it really easy to add cool visual effects to your data transitions. This is a testimony to its solid theoretical core.

We now have our complete timeline chart, which transitions smoothly in response to data changes initiated by the user.

Summary

Following on from the bar chart in Chapter 16, this chapter extended the update pattern, showing how to use a second data-join on nested data to create a novel chart. It's important to emphasize that this ability to create novel visualizations is D3's great strength: you are not tied to the particular functionality of a conventional charting library but can achieve unique transformations of your data. As our Nobel Prize bar chart showed, it's easy to build conventional dynamic charts, but D3 allows for so much more.

We also saw how easy it is to liven up your visualizations with engaging transformations once a solid update pattern is in place.

In the next chapter, we will build the map component of our Nobel-viz using D3's impressive topographic library.

## CHAPTER 18

Mapping with D3

Building and customizing map visualizations is one of D3's core strengths. It has some very sophisticated libraries, allowing for all kinds of projections, from the workhorse Mercator and orthographic to more esoteric ones such as conicEquidistant. Mapping seems to be something of an obsession for Mike Bostock and Jason Davies, D3's core devs, and their attention to detail is striking. If you have a mapping problem, chances are D3 can do the heavy lifting required.[1] In this chapter, we'll use our Nobel Prize visualization (Nobel-viz) map (Figure 18-1) to introduce the core D3 mapping concepts.

---

1 The math of projections, particularly interpolative transitions and the like, can get quite involved.

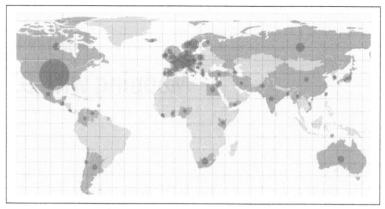

Figure 18-1. This chapter's target element

Available Maps

The most popular mapping format is the aging Shapefile (*https://en.wikipedia.org/wiki/Shapefile*), developed for geographic information system (GIS) software. There are many free and proprietary desktop programs[2] to manipulate and produce Shapefiles.

Unfortunately, Shapefiles were not designed for the Web, which would far rather deal in a JSON-based map format, and demands small, efficient representations to limit bandwidth and related lag.

The good news is that there are many convenient ways to convert Shapefiles to our preferred TopoJSON format,[3] meaning you can manipulate your Shapefiles in software and then convert them to a web-friendly format. The standard way of finding maps for web dataviz is to first look for TopoJSON or GeoJSON versions, then search among the richer pool of Shapefiles, and, as a last resort, roll your own using a Shapefile, or equivalent, editor. Depending on how much map visualization you intend to do, there will probably be an off-the-shelf solution. For things like world maps or continental projections (e.g., the popular Albers-USA), you can usually find a number of solutions with different degrees of accuracy.

For our Nobel map, we want a global mapping, at least showing all 58 Nobel Prize–winning nations, with labeled shapes for pretty

---

2 I use and thoroughly recommend the open source QGIS (*http://www.qgis.org/en/site/*).

3 Python's topojson.py and the TopoJSON command-line program.

much all of them. Luckily, D3 provides a number of example world maps, one at 50m grid resolution, the other a smaller 110m resolution map. The latter is fine for our fairly crude requirements.[4]

D3's Mapping Data Formats

D3 makes use of two JSON-based geometric data formats, GeoJSON (*http://geojson.org/*) and TopoJSON (*https://github.com/mbostock/topojson*), an extension of GeoJSON devised by Mike Bostock that encodes topology. GeoJSON is more intuitive to read, but TopoJSON is far more efficient in most cases. Typically, maps are converted to TopoJSON for web delivery, where size is an important consideration. The TopoJSON is then converted to GeoJSON via D3 on the browser, to simplify SVG path creation, feature optimization, and so on.

 There is a nice summation of the differences between TopoJSON and GeoJSON on Stack Overflow (*http://bit.ly/2621NJg*).

Let's have a look at the two formats now. Understanding their basic structure is important and a little effort there will pay off, especially as your mapping endeavors become more ambitious.

GeoJSON

GeoJSON files contain one `type` object, one of Point, MultiPoint, LineString, MultiLineString, Polygon, MultiPolygon, GeometryCollection, Feature, or FeatureCollection. The case of the type member values must be CamelCase (*http://bit.ly/1V2p2Yr*), as shown here. They may also contain a `crs` member, specifying a particular coordinate reference system.

FeatureCollections are the largest GeoJSON container, and maps with more than one region are usually specified with these. Feature-

---

4 As we'll see, it does lack a couple of our Nobel Prize countries, but these are too small to be clickable and we have the coordinates of their centers, allowing for a visual cue to be overlaid.

Collections contain a `features` array, each element of which is a GeoJSON object of a type listed in the previous paragraph.

Example 18-1 shows a typical FeatureCollection containing an array of country maps, the boundaries of which are specified by Polygons.

Example 18-1. The GeoJSON mapping data format

```
{
  "type": "FeatureCollection", ❶
  "features": [ ❷
    {
      "type": "Feature",
      "id": "AFG",
      "properties": {
        "name": "Afghanistan"
      },
      "geometry": { ❸
        "type": "Polygon",
        "coordinates": [
          [
            [
              61.210817, ❹
              35.650072
            ],
            [
              62.230651,
              35.270664
            ],
            ...
          ]
        ]
      }
    },
    ...
    {
      "type": "Feature",
      "id": "ZWE",
      "properties": {
        "name": "Zimbabwe"
      },
      "geometry": {
        "type": "Polygon",
        "coordinates": [
          [
            [...
      }
    }
  ]
}
```

❶ Each GeoJSON file contains a single object wth a type and containing...

❷ ...an array of Features—in this case, country objects...

❸ ...with coordinate-based, polygonal geometry.

❹ Note that the geographic coordinates are given in [Longitude, Latitude] pairs, the reverse of conventional geographic positioning. This is because GeoJSON use an [X,Y] coordinate scheme.

Although GeoJSON is more succinct than Shapefiles and in the preferred JSON format, there is a lot of redundancy in the encoding of maps. For example, shared boundaries are specified twice and the floating-point coordinate format is fairly inflexible and, for many jobs, too precise. The TopoJSON format was designed to address these issues and produce a far more efficient way of delivering maps to the browser.

TopoJSON

Developed by Mike Bostock, TopoJSON is an extension to GeoJSON that encodes topology, stitching geometries together from a shared pool of line segments called arcs. Because they reuse these arcs, TopoJSON files are typically 80% smaller than their GeoJSON equivalents! In addition, taking a topological approach to map representation enables a number of techniques that use topology. One of these is topology-preserving shape simplification,[5] which can eliminate 95% of map points while retaining sufficient detail. Cartograms and automatic map coloring are also facilitated. Example 18-2 shows the structure of a TopoJSON file.

Example 18-2. Structure of our TopoJSON world map

```
{
    "type":"Topology",    ❶
    "objects:{            ❷
        "countries":{
            "type": "GeometryCollection",
            "geometries": [{
```

---

5 See *http://bost.ocks.org/mike/simplify/* for a very cool example.

```
      "_id":24, "arcs":[[6,7,8],[10,11,12]], ... ❸
   ...},
   "land":{...},
},
"arcs":[[[67002,72360],[284,-219],[209..]], <-- arc number 0 ❹
        [[70827,73379],[50,-165]], ...      <-- arc number 1
...]
"transform":{        ❺
   "scale":[
       0.003600036...,
       0.001736468...,
   ],
   "translate":[
       -180,
       -90
   ]
 }
}
```

❶ TopoJSON objects have a Topology type and must contain an
   objects object and an array of arcs.

❷ In this case, the objects are countries and land, both being arc-
   defined GeometryCollections.

❸ Each geometry (in this case defining a country shape) is defined
   by a number of arc paths, comprising continuous arcs referenced by their index in the arcs array ❹.

❹ An array of component arcs used to construct the objects. The
   arcs are referenced by index.

❺ Numbers needed to quantize positions as integers rather than
   floats.

Given that you probably won't be manipulating TopoJSON files
directly but instead converting Shapefiles or GeoJSON files into
them, and that D3 converts the arc-based shapes into SVG paths, the
most important thing to know is how to create efficient TopoJSON
files from existing GeoJSON and ESRI (*http://www.esri.com/*) shapefiles. Handily, D3 provides topojson, a command-line utility to do
just this.

Converting Maps to TopoJSON

You can install TopoJSON via the node repositories (see Chapter 1), using the -g flag to make it a global install.

```
$ npm install -g topojson
```

With topojson installed, converting an existing GeoJSON or Shapefile into TopoJSON is as easy as can be. Here we call topojson from the command line on a GeoJSON *geo_input.json* file, specifying an output file *topo_output.json*:

```
$ topojson -o topo_output.json geo_input.json
```

Alternatively, you can pipe the result to a file:

```
$ topojson geo_input.json > topo_output.json
```

topojson will also convert ESRI shapefiles:

```
$ topojson -o topo_output.json input.shp
```

topojson can also convert CSV files into TopoJSON, where each CSV row represents a point feature.

topojson has a number of useful options, such as quantization, which allows you to specify your map's precision. Playing around with this option can result in a much smaller file with little perceptible reduction in quality. Simplification is a similar option, allowing you to play with the balance of detail and file size. You can see the full spec on the TopoJSON GitHub page (*https://github.com/mbostock/topojson/wiki/Command-Line-Reference*).

If you want to convert your map files programmatically, there is a handy Python library for the job, *topojson.py*. You can find it on GitHub (*https://github.com/calvinmetcalf/topojson.py*).

Now that we've got our map data in a light, efficient, web-optimized format, let's see how we use JavaScript to turn it into interactive web maps.

D3 Geo, Projections, and Paths

D3 has a client-side topojson library, dedicated to dealing with TopoJSON data. This converts the optimized, arc-based TopoJSON to the coordinate-based GeoJSON, ready to be manipulated by D3's projections and paths, objects in the d3.geo library.

Example 18-3 shows the process of extracting the GeoJSON features needed by our Nobel map from the TopoJSON *world-100m.json* map. This provides us with the coordinate-based polygons representing our countries and their borders.

In order to extract the GeoJSON features we require from the TopoJSON `world` object just delivered to the browser, we use topo `json`'s `feature` and `mesh` methods. `feature` returns the GeoJSON Feature or FeatureCollection for the specified object and `mesh` the GeoJSON MutliLineString geometry object representing the mesh for the specified object.

The `feature` and `mesh` methods take as their first argument the TopoJSON object and as their second a reference to the feature we want to extract (`land` and `countries` in Example 18-3). In our world map, `countries` is a FeatureCollection with a `features` array of countries (Example 18-3, ❷).

The `mesh` method has a third argument, which specifies a filter function, taking as arguments the two geometry objects (`a` and `b`) sharing the mesh arc. If the arc is unshared, then `a` and `b` are the same, allowing us to filter out external borders in our world map (Example 18-3, ❸).

Example 18-3. Extracting our TopoJSON features

```
queue() ❶
    .defer(d3.json, "data/world-110m.json") // world map
    //...
    .await(ready);
//...
function ready(error, worldMap...){
  //...
  nbviz.initMap(worldMap, ...
}
//...
nbviz.initMap = function(world, ...){

    var land = topojson.feature(world, world.objects.land),
        countries = topojson
          .feature(world, world.objects.countries)
          .features, ❷
        borders = topojson.mesh(
          world, world.objects.countries, function(a, b){
            return a !== b; ❸
          });
```

❶ Uses D3's queue to asynchronously load the map data in TopoJSON format.

❷ Uses `topojson` to extract our desired features from the TopoJSON data, delivering them in the GeoJSON format.

❸ Filters for only internal borders, shared between countries. If an arc is only used by one geometry (in this case, a country), then a and b are identical.

Map presentation in D3 generally follows a standard pattern. We first create a D3 `projection`, using one of D3's many and varied alternatives. We then create a `path` using this `projection`. This `path` is then used to convert the features and meshes extracted from our TopoJSON object into the SVG paths displayed in the browser window. Let's now look at the rich subject of D3 `projections`.

Projections

Probably the chief challenge for maps, since the time it was appreciated that the Earth is spheroidal, is that of representing a three-dimensional globe, or significant parts of it, in a two-dimensional form. In 1569, the Flemish cartographer Gerardus Mercator famously resolved this by extending lines from the Earth's center to significant boundary coordinates and then projecting them onto a surrounding cylinder. This had the useful property of representing lines of constant course, known as *rhumb lines*, as straight line segments, a very useful feature for the seafaring navigators intended to use the map. Unfortunately, the projection process distorts distances and size, magnifying the scale as one moves from the equator to the pole. As a result of this, the huge African continent appears not much bigger than Greenland when in reality it is around 14 times the size.

All projections are, like Mercator's, a compromise, and what's great about D3 is that the rich array of choices means one can balance these compromises to find the right projection for the job.[6] Figure 18-2 shows some alternative `projections` for our Nobel map,

---

6 The extended set of D3 `projections` (*https://github.com/d3/d3-geo-projection*) is part of an extension of D3, not in the main core.

including the equirectangular one chosen for the final visualization. The constraint was to show all Nobel Prize–winning countries within the rectangular window and to try to maximize the space available, particularly in Europe where there are many countries that are small geographically but have a relatively large prize haul.

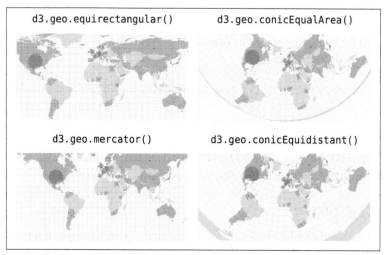

Figure 18-2. Some alternative mapping projections for the Nobel map

To create a D3 `projection`, just use one of the applicable `d3.geo` methods:

```
var projection = d3.geo.equirectangular()
...
```

D3 `projections` have a number of useful methods. It's common to use the `translate` method to translate the map by half the width and height of the container, overriding the default of [480, 250]. You can also set the precision, which affects the degree of *adaptive resampling* used in the `projection`. Adaptive resampling is a clever technique to increase the accuracy of projected lines while still performing efficiently.[7] The scale of the map and its center's longitude and latitude can be set by the `scale` and `center` methods.

Putting the `projection` methods together, the following code is that used by our Nobel-viz world equirectangular map. Note that it's hand-tweaked to maximize the space given to Nobel Prize–winning

---

7 See *http://bl.ocks.org/mbostock/3795544* for a nice demonstration.

countries. The two poles are truncated, there being no winners in either the Arctic or Antarctic (note that equirectangular maps assume a width/height ratio of 2):

```
var projection = d3.geo.equirectangular()
    .scale(193 * (height/480)) ❶
    .center([15,15]) ❷
    .translate([width / 2, height / 2])
    .precision(.1);
```

❶   Enlarged slightly; the default height is 480 and scale 153.

❷   Centered at 15 degrees east, 15 degrees north.

With our equirectangular `projection` defined, let's see how you use it to create a `path`, which will in turn be used to create the SVG maps.

Paths

Once you've settled on an appropriate `projection` for your map, you use it to create a D3 geographic `path` generator, which is a specialized variant of the SVG `path` generator (`d3.svg.path`). This `path` takes any GeoJSON feature or geometry object, such as a Feature-Collection, Polygon, or Point, and returns the SVG path data string for the d element. For example, with our map `borders` object, the geographic border coordinates describing a `MultiLineString` are converted into path coordinates for SVG.

Generally, we create our `path` and set its `projection` in one go:

```
var projection = d3.geo.equirectangular()
// ...

var path = d3.geo.path()
            .projection(projection);
```

Typically, we use the `path` as a function to generate the d attribute to an SVG path, using GeoJSON data bound using the `datum` method (used to bind a single object—not array—and shorthand for `data([objects])`). So to use the borders data we just extracted using `topojson.mesh` to draw our country borders, we use the following:

```
// BOUNDRY MARKS
svg.insert("path", ".graticule") // insert before the graticule
    .datum(borders)
```

```
.attr("class", "boundary")
.attr("d", path);
```

Figure 18-3 shows output from the Chrome Console for the
TopoJSON borders object, extracted from our world-map data, and
the resultant path generated by our D3.geo path, using the equirectangular projection.

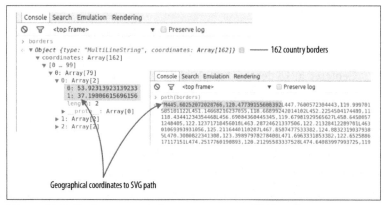

Figure 18-3. Path generator, from geometry to SVG path

The geo-path generator is the mainstay of D3 map presentations. I
recommend playing around with different projections with simple
geometries to get a feel for things, investigating the astonishing
number of examples found at bl.ocks.org (*http://bl.ocks.org/
mbostock*) and the docs on D3's GitHub page (*https://github.com/
mbostock/d3/wiki/Geo-Projections*), and checking out this great little
demo (*http://bl.ocks.org/mbostock/3711652*).

Now let's look at one of the useful d3.geo components you'll use in
your maps, the graticule (or map grid).

Graticules

A useful component of d3.geo and one used in our Nobel map is the
graticule, one of the geo shape generators.[8] This creates a global
mesh of meridians (lines of longitude) and parallels (lines of latitude), spaced by default at 10 degrees. When our path is applied to

---

8 See the D3 GitHub (*https://github.com/mbostock/d3/wiki/Geo-Paths#shape-generators*)
for a full list.

this `graticule`, it generates a suitably projected grid, as shown back in Figure 18-1.

Example 18-4 shows how to add a `graticule` to your map. Note that if you want your grid to overlay your map paths, then its SVG path should come after the map paths in the DOM tree. As you'll see, you can use D3's `insert` method to enforce this order.

Example 18-4. Creating a graticule

```
var graticule = d3.geo.graticule()
                 .step([20, 20]); ❶

svg.append("path")
   .datum(graticule) ❷
   .attr("class", "graticule")
   .attr("d", path); ❸
```

❶ Create `graticule`, overriding the default 10 degree steps.

❷ Note the `datum` shorthand for data([`graticule`]).

❸ Use the `path` generator to receive the `graticule` data and return a grid path.

Now that we have our grid overlay and the ability to turn our map file into SVG paths with the required `projection`, let's put the elements together.

Putting the Elements Together

Using the `projection`, `path`, and `graticule` components discussed, we'll now create the basic map. This map is intended to respond to user events, highlighting those countries represented by the selected winners, and reflecting the number of winners with a filled red circle at the countries' centers. We'll deal with this interactive update separately.

Example 18-5 shows the code required to build a basic global map. It follows what should now be a familiar pattern, getting the `mapCon tainer` from its div container (id `nobel-map`), appending an `<svg>` tag to it, and then proceeding to add SVG elements, which in this case are D3-generated map paths.

Our map has fixed components (e.g., the choice of `projection` and `path`) that are not dependent on any data change and are defined outside the initializing `nbviz.initMap` method. `nbviz.initMap` is called when the visualization is initialized with data from the server. It receives the TopoJSON `world` object and uses it to build the basic map with the `path` object. Figure 18-4 shows the result.

Example 18-5. Building the map basics

```
// DIMENSIONS AND SVG
var mapContainer = d3.select('#nobel-map');
var boundingRect = mapContainer.node().getBoundingClientRect();
var width = boundingRect.width
    height = boundingRect.height;
var svg = mapContainer.append('svg');
// OUR CHOSEN PROJECTION
var projection = d3.geo.equirectangular()
    .scale(193 * (height/480))
    .center([15,15])
    .translate([width / 2, height / 2])
    .precision(.1);
// CREATE PATH WITH PROJECTION
var path = d3.geo.path()
        .projection(projection);
// ADD GRATICULE
var graticule = d3.geo.graticule()
    .step([20, 20]);
svg.append("path")
    .datum(graticule)
    .attr("class", "graticule")
    .attr("d", path);
// A RADIUS SCALE FOR OUR CENTROID INDICATORS
var radiusScale = d3.scale.sqrt()
    .range([nbviz.MIN_CENTROID_RADIUS, nbviz.MAX_CENTROID_RADIUS]);
// OBJECT TO MAP COUNTRY NAME TO GEOJSON OBJECT
var cnameToCountry = {};
// INITIAL MAP CREATION, USING DOWNLOADED MAP DATA
nbviz.initMap = function(world, names) { ❶
    // EXTRACT OUR REQUIRED FEATURES FROM THE TOPOJSON
    var land = topojson.feature(world, world.objects.land),
        countries = topojson.feature(world, world.objects.countries)
                    .features,
        borders = topojson.mesh(world, world.objects.countries,
                    function(a, b) { return a !== b; });
    // MAIN WORLD MAP
    svg.insert("path", ".graticule") ❷
        .datum(land)                  ❸
        .attr("class", "land")
        .attr("d", path)
```

```
    ;
    // COUNTRY PATHS
    svg.insert("g", ".graticule")
        .attr("class", 'countries');
    // COUNTRIES VALUE-INDICATORS
    svg.insert("g")
        .attr("class", "centroids");
    // BOUNDARY LINES
    svg.insert("path", ".graticule")
        .datum(borders)
        .attr("class", "boundary")
        .attr("d", path);

    // CREATE OBJECT MAPPING COUNTRY NAMES TO GEOJSON SHAPES
    var idToCountry = {};
    countries.forEach(function(c) {
        idToCountry[c.id] = c;
    });

    names.forEach(function(n) {
        cnameToCountry[n.name] = idToCountry[n.id]; ❹
    });

};
// ...
// DRAW MAP ON DATA LOAD
nbviz.drawMap(world, names, countryData);
```

❶ world TopoJSON object with the country features with a names
    array connecting country names to country feature ids (e.g.,
    {id:36, name: *Australia*}).

❷ Note that we insert this path before the graticule grid, keeping
    the grid overlay on top.

❸ Uses datum to assign the whole land object to our path.

❹ Object that, if given country-name key, returns its respective
    GeoJSON geometry.

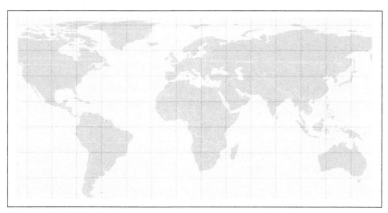

Figure 18-4. The basic map

With our map shapes in place, we can use a little CSS to style
Figure 18-4, adding a light azure for the oceans and light gray for the
land. The `graticule` is a half-transparent dark gray and the country
boundaries white:

```css
/* NOBEL-MAP STYLES */
#nobel-map {
    background: azure;
}

.graticule {
    fill: none;
    stroke: #777;
    stroke-width: .5px;
    stroke-opacity: .5;
}

.land {
    fill: #ddd;
}

.boundary {
    fill: none;
    stroke: #fff;
    stroke-width: .5px;
}
```

With the SVG map assembled, let's see how we use the winners dataset to draw the Nobel Prize–winning countries and the red indicator
for number of wins.

Updating the Map

The first time our Nobel map gets updated is when the visualization is initialized. At this point the selected dataset is unfiltered, containing all the Nobel Prize winners. Subsequently, in response to filters applied by the user (e.g., all the Chemistry winners or those from France), the dataset will change and our map changes to reflect that.

So updating the map involves sending it a dataset of the Nobel Prize–winning countries with their current prize haul, dependent on the user filters applied. To do this, we use an updateMap method:

```
nbviz.updateMap = function(countryData) { //...
```

The countryData array has this form:

```
[
  {
    code: "USA",
    key: "United States",
    population: 319259000,
    value: 336 ❶
  },
  // ... 56 more countries
]
```

❶ The number of winners for the US in the currently selected dataset.

We want to convert this array before sending it to our D3 map. The following code does this job, providing an array of country objects with properties geo (the country's GeoJSON geometry), name (the country name), and number (the country's number of Nobel Prize winners).

```
var mapData = countryData
    .filter(function(d) {
        return d.value > 0; ❶
    })
    .map(function(d) {
    return {
        geo: cnameToCountry[d.key], ❷
        name: d.key,
        number: d.value
    };
});
```

❶ Filters out countries with no winners—we only display winning countries on the map.

❷ Uses the country's key (its name in this case) to retrieve its Geo-JSON feature.

We want to display a red circular indicator at the center of our winning countries, indicating the number of prizes won. The circles' areas should be proportional to the number of prizes won (absolute or per capita), which means (by circle area = pi × radius-squared) their radius should be a function of the square root of that prize number. D3 provides a handy `sqrt` scale for just such a need, allowing you to set a domain (min and max prize number in this case) and a range (min and max indicator radius).

Let's see a quick example of the `sqrt` scale in action. In the following, we set a scale with a domain between 0 and 100 and a zero-based range with a maximum area of 25 (5 × 5). This means calling the scale with 50 (half the range) should give the square root of half the maximum area (12.5):

```
var sc = d3.scale.sqrt().domain([0, 100]).range([0, 5]);
sc(50) // returns 3.5353..., the square root of 12.5
```

To create our indicator radius scale, we create a `sqrt` scale using the maximum and minimum radii specified in *nbviz_core.js* to set its range:

```
var radiusScale = d3.scale.sqrt()
    .range([nbviz.MIN_CENTROID_RADIUS,
    nbviz.MAX_CENTROID_RADIUS]);
```

In order to get the domain to our scales, we use this `mapData` to get the maximum number of winners per country and use that value as the domain's upper value, with 0 for its lower:

```
var maxWinners = d3.max(mapData.map(function(d) {
    return d.number;
}));
// DOMAIN OF VALUE-INDINCATOR SCALE
radiusScale.domain([0, maxWinners]);
```

To add our country shapes to the existing map, we bind `mapData` to a selection on the `countries` group of class `country` and implement an update pattern (see "The Update Pattern" on page 430) to first add any country shapes required by the `mapData`. Instead of removing unbound country paths, we use the CSS `opacity` property to make the bound countries visible and the unbound invisible. A two-second transition is used to make these countries fade in and out appropriately. Example 18-6 shows the update pattern.

Example 18-6. Updating the country shapes

```
nbviz.updateMap = function(countryData) {
// mapData = filtered countryData
//  ...
    // BIND MAP DATA TO THE COUNTRY PATHS USING THE NAME KEY
    var countries = svg.select('.countries').selectAll('.country')
        .data(mapData, function(d) {
            return d.name;
        });
    // ENTER AND APPEND ANY NEW COUNTRIES
    countries.enter()
        .append('path')
        .attr('class', 'country')
        .on('mouseenter', function(d) { ❶
            // console.log('Entered ' + d.name);
            d3.select(this).classed('active', true);
        })
        .on('mouseout', function(d) {
            // console.log('Left ' + d.name);
            d3.select(this).classed('active', false);
        })
        ;
    // UPDATE ALL BOUND COUNTRIES
    countries
        .attr('name', function(d) {
            return d.name;
        })
        .classed('visible', true) ❷
        .transition().duration(nbviz.TRANS_DURATION) ❸
        .style('opacity', 1)
        .attr('d', function(d) {
            return path(d.geo); ❹
        });
    // REMOVE ANY UNBOUND COUNTRIES
    countries.exit()
        .classed('visible', false)
        .transition().duration(nbviz.TRANS_DURATION) ❺
        .style('opacity', 0);
    //...
};
```

❶ Classes a country as active as the mouse cursor enters it, and as inactive as it leaves.

❷ We keep track of the visible and invisible (opacity of 0) countries by using a visible class. We'll use this in "Building a Simple Tooltip" on page 488 to decide whether to show a mouse tooltip over a country.

❸ Fades in any newly data-bound countries over two seconds by increasing their opacity to 1.

❹ Builds the country's path using its geo GeoJSON feature.

❺ Fades out any data-unbound countries by setting their opacity to 0 over two seconds—nbviz.TRANS_DATA-UNBOUND is 2000 (ms).

Note that we add a CSS country class to countries in mapData, setting their color to a light khaki green. In addition to this the mouse events are used to class the country active if the cursor is over it, highlighting it with a darker green. Here are the CSS classes:

```
.country{
    fill: rgb(175, 195, 186); /* light green */
}

.country.active{
    fill: rgb(155, 175, 166); /* dark green */
}
```

The update pattern shown in Example 18-6 will smoothly transition from old to new datasets, produced in response to user-applied filters and passed to updateMap. All we need now is to add similarly responsive filled circular indicators, centered on the active countries and reflecting their current value, either an absolute or relative (per capita) measure of their Nobel Prize haul.

Adding Value Indicators

To add our circular value indicators, we want an update pattern that mirrors that used to create our country SVG paths. We want to bind to the mapData dataset and append, update, and remove our indicator circles accordingly. As with the country shapes, we'll adjust the indicators' opacity to add and remove them from the map.

The indicators need to be placed at the center of their respective countries. D3's path generator provides a number of useful utility methods for dealing with GeoJSON geometries. One of them is centroid, which computes the projected centroid for the specified feature:

```
// Given the GeoJSON of country (country.geo)
// calculate x, y coords of center
var center = path.centroid(country.geo);
// center = [x, y]
```

While `path.centroid` does a pretty good job as a rule, and is very useful for labeling shape, boundaries, and so on, it can produce strange results, particularly with highly concave geometries. Handily, the world country data we stored in "Getting Country Data for the Nobel Dataviz" on page 138 contains the central coordinates of all our Nobel Prize countries.

We'll first write a little method to retrieve those given a `mapData` object:

```
var getCentroid = function(d) {
    var latlng = nbviz.data.nationalData[d.name].latlng;  ❶
    return projection([latlng[1], latlng[0]]);  ❷
};
```

❶ Get the latitude and longitude of our country's center by name, using the stored world country data.

❷ Use our equirectangular `projection` to turn these into SVG coordinates.

As shown in Example 18-7, we bind our `mapData` to the selection of all elements of class `centroid` in the `centroids` group we added in Example 18-5. The data is bound via the `name` key.

Example 18-7. Adding prize-haul indicators to the Nobel countries' centroids

```
nbviz.updateMap = function(countryData) {
//...
    // BIND MAP DATA WITH NAME KEY
    var centroids = svg.select('.centroids')
        .selectAll(".centroid")
        .data(mapData, function(d) {
            return d.name;  ❶
        });
    // ENTER TO APPEND INDICATORS
    centroids.enter().append('circle')
        .attr("class", "centroid");
```

```
// UPDATE RADIUS AND OPACITY OF INDICATORS
centroids.attr("name", function(d) {
    return d.name;
})
    .attr("cx", function(d) {
        return getCentroid(d)[0]; ❷
    })
    .attr("cy", function(d) {
        return getCentroid(d)[1];
    })
    .classed('active', function(d) {
        return d.name === nbviz.activeCountry; ❸
    })
    .transition().duration(nbviz.MAP_DURATION) ❹
    .style('opacity', 1)
    .attr("r", function(d) {
        return radiusScale(+d.number); ❺
    });
// MAKE UNBOUND INDICATORS INVISIBLE
centroids.exit()
    .style('opacity', 0);

};
```

❶ Binds the data to the centroid elements using the name key.

❷ Uses our getCentroid method to turn geo-coords into SVG coords.

❸ If the country is currently selected, class it active.

❹ Fades in newly active indicators over two seconds.

❺ Our sqrt scale adjusts the radius to keep the indicator circle area proportionate to number of winners (either absolute or per capita).

Using a bit of CSS, we can make the indicators red and slightly transparent, allowing map details and, where they are densely packed in Europe, other indicators to show through. If the country is selected by the user, using the country filter on the UI bar, it is classed as active and given a golden hue. Here's the CSS to do that:

```
.centroid{
    fill: red;
    fill-opacity:0.3;
    pointer-events:none; ❶
}
```

```
.centroid.active {
    fill:goldenrod;
    fill-opacity:0.6;
}
```

❶ This allows mouse events to propagate to country shapes below the circles, allowing the user to still click on them.

The active centroid indicators we just added are the last element of our Nobel Prize map. Now let's take a look at the complete article.

Our Completed Map

With the country and indicator update patterns in place, our map should respond to user-driven filtering with a smooth transition. Figure 18-5 shows the result of selecting Nobel Prizes for Economics. Only winning countries remain highlighted and the value indicators are resized, reflecting American dominance of this category.

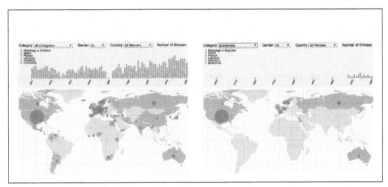

Figure 18-5. (A) Shows the map with the full Nobel dataset; (B) Prizes are filtered by category, showing the Economics winners (and the dominance of the US economists)

The map as it stands in not interactive but does show when a user hovers over a particular country with a mouse, by calling the mouseenter and mouseout callback functions and adding or removing an active class. These callbacks could easily be used to add more functionality to the map, such as tooltips or the use of the couries as clickable data filters. Let's now use these to build a simple tooltip, to show the country the mouse is hovering over and some simple prize information.

Building a Simple Tooltip

Tooltips and other interactive widgets are the kind of thing commonly demanded of data visualizers and though they can get quite involved, particularly if they themselves are interactive (e.g., menus that appear on mouse hover), there are some simple recipes that are very handy to know. In this section, I'll show how to build a simple but pretty effective tooltip. Figure 18-6 shows what we're aiming to build.

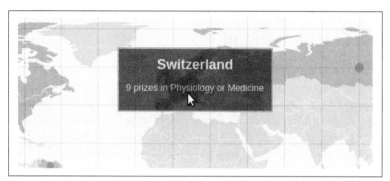

Figure 18-6. A simple tooltip for our Nobel Prize map

Let's remind ourselves of our current `countries` update, with `mouseenter` and `mouseout` callback functions:

```
// ENTER AND APPEND ANY NEW COUNTRIES
countries.enter()
    .append('path')
    .attr('class', 'country')
    .on('mouseenter', function(d) {
        d3.select(this).classed('active', true);
    })
    .on('mouseout', function(d) {
        d3.select(this).classed('active', false);
    })
    ;
```

In order to add a tooltip to our map, we need to do three things:

1. Create a tooltip box in HTML with placeholders for the information we want to display—in this case, country name and number of wins in the selected prize category.

2. Display this HTML box over the mouse when the user moves it into a country and hide it when they move the mouse out.

3. Update the box when displayed using the data bound to the country underneath the mouse.

We create the HTML for the tooltip by adding a content block to the Nobel-viz map section, with id map-tooltip, an <h2> header for its title, and a <p> tag for the tooltip's text:

```
<!-- templates/index.html  -->
    <!-- ... -->
    <div id="nobel-map">
      <div id="map-tooltip">
        <h2></h2>
        <p></p>
      </div>
    <!-- ... -->
```

We'll also need some CSS for the tooltip's look and feel, added to our *style.css* file:

```
/* css/style.css */
/* MAP TOOLTIP */
#map-tooltip {
    position: absolute;
    pointer-events:none;  ❶
    color:#eee;
    font-size:12px;
    opacity:0.7; /* a little transparent */
    background:#222;
    border:2px solid #555;
    border-color: goldenrod;
    padding:10px;
    left: -999px;  ❷
}

#map-tooltip h2 {
    text-align: center;
    padding: 0px;
    margin: 0px;
}
```

❶ Setting pointer-events to none effectively lets you click on things underneath the tooltip.

❷ Initially, the tooltip is hidden far to the (virtual) left of the browser window, using a large negative x index.

With our tooltip's HTML in place and the element hidden to the left of the browser window (left is –999 pixels), we just need to extend our mousein and mouseout callback functions to display or hide the tooltip. The `mousein` function, called when the user moves the mouse into a country, does most of the work:

```
// ...
countries.enter()
    .append('path')
    .attr('class', 'country')
    .on('mouseenter', function(d) {

        var country = d3.select(this);
        // don't do anything if the country is not visible
        if(!country.classed('visible')){ return; }

        // get the country data object
        var cData = country.datum();
        // if only one prize, use singular 'prize'
        var prize_string = (cData.number === 1)?
            ' prize in ': ' prizes in ';
        // set the header and text of the tooltip
        tooltip.select('h2').text(cData.name);
        tooltip.select('p').text(cData.number
            + prize_string + nbviz.activeCategory);
        // set the border color according to selected
        // prize category
        var borderColor =
          (nbviz.activeCategory === nbviz.ALL_CATS)?
            'goldenrod':
            nbviz.categoryFill(nbviz.activeCategory);
        tooltip.style('border-color', borderColor);

        var mouseCoords = d3.mouse(this); ❶
        var w = parseInt(tooltip.style('width')), ❷
            h = parseInt(tooltip.style('height'));
        tooltip.style('top', (mouseCoords[1] - h) + 'px'); ❸
        tooltip.style('left', (mouseCoords[0] - w/2) + 'px');

        d3.select(this).classed('active', true);
    })
```

❶ D3's mouse method returns the mouse coordinates (here, relative to the parent map group) in pixels, which we can use to position the tooltip.

❷ We get the computed width and height of the tooltip box, which has been adjusted to accommodate our country title and prize string.

❸ We use the mouse coordinates and the width and height of the tooltip box to position the box centered horizontally and roughly above the mouse cursor (the width and height don't include our 10px of padding around the tooltip's `<div>`).

With the `mouseenter` callback function written, we now only need a `mouseout` to hide the tooltip by placing it far to the left of the browser window:

```
countries.enter()
    .append('path')
    .attr('class', 'country')
    // ...
    .on('mouseout', function(d) {
        tooltip.style('left', '-9999px');
        d3.select(this).classed('active', false);
    })
```

With the `mouseenter` and `mouseout` functions operating in concert, you should see the tooltip appearing and disappearing where needed, just as shown in Figure 18-6.

Now that we've built the map component of our Nobel dataviz, let's summarize what we've learned before moving on to show how user input drives the visualization.

Summary

D3 mapping is a rich area, with many varied projections and lots of utility methods to help with manipulating geometries. But building a map follows a fairly standard procedure, as demonstrated in the chapter: you first choose your projection—say, a Mercator or maybe the Albers conic projection commonly used for mapping the US. You then use this projection to create a D3 `path` generator, which turns GeoJSON features into SVG paths, creating the map you see. The GeoJSON will normally be extracted from more efficient TopoJSON data.

This chapter also demonstrated how easy it is with D3 to interactively highlight your map and deal with cursor movements. Taken together, the basic set of skills learned should allow you to start building your own mapping visualizations.

Now that we've constructed all of our SVG-based graphical elements, let's see how well D3 works with conventional HTML elements by building our winners' list and an individual's biography box.

## CHAPTER 19

Visualizing Individual Winners

We want our Nobel Prize visualization (Nobel-viz) to include a list of currently selected winners and a biography box (aka bio-box) to display the details of an individual winner (see Figure 19-1). By clicking on a winner in the list the user can see his or her details in the bio-box. In this chapter, we'll see how to build the list and bio-box, how to repopulate the list when the user selects new data (with the menu bar filters), and how to make the list clickable. We'll also see how an AJAX call to our Eve API is used to get the biography data needed to update the bio-box (see "Delivering Data to the Nobel Prize Visualization" on page 356).

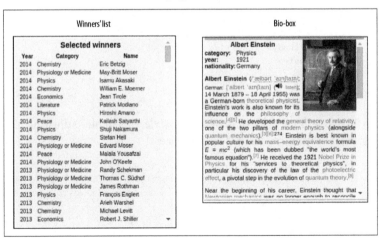

Figure 19-1. The chapter's target elements

As this chapter will demonstrate, D3 isn't just for building SVG visualizations. You can bind data to any DOM element and use it to change its attributes and properties or its event-handling callback functions. D3's data joining and event handling (achieved via the on method) play very well with common user interfaces such as the clickable list of this chapter and selection boxes.[1]

Let's deal first with the list of winners and how it is built with the dataset of currently selected winners.

Building the List

We build our list of winners (see Figure 19-1) using an HTML table with Year, Category, and Name columns. The basic skeleton of this list is provided in the Nobel-viz's *index.html* file:

```
<!DOCTYPE html>
<meta charset="utf-8">
<body>
...
    <div id="nobel-list">
      <h2>Selected winners</h2>
      <table>
        <thead>
          <tr>
            <th id='year'>Year</th>
            <th id='category'>Category</th>
            <th id='name'>Name</th>
          </tr>
        </thead>
        <tbody>
        </tbody>
      </table>
    </div>
...
</body>
```

We'll use a little CSS in *style.css* to style this table, adjusting the width of the columns and their font size:

```
/* WINNERS LIST */
#nobel-list { overflow: scroll; overflow-x: hidden; } ❶

#nobel-list table{ font-size: 10px; }
#nobel-list table th#year { width: 30px }
```

---

1 We'll cover selection boxes (as data filters) in Chapter 20.

```
#nobel-list table th#category { width: 120px }
#nobel-list table th#name { width: 120px }

#nobel-list h2 { font-size: 14px; margin: 4px;
text-align: center }
```

❶ overflow: scroll clips the content of the list (keeping it within our nobel-list container) and adds a scroll bar so we can access all the winners. overflow-x: hidden inhibits the addition of a horizontal scroll bar.

In order to create the list, we will add <tr> row elements (containing a <td> data tag for each column) to the table's <tbody> element for each winner in the current dataset, producing something like this:

```
...
<tbody>
  <tr>
    <td>2014</td>
    <td>Chemistry</td>
    <td>Eric Betzig</td
  </tr>
  ...
</tbody>
...
```

To create these rows, an updateList method will be called by our central onDataChange when the app is initialized and subsequently when the user applies a data filter and the list of winners changes (see "Basic Data Flow" on page 392). The data received by updateList will have the following structure:

```
// data =
[{
  name:"C\u00e9sar Milstein",
  category:"Physiology or Medicine",
  gender:"male",
  country:"Argentina",
  year: 1984
  _id: "5693be6c26a7113f2cc0b3f4"
},
...
]
```

Example 19-1 shows the updateList method. The data received is first sorted by year and then, after any existing rows have been removed, used to build the table rows.

Example 19-1. Building the selected winners list

```
nbviz.updateList = function(data) {

    var rows, cells;
    // Sort the winners' data by year
    var data = data.sort(function(a, b) {
        return +b.year - +a.year;
    });
    // Bind our winner's data to the table rows
    rows = d3.select('#nobel-list tbody')
        .selectAll('tr')
        .data(data);

    rows.enter().append('tr') ❶
        .on('click', function(d) {
            console.log('You clicked a row ' + JSON.stringify(d));
            nbviz.displayWinner(d); ❷
        });
    // Fade out excess rows over 2 seconds
    rows.exit()
        .transition().duration(nbviz.TRANS_DURATION)
        .style('opacity', 0)
        .remove();

    cells = rows.selectAll('td') ❸
        .data(function(d) {
            return [d.year, d.category, d.name];
        });

    // Append data cells, then set their property text
    cells = cells.enter().append('td');
    cells.text(function(d) {
            return d;
        });

    // Display a random winner if there is one or more
    if(data.length){
      nbviz.displayWinner(
        data[Math.floor(Math.random() * data.length)]); ❹
    }
};
```

❶ Appends any necessary row tags and adds a callback function for when the user clicks a row.

❷ When the user clicks on a row, this click-handler function will pass the winner data bound to that row to a `displayWinner` method, which will update the bio-box accordingly.

---

❸ Here we bind an array containing year, category, and name of the winner to the row's data cells. In the next statement, we enter this data and create the cell tags.

❹ Each time the data is changed, we select a winner at random from the new dataset and display him or her in the bio-box.

As the user moves the cursor over a row in our winners' table, we want to highlight the row and also to change the style of pointer to cursor to indicate that the row is clickable. Both of these details are fixed by the following CSS, added to our *style.css* file:

```
#nobel-list tr:hover{
    cursor: pointer;
    background: lightblue;
}
```

Our updateList method calls a displayWinner method to build a winner's biography box when a row is clicked or when the data changes (with a random choice). Let's now see how the bio-box is built, using an AJAX request for data from our Eve API.

Building the Bio-Box

The bio-box receives a winner object missing the mini_bio field. In order to get the biographical text needed, it makes a request to our data API using the winner's id to specify the resource required. This data is used to update an HTML skeleton.

The bio-box's HTML skeleton is provided in the *index.html* file consisting of content blocks for the biographical elements and a read more footer providing a Wikipedia link to further information on the winner:

```
<!DOCTYPE html>
<meta charset="utf-8">
<body>
...
    <div id="nobel-winner">
      <div id="picbox"></div>
      <div id='winner-title'></div>
      <div id='infobox'>
        <div class='property'>
          <div class='label'>Category</div>
          <span name='category'></span>
        </div>
      </div>
```

```
          <div class='property'>
            <div class='label'>Year</div>
            <span name='year'></span>
          </div>
          <div class='property'>
            <div class='label'>Country</div>
            <span name='country'></span>
          </div>
        </div>
        <div id='biobox'></div>
        <div id='readmore'>
          <a href='#'>Read more at Wikipedia</a></div>
      </div>
  ...
  </body>
```

A little CSS in *style.css* sets the positions of the list and bio-box elements, sizes their content blocks, and provides borders and font specifics:

```
/* WINNER INFOBOX */

#nobel-winner {
    font-size: 11px;
    overflow: auto;
    overflow-x: hidden;
    border-top: 4px solid;
}

#nobel-winner #winner-title {
    font-size: 12px;
    text-align: center;
    padding: 2px;
    font-weight: bold;
}

#nobel-winner #infobox .label {
    display: inline-block;
    width: 60px;
    font-weight: bold;
}

#nobel-winner #biobox { font-size: 11px; }
#nobel-winner #biobox p { text-align: justify; }

#nobel-winner #picbox {
    float: right;
    margin-left: 5px;
}
#nobel-winner #picbox img { width:100px; }
```

```
#nobel-winner #readmore {
    font-weight: bold;
    text-align: center;
}
```

With our content blocks in place, we need to make a callback to our data API to get the data needed to fill them. Example 19-2 shows the displayWinner method used to build the box. The id (a MongoDB id) field of _wData is used to create a resource string that will be used by our getDataFromAPI method to make an AJAX call back to the data server (see Example 15-4 for details). The response from this call is passed to an anonymous callback function as wData and used to build the box with D3.

Example 19-2. Updating a selected winner's biography box

```
nbviz.displayWinner = function(_wData) {

    nbviz.getDataFromAPI('winners/' + _wData._id, {}, ❶
        function(error, wData) {

            if(error){
                return console.warn(error);
            }

            var nw = d3.select('#nobel-winner');
            nw.style('border-color',
                    nbviz.categoryFill(wData.category)); ❷

            nw.select('#winner-title').text(wData.name);


            nw.selectAll('.property span') ❸
                .text(function(d) {
                    var property = d3.select(this).attr('name');
                    return wData[property];
                });

            // Add the biographic HTML
            nw.select('#biobox').html(wData.mini_bio);
            // Add an image if available or hide the old one
            if(wData.bio_image){ ❹
                nw.select('#picbox img')
                    .attr('src', 'static/images/winners/'
                        + wData.bio_image)
                    .style('display', 'inline');

            }
            else{
```

```
                nw.select('#picbox img').style('display', 'none');
            }

            nw.select('#readmore a').attr('href',
                'http://en.wikipedia.org/wiki/' + wData.name);
        } // End anonymous function
    );
};
```

❶ Creates a resource string using the winner object's MongoDB id.
We pass an empty query object {} to get the full resource. This
will include the mini_bio field, containing the biographical
body text. The response is passed to an anonymous function as
a wData object.

❷ Our nobel-winner element has a top border (CSS: border-top:
4px solid), which we will color according to the winner's category, using the categoryFill method defined in *nbviz_core.js*.

❸ We select the <span> tags of all the divs with class property.
These are of the form <span name=*category*></span>. We use
the span's name attribute to retrieve the correct property from
our Nobel winner's data and use it to set the tag's text.

❹ Here we set the src (source) attribute on our winner's image if
one is available. We use the image tag's display attribute to hide
it (setting it to none) if no image is available or show it (the
default inline) if one is.

Now that we've seen how we add a bit of personality to our Nobel-
viz by allowing users to display a winner's biography, let's summarize
this chapter before moving on to see how the menu bar is built.

Summary

In this chapter, we saw how D3 can be used to build conventional
HTML constructions, not just SVG graphics. D3 is just as at home
building lists, tables, and the like as it is displaying circles or changing the rotation of a line. Wherever there is changing data that needs
to be reflected by elements of a web page, D3 is likely able to solve
the problem elegantly and efficiently.

We saw how an AJAX call to our RESTful Eve API was used to get the biographical text necessary for an individual's bio-box. Although our visualization deals with a relatively small dataset, the ability to grab multivariate dynamic data on demand, driven by the users and their interests, is crucial as data visualizations get more ambitious and caching all the data required becomes unfeasible.

With our winners' list and biography box covered, we've seen how all the visual elements in our Nobel-viz are built. It only remains to see how the visualization's menu bar is built and how the changes it enables, to both the dataset and the measure of prizes, are reflected by these visual elements.

## CHAPTER 20

The Menu Bar

The previous chapters showed how to build the visual components of our interactive Nobel Prize visualization, the time chart to display all Nobel Prize winners by year, a map to show geographic distributions, a list to display the currently selected winners, and a bar chart to compare absolute and per capita wins by country. In this chapter, we will see how the user interacts with the visualization by using selectors and buttons (see Figure 20-1) to create a filtered dataset that is then reflected by the visual components. For example, selecting Physics in the category-select box filters will display only Physics prize winners in the Nobel Prize visualization (Nobel-viz) elements. The filters in our menu bar are cumulative, so we can, for example, select only those female chemists from France to have won the Nobel Prize.[1]

Figure 20-1. This chapter's target menu bar

---

1 Remarkably, Marie Curie and her daughter Irène Joliot-Curie hold this distinction.

In the sections ahead, I will show you how to use D3 to build the menu bar and how JavaScript callbacks are used to respond to user-driven changes.

Creating HTML Elements with D3

Many people think of D3 as a specialized tool for creating SVG visualizations composed of graphical primitives such as lines and circles. Though D3 is great for this (the best there is), it's equally at home creating conventional HTML elements such as tables or selector boxes. For tricky, data-driven HTML complexes like hierarchical menus, D3's nested data-joins are an ideal way to create the DOM elements and the callbacks to deal with user selections.

We saw in Chapter 19 how easy it is to create `table` rows from a selected dataset or fill in the details of a biography box with a winner's data. In this chapter, we'll show how to populate selectors with options based on changing datasets and how to attach callback functions to user interface elements such as selectors and radio boxes.

 If you have stable HTML elements (e.g., a select box whose options are not dependent on changing data), it's best to write them in HTML and then use D3 to attach any callback functions you need to deal with user input. As with CSS styling, you should do as much as possible in vanilla HTML. It keeps the code base cleaner and is easier to understand by others devs and non devs. In this chapter I stretch this rule a bit to demonstrate the creation of HTML elements, but it's pretty much always the way to go.

Building the Menu Bar

As discussed in "The HTML Skeleton" on page 382, our Nobel-viz is built on HTML `<div>` placeholders, fleshed out with JavaScript and D3. As shown in Example 20-1, our menu bar is built on the `nobel-menu` `<div>`, placed above the main chart holder, and consists of three selector filters (by the winners' category, gender, and country) and a couple of radio buttons to select the country prize-winning metric (absolute or per capita).

Example 20-1. The HTML skeleton for the menu bar

```
<!-- ... -->
<body>
<!-- ... -->
  <!-- THE PLACEHOLDERS FOR OUR VISUAL COMPONENTS  -->
    <div id="nbviz">
      <!-- BEGIN MENU BAR -->
      <div id="nobel-menu">
        <div id="cat-select">
          Category
          <select></select>
        </div>
        <div id="gender-select">
          Gender
          <select>
            <option value="All">All</option>
            <option value="female">Female</option>
            <option value="male">Male</option>
          </select>
        </div>
        <div id="country-select">
          Country
          <select></select>
        </div>
        <div id='metric-radio'>
          Number of Winners: 
          <form>
            <label>absolute
              <input type="radio" name="mode" value="0" checked>
            </label>
            <label>per-capita
              <input type="radio" name="mode" value="1">
            </label>
          </form>
        </div>
      </div>
      <!-- END MENU BAR  -->
  <div id='chart-holder'>
<!-- ... -->
</body>
```

Now we'll add the UI elements in turn, starting with the selector filters.

Building the Category Selector

In order to build the category selector, we're going to need a list of option strings. Let's create that list using the CATEGORIES list defined in *nbviz_core.js*:

```
/* nbviz_menu.js */
/* global $, _, crossfilter, d3  */
(function(nbviz,  _, $) {
    'use strict';

    var catList = [nbviz.ALL_CATS].concat(nbviz.CATEGORIES); ❶
```

❶ Creates the category selector's list ['All Categories', 'Chem
istry', 'Economics', …] by concatenating the list ['All
Categories'] and the list ['Chemistry', 'Economics', …].

We're now going to use this category list to make the options tags.
We'll first use D3 to grab the #cat-select select tag:

```
//...
    var catSelect = d3.select('#cat-select select');
```

With catSelect to hand, let's use some standard D3 data binding to
turn our catList list of categories into HTML option tags:

```
catSelect.selectAll('option')
    .data(catList).enter()
    .append('option') ❶
    .attr('value', function(d) { return d; }) ❷
    .html(function(d) { return d; });
```

❶ After data binding, append an option for each catList
member.

❷ We are setting the option's value attribute and text to a category (e.g., <option value="Peace">Peace</option>).

The result of the preceding append operations is the following catselect DOM element:

```
<div id="cat-select">
  "Category "
  <select>
    <option value="All Categories">All Categories</option>
    <option value="Chemistry">Chemistry</option>
    <option value="Economics">Economics</option>
    <option value="Literature">Literature</option>
    <option value="Peace">Peace</option>
    <option value="Physics">Physics</option>
    <option value="Physiology or Medicine">
    Physiology or Medicine</option>
  </select>
</div>
```

Now that we have our selector, we can use D3's on method to attach an event-handler callback function, triggered when the selector is changed:

```
catSelect.on('change', function(d) {
        var category = d3.select(this).property('value'); ❶
        nbviz.filterByCategory(category); ❷
        nbviz.onDataChange(); ❸
    });
```

❶ `this` is the select tag, with the `value` property as the selected category option.

❷ We call the `filterByCategory` method defined in *nbviz_core.js* to filter our dataset for prizes in the category selected.

❸ `onDataChange` triggers the visual-component update methods that will change to reflect our newly filtered dataset.

Figure 20-2 is a schematic of our select callback. Selecting Physics calls the anonymous callback function attached to our selector's change event. This function initiates the update of the Nobel-viz's visual elements.

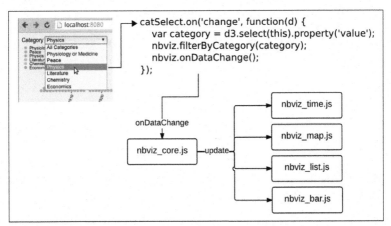

Figure 20-2. The category select callback

Within the category selector's callback, we first call the `filterByCa tegory` method[2] to select only the Physics winners and the `onData`

---

2 Defined in the *nbviz_core.js* script.

Change method to trigger an update of all the visual components. Where applicable, these will reflect the changed data. For example, the map's distribution circular indicators will resize, vanishing in the case of countries with no Nobel Physics winners.

Adding the Gender Selector

We have already added the HTML for our gender selector and its options, in the menu bar's description in *index.html*:

```
<!-- ... -->
    <div id="gender-select">
      Gender
      <select>
        <option value="All">All</option>
        <option value="female">Female</option>
        <option value="male">Male</option>
      </select>
    </div>
<!-- ... -->
```

All we need now do is select the gender `select` tag and add a callback function to handle user selections. We can easily achieve this using D3's on method:

```
d3.select('#gender-select select')
    .on('change', function(d) {
        var gender = d3.select(this).property('value');
        if(gender === 'All'){
            nbviz.genderDim.filter(); ❶
        }
        else{
            nbviz.genderDim.filter(gender);
        }
        nbviz.onDataChange();
    });
```

❶ Calling the gender dimension's filter without an argument resets it to allow all genders.

First we select the selector's option value. We then use this value to filter the current dataset. Finally, we call `onDataChange` to trigger any changes to the Nobel-viz's visual components caused by the new dataset.

To place the gender `select` tag, we use a little CSS, giving it a left margin of 20 pixels:

```
#gender-select{margin-left:20px;}
```

Adding the Country Selector

Adding the country selector is a little more involved than adding those of category and gender. The distribution of Nobel Prizes by country has a long tail (see Figure 16-1), with lots of countries having one or two prizes. We could include all of these in our selector, but it would make it rather long and cumbersome. A better way is to add groups for the single- and double-winning countries, keeping the number of select options manageable and adding a little narrative to the chart, namely the distributions of small winners over time, which might conceivably say something about changing trends in the Nobel Prize award allocation.[3]

In order to add our single- and double-country winner groups, we will need the crossfiltered country dimension to get the group sizes by country. This means creating the country selector after our Nobel Prize dataset has loaded. To do this, we put it in an nbviz.initUI method, called in our main *nbviz_main.js* script after the crossfilter dimensions have been created (see "Filtering Data with Crossfilter" on page 400).

The following code creates a selection list. Countries with three or more winners get their own selection slot, below the All Winners selection. Single- and double-country winners are added to their respective lists, which will be used to filter the dataset if the user selects the Single Winning Countries or Double Winning Countries from the selector's options.

```
nbviz.initUI = function() {
    var ALL_WINNERS = 'All Winners';
    var SINGLE_WINNERS = 'Single Winning Countries';
    var DOUBLE_WINNERS = 'Double Winning Countries';

    var nats = nbviz.countrySelectGroups = nbviz.countryDim
        .group().all() ❶
        .sort(function(a, b) {
            return b.value - a.value; // descending
        });

    var fewWinners = {1:[], 2:[]}; ❷
    var selectData = [ALL_WINNERS];
```

---

3 It does show that among single winners, the Nobel Prize for Peace predominates, followed by literature.

```
nats.forEach(function(o) {
    if(o.value >= 3){ ❸
        selectData.push(o.key);
    }
    else{
        fewWinners[o.value].push(o.key); ❹
    }
});

selectData.push(
    DOUBLE_WINNERS,
    SINGLE_WINNERS
);
```

❶ Sorted group array of form ({key:"United States", value:
336}, ...) where value is the number of winners from that
country.

❷ An object with lists to store single and double winners.

❸ Countries with more than two winners get their own slot in the
selectData list.

❹ Single- and double-winning countries are added to their respective lists based on the group size (value) of 1 or 2.

Now that we have our selectData list with corresponding fewWin
ners arrays, we can use it to create the options for our country selector. We first use D3 to grab the country selector's select tag and
then add the options to it using standard data binding:

```
var countrySelect = d3.select('#country-select select');

countrySelect.selectAll('option')
    .data(selectData).enter()
    .append('option')
    .attr('value', function(d) { return d; })
    .html(function(d){ return d; });
```

With our selectData options appended, the selector looks like
Figure 20-3.

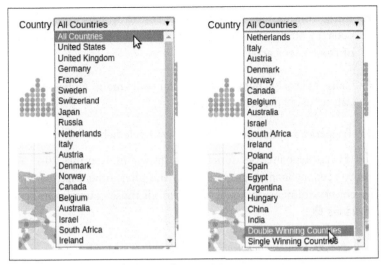

Figure 20-3. Selector for prizes by country

Now all we need is a callback function, triggered when an option is selected, to filter our main dataset by country. The following code shows how it's done. First we get the select's value property (1), a country or one of ALL_WINNERS, DOUBLE_WINNERS, or SINGLE_WIN NERS. We then construct a list of countries to send to our national filter method, nbviz.filterByCountries (defined in *nbviz_core.js*).

```
countrySelect.on('change', function(d) {

    var countries;
    var country = d3.select(this).property('value');

    if(country === ALL_WINNERS){ ❶
        countries = [];
    }
    else if(country === DOUBLE_WINNERS){
        countries = fewWinners[2];
    }
    else if(country === SINGLE_WINNERS){
        countries = fewWinners[1];
    }
    else{
        countries = [country];
    }

    nbviz.filterByCountries(countries); ❷
    nbviz.onDataChange(); ❸
});
```

❶ These conditionals make a `countries` array, depending on the country string. This array is empty, single-valued, or with one of `fewWinners` arrays.

❷ Calls `filterByCountries` to filter our main Nobel-winners dataset using the array of countries.

❸ Triggers an update to all the Nobel-viz's elements.

The `filterByCountries` function is shown in Example 20-2. An empty `countryNames` argument resets the filter; otherwise, we filter the country dimension `countryDim` for all those countries in coun tryNames ❶.

Example 20-2. Filter by countries function

```
nbviz.filterByCountries = function(countryNames) {

    if(!countryNames.length){ ❶
        nbviz.countryDim.filter();
    }
    else{
        nbviz.countryDim.filter(function(name) { ❷
            return countryNames.indexOf(name) > -1;
        });
    }

    if(countryNames.length === 1){ ❸
        nbviz.activeCountry = countryNames[0];
    }
    else{
        nbviz.activeCountry = null;
    }
};
```

❶ Resets the filter if the `countryNames` array is empty (the user chose All Countries).

❷ Here, we create a filter function on our `crossfilter` country dimension, which returns `true` if a country is in the `country Names` list (containing either a single country or all single or double winners).

❸ Keeps a record of any single selected country in order—for example, to highlight it in the map and bar chart.

Now that we've built the filter selectors for our category, gender, and country dimensions, all we need to do is add the callback function to deal with changes to the prize-winning metric radio button.

Wiring Up the Metric Radio Button

The metric radio button has already been built in HTML, consisting of a form with `radio` inputs:

```
<div id='metric-radio'>
  Number of Winners:  ❶
  <form>
    <label>absolute
      <input
        type="radio" name="mode" value="0" checked> ❷
    </label>
    <label>per-capita
      <input type="radio" name="mode" value="1">
    </label>
  </form>
</div>
```

❶   is used to create a nonbreaking space between the form and its label.

❷ Inputs of type `radio` sharing the same name (`mode`, in this case) are grouped together, and activating one deactivates all others. They are differentiated by value (0 and 1 in this case). Here we use the `checked` attribute to activate value 0 initially.

With the radio button form in place, we need only select all its inputs and add a callback function to deal with any button presses triggering a change:

```
d3.selectAll('#metric-radio input').on('change', function() {
    var val = d3.select(this).property('value');
    nbviz.valuePerCapita = parseInt(val); ❶
    nbviz.onDataChange();
});
```

❶ Update the value of `valuePerCapita` before calling `onData Change` and triggering a redraw of the visual elements.

We are storing the current state of the button with our `valuePerCa pita` integer. When the user selects a radio box, this value is changed and a redraw with the new metric is triggered with `onData Change`.

We now have the menu bar elements to our Nobel-viz, allowing users to refine the displayed dataset and drill down to subsets they are most curious about.

Summary

In this chapter, we saw how to add selectors and radio-button elements to our Nobel Prize visualization. There are a number of other user interface HTML tags, such as button groups, groups of checkboxes, time pickers, and plain buttons.[4] But implementing these controllers involves the same patterns as shown in this chapter. A list of data is used to append and insert DOM elements, setting properties where appropriate, and callback functions are bound to any change events. This is a very powerful method that plays very well with such D3 (and JS) idioms as method chaining and anonymous functions. It will quickly become a very natural part of your D3 workflow.

---

4 There are also native sliders in HTML5, where before one relied on jQuery plugins.

## CHAPTER 21

Conclusion

Although this book had a guiding narrative—the transformation of some basic Wikipedia HTML pages into a modern, interactive JavaScript web visualization—it is meant to be dipped into as and when required. The different parts are self-contained, allowing for the existence of the dataset in its various stages, and can be used independently. Let's have a short recap of what was covered before moving on to a few ideas for future visualization work.

Recap

This book was divided into five parts. The first part introduced a basic Python and JavaScript dataviz toolkit, while the next four showed how to retrieve raw data, clean it, explore it, and finally transform it into a modern web visualization. This process of refinement and transformation used as its backbone a dataviz challenge: to take a fairly basic Wikipedia Nobel Prize list and transform the dataset contained into something more engaging and informative. Let's summarize the key lessons of each part now.

Part I, "Basic Toolkit"

Our basic toolkit consisted of:

- A language-learning bridge between Python and JavaScript. This was designed to smooth the transition between the two languages, highlighting their many similarities and setting the scene for the bilingual process of modern dataviz. With the advent of a the latest JavaScript, based on ECMAScript 2015 (sixth edition) (*http://www.ecma-international.org/ecma-262/6.0/*) and soon to be available on all browsers, Python and JavaScript share even more in common, making switching between them that much less stressful.

- Being able to read from and write to the key data formats (e.g., JSON and CSV) and databases (both SQL and NoSQL) with ease is one of Python's great strengths. We saw how easy it is to pass data around in Python, translating formats and changing databases as we go. This fluid movement of data is the main lubricant of any dataviz toolchain.

- We covered the basic web development (webdev) skills needed to start producing modern, interactive, browser-based dataviz. By focusing on the concept of the single-page application (*https://en.wikipedia.org/wiki/Single-page_application*) rather than building whole websites, we minimize conventional web-dev and place the emphasis on programming your visual creations in JavaScript. An introduction to Scalable Vector Graphics (SVG), the chief building block of D3 visualizations, set the scene for the creation of our Nobel Prize visualization in Part V.

Part II, "Getting Your Data"

In this part of the book, we looked at how to get data from the Web using Python, assuming a nice, clean data file hasn't been provided to the data visualizer:

- If you're lucky, a clean file in an easily usable data format (i.e., JSON or CSV) is at an open URL, a simple HTTP request away. Alternatively, there may be a dedicated web API for your dataset, with any luck a RESTful one. As an example, we looked at using the Twitter API (via Python's Tweepy library). We also saw how to use Google spreadsheets, a widely used data sharing resource in dataviz.

- Things get more involved when the data of interest is present on the Web in human-readable form, often in HTML tables, lists, or hierarchical content blocks. In this case, you have to resort to *scraping*, getting the raw HTML content and then using a parser to make its embedded content available. We saw how to use Python's lightweight BeautifulSoup scraping library and the much more featureful and heavyweight Scrapy, the biggest star in the Python scraping firmament.

Part III, "Cleaning and Exploring Data with Pandas"

In this part, we turned the big guns of Pandas, Python's powerful programmatic spreadsheet, on the problem of cleaning and then exploring datasets. We first saw how Pandas is part of Python's NumPy ecosystem, leveraging the power of very fast, powerful low-level array processing libraries but making them accessible. The focus was on using Pandas to clean and then explore our Nobel Prize dataset:

- Most data, even that which comes from official web APIs, is dirty. And making it clean and usable will occupy far more of your time as a data visualizer than you probably anticipated. Taking the Nobel dataset as an example, we progressively cleaned it, searching for dodgy dates, anomalous datatypes, missing fields, and all the common grime that needs cleaning before you can start to explore and then transform your data into a visualization.

- With our clean (as we could make it) Nobel Prize dataset in hand, we saw how easy it is to use Pandas and Matplotlib to interactively explore data, easily creating inline charts, slicing the data every which way, and generally getting a feel for it, looking for those interesting nuggets you want to deliver with visualization.

Part IV, "Delivering the Data"

In this part, we saw how easy it is to create a minimal data API using Flask, to deliver data both statically and dynamically to the web browser:

- First we saw how to use Flask to serve static files and then how to roll your own basic RESTful API, serving data from a local database. Flask's minimalism allows you to create a very thin data-serving layer between the fruits of your Python data processing and their eventual visualization on the browser.

- The glory of open source software is that you can often find robust, easy-to-use libraries that solve your problem better than you could. Two Flask-based RESTful APIs were demonstrated that let you serve your data for the price of a small configuration file. Python Eve is a great MongoDB-based RESTful API library, while Flask-Restless makes serving data from SQL databases easy.

Part V, "Visualizing Your Data with D3"

I think it's fair to say that this was an ambitious part, but I was determined to demonstrate the construction of a multi-element visualization, such as the kind you may well end up being employed to make. One of the joys of D3 is the huge number of examples (*http://bit.ly/1ZWYnAC*) that can easily be found online, but most of them demonstrate a single technique and there are few showing how to orchestrate multiple visual elements. In these D3 chapters, we saw how to synchronize the update of a timeline (featuring all the Nobel Prizes), a map, a bar chart, and a list as the user filtered the Nobel Prize dataset or changed the prize-winning metric (absolute or per capita).

Data for the Nobel Prize visualization was provided as both static files and through a RESTful API, courtesy of Python Eve and Flask. The methods shown should scale for much larger datasets. Once you have mastered retrieving data dynamically from an API, the sky's the limit in terms of the amount of data you can use to drive your visualization.

Mastery of the core themes demonstrated in these chapters should allow you to let loose your imagination and learn by doing. I'd recommend choosing some data close to your heart and designing a D3 creation around it.

Future Progress

As mentioned, the Python and JavaScript data processing and visualization ecosystems are incredibly active right now and are building from a very solid base.

While the business of acquiring and cleaning datasets learned in Part II and Chapter 9 improves incrementally, getting a lot easier as your craft skills (e.g., your Pandas fu) improve, Python is throwing out new and powerful data processing tools with abandon. There's a fairly comprehensive list (*https://wiki.python.org/moin/Numeri cAndScientific*) at the Python wiki. Here are a few ideas you might want to use to create some visualizations.

Visualizing Social Media Networks

The advent of social media has provided a huge amount of interesting data, often available from a web API or eminently scrapeable. There are also curated collections of social media data such as Stanford's Large Network Dataset Collection (*https://snap.stanford.edu/ data/*) or the UCIrvine collection (*https://networkdata.ics.uci.edu/ resources.php*). These datasets can provide an easy testing ground for adventures in network visualization, an increasingly popular area.

The two most popular Python libraries for network analysis are Graph-tool (*https://graph-tool.skewed.de/*) and NetworkX (*https:// networkx.github.io/*). While Graph-tool is more heavily optimized, NetworkX is arguably more user-friendly. Both libraries produce graphs in the common GraphML (*http://graphml.graphdrawing.org/*) and GML (*http://bit.ly/1S9TRIW*) formats. NetworkX can also produce a variety of JSON formats, which play well with D3's force layouts (*http://bit.ly/1UEG5je*). There's a nice, integral example on the NetworkX website of turning a NetworkX graph into a D3 visualization (*http://bit.ly/1PyKnam*). There's a handy Gist from Anders Eriksen showing how to convert GraphML format to a D3-ready JSON (*http://bit.ly/1rtGiy3*) for force-directed layouts. There's also a handy tool from Keiichiro Ono (*http://bit.ly/1ZX2ooH*), which allows you to convert GraphML and GML to D3-ready JSON.

As well as the examples at its website, there's a nice introduction to NetworkX at Udacity (*http://bit.ly/1tANSsE*). For a nice case study showing NetworkX and D3 in action, Lynn Cherny's quick and dirty intro (*http://bit.ly/1UThGJx*) is a great starting point.

Interactive Mapping with Leaflet and Folium

In Chapter 18 you were introduced to D3's impressive mapping abilities. D3 maps are supremely adaptable and, as with most things D3, you can achieve pretty much any effect you want. The huge number of geometric projections provided really broaden the scope of map visualizations. JavaScript's very popular Leaflet (*http://leafletjs.com/*)

library offers a faster route to mobile-friendly interactive maps. It doesn't have the low-level customization D3 offers, but you do get a lot of functionality for free, including pop-ups, zooming, integration with map databases such as Openstreetmap (*https://www.openstreet map.org/#map=5/51.500/-0.100*), and more. Leaflet has a huge range of plugins (*http://leafletjs.com/plugins.html*) to extend its basic functionality, which testifies to its large and enthusiastic user base. Leaflet plays nicely with D3 so you can combine the latter's data binding strengths with the former's convenience. There are a few nice examples at bl.ocks.org such as this overlaying example (*http://bl.ocks.org/ d3noob/9267535*) and Mike Bostock's (*https://bost.ocks.org/mike/leaf let/*) original demonstration.

Python's Folium (*https://folium.readthedocs.org/en/latest/*) library provides a great way to combine the strength of Python's data-processing ecosystem with Leaflet's easy browser-based mapping. As well as binding data to maps based on tilesets (OpenStreetMap by default), Folium can output the results of your Python analysis as visual markers using Vega (*https://vega.github.io/vega/*), a popular JSON-based visualization grammar that can be used to create interactive visualizations in the browser (as well as other platforms). It does this using Vincent (*https://vincent.readthedocs.org/en/latest/*), a Python-to-Vega translator that is designed to play nicely with Python data structures (lists, dicts, etc.) and also Pandas `Data Frames`.

There is a huge scope for geographic visualizations, and maps do tend to engage people's attention. Many social media datasets, such as Twitter's tweets (see "Using the Twitter API with Tweepy" on page 143 to see how Python can harvest tweets), have geo-tagged data or some clue (place of origin of sender) from which the geographic location can be fairly reliably derived. We saw that sites like flightaware (*http://uk.flightaware.com/commercial/flightxml/*) provide a paid API providing international flight tracking, and there are free resources such as openflights (*http://openflights.org/data.html*) providing curated datasets of flight routes and airports.

Machine-Learning Visualizations

Machine learning is more than a little in vogue at the moment and Python offers a fantastic set of tools to allow you to start analyzing and mining your data with a huge range of algorithms, from the supervised to unsupervised, from basic regression algorithms (such as linear or logistic regression) to more esoteric, cutting-edge stuff like the family of Ensemble Algorithms such as Random Forest. See this nice tour (*http://bit.ly/1YynBq6*) of the different flavors of algorithm.

Premier among Python's machine-learning stable is Scikit-learn (*http://scikit-learn.org/stable/tutorial/basic/tutorial.html*), which is part of the NumPy ecosystem, also building on SciPy and Matplotlib. Scikit-learn provides an amazing resource for efficient data mining and data analysis. Algorithms that only a few years back would have taken days or weeks to craft are available with a single import, well designed, easy to use, and able to get useful results in a few lines of code.

Tools like Scikit-learn enable you to discover deep correlations in your data, if they exist. There's a nice demonstration (*http://www.r2d3.us/visual-intro-to-machine-learning-part-1/*) at r2d3 that both introduces some machine-learning techniques and uses D3 to visualize the process and results. It's a great example of the creative freedom mastery that D3 provides and the way in which good web dataviz is pushing the boundaries, making novel visualizations that engage in a way that hasn't been possible before—and, of course, are available to everybody.

There's a great collection (*http://bit.ly/1YynF9k*) of IPython (Jupyter) Notebooks for statistics, machine learning, and data science at the IPython GitHub repo. Many of these demonstrate visualization techniques that can be adapted and extended in your own works.

Final Thoughts

The suggestions in the previous section just scratch the surface of where you might take your new Python and JavaScript dataviz skills. Hopefully this book has provided a solid bedrock on which to build your web dataviz efforts for the many jobs now opening up in the field or just to scratch a personal itch. The ability to harness Python's immensely powerful data wrangling and general-purpose abilities to JavaScript's (D3 being prominent here) increasingly powerful and mature visualization libraries represents the richest dataviz stack I know. Skills in this area are already very bankable, but the pace of change and scale of interest is increasing at a rapid rate. I hope you find this exciting and emergent field as fulfilling as I do.

Moving from Development to Production

In this appendix, we'll skim the surface of some big subjects and hopefully provide a good starting point and some sensible directions to follow. How far you need to develop these skills will depend on the scope of your job or projects. Hopefully you won't be required to extend your authentication or deployment skills too far, or you'll quickly find yourself doing more webdev and systems admin than dataviz. But testing is a generic programming skill for life and you probably want to be strengthening that core as you go. Decent project configuration skills are a very dependable asset, too. Using the following sections, I'd recommend taking your first Flask app with JavaScript project and making sure you can serve it on Apache with basic authentication, some unit tests, and at least two configuration states (e.g., production and development).

In covering the webdev sections of this book, the aim has been to give you a lightweight, pared-down starting point so that you can learn anything else you require on a need-to-know basis. In this sense, it's been set in a development environment. Sometimes, if you're working on a fast and dirty prototype, you won't need to stray too far from your development setup. But often, out there in the real world, you'll be working on a project that demands different environments for development and production (and maybe one for tests as well). Although both environments use testing, things like authentication and deployment usually have an end user in sight.

In the following sections, I'll give a brief overview of some of the key things you should be aware of on a project when you're moving to a production environment, using our development Nobel Prize visualization (Nobel-viz) single-page app as a starting point.

The Starting Directory

Let's remind ourselves of our Nobel-viz's development files. Example A-1 shows the basic Flask directory structure we're starting with. We also have an *api* subdirectory containing our Flask-based Eve web API; this could be anywhere on your system or, as is often the case, deployed to the cloud (see "Deploying Flask Apps" on page 541).

Example A-1. Our project's file structure

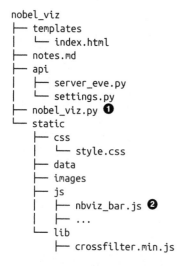

```
nobel_viz
├── templates
│   └── index.html
├── notes.md
├── api
│   ├── server_eve.py
│   └── settings.py
├── nobel_viz.py ❶
└── static
    ├── css
    │   └── style.css
    ├── data
    ├── images
    ├── js
    │   ├── nbviz_bar.js ❷
    │   ├── ...
    └── lib
        ├── crossfilter.min.js
```

❶ Our main Flask server, providing the entry point to our Nobel-viz single-page app.

❷ Our JavaScript files.

Configuration

As projects start to grow from the small-scale, prototyping phase, they often start to need different configurations for development and production (and testing, too, for that matter). These configurations may use different databases, web APIs, and URLs. You won't want to be doing development using the same database as your production server. Flask-based projects can take advantage of Flask's flexible configuration system to create these different environments.

Configuring Flask

You can configure Flask through the apps config object (essentially a dictionary). This can be accessed through the Flask app created in *nobel_viz.py*. Here, we set the DEBUG variable to True:

```
# nobel_viz/nobel_viz.py
app = Flask(__name__)
app.config['DEBUG'] = True
```

Flask provides a number of ways to initialize the config instance. For example, you can use an environment variable that points to the location of a *settings.cfg* file:

```
// ENV_NBIZ_SETTINGS = / path / to / settings.cfg
app.config.from_envvar('ENV_NBVIZ_SETTINGS')
```

This *.cfg* config file is actually a Python file, which will be processed to seed the config dictionary. Setting our configuration from an environment variable means we only need to change the path it defines to change our Flask setup. So setting ENV_NBIZ_SETTINGS to point to settings_debug.cfg gives us a debug environment:[1]

```
# settings_debug.cfg
# Debug config
DEBUG = True
EVE_API = 'http://localhost:5000/api/'
...
```

Note that only fully uppercase variables will be used to create values in config; everything else will be ignored.

The way I configure Flask is through the class-inheritance model, which makes it easy to build from default settings. To do this we cre-

---

1 To set a environment variable in OS X or Linux, the export command should do the trick (e.g., export ENV_NBIZ_SETTINGS='/path/to/settings_debug.cfg). In Windows, you usually do this using the set command, which will persist for the current CMD session or with a menu option as described in this Stack Exchange thread (*http://bit.ly/1YxqPKL*).

ate a *config.py* file in our root directory with a `Config` class and its subclasses:

```
# nobel_viz/config.py
class Config(object):
    DEBUG = False
    TESTING = False
    DATABASE_URI = 'sqlite://:memory:'
    EVE_API = 'http://localhost:5000/api/'

class ProductionConfig(Config):
    DATABASE_URI = 'mysql://user@localhost/prod_db'
    EVE_API = 'http://foo.com:5000/api/'

class DevelopmentConfig(Config):
    DEBUG = True

class TestingConfig(Config):
    TESTING = True
```

With this config file in the same directory as the Flask server file (*nobel_viz.py*), you can update the app's `config` from the required class using its `from_object` method like so:

```
# nobel_viz/nobel_viz.py
# ...
app.config.from_object('config.DevelopmentConfig')
```

So we could set our project's configuration with an environment variable and use Python's os module to read it and configure accordingly. In OS X or Linux, we use the following command to set the environment variable:

```
$ export NBVIZ_CONFIG=config.DevelopmentConfig
```

In Windows, we use `set` instead of `export`:

```
> set NBVIZ_CONFIG=config.DevelopmentConfig
```

To configure our project based on `NBVIZ_CONFIG`, we can use Python's os (operating system) module to get its value and use that with the `config.from_object` method:

```
...
app = Flask(__name__)

import os

cfg_var = os.environ.get('NBVIZ_CONFIG')
if not cfg_var:
    raise RuntimeError('The environment variable NBVIZ_CONFIG'\
```

```
                                ' is not set. Please set to enable configuration'
        )

    app.config.from_object(cfg_var)
    ...
```

Now that we can configure our app by setting a single environment variable, let's see how we can pass configuration variables to the app.

Configuring the JavaScript App

There are a number of ways we can pass configuration settings to our JavaScript app. We could initiate a web session and configure based on user authentication (as described later in this appendix) or use a configuration JSON file mirroring the current environments[2] (e.g., production or development). One simple method, which suffices for many jobs, is to use Flask's templating system to pass variables from Python to JavaScript. Let's cover that now.

Although we have a templated *index.html* file, we haven't up to now been making use of Flask's templating library, Jinja2 (see "Templating with Jinja2" on page 333).

Let's use a little template now to pass the configuration-dependent address of our RESTful Eve API. This is defined in our Flask *config.py* file:

```python
# config.py

class Config(object):
    #...
    EVE_API = 'http://localhost:5000/api/'

class ProductionConfig(Config):
    DATABASE_URI = 'mysql://user@localhost/prod_db'
    EVE_API = 'http://foo.com:5000/api/'
```

We'll pass the value of EVE_API to JavaScript by using a little templating to set a global $EVE_API variable in our *index.html* file, declaring the variable before our Nobel-viz scripts:

```html
<!-- index.html -->
...
  <script>
    $EVE_API = {{ config.EVE_API|tojson|safe }}; ❶
```

---

2 We want to make sure this file isn't available to a general web request.

```
</script>

<script src="static/js/nbviz_core.js" ></script>
...
```

❶ The config object is available to templates. Here we pass the
EVE_API variable through a couple of filters to first convert it to
JSON representation, and then mark the value safe to send
through to HTML without escaping.

We can now use the $EVE_API variable in our getDataFromAPI
method to use different API addresses dependent on our Flask
configuration:

```
// nbviz_core.js
//...
// var API_URL = 'http://localhost:5000/api/';
nbviz.getDataFromAPI = function(resource, data, callback){
    $.getJSON($EVE_API + resource, data)
        .done(function(resp_data){
        //...
```

By using Jinja2's tojson filter, you can pass whole dictionaries from
Python to JavaScript, allowing for as much configurability as you
need.

Using templates, we can alter aspects of the visualization on an environment (dev or prod) by environment basis. But what if we wished
to restrict use of our app to certain users or change the dataset
visualized according to individuals or members of a group. For
example, a dashboard may reveal specific information for adminis-
trators that should be hidden from normal users. At this point, we
need to start dealing with the issues of user authentication.

Authentication

Often we want to limit access to a particular web page (in our case, a
visual single-page app) to particular users, or change the look and
feel based on the user's status (e.g., a user versus admin view). Generally this requires creating a login page through which users must
pass (with the correct password) before being delivered the right
visualization.

There are lots of ways for a website to authenticate users, from the old but not particularly safe[3] basic authentication (*https://en.wikipe dia.org/wiki/Basic_access_authentication*) to more modern types such as OAuth (*https://en.wikipedia.org/wiki/OAuth*), a not altogether successful attempt to impose some open standards for authorization. As you'd expect, Flask offers a number of plugins to provide authentication, the most popular of which is Flask-login, which we'll cover in brief now.

Before adding a login stage to our visualization, we need to install Flask-login with a call to `pip`:

```
$ pip install flask-login
```

With Flask-login installed, the first thing you need to do is create a login manager. We'll add the login code to our *nobel_viz.py* module for simplicity, but as authentication gets more involved it's worth parceling it off to a separate module. So, after declaring our Flask app, we use it to initialize a login manager:

```
# nobel_viz.py

# ...
import flask.ext.login as flask_login

app = Flask(__name__)
# ...
login_manager = flask_login.LoginManager()
login_manager.init_app(app)
login_manager.login_view = "login"  ❶
```

❶ The `login_view` variable tells Flask-login where the login page is, which in our case is at the address /login.

Now that we have our login manager, we need a little code for user handling:

```
# FOR DEMO ONLY!!! NEVER STORE PASSWORDS IN PLAIN TEXT
users = {'groucho': {'pw': 'swordfish'}}  ❶

class User(flask_login.UserMixin):  ❷
    pass
```

---

3 Credentials for basic authentication are not encrypted or hashed in any way, making HTTPS pretty much essential.

```
@login_manager.user_loader
def user_loader(name):  ❸

    if name not in users:  # only groucho may pass
        return

    user = User()
    user.id = name
```

❶ We'll use this little dictionary for user lookup, but you would normally retrieve these details using a database call. Flask-login allows full flexibility here.

❷ We subclass the basic Flask-login UserMixin class, which provides some sensible defaults (*http://bit.ly/1Qccba1*). Note that we don't have to inherit from UserMixin but would then need to implement some basic properties or methods (e.g., is_authenticated).

❸ Called after a user submits a login form with the user's id (here we're using a name to identify the user).

Unauthorized users trying to access one of our protected pages will be sent to the login view. For a standard GET request, this login method will return a login page, rendered from a template. A POST request will see the form processed; if the passwords match, the user will be logged in to the session. Here's the code for the login route:

```
@app.route('/login', methods=['GET', 'POST'])
def login():

    if flask.request.method == 'GET':
        return render_template('login.html')  ❶

    name = flask.request.form['name']
    # FOR DEMO PURPOSES ONLY:
    # password should never be in plaintext!
    if users.get(name) and\
    flask.request.form['pw'] == users[name]['pw']:
        user = User()
        user.id = name
        # Authenticate the user session
        flask_login.login_user(user)
        return flask.redirect(flask.url_for('root'))  ❷

    return '<h2>A Bad Login Attempt</h2>' \
    '<p>Wrong name and/or password given</p>'  ❸
```

❶ If the request is a GET, then direct the user to our login page; otherwise, we'll be processing the contents of the posted login form.

❷ On logging in the user, we'll redirect them to the root of our single-page visualization.

❸ The login POST has failed with incorrect form fields. We'll return this placeholder; normally you'd probably return a proper failed login template with suitable failure warnings.

The *login.html* template is a simple form with input fields for password and name:

```html
<!DOCTYPE html>
<meta charset="utf-8">
<!-- IMPORT THE VISUALIZATIONS CSS STYLING -->
<link rel="stylesheet" href="static/css/style.css">

<style type="text/css" media="screen">
  div#login {text-align: center;}
</style>

<body>
  <div id="login">
    <h2>Login with name and password:</h2>
    <form action='login' method='POST'>
      <input
      type='text' name='name' id='name' placeholder='name'>
      </input>
      <input
      type='password' name='pw' id='pw' placeholder='password'>
      </input>
      <input type='submit' name='submit'></input>
    </form>
  </div>
</body>
```

To login-protect a route (in this case our Nobel-viz address), we add Flask-login's `login_required` decorator:

```python
@app.route('/')
@flask_login.login_required
def root():
    return render_template('index.html')
```

Putting all the login elements together means that when you visit the Nobel-viz for the first time, you will be directed to a login page like

Figure A-1. Filling in the correct name and password (name: Groucho; password: swordfish) will redirect you to the visualization.

Figure A-1. A simple Flask-login page

Flask-login is an eminently extensible and fairly unopinionated login framework. It's easy to override and customize various stages of the login process. For example, by default, unauthorized users will be redirected to the login page. You can specialize this handling by defining your own unauthorized_handler. Here we follow the default and redirect to a login page, adding a little debug output message.

```
@login_manager.unauthorized_handler
def unauthorized_callback():

    app.logger.debug('An unauthorized user!')
    return redirect('/login')
```

You can easily customize Flask-login through the set of callbacks and configuration variables (*http://bit.ly/1WRONB0*). A nice example of a such tailoring is found in Miguel Grinberg's demonstration of OAuth authorization (*http://bit.ly/1Xuo3GH*).

Now that you've seen how a basic login process works, let's see how you would deploy a Flask app on a conventional web server.

Testing Flask Apps

A programming quote from Bruce Eckel sums up how many feel about the importance of testing:

> "If it's not tested, it's broken."

Of course, there is much disagreement about how much testing should be done and how much time you want to allocate to it. Writing testing procedures can be pretty onerous and since writing tests involves preempting fail points, how do you know you've caught them all? In fact, with a program of any great complexity you probably can't. Nevertheless, testing is a fundamental aspect of modern programming and, in the examples to come, we'll see how you can write little test procedures to try to catch your code misbehaving.

Testing is becoming an unavoidable aspect of modern programming and is a best practice for any medium- to large-sized project, particularly a collaborative one. Testing is important during development but, arguably, vital in production. Python's unittest (*https://docs.python.org/2/library/unittest.html*) is a built-in testing library that provides a basic test framework. There are also various third-party libraries, such as pytest (*http://pytest.org/*) and nose (*https://nose.readthedocs.org/en/latest/*), that build on unittest, simplifying the syntax and generally making it easier to write tests. Let's see how to use unittest to run some basic tests on our Flask app. We'll use the login process we just created as a test example.[4]

We'll put our tests in a *test_nbviz.py* file in our project's root directory. By convention, test files should begin with test_ (test runners like py.test require this by default in order to discover a project's tests). As the tests get more extensive, it's sensible to stick them in their own subdirectory. The first thing we'll do in the test_nbviz module is import our nobel_viz Flask app and the unittest library:

```
# test_nbviz.py
import nobel_viz
import unittest
```

The unittest library has a number of classes to help structure your tests. We'll subclass a TestCase to set up our tests. TestCases take a setUp and tearDown method, which are called before and after each test, respectively. These are used to set up a clean test context and then clean up afterward. So, for example, if you were testing a database operation, you would initialize a clean test database in setUp and then drop it in tearDown. For our test, we'll just use setUp to provide a test_client from our nobel_viz app. These test clients provide a handy way to make requests to our app. Here's the initial NVizTestCase code:

---

4 This is adapted from the example (*http://flask.pocoo.org/docs/0.10/testing/*) in the Flask docs.

```
import nobel_viz
import unittest


class NVIzTestCase(unittest.TestCase):

    def setUp(self):
        nobel_viz.app.config['TESTING'] = True
        self.app = nobel_viz.app.test_client()

    def tearDown(self):
        pass
```

Now let's write a couple of helper methods to NVizTestCase to use our freshly set up test_client to make login and logout requests to the nobel_viz app:

```
# ...
    def login(self, name, password):
        return self.app.post('/login', data=dict(
            name=name, pw=password
            ), follow_redirects=True)

    def logout(self):
        return self.app.get('/logout', follow_redirects=True)
```

Now we just need add a login+logout test to our test case. Once again, convention dictates that tests start with test_:

```
# TESTS
    def test_login_logout(self):
        # log in with valid name and password
        resp = self.login('groucho', 'swordfish')
        # check we have been redirected to Nobel-viz page
        assert nobel_viz.app.config['APP_TITLE'] in resp.data  ❶
        # log out and test for the logout string in the response
        resp = self.logout()
        assert 'Logged Out!' in resp.data
        # log in with invalid name and password
        resp = self.login('chico', 'shark')
        assert 'Bad Login Attempt' in resp.data
```

If you want to run this test module from the command line, you can just add a __name__ test to the end of the file to call unittest:

```
# ...
if __name__ == '__main__':
    unittest.main()
```

Running the test file from the project root should then produce a test output, showing that our login and logout tests have passed:

```
$ python test_nbviz.py
.
- - - - - - - - - - - - - - - - - - - - - - - - - - - - - - - - - - - - - - - - - - - - - -
Ran 1 test in 0.019s
OK
```

While you can run individual test files in this way, it's sensible to use a dedicated test runner to do this. These libraries add extra functionality to the standard Python test suite, including robust test-discovery mechanisms, which remove a lot of the bookkeeping code from the test process. My personal fave is pytest (*http://pytest.org/latest/*), which is one of the Anaconda packages (*http://docs.contin uum.io/anaconda/pkg-docs*). Should you wish you install manually, a pip command will do the job:

```
$ pip install pytest
```

With pytest installed you just run it from the project root and it will automatically search through all subdirectories and files beginning with test_ looking for unit tests, running any it finds, and producing a status report:

```
$ py.test
================================ test session starts =========
platform linux2 -- Python 2.7.6, pytest-2.8.7, py-1.4.31,   ...
rootdir: /home/kyran/workspace/nobel_viz, inifile:
collected 1 items

test_nbviz.py .

============================== 1 passed in 0.14 seconds =======
```

On failure of a test, pytest reports are richer than the unittest standard, providing contextual feedback showing the failure point in the code. pytest adds a lot of useful function to Python testing and simplifies a lot of the boilerplate code. I highly recommend using it.

As befits such a big subject, Python testing can get very complex. But you can do an awful lot with the built-in unittest framework and extensions such as pytest. I'd recommend taking a few simple Python functions you're using and trying to create some succinct, efficient tests to probe for as many fail points in as few lines of code as possible. Like most things programming, testing is a craft that is learned in the doing.

Now let's have a brief intro to JavaScript testing, a rather more varied and colorful area.

Testing JavaScript Apps

Unlike Python, JavaScript doesn't have a built-in testing library, but it does have an impressive number of third-party ones. In fact, even for an experienced JavaScripter, the choice can be bewildering. This problem is compounded by the fact that JavaScript is in flux at the moment, with the new version (ECMAScript 6) promising much easier modular testing, while the Node ecosystem (using Node's modular, `require`-based import system) is developing some impressive dedicated testing libraries (e.g., Tape (*https://github.com/substack/tape*)).

JavaScript also has to deal with the difficulties of testing user interaction on the client browser, which is still something of a black art. To keep things manageable, this section will deal with a simple example of testing, using a few of our core Nobel-viz methods. We'll use the well-established Jasmine (*http://jasmine.github.io/2.4/intro duction.html*) behavior-driven framework.

There are a number of ways to install Jasmine, but the simplest (and the one we're using) is to download a zip file of the latest release (*http://bit.ly/1tujTC2*) from GitHub. Now we'll create a *tests* directory and unzip the Jasmine folder in it, giving a folder structure like the following (*NBVizSpec.js* is the file we'll be writing our tests to). We also copy the *SpecRunner.html* file to our project's root:

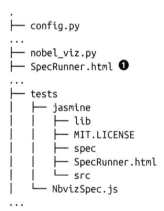

❶ Copied from the unzipped Jasmine folder

Out of the box, Jasmine is configured to deliver the results of any tests you run to the browser by opening a *SpecRunner.html* file. This file calls in some Jasmine JavaScript libraries and some CSS styling. Let's copy the default (shown in the file tree) to our project root and make a few changes to enable us to test the JavaScript methods in our core Nobel-viz module (*nbviz_core.js*):

```html
<!-- SpecRunner.html -->
<!DOCTYPE html>
<html>
<head>
  <meta charset="utf-8">
  <title>Jasmine Spec Runner v2.4.1</title>

  <link rel="shortcut icon" type="image/png"
  href="tests/jasmine/lib/jasmine-2.4.1/jasmine_favicon.png"> ❶
  <link rel="stylesheet"
    href="tests/jasmine/lib/jasmine-2.4.1/jasmine.css">

  <script src="tests/jasmine/lib/jasmine-2.4.1/jasmine.js">
  </script>
  <script
  src="tests/jasmine/lib/jasmine-2.4.1/jasmine-html.js">
  </script>
  <script
  src="tests/jasmine/lib/jasmine-2.4.1/boot.js"></script>

  <!-- include source files here... -->
  <!-- OUR MAIN JS LIBS -->
  <script
    src="https://cdnjs.cloudflare.com/ajax/libs/d3/3.5.16/
    d3.js">
  </script>
  <script
    src="https://cdnjs.cloudflare.com/ajax/libs/topojson/
    1.6.20/topojson.min.js">
  </script>
  <script
    src="https://cdnjs.cloudflare.com/ajax/libs/queue-async/
    1.0.7/queue.min.js">
  </script>
  <script src="static/lib/crossfilter.min.js"></script>
  <!-- OUR JS FILES TO TEST -->
  <script src="static/js/nbviz_core.js"></script>

  <!-- include spec files here... -->
  <!-- OUR TEST SCRIPTS -->
  <script src="tests/NbvizSpec.js"></script>
</head>

<body>
```

```
</body>
</html>
```

❶ We've adjusted the hrefs for the CSS files and the src for the JavaScript files to point them to our local Jasmine library.

With our *SpecRunner.html* configured, we need to write some tests to *NbvizSpec.js*. The structure of Jasmine tests is guided by the principles of behavior-driven development (BDD) (*https://en.wikipe dia.org/wiki/Behavior-driven_development*), an extension of test-driven development (TDD). Test blocks are written using Jasmine's describe method, the first argument of which is a descriptive string. These describe blocks contain annotated tests written using Jasmine's it function, which contains one or more expect functions, each with a test clause.

Let's first define our describe function to test the core functions of the Nobel-viz. We'll also add a little test data to it:

```
// tests/NbvizSpec.js
describe("Nbviz core functions", function() {
    var testData = [
        {name: 'Albert Einstein', country:'Switzerland',
          sex:'male', category:'Physics'},
        {name: 'Paul Dirac', country:'England',
          sex:'male', category:'Physics'},
        {name: 'Marie Curie', country:'Poland',
          sex:'female', category:'Chemistry'}
    ];
    var result;

    // ...
```

For a first test, let's test our categoryFill method, which takes a Nobel Prize category and produces a CSS color hex string. We know that, if the method is working, the Chemistry category should produce the pinkish hex color #ff7aad:

```
// ...
    it('should show correct color for category', function() {
        var col = nbviz.categoryFill('Chemistry');
        expect(col.toString()).toBe('#ff7aad'); ❶
    });
// ...
```

❶ expect is initialized with a value (in this case, the string version of col), which is then tested by one of its methods—in this case, an equality (===) check.

Now let's add a little test of our `filterByCountries` method, which takes a list of countries and filters our dataset (`testData`, in this case) for winners from those countries. We'll first call the `makeFilterAndDimensions` (see Example 15-8) method with our test data to create a Crossfilter filter and the category, country, and gender dimensions we use in the visualization:

```
// ...
    it('should filter winners by countries', function() {

        nbviz.makeFilterAndDimensions(testData);

        nbviz.filterByCountries(['Poland']);
        result = nbviz.countryDim.top(Infinity);

        expect(result.length).toBe(1); ❶
        expect(result[0].name).toBe('Marie Curie');

        nbviz.filterByCountries([]); ❷
        result = nbviz.countryDim.top(Infinity);

        expect(result.length).toBe(3);
        expect(result[2]).toEqual(testData[1]); ❸
    });
// ...
```

❶ Checks that the result of filtering by Poland returns the one Polish winner in `testData` and that her name is Marie Curie.

❷ We reset the filter with an empty list and then check that the result is the length or our full test dataset.

❸ The `crossfilter` result should be sorted on country with Paul Dirac (England) last (index 2). This should be equal to the second object (index 1) in the test data. `toEqual` is similar to `toBe` but does a deep equality check of the two objects. See this thread (*http://stackoverflow.com/questions/22413009/jasmine-javascript-testing-tobe-vs-toequal*) for further details.

We would probably write a test for each of our Crossfilter methods and other significant core methods. For now, let's run these two tests. In order to see the result of the two tests, open *SpecRunner.html* in a web browser. This should produce something like Figure A-2 showing that the two tests have succeeded.

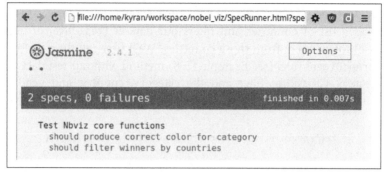

Figure A-2. Running Jasmine's SpecRunner.html in a local browser

Jasmine produces useful feedback should one of your tests fail. Let's change our winner name check from Marie Curie to another well-known prize winner:

```
expect(result[0].name).toBe('Albert Einstein');
```

Running the tests now gives Figure A-3, with the name failure and a stack trace.

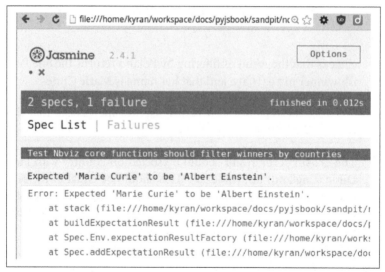

Figure A-3. Failing a test with Jasmine

JavaScript has a lot of testing libraries and, as mentioned, when one starts trying to test interactive elements, things get difficult very quickly. Extending Jasmine with a good test runner like Karma (*http://karma-runner.github.io/*) (a framework-agnostic runner) would be a good initial step. For testing Node.js modules, Tape (*https://github.com/substack/tape*) is a nice, simple library.[5] As projects get more involved, you may want to look at a continuous integration testing setup like Travis CI (*https://travis-ci.org/*) (for GitHub-based projects).

Now that we've had a little taste of Python and JavaScript testing, let's dip our toes in the waters of an equally big subject: deploying a Flask app to the Web.

Deploying Flask Apps

In development, you are likely running Flask on a port (5000 by default) of localhost. In production, you'll probably want to direct your Flask app through a dedicated server such as Apache or Nginx (by far the most popular servers, with around two-thirds of the market share). The Web Server Gateway Interface (WSGI) (*https:// en.wikipedia.org/wiki/Web_Server_Gateway_Interface*) provides a handy specification for hooking up Python web apps to heavyweight servers. We'll now see how Flask makes use of this with the most popular web server, Apache.

Configuring Apache

With Apache, you'll need the `mod_wsgi` module installed (see the installation instructions (*http://bit.ly/1Yyr5Ja*)).

On a typical Ubuntu-based server, you would use something like this to install the Apache WSGI module:

```
$ sudo apt-get install libapache2-mod-wsgi
```

With the WSGI module installed, the first sensible step is to either add your app's root directory to Apache's default *var/www* gateway directory or create a symbolic link to it (e.g., with the Nobel-viz root at */home/kyran/workspace/nobel_viz*). On a Unix or OS X box, you would create a symbolic link like so, with superuser status:

```
$ ln -s /home/kyran/workspace/nobel_viz /home /var/www
```

---

5 See this article (*http://bit.ly/1UEI5YK*) for a detailed reason why Tape might save you a lot of time and stress.

To use the WSGI module, you need to define a *.wsgi* file (regardless of the suffix, a Python module) for your app. This will act as the Apache initializer for your app, web API, and so on. Place the wsgi file in your project's root directory (in our case, *nobel_viz*):

```
# /home/kyran/workspace/nobel_viz/nobel_viz.wsgi
import sys
import os
# Add our app's directory to the system path
sys.path.insert(0, '/var/www/nobel_viz')

activate_this = '/home/kyran/.virtualenvs/pyjsbook/bin'\
'/activate_this.py' ❶
execfile(activate_this, dict(__file__=activate_this))

os.environ["NBVIZ_CONFIG"] = "config.DevelopmentConfig" ❷

from server import app as application ❸
```

❶ If using a Python virtual environment (as you should), then you need to activate it (making its libraries available) using its acti vate_this module.

❷ Here we pass an environment variable to the app's environment, in this case the NBVIZ_CONFIG configuration variable we discussed earlier in the appendix.

❸ The Flask app defined in our nobel_viz.py module. The WSGI module needs it to be imported as application.

With nobel_viz.wsgi written, we need to point Apache to it, using a standard configuration file added to the */etc/apache2/sites-enabled* directory:

```
# /etc/apache2/sites-enabled/nobel-viz.conf

NameVirtualHost *:80

<VirtualHost *:80>
        ServerName http://nobelviz.com ❶
        WSGIScriptAlias / /var/www/nobel_viz/nobel_viz.wsgi ❷
        <Directory /var/www/nobel_viz/>
                Order allow,deny
                Allow from all
        </Directory>
        ErrorLog ${APACHE_LOG_DIR}/error.log
        LogLevel info
```

```
        CustomLog ${APACHE_LOG_DIR}/access.log combined
</VirtualHost>
```

❶   Assuming our Nobel-viz is running on its own dedicated server
     with DNS name.

❷   The location of our *.wsgi* configuration file.

With the WSGI module installed and *nobel_viz.wsgi* and *nobel-
viz.conf* in place, we need to restart Apache. On a standard Linux-
based server, this is done thusly:

```
$ sudo service apache2 restart
```

If you now go to either the address *http:localhost* or, assuming it is
up and running, *http://nobelviz.com*, you should find your Flask app
being served by Apache.

Deploying to Nginx servers (the second most popular out there) is
just as easy, using the uWSGI (*https://uwsgi-docs.readthedocs.org/en/
latest/*) application server. Check out this fine tutorial (*http://
vladikk.com/2013/09/12/serving-flask-with-nginx-on-ubuntu/*) for a
detailed rundown.

Similar principles to those just outlined should see you up and running on the popular production servers. Check the official docs for a
comprehensive rundown (*http://flask.pocoo.org/docs/0.10/deploy
ing/*).

Logging and Error Handling

Logging is a fundamental part of a production setup and another big
topic that can easily mushroom as projects increase in size. On a few
projects I've worked on, a centralized logging setup such as GrayLog
(*https://www.graylog.org/*) or Logstash (*http://logstash.net/*) has
proved useful. It's great to be able to pool all logging to one place,
and web-based access is another boon.

There's a nice section in the Flask docs on error handling (*http://
flask.pocoo.org/docs/0.10/errorhandling/*), which makes a very sensible point: you will generally only look at a log-file for application
errors when a user reports an error. It's better practice to receive an
email alert as soon as an exception occurs. Python has a handy log
handler (SMTPHandler) for just this occasion, based on the Simple

Mail Transfer Protocol (SMTP) (*https://en.wikipedia.org/wiki/ Simple_Mail_Transfer_Protocol*).

In the following code, we set up a Python SMTP logging handler to send an email to the Nobel-viz admin if the Flask server throws an error. You'll need access to a mail host to do this, and while you could run one on the same machine as the Flask app (access on 127.0.0.1), you'll usually want to use an external SMTP mail server, accessed by username and password.

```python
# ...
app = Flask(__name__)
#...
ADMINS = ['nvizadmin@kyrandale.com']
if not app.debug:
    import logging
    from logging.handlers import SMTPHandler
    mail_handler = SMTPHandler(
        mailhost = ('smtp.foo.com', 495) # mail server, port
        fromaddr = 'server-error@nobelviz.com',
        toaddr = ADMINS,
        subject = 'Your Application Failed'),
        credentials = (app.config.SMTP_USER,\
        app.config.SMTP_PASSWORD)
    mail_handler.setLevel(logging.ERROR)
    app.logger.addHandler(mail_handler)
```

There are some handy error-handling pointers (*http:// flask.pocoo.org/docs/0.10/errorhandling/*) in the Flask docs. They build on Python's already solid built-in logging (*https:// docs.python.org/2/library/logging.html*) library, which I recommend becoming familiar with. At its most basic, it pretty much replaces the need to use the print statement ever again, outside of providing output to a command-line application. But it has a fair number of bells and whistles beyond that. The basic logging tutorial (*https:// docs.python.org/2/howto/logging.html#logging-basic-tutorial*) is a good starting point. The logging module is also covered succinctly in one of Doug Hellman's Weekly Modules (*https://pymotw.com/2/ logging/*). For a nice overview of some logging and exception patterns, see this loggly blog post (*https://www.loggly.com/blog/ exceptional-logging-of-exceptions-in-python/*).

Index

A

acknowledgments, xiii
AJAX, 352-356, 497-500
Anaconda
    development setup, 1-4
    libraries included in, 3
Apache, 541-543
append method (D3 library), 413
arrays, 31-32
attributions, xi
audience, 369
authentication, 528
axes (D3 library), 436-442, 451

B

Babel.js, 19
bar charts (Matplotlib), 274-278
bar charts, planning for, 375 (see also D3 library)
basic authentication, 529
BeautifulSoup
    basic web scraping with, 147
    installing, 147
    parsing data with, 149
    vs. Scrapy library, 161
    selecting tags, 149-158
Bokeh, xx, 282
boolean operators, 30
Bootstrap library, 371
Bostock, Mike, 467

C

CamelCase, 18
categorizing measurements, 208-210
category labels, 452
Chrome/Chromium
    downloading, 5
    web-developer kit, 88, 93, 102-104
circles, creating in SVG, 111
classes, 37-42
closures, 50-53
code examples, using, xi, xv, 1
code-linting, 91
collections module, 44
command prompt, 93
comments, xii, 27
conditional statements, 36
contact information, xi, xv
content delivery networks (CDN), 5
Continuum Analytics, 1
cross-origin resource sharing (CORS), 354, 363
Crossfilter library
    benefits of, 400
    filter creation, 400
    overview of, xxviii
CSS (Cascading Style Sheets)
    applying to HTML, 99-101, 386-389
    applying to SVG, 112
    applying with D3 library, 409-412
CSV (comma-separated values) files
    creating, 61
    loading into DataFrames, 217

manipulating, 62
curl, testing APIs with, 349
curly brackets, 26

D

D3 library
  bar charts
    accessing bound data, 429
    adding DOM elements,
      412-418
    axes/labels, 436-442
    data binding, 423
    enter method, 425-429
    integrating datasets, 418
    key components, 408
    scales, 418
    transitions, 442-447
    update pattern, 430-436
  benefits of, 407
  bio-box visualizations
    building the bio-box, 497-500
    building the list, 494-497
    overview of, 493
  map visualizations
    adding value indicators,
      484-487
    available maps, 466
    benefits of, 465
    building maps, 477-480
    completed map, 487-487
    d3.geo library, 471-477
    data formats, 467-471
    tooltips, 488-491
    updating maps, 481-484
  menu bars
    building, 504
    HTML element creation, 504
    target visualization, 503
  overview of, xxvii
  recap of, 518
  timeline charts
    axes, 451
    framework for, 449
    labels, 452
    nested data-join, 456-460
    nesting data, 454
    ordinal scales, 450
    transitions, 460-463

working with selections, 408-412
D3.js, 16
data binding (D3 library)
  accessing bound data, 429
  axes/labels, 436-442
  benefits of, 423
  enter method, 425-429
  transitions, 442-447
  update pattern, 430-436
data cleaning
  dealing with times/dates, 253-256
  dirty data examples, 231
  finding duplicates, 242-245
  finding mixed types, 239
  full clean_data function, 256
  importance of, 229-231
  inspecting data, 231-234
  merging DataFrames, 258
  recap of, 517
  removing duplicates, 246-252
  removing rows, 241
  replacing strings, 239-241
  saving cleaned data sets, 257
  selecting data in Pandas, 235-239
  sorting data, 245-246
data collection
  approaches to, 129
  from Web APIs, 134-140
  parsing data, 149
  recap of, 516
  requests library for, 129-140
  scraping data, 146-148
  Scrapy library for, 161-194
  selecting tags, 149-158
  using libraries, 140-146
data containers, 31-32
data delivery (see also Flask)
  dynamic data, 340-344
  recap of, 517
  selecting delivery method, 344
  serving data, 330-335, 382
  static files, 336-340, 382
data exploration
  age/life expectancy, 316-322
  birth vs. current country, 323
  discovering stories, 293
  environment set up, 294-296
  gender disparities, 297-304

integrated plotting, 296
national trends, 304-315
data nesting (D3 library), 454
data processing, compared, 23-25
data sharing
  benefits of Python for, 59
  CSV file creation, 61
  CSV/TSV and row-column formats, 62-65
  date/time handling, 66-68, 84
  JSON data, 65
  MongoDB, 79-84
  SQL databases, 69-79
  target list of data objects, 60
data visualization (dataviz)
  approach to learning, xv, xxviii
  future progress
    interactive mapping, 519
    machine-learning, 520
    social media networks, 519
  guiding principle of, ix
  history of, xvii
  measurement categories in, 208
  overview of
    basic toolkit, 515
    D3 library for, 518
    data cleaning, 517
    data collection, 516
    data delivery, 517
  prerequisites to learning, xvi, xix, xxix
  recommended books, xxxii
  theory of, xxix
  tools presented, ix, xx, xxiii (see also Matplotlib)
data-join method (D3 library), 431
databases
  development setup, 6
  loading into DataFrames, 220
  MongoDB, 79-84
  SQL, 69-79
DataFrames (Pandas)
  altering views vs. copies, 247
  columns property, 210
  creating from Series, 223-225
  creating/saving DataFrames, 214
  indices, 210, 235-239
  inspecting contents, 210

loading CSV data, 217
loading Excel files, 218
loading JSON data, 215
loading MongoDB tables, 221
loading SQL tables, 220
merging, 258
selecting groups (subsets), 213, 235-239
working with rows/columns, 211
Dataset library, 77-79
dataviz toolchain
  cleaning/exploring data, 195
  delivering data, 327
  getting data, 127
    (see also data collection)
  overview of, xxv
  recap of, 515
  visualizing data, 367
dates, 66-68, 84, 253-256
development setup
  accompanying code, 1
  databases, 6
  integrated development environments, 8
  JavaScript, 5-6
  Python, 1-4
dicts, 31-32
dimensions, 388, 413
Django, 331
doc-strings, 27
Document Object Model (DOM), 94, 412-418
duplicates
  finding, 242-245
  removing, 246-252
dynamic data delivery, 340-344

E

elements
  appending/inserting, 412
  getting dimensions of, 413
Elements tab (Chrome), 102
elif statements, 36
else statements, 36
enter method (D3 library), 425-429
environment variables, adjusting, 3
errata, xii
error handling, 543

Eve RESTful APIs, 348-351, 497-500
eve-sqlalchemy extension, 360
Excel files
    loading into DataFrames, 218

F

FacetGrids (Seaborn), 285-288
feature method (TopoJSON), 472
feedback, xv
figures
    OOP approach to, 269-273
    setting sizes in Matplotlib, 266
file I/O, 36
file organization, 331
files
    creating CSV files, 61
filter function, 49
Flask
    dynamic data delivery, 340-344
    file organization, 331, 380
    installing, 332
    overview of, xxvii
    production environment
        configuration, 524-527
        deploying apps, 541-543
        starting directory, 524
        testing apps, 532-535
    RESTful API with, 340-344
    RESTful data with
        adapting plugins for, 347
        Ajax API access, 352-356
        MongoDB plugin, 348-351
        Nobel Prize visualization,
            356-361
        SQL plugins, 361-365
        serving data with, 332
Flask-Restless, RESTful APIs, 347
Folium, 519
for loops, 33-35
frameworks, 90
functional methods
    array methods, 47-49
    vs. for loops, 33-35
functions, 32

G

<g> element (SVG), 110

geographic information system (GIS),
    466
GeoJSON, 467
ggplot library, 282
Gizma, 446
Google spreadsheets, 140-143
graticules (D3 library), 476
grouping/ungrouping elements
    (SVG), 120-121

H

HATEEOAS, 350
Hello World!, 23
heterogeneous datasets, 208-210
hierarchy layouts (D3 library), 456
historical trends, 301-304
HTML (Hypertext Markup Lan-
    guage)
    conversion to DOM, 94
    creating elements with D3, 504
    CSS application, 99-101
    markup tags, 97-99
    web visualization skeleton, 95,
        382-386
HTTP (Hypertext Transfer Protocol)
    serving web pages with, 94
    status codes, 131
    verbs, 134-138

I

identity scales (D3 library), 421
if statements, 36
injection attacks, 336
insert method (D3 library), 417
integrated development environ-
    ments (IDEs)
    development setup, 8
    vs. browser tools, 93
integrated plotting, 296
Intelligent Development Environ-
    ment (IDE), 90
interactive mapping, 519
interpolate method (D3 library), 420
IPython
    environment set up, 294-296
    interpreter, 15, 93
iteration, 33-35

J

Java, xxi
JavaScript
  benefits of, xx
  configuring apps, 527-528
  development setup, 5-6
  including scripts, 19
  vs. Python (see language-learning
    bridge)
  for SVG, 123-125
  testing apps, 536-541
  for web visualizations, 101,
    390-403
JavaScript converters, xx
Jinja2, 333
JSBin, 16
JSON (JavaScript Object Notation)
  for data sharing, 65
  loading into DataFrames, 215
  for web visualizations, 102

L

labels (D3 library), 436-442
lambdas, 49
language-learning bridge
  code access, 15
  code interaction (JavaScript), 16
  code interaction (Python), 15
  language differences, 14
  language similarities, 14
  overview of, 13
  practical differences
    closures, 50-53
    collections, 44
    functional array methods,
      47-49
    lambdas, 49
    list comprehensions, 47-49
    list enumeration, 43
    map, reduce, and filter func-
      tions, 49
    method chaining, 43
    module pattern, 50-53
    this vs. that keywords, 53
    tuple unpacking, 44
    underscore library, 46
  programming basics
    boolean operators, 30

CamelCase, 18
classes, 37-42
comments, 27
conditionals, 36
curly brackets, 26
data containers, 31-32
data processing, 23-25
doc-strings, 27
file I/O, 36
functions, 32
Hello World!, 23
iteration, 33-35
module importing, 19-21
namespaces, 21
numeric types, 29
PEP-8, 18
prototypes, 37-42
script inclusion, 19-21
string construction, 25
string quoting, 29
style guidelines, 18
underscores, 18
use strict directive, 18
variables, declaring, 28
whitespace, 26
  reference guide/cheat sheet, 54-56
lattice plots, 285
layering elements (SVG), 122
Leaflet, 519
legends, 452
libraries
  choosing, xxiv
  installing extra, 3
  installing locally, 6
  smaller supporting libraries, xxviii
  using to access Web APIs, 140-146
linear scales (D3 library), 420
lines, creating in SVG, 113
linter, 92
lists
  vs. arrays, 31-32
  enumerating, 43
  list comprehensions, 47-49
log scales (D3 library), 421
logging, 543
lxml, 147

M

machine-learning visualizations, 520
map function, 49
maps, planning for, 373-374, 519
Matplotlib
  axes and subplots, 270-273
  benefits of, 261
  configuring, 265
  creating plots in, 261
  ggplot library for, 282
  interactive plotting, 264-269
  labels and legends in, 266
  OOP approach to figures, 269-273
  overview of, xxvi
  plot types
    bar charts, 274-278
    scatter plots, 278-282
  point measurements in, 266
  Python-produced visualizations,
    xx
  saving charts, 269
  Seaborn library for, 282-290
  setting figure sizes, 266
  starting interactive sessions, 262
  titles and axes labels in, 267
matrix transformations (SVG), 119
menu bars
  building
    category selectors, 505
    country selectors, 509
    gender selectors, 508
    metric radio buttons, 513
    overview of, 504
  HTML element creation, 504
  planning for, 371
  target visualization, 503
mesh method (TopoJSON), 472
method chaining, 43
modules
  importing, 19-21
  module pattern, 50-53
MongoDB
  accessing, 81
  accessing with constants, 80
  benefits of, 79, 84
  creating collections, 80
  documentation, 83
  installing, 6
  loading into DataFrames, 221
  ObjectIds, 82
  query expressions, 82
  RESTful API with Eve, 348-351

N

namespaces, 21
national trends, 304-315
Nobel Prize visualization
  basic skills needed, xxiv
  cloning copy of, 1
  delivering data to, 356-361
  goals of, xv
  tools presented, xxv
  Wikipedia page for, xxv
  working copy of, xv
Notebook (IPython), 294
NumPy (Numeric Python) library
  array indexing and slicing, 201
  basic operations, 202
  benefits of, 197
  calculating moving averages, 205
  creating array functions, 204
  creating arrays, 200
  ndarray objects, 198

O

OAuth, 529
objects, 31-32
ordinal scales (D3 library), 422, 450

P

Pairgrids (Seaborn), 289-290
Pandas
  altering views vs. copies, 247
  benefits of, 207
  cleaning data with, 229-259
  creating Series, 223-225
  creating/saving DataFrames,
    214-222
  DataFrames, 210-214
  development of, 207
  exploring data with, 293
  groupby method, 297
  heterogeneous datasets and,
    208-210
  integrated plotting in, 296

overview of, xxvi
Panel class, 225
unstacking groups in, 299-300
Panel class (Pandas), 225
paths (D3 library), 475-476
paths (SVG), 116-119
PEP-8, 18
pipelines (Scrapy library)
concept of, 185-187
scraping text and images with, 187-193
specifying with multiple spiders, 193
polygons, creating in SVG, 113
power scales (D3 library), 421
production environment
authentication, 528
configuration, 524-527
deploying Flask apps, 541-543
logging/error handling, 543
moving to from development, 523
starting directory, 524
testing Flask apps, 532-535
testing JavaScript apps, 536-541
projections (D3 library), 473-475
prototypes, 37-42
PyCharm, 8
PyDev, 8
Python
benefits of, xx
consuming data from Web APIs with, 134-140
development setup, 1-4
drawbacks of, xx
Gspread library, 140-143
IDEs for, 8
improvements to, xxii
vs. JavaScript (see language-learning bridge)
reading/writing data with (see data sharing)
requests library, 129-140
Scrapy library for, 161-194
Tweepy library, 143-146
version 2 vs. version 3, 2
web scraping tools, 147
Python-to-JavaScript conversion, xx

Q

Qt console (IPython), 294
quantitative scales, 419-422
quantize/quantile scales (D3 library), 421

R

R, xxi
rectangles, creating in SVG, 113
reduce function, 49
requests library
benefits of, 129
downloading/installing, 130
getting data files with, 130-134
overview of, xxviii
RESTful Web APIs and, 135-140
web scraping with, 147
responsive web design (RWD), 371
REST (Representational State Transfer), 134, 340-344
rotating (SVG), 119
row-column file format, 62

S

sandboxing, 4
scales (D3 library)
benefits of, 418
categories of, 419
ordinal scales, 422, 450
quantitative scales, 419-422
scaling (SVG), 119
scatter plots (Matplotlib), 278-282
SciPy (Sciency Python) library
benefits of, 197
Seaborn library and, 282
scraping data (see web scraping)
Scrapy library
vs. BeautifulSoup, 161
benefits and drawbacks of, 161
caching web pages, 180
establishing targets, 164
overview of, xxv
pipelines in, 185-187
Scrapy shell, 166-170
selecting with relative xpaths, 170
setting up, 163
spider production, 171-177

targeting HTML with xpaths, 165
yielding requests, 181-185
scripts, including, 19-21
Seaborn library
    benefits of, 282
    FacetGrids in, 285-288
    overview of, xxviii
    Pairgrids, 289-290
    working with, 283-285
selections (D3 library), 408-412
self variable, 40
Series (Pandas), 223-225
Shapefile, 466
SimpleHTTPServer, 330
single-line servers, 330
single-page applications (SPAs), 88
size, 372, 386, 413
skewing (SVG), 119
SOAP (Simple Object Access Proto-
    col), 134
social media networks, 519
Sources tab (Chrome), 103
SPA (single-page applications), 330
spiders (Scrapy)
    producing, 171-177
    specifying multiple, 193
SQLAlchemy
    adding instances, 72
    benefits of, 69
    database engine creation, 69
    database table definition, 70
    Dataset module, 77-79
    loading into DataFrames, 220
    overview of, xxviii
    queries, 74-77
SQLite
    installing, 6
    loading into DataFrames, 220
static file delivery, 336-340, 382
Statsmodels library, 282
stories, discovering, 294
strings
    constructing, 25
    quoting, 29
    replacing, 239-241
style guidelines, 18
supplemental material, obtaining, xi
SVG (Scalable Vector Graphics)

<g> elements, 110
circles, 111
CSS application, 112
geometric operations on, 119
grouping/ungrouping elements,
    120-121
JavaScripted SVG, 123-125
layering/transparency, 122
lines, rectangle, and polygons, 113
paths, 116-119
providing SVG frames, 413
resurgence of, 109
svg elements, 110
text handling in, 114-115
for web page contents, 108
switch statements, 36
system files, 61

T

Tableau, xxii
Terminal (xterm), 93
text
    SVG vs. rasterized canvas context,
        114-115
text editors, selecting, 91
'that', as proxy for JS this, 53
this keyword, 40, 53
timeline charts
    axes, 451
    framework for, 449
    labels, 452
    nested data-join, 456-460
    nesting data, 454
    ordinal scales, 450
    transitions, 460-463
times, 66-68, 84, 253-256
TopoJSON, 466, 469-471
transitions (D3 library), 442-447
translating (SVG), 119
transparency (SVG), 122
trellis plots, 285
TSV (tab-separated value) files, 62
tuples, unpacking, 44
Twitter API, 143-146
typographical conventions, x

U

underscore library, 46
underscores, 18
update pattern (D3 library), 430-436
URL globbing parsers, 350
use strict directive, 18

V

variables, declaring, 28
virtual environments, 4
visualization implementation
  core components, 380
  CSS styling, 386-389
  file organization, 380
  HTML skeleton for, 382-386
  JavaScript engine
    basic data flow, 392
    benefits of modularity, 390
    core code, 393
    data-driven updates, 398
    filtering data, 400
    importing scripts, 390
    initialization, 395
    ready function, 396
  recap of, 517
  running the app, 404
  serving data, 382
visualization planning
  audience, 369
  bar charts, 375
  biography and photo, 376 (see
    also D3 library)
  complete visualization, 377
  list of winners, 375
  maps, 373-374
  menu bars, 371
  recap of, 517
  size and colors, 372
  visual element selection, 370

W

Web APIs
  consuming data from, 134-140
  types of, 134
  using libraries to access, 140-146
web development
  adding content, 108

basic pages, 105-107
building web pages, 93-102
challenges of, xviii
Chrome's Developer Tools,
    102-104
divide from programming, xvi
overview of, 87
SPAs, 88
SVG for, 109-125
tools required, 88-93
web scraping
  basics of, 147
  benefits of, 146
  caching web pages, 154
  parsing data, 149
  purpose of, 146
  Scrapy library for, 161-194
  selecting tags, 149
  selection patterns, 151-154
  tools for, 147
web visualizations (see also visualiza-
    tion implementation; visualization
    planning)
  adding content, 108
  basic pages, 105-107
  content markup, 97-99
  CSS application, 99-101, 386-389
  data formats, 101
  DOM manipulations, 94
  elements of, 93
  HTML skeleton for, 95, 382-386
  JavaScript for, 101
  serving pages with HTTP, 94
whitespace, 26
WingIDE, 8
wrapper libraries
  Google spreadsheets, 140-143
  Twitter, 143-146
WSGI (Web Server Gateway Inter-
    face), 541-543

X

XML-RPC APIs, 134
xpaths
  selecting with relative, 170
  targeting HTML with, 165
  testing with Scrapy shell, 166-170
xterm (Terminal), 93

About the Author

Kyran Dale is a journeyman programmer, ex–research scientist, recreational hacker, independent researcher, occasional entrepreneur, cross-country runner, and improving jazz pianist. During 15-odd years as a research scientist, he hacked a lot of code, learned a lot of libraries, and settled on some favorite tools. These days he finds Python, JavaScript, and a little C++ go a long way to solving most problems out there. He specializes in fast prototyping and feasibility studies with an algorithmic bent but is happy to just build cool things.

Colophon

The animals on the cover of *Data Visualization with Python and JavaScript* are the blue-banded bee (*Amegilla cingulata*), the orchid bee (of the *Euglossini* tribe), and the blue carpenter bee (*Xylocopa caerulea*). Bees are crucial to agriculture, as they pollinate crops and other flowering plants while they collect pollen and nectar.

The blue-banded bee is native to Australia, in all kinds of habitats including woodlands, heath, and even urban areas. As its Latin name suggests, its distinctive physical feature is the iridescent blue bands on its abdomen: males have five, while females have four. These bees practice what is known as "buzz pollination," meaning they use vibration to shake pollen loose. This species can vibrate a flower at an astonishing 350 times per second. Many plants, including tomatoes, are pollinated most efficiently in this manner.

The orchid bee is a colorful insect found in the rainforests of Central and South America. They have shiny metallic coloration in vivid shades of green, blue, gold, purple, and red. They are not as hairy as most bee species, and have long tongues almost twice the length of their body. Male orchid bees have specialized legs with small hollows that collect and store fragrant compounds, which are then released at a later time (perhaps in a mating display). Several orchid species hide their pollen in a particular spot marked with a scent the male orchid bee is attracted to, thus relying solely on this species for pollination.

The blue carpenter bee is a large insect (on average, 0.91 inches long) covered in light blue hair. It is widely distributed in Southeast

Asia, India, and China. They are so named because nearly all species nest within dead wood, bamboo, or timbers of manmade structures. They bore holes by vibrating their bodies and scraping their mandibles against the wood (however, carpenter bees feed on nectar; the wood they bore through is discarded). They are solitary and so do not form large colonies, but it is possible for several individuals to build nests in the same area.

Many of the animals on O'Reilly covers are endangered; all of them are important to the world. To learn more about how you can help, go to *animals.oreilly.com*.

The cover image is from *Insects Abroad*. The cover fonts are URW Typewriter and Guardian Sans. The text font is Adobe Minion Pro; the heading font is Adobe Myriad Condensed; and the code font is Dalton Maag's Ubuntu Mono.

Have it your way.

Get even more for your money.

Join the O'Reilly Community, and register the O'Reilly books you own. It's free, and you'll get:

- $4.99 ebook upgrade offer
- 40% upgrade offer on O'Reilly print books
- Membership discounts on books and events
- Free lifetime updates to ebooks and videos
- Multiple ebook formats, DRM FREE
- Participation in the O'Reilly community
- Newsletters
- Account management
- 100% Satisfaction Guarantee

Signing up is easy:

1. Go to: oreilly.com/go/register
2. Create an O'Reilly login.
3. Provide your address.
4. Register your books.

Note: English-language books only

To order books online:
oreilly.com/store

For questions about products or an order:
orders@oreilly.com

To sign up to get topic-specific email announcements and/or news about upcoming books, conferences, special offers, and new technologies:
elists@oreilly.com

For technical questions about book content:
booktech@oreilly.com

To submit new book proposals to our editors:
proposals@oreilly.com

O'Reilly books are available in multiple DRM-free ebook formats. For more information:
oreilly.com/ebooks

CPSIA information can be obtained
at www.ICGtesting.com
Printed in the USA
LVOW02s1904071116
511968LV00006B/60/P